Mapping My Way Home

A Gitxsan History

Neil J. Sterritt

Smithers, BC Canada
April 2016

Neil J. Sterritt © 2016

Creekstone Press, 7456 Driftwood Road
Smithers BC V0J 2N7 Canada
www.creekstonepress.com

All rights reserved. No part of this book may be reproduced in any form or by any means without permission from the publisher (or in the case of photocopying in Canada, without a license from Access Copyright, the Canadian Copyright Licensing Agency). Reviewers, however, are welcome to quote brief passages.

Library and Archives Canada Cataloguing in Publication

Sterritt, Neil J., author
Mapping my way home: a Gitxsan history / Neil J. Sterritt.

Includes bibliographical references and index.
ISBN 978-1-928195-01-6 (hardback).—ISBN 978-1-928195-02-3 (paperback)

1. Hazelton (B.C.)—History. 2. Hazelton (B.C.)—Biography. 3. Gitanmaax (First Nation)—History. 4. Gitanmaax (First Nation)—Biography. 5. Gitksan Indians—British Columbia—Hazelton—History. 6. Gitksan Indians—British Columbia—Hazelton—Biography. I. Title.

FC3849.H39S74 2016   971.1'85   C2015-908532-2

Editors: Lynn Shervill and Sheila Peters
Design: Tom Grasmeyer, Bulkley Valley Printers Ltd.
Cover design: Hans Saefkow, Bulkley Valley Printers Ltd.
The cover photograph of Temlaham Ranch with Stekyawden rising behind was taken by Jamie Sterritt.
The North arrow used throughout the book and on the cover was created by Jamie Sterritt (www.sahetxw.com).
The handwritten background image on the cover is taken from one of the author's fieldbooks.
Maps: Morgan Hite (www.hesperus-wild.org)
Index: Patricia Buchanan

Throughout the book, the terms 'right bank' and 'left bank' are used to designate the riverside location of villages, homes, etc. The direction is determined by facing downriver.

The spelling of Gitxsan names has been fluid as explorers, anthropologists and the Gitxsan themselves began to record what had been an oral culture. To avoid confusion and cumbersome insertions, the author has taken the liberty, where appropriate, of using the most common current spelling in some quoted material.

Where photos have abbreviated credits:
NBS photo: Neil B. Sterritt
NJS photo: Neil J. Sterritt (the author)
RBCM & A: Royal British Columbia Museum and Archives
NAC: National Archives of Canada
MA: Manitoba Archives
Wherever possible photo credits have been provided and permission received;
if further information is available please contact info@creekstonepress.com.

Mapping My Way Home is typeset in Minion Pro on Rolland Opaque White 60 lb. paper
and printed and bound by Friesens in Canada.

To Barbara, my wife and fellow traveller. Without her understanding, support, patience and encouragement, the book might never have seen daylight. Thank you.

Contents

ix **FOREWORD**

xiii **MAPS**

    Map 1   Migration Routes to the Gitxsan Ancestral Villages xiii

    Map 2   Gitanmaax & Old Hazelton 1946 xiv

    Map 3   Gitanmaax & Hazelton Local Area xv

    Map 4   Central Skeena xvi

    Map 5   Skeena River Watershed xvii

    Map 6   Fur Trade in Western Canada. xviii

    Map 7   Pacific Northwest xix

    Map 8   Northern British Columbia. xx

    Map 9   Routes to the Omineca Gold Fields xxi

    Map 10   Yukon Telegraph Trail xxii

    Map 11   Eastern Canada and New England. xxiii

xxiv **FAMILY TREES**

    Key to Family Trees xxiv

    Hankin Family Tree xxv

    Starrett and Cummins Family Tree xxvi

    Russell and Weir Family Tree xxvii

    Haaxxw Family Tree. xxviii

    Wiik'aax Family Tree xxix

    Sterritt Family Tree xxx

1 **INTRODUCTION**

11 **THE ALUUGIGAT**

    Chapter 1   From Asia by Land 13

    Chapter 2   Wiigyet: The Essence of Human Frailty 18

                      Wiigyet brings light to the world 19

                      Wiigyet brings water to the world. 21

                      How the lynx got tufted ears 21

                      Wiigyet and the abalone 23

    Chapter 3   Temlaham: The Ancestral Place. 25

		Ska'woo 26

        Ska'woo 26

        Madiik 28

        The Dispersal 29

Chapter 4   Gitanmaax: The Torchlight People 32

Chapter 5   Kispiox: The Hiding Place 39

        Yee'l and Ts'iiyee 39

        Liluxws/Kispiox Jim 46

Chapter 6   Gitangasx, Kisgegas and Bear Lake 53

        The Tsetsaut 55

        Bear Lake 59

Chapter 7   Hagwilget: The Gentle People 65

Chapter 8   The Halayt 71

Chapter 9   Gitxsan Time, Territory and Technology 75

        The Seasonal Cycle 76

        Bridges 84

91   The K'amksi'waa

Chapter 10   From Europe by Sea 93

Chapter 11   Ayton's River 97

Chapter 12   Voyages of Discovery (1822-1885) 102

        William Brown 102

        Simon McGillivray 107

        William Downie 112

        Charles Morison 115

Chapter 13   Thomas Hankin: Skeena Merchant 125

143   The Confluence

Chapter 14   Missionaries, Merchants and Miners 145

Chapter 15   Wiilaxhaa/Charles Martin 161

        A Man of the Cloth 164

        On the Yukon Telegraph 168

        Hazelton Merchant 173

        Land Rights Advocate 175

Chapter 16   Starrett and Cummins: Tracing Family, Father's Side 183

Chapter 17   Russell and Weir: Tracing Family, Mother's Side 193

Chapter 18   Haaxxw/Charlie Sterritt 205

Chapter 19   Wii Bowax/Percy Sterritt 221

Chapter 20   Wiik'aax/Neil B. Sterritt 235

	Luu Uuxs/Kathleen (Kate) Morrison	236
	Early Years	241
	Trapping at Xsuwii Aks	247
	Am Hat'al—Western Redcedar in the 20th Century	250
	The War Years and After	257
	Wiik̲'aax	263
Chapter 21	The *Ansgiyast* (Cemetery)	268
	Reincarnation	270
	Charlie Yeomans	276
	Spookxw/James Spaagh	279
Chapter 22	The Land Question	284
	Captain Cook	286
	Joseph Trutch	289
	The McKenna-McBride Royal Commission	290
	Native Brotherhood of British Columbia	296
	Calder v. BC	298
Chapter 23	Delgamuukw v. BC	302
	The Legacy of Delgamuukw	319

323 **GITXSAN SPELLING AND PRONUNCIATION GUIDE**

325 **GLOSSARY**

336 **ACKNOWLEDGEMENTS**

337 **ABOUT THE AUTHOR**

338 **REFERENCES**

344 **INDEX**

Foreword

MAPPING MY WAY HOME IS A RARE ACHIEVEMENT, BRINGING THE MYSTERIOUS CRAFTS OF WAYFINDING, THE ENIGMATIC TRUTHS OF HISTORY, AND THE DREAMLIKE REALITIES OF home together in one glorious adventure story, covering tens of thousands of years of human enterprise and experience from Asia, Europe, Africa, Australia and the Americas to the homeland of the Gitxsan in the mountains of northwest British Columbia, along by the Skeena, 'the river of mists'…and reminding us that to the first peoples of the Americas, "for at least 14,000 years, the rest of the world did not exist."

The mapping itself is along the lines of what should be called the Sterritt Projection, for like the famous cartographer Mercator, Neil Sterritt offers us a new way of navigating the world, not only by imagining curved surfaces as straight lines but by taking the two classic metaphors of genealogy—the tree and the river—and combining them with the two models of history that geology proposes—time as an arrow and time as a cycle. And he does this with a storyteller's instinct for unlikely moments and unforgettable people and unmistakable words and deeds.

His story begins with the defining moment when humans make a new place their home, naming the rivers and mountains and plants and animals, building settlements and harvesting resources and creating secular and sacred customs that reflect their imaginations and desires as well as their realities and needs. For all of us in the Americas, this is the moment when the first peoples—*Aluugigat*—travelled across the Bering land bridge to America and settled throughout the northern and southern continents; the moment when the first wanderers became the first settlers. Later, along came some newcomers—*K'amksi'waa*, a Gitxsan word for driftwood, bleached white and coming and going with the flow of the river and the tide of the sea—in a new wave of wandering.

This is the history that Neil Sterritt offers us; and it is an inspiring one—reversing the settler/wanderer story that has plagued relations between aboriginal and non-aboriginal peoples around the world for centuries, and rendering a history of the Gitxsan that celebrates what he calls a confluence of fresh water and salt water, river and sea, *Aluugigat* and *K'amksi'waa*. For in this wayfinder's mapping, the first peoples are the settlers of this land, and the newcomers are the wanderers, the nomads. But they too want to make a home in this new world. This book gives us a lesson in how that has been done in Gitxsan territory, and how it has sometimes been undone; and it reminds us that doing so with respect is a work in progress.

Replacing the nouns of historical occasions and family trees with the verbs of family relations and flowing—sometimes overflowing—rivers, it provides us with a new grammar of assent, a new way of saying 'yes' to the customs and courtesies as well as the conflicts and collaborations—the bridging and braiding of cultures—that have shaped this place and its peoples in the way sagas and epics and visionary narratives and national literatures of the world have done for millennia. This is no small thing. It offers a new way of believing in others, and in ourselves. And in stories that come to rest somewhere in that domain between here and nowhere, between 'once upon a time' and 'right now'—where stories take place. There is no earlier or later in the Torah, say scholars as well as poets. "The past is never dead. It isn't even past," said William Faulkner. And chronicles of events and characters such as this becomes ceremonies of belief in lives lived like a tale that is told, lives full of sorrows and joys, disconcerting surprises and sudden rightnesses. That belief takes hold when we read the story and enter into the history, and it stays with us when we have closed the book. Recognizing the wonderful strangeness in the histories and heritages—and the languages—of others, we see and hear it in our own. And our children will delight in the stories in this book as much as we will.

All great storytellers are good listeners…and as a listener Neil is in a special class, in company with the poet and Nobel laureate Seamus Heaney, a storyteller and peacemaker who shares Sterritt's Ulster heritage. It was once said of Heaney that he makes people make sense by the quality of his attention. I have watched Neil do just that many, many times (which is why he is such a gifted negotiator and mediator); and one of the things that makes this such a remarkable book is that he has listened to the stories of his people—his peoples—with the diligent intelligence of a scholar and the delighted imagination of a storyteller—and joined his Gitxsan tradition by telling them in his own voice, a voice full of the mystery of the rivers and trees and mountains and mists of the land and the frogs and fireweed and wolves and eagles of the clans, and full of mischief inherited from Wiigyet, the creator/trickster of Gitxsan mythology to bring light and water to nourish the world.

Neil Sterritt is a mischief-maker too, and this book has a rich vein of humour running through, holding us close to life and love and laughter. It is filled with marvelous accounts of the land and the livelihoods of the people and the plants and animals and sovereign spirits that have sustained them for thousands of years, and in the way of storytelling that nourishes us too. This is a natural history that includes humans among natural species, and it brings the deep time of geology into conversation with the real time of geography. Its cultural history is rich with both spiritual illuminations and technological insights, telling us how the cambium layer of the hemlock tree was made into food, how fish traps were made, and how bridges were built and canals dug using methods that astonished those who came after. There are fascinating details of trade and commerce and fishing and trapping and mining and logging both before and after contact between *Aluugigat* and *K'amksi'waa;* and of games of skill and strength and chance, like the contests between packers to see who can throw a diamond hitch on a horse or mule the fastest, with the ropes whistling and snapping in a blur. This book is a lot of fun, as well as a wealth of information. Commenting on the apparent preferences of aboriginal and non-aboriginal citizens for a location in the old cemetery, he notes that Gitxsan always wanted to face the river, or later the road, where they could be seen; while the whites preferred a cemetery plot on the hillside, what he describes as 'a room with a view'. But rather than signifying some deep difference between Them and Us, which Neil discounts, it signals a difference in customs. Neither more nor less.

A thoughtful wanderer once remarked that a seagoing traveller has a more vivid impression that the ocean is made up of waves than that it is made of water. Neil Sterritt brings that kind of understanding to bear on his discussion of language, paying affectionate attention to the Gitxsan language—its patterns and its pauses—and on his concern for what he calls the 'land question'. This is not a polemical book, and is refreshingly free of colonial, anti-colonial and postcolonial rhetoric; but as he makes clear in the final chapter, that question is one for all of us, not just the Gitxsan. It has to do with a future that we share, and—thanks to this book—a past we can understand. And it is urgent.

One of my favourite stories told by Neil himself, not mentioned in the book, involves a confrontation between the Gitxsan and the government over fishing rights. Exasperated by decades of aggravation and increasingly frequent arrests, Gitxsan leaders announced that the community would be fishing at a particular time and place prohibited by the government regulations but sanctioned by centuries of Gitxsan practice, and by healthy fish stocks. The police, along with officials from the department of fisheries, arrived in force, and ready for trouble; but they were stopped short by a blockade organized in what I have heard Neil mischievously describe (with a big smile on his face) as traditional Gitxsan battle order: children in front, carrying kid's stuff; women next, the guardians of place; and the men hiding safely behind, urging everyone on. The authorities demanded the people move, but the Gitxsan refused. A classic stand-off. Then the authorities moved menacingly forward…at which point the children reached into their kiddy bags, pulled out some mysterious missiles…and threw a volley of marshmallows at the advancing forces. Startled and scared—after all, they were in Gitxsan territory—the authorities covered their heads, turned their backs and ran for cover, their embarrassing retreat caught on camera by the large media contingent that the Gitxsan had invited along. It made the evening news and newspaper headlines throughout the west, and became known as the Marshmallow War. It also prompted the government to negotiate a responsible agreement on that fishery with the Gitxsan, whose children were both the heroes of the day and the reason Neil Sterritt has dedicated his life to showing all of us, in the gentlest way possible, that understanding history and heritage—our own past as well as that of others—offers the only way forward.

I still have my membership pin for the Tillicum Club, sponsored by the Vancouver *Province* in the 1950s to promote children's stories from all the aboriginal coast cultures. Shaped like a souvenir-shop totem pole, its motto—in the Chinook creole that facilitated communication and commerce between peoples of the coast and interior of British Columbia—is *Klahowya Tillicum*: "Greetings, Friend." With luminous integrity, Neil Sterritt's book greets us all as friends, bringing shrewd common sense, a subtle but stern sense of ceremony, a deep but not bottomless patience, and a wonderful sense of humour to his history of home. Written with the grace of a storyteller and the generosity of a wise man, it will deepen everyone's sense of family, and heritage, and home.

—J. Edward Chamberlin

J. Edward Chamberlin is Professor Emeritus of English and Comparative Literature at the University of Toronto. He was the Senior Research Associate with the Royal Commission on Aboriginal Peoples in Canada, worked with Justice Thomas Berger on the Mackenzie Valley Pipeline Hearings and has worked extensively with indigenous peoples around the world. His books include *If This Is Your Land, Where Are Your Stories* (the title quoting a Gitxsan elder in the 1980s); *Horse: How the Horse Has Shaped Civilizations* and *Island: How Islands Transform the World*.

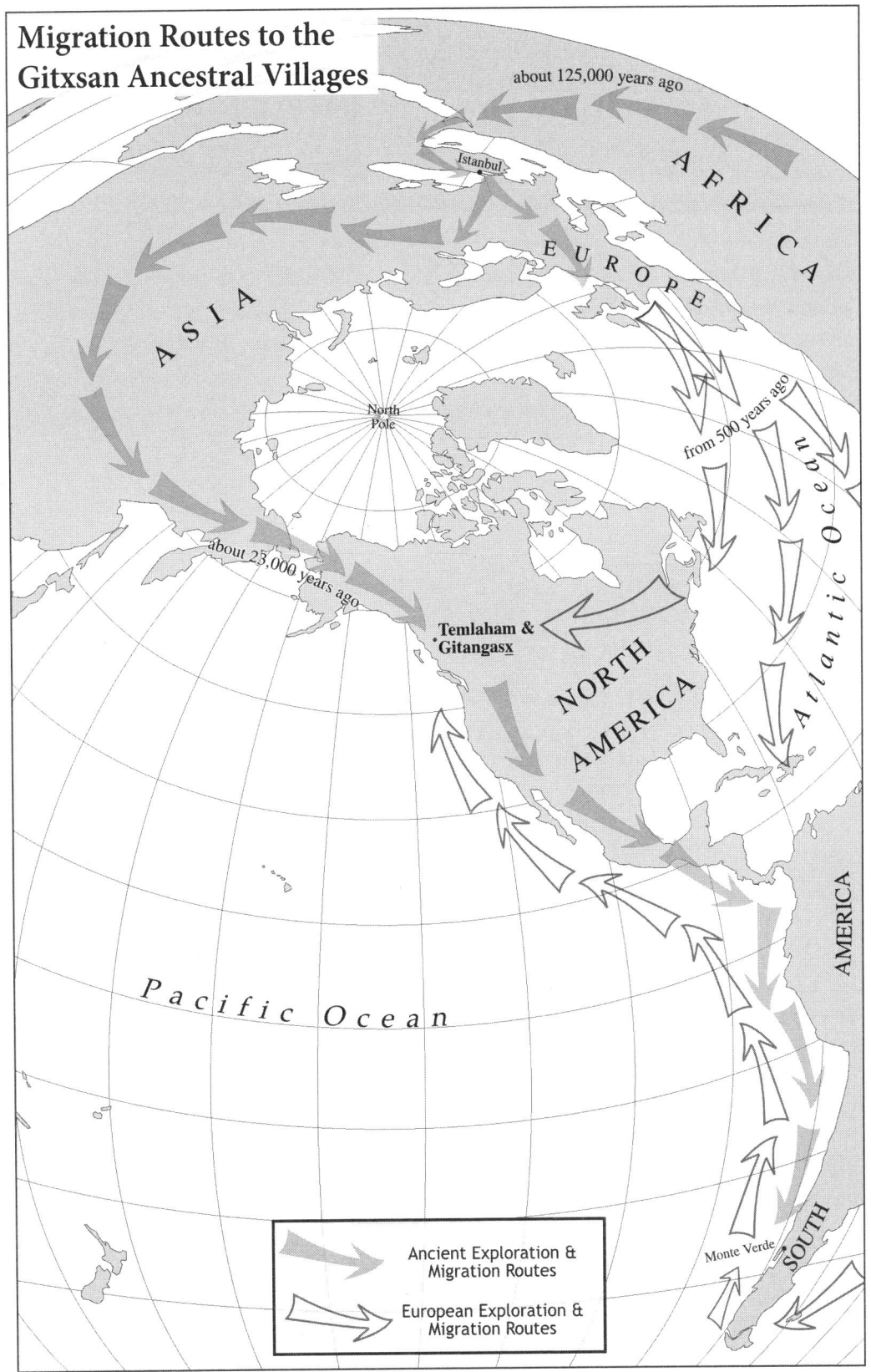

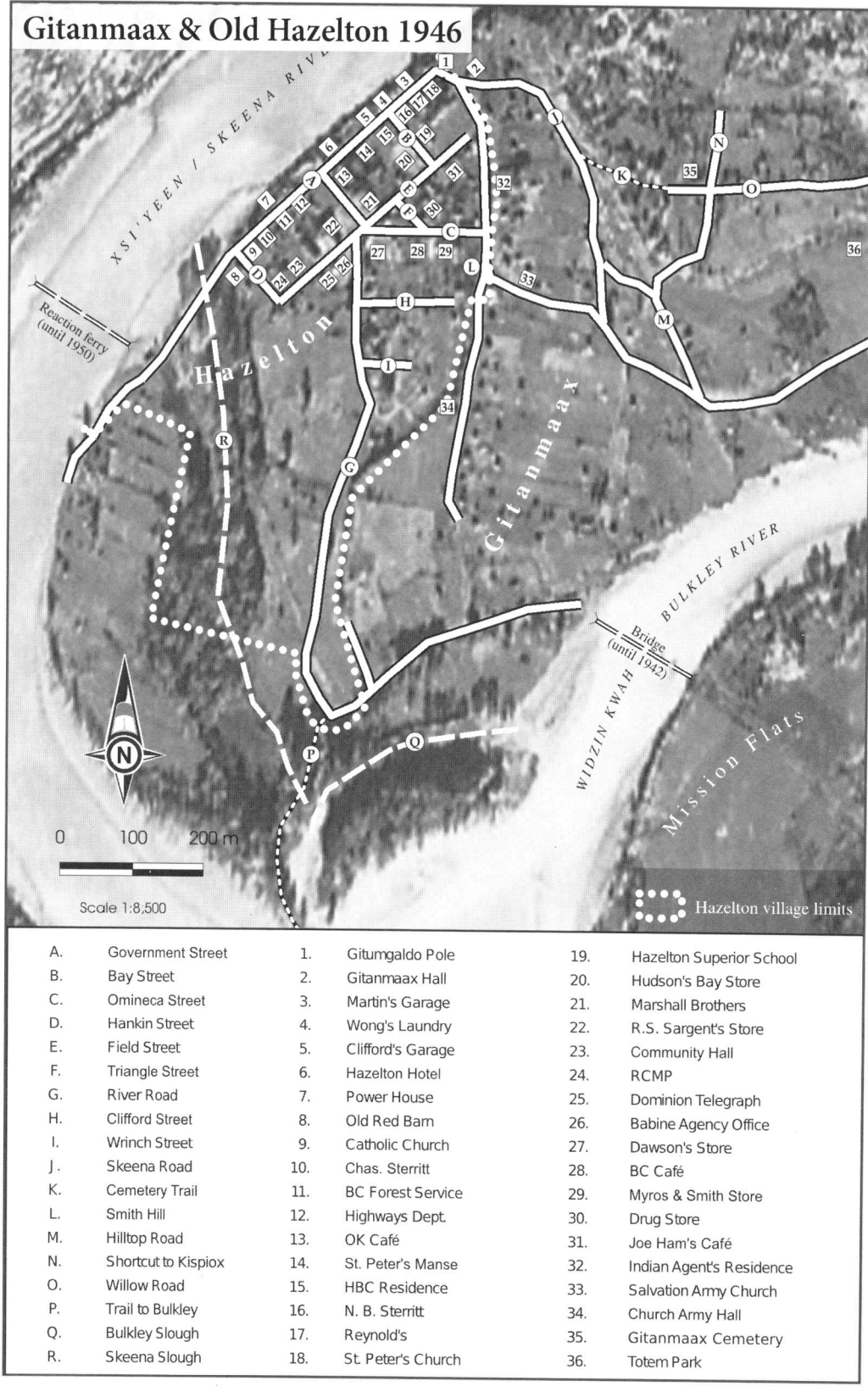

Gitanmaax & Old Hazelton 1946

A.	Government Street	1.	Gitumgaldo Pole	19.	Hazelton Superior School
B.	Bay Street	2.	Gitanmaax Hall	20.	Hudson's Bay Store
C.	Omineca Street	3.	Martin's Garage	21.	Marshall Brothers
D.	Hankin Street	4.	Wong's Laundry	22.	R.S. Sargent's Store
E.	Field Street	5.	Clifford's Garage	23.	Community Hall
F.	Triangle Street	6.	Hazelton Hotel	24.	RCMP
G.	River Road	7.	Power House	25.	Dominion Telegraph
H.	Clifford Street	8.	Old Red Barn	26.	Babine Agency Office
I.	Wrinch Street	9.	Catholic Church	27.	Dawson's Store
J.	Skeena Road	10.	Chas. Sterritt	28.	BC Café
K.	Cemetery Trail	11.	BC Forest Service	29.	Myros & Smith Store
L.	Smith Hill	12.	Highways Dept.	30.	Drug Store
M.	Hilltop Road	13.	OK Café	31.	Joe Ham's Café
N.	Shortcut to Kispiox	14.	St. Peter's Manse	32.	Indian Agent's Residence
O.	Willow Road	15.	HBC Residence	33.	Salvation Army Church
P.	Trail to Bulkley	16.	N. B. Sterritt	34.	Church Army Hall
Q.	Bulkley Slough	17.	Reynold's	35.	Gitanmaax Cemetery
R.	Skeena Slough	18.	St. Peter's Church	36.	Totem Park

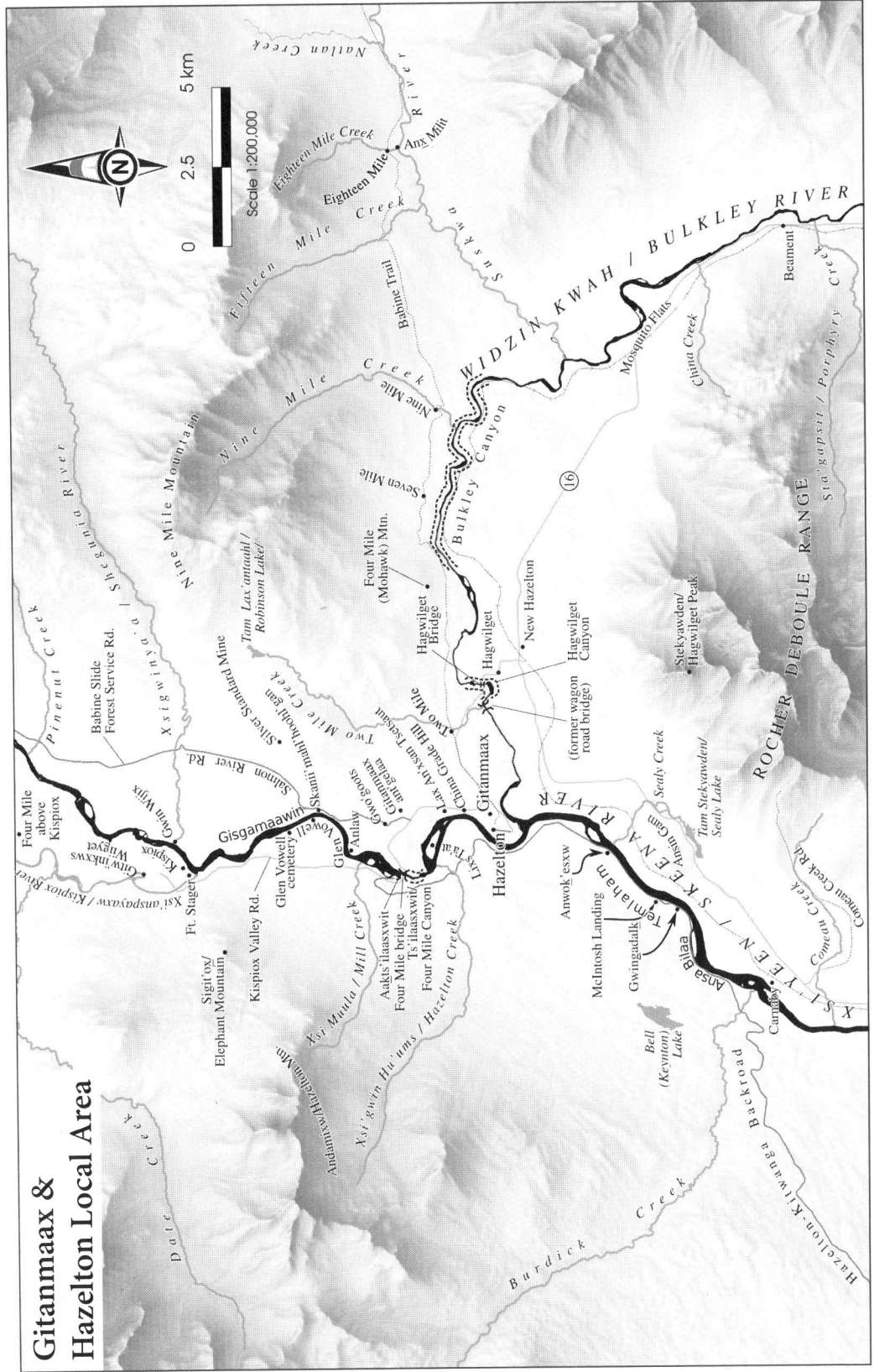

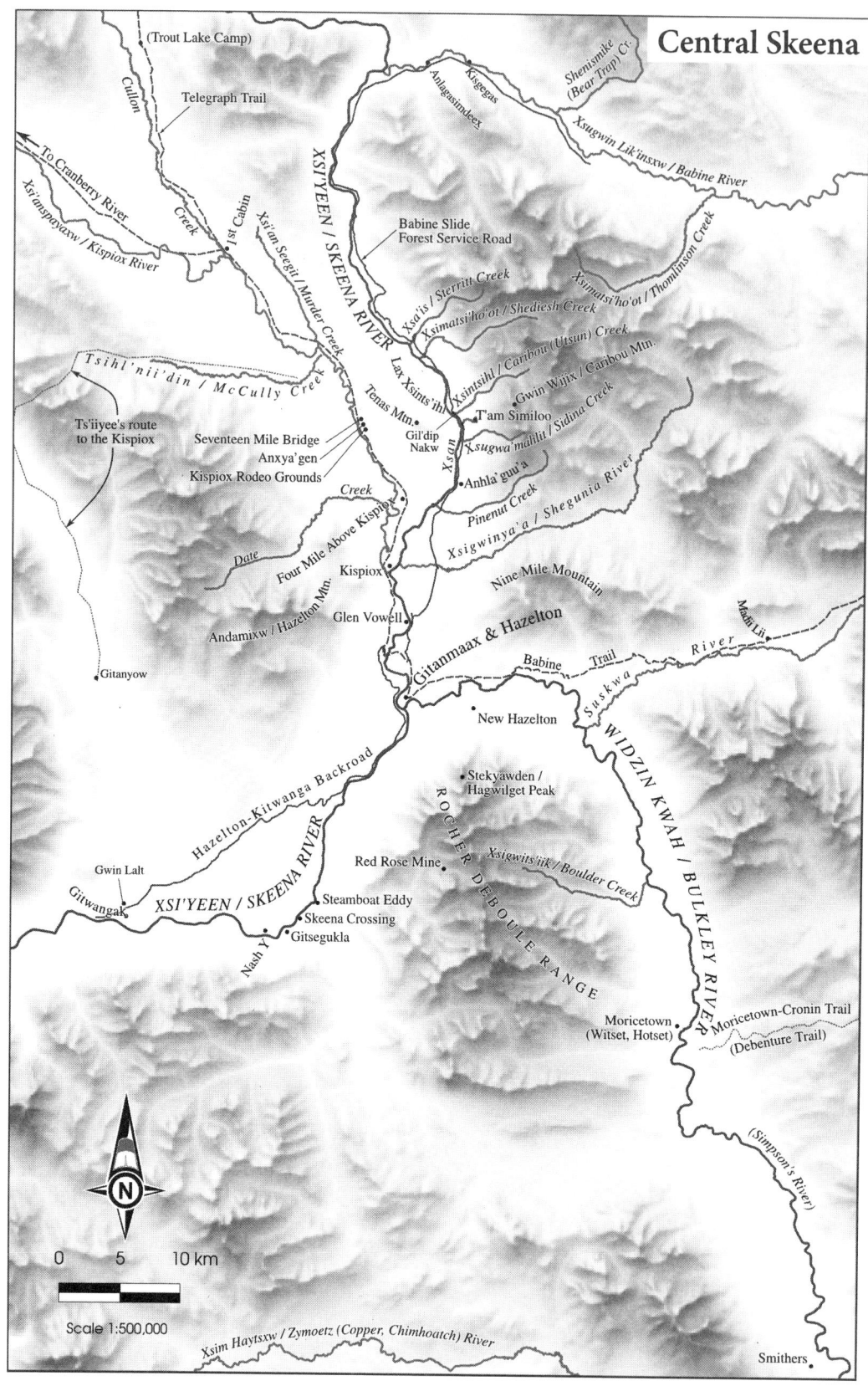

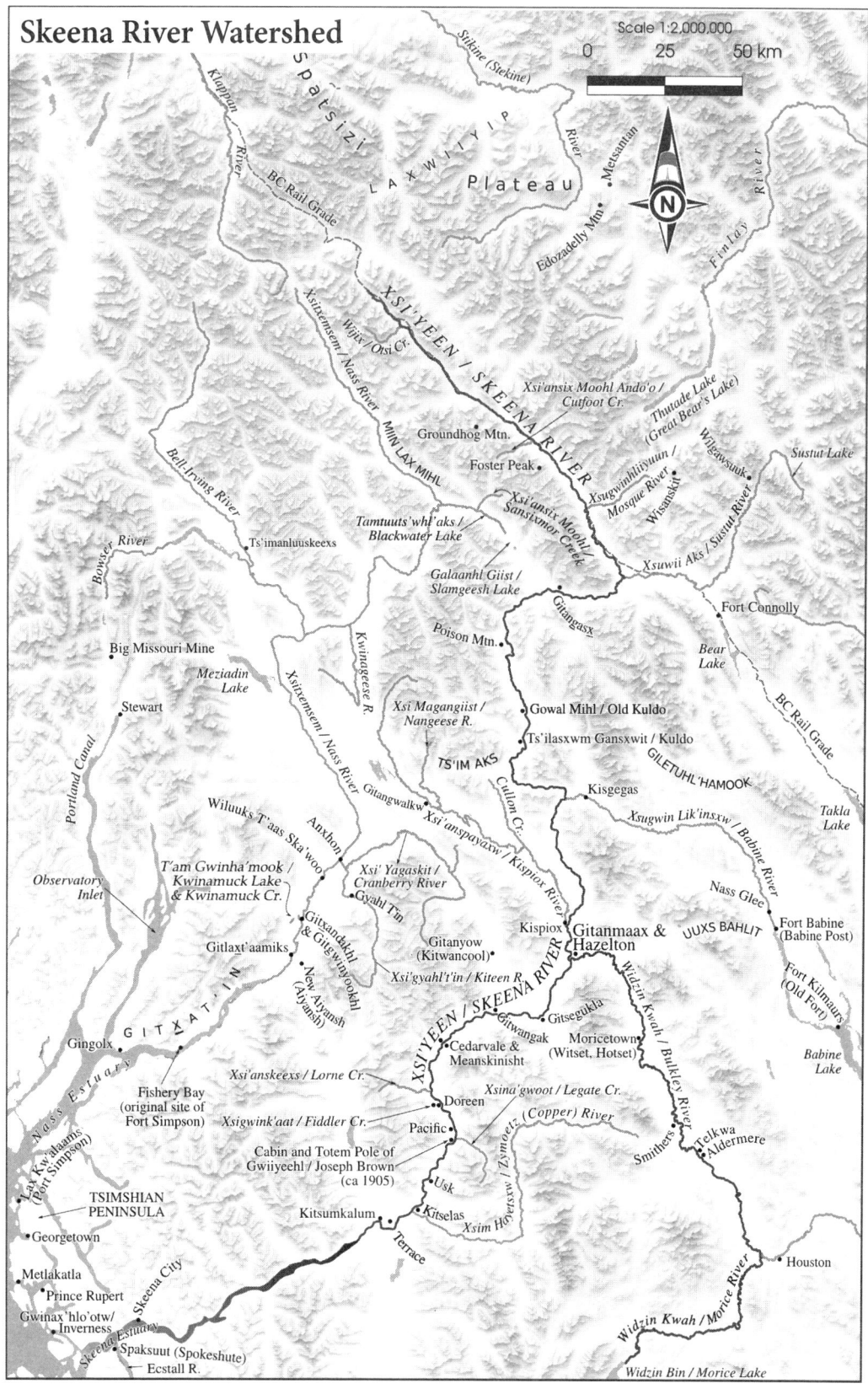

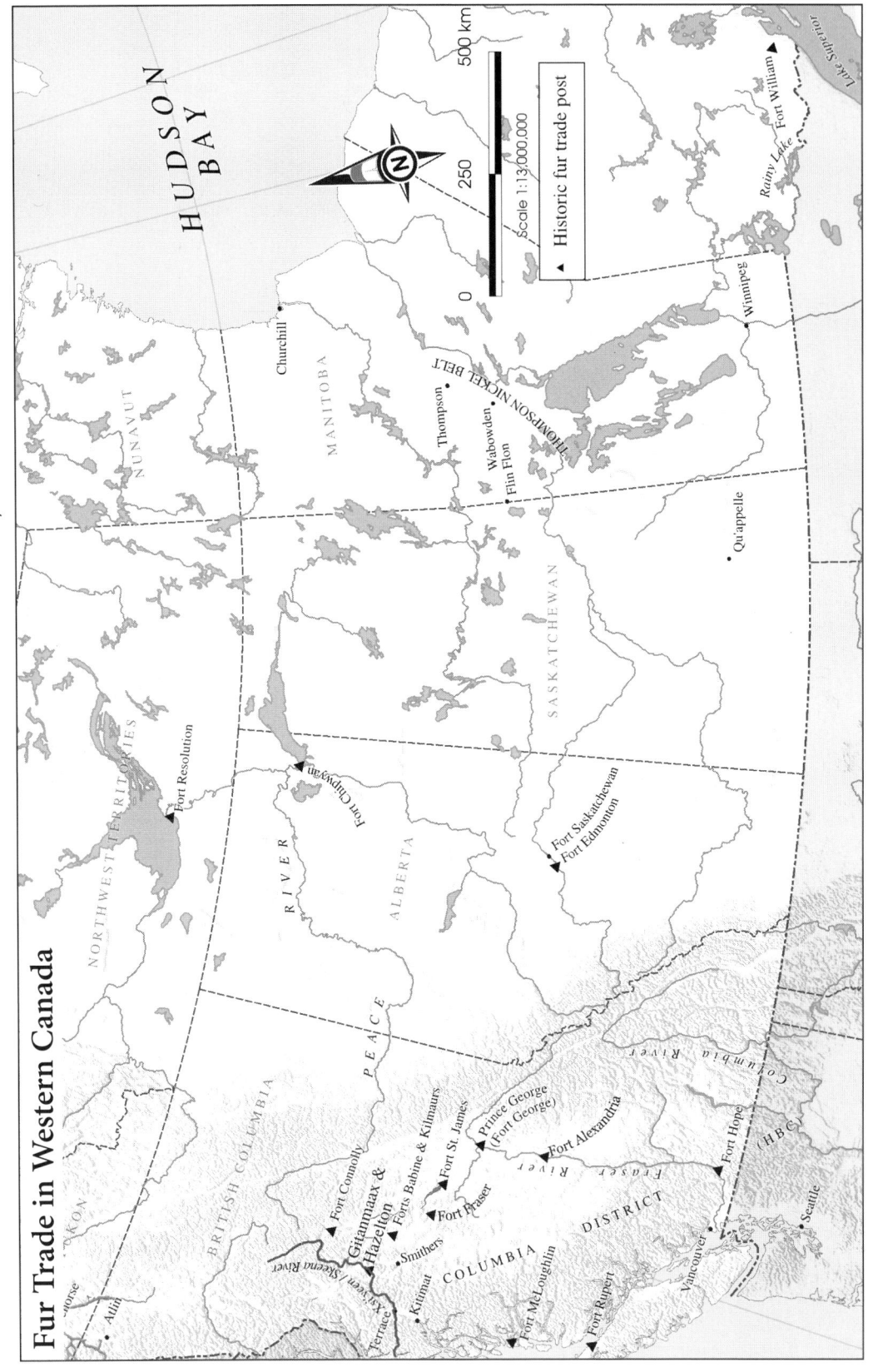

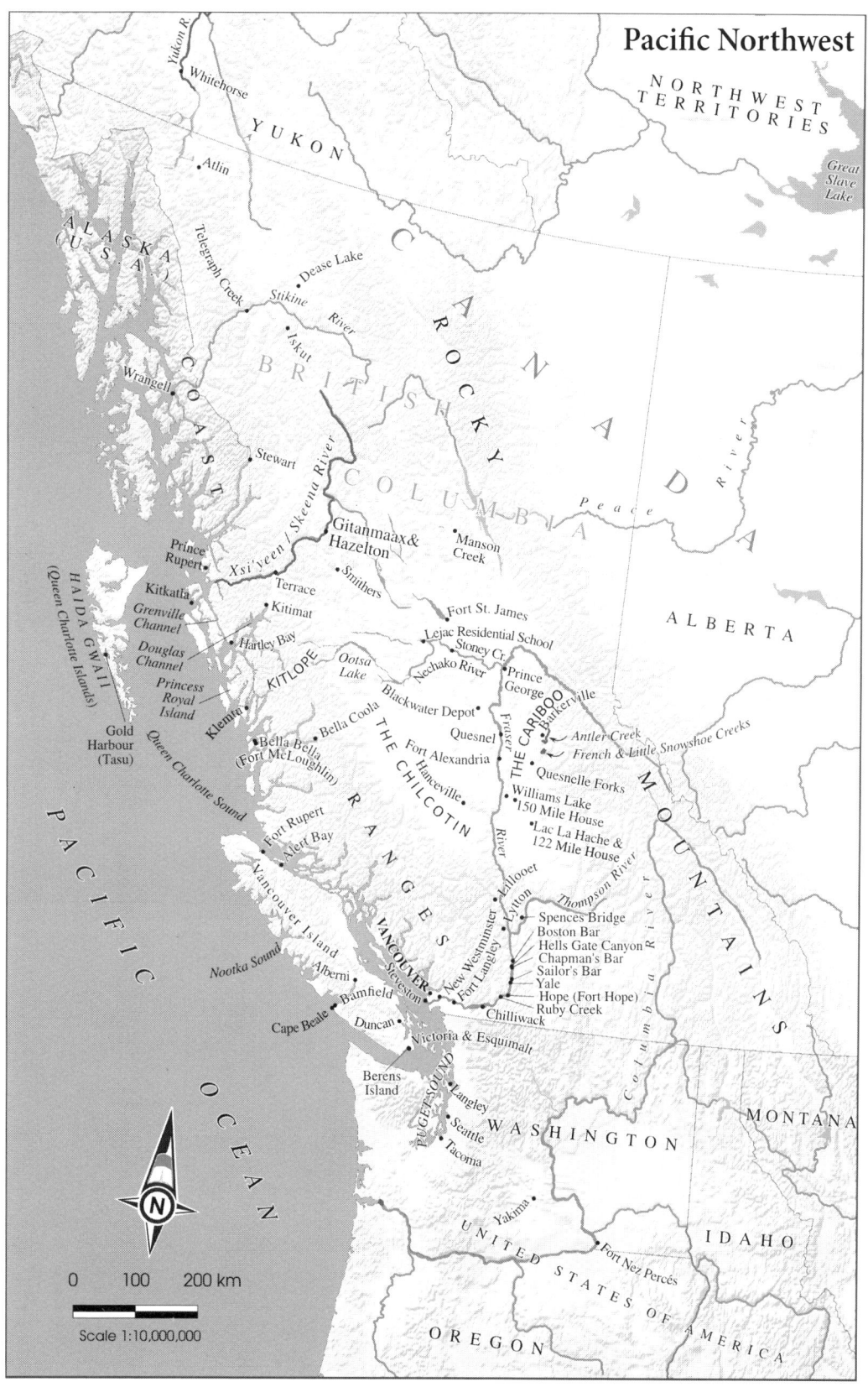

Neil J. Sterritt

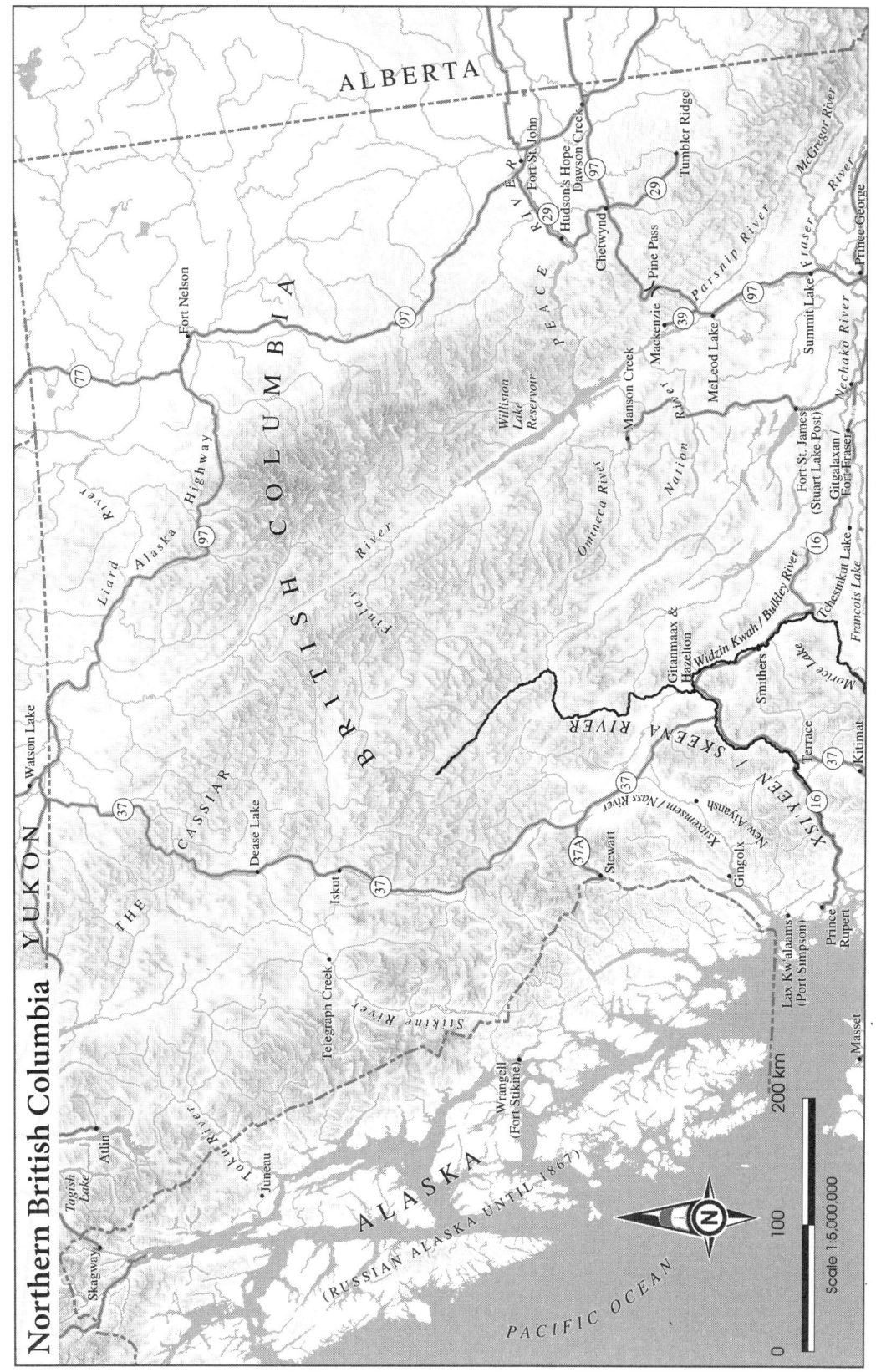

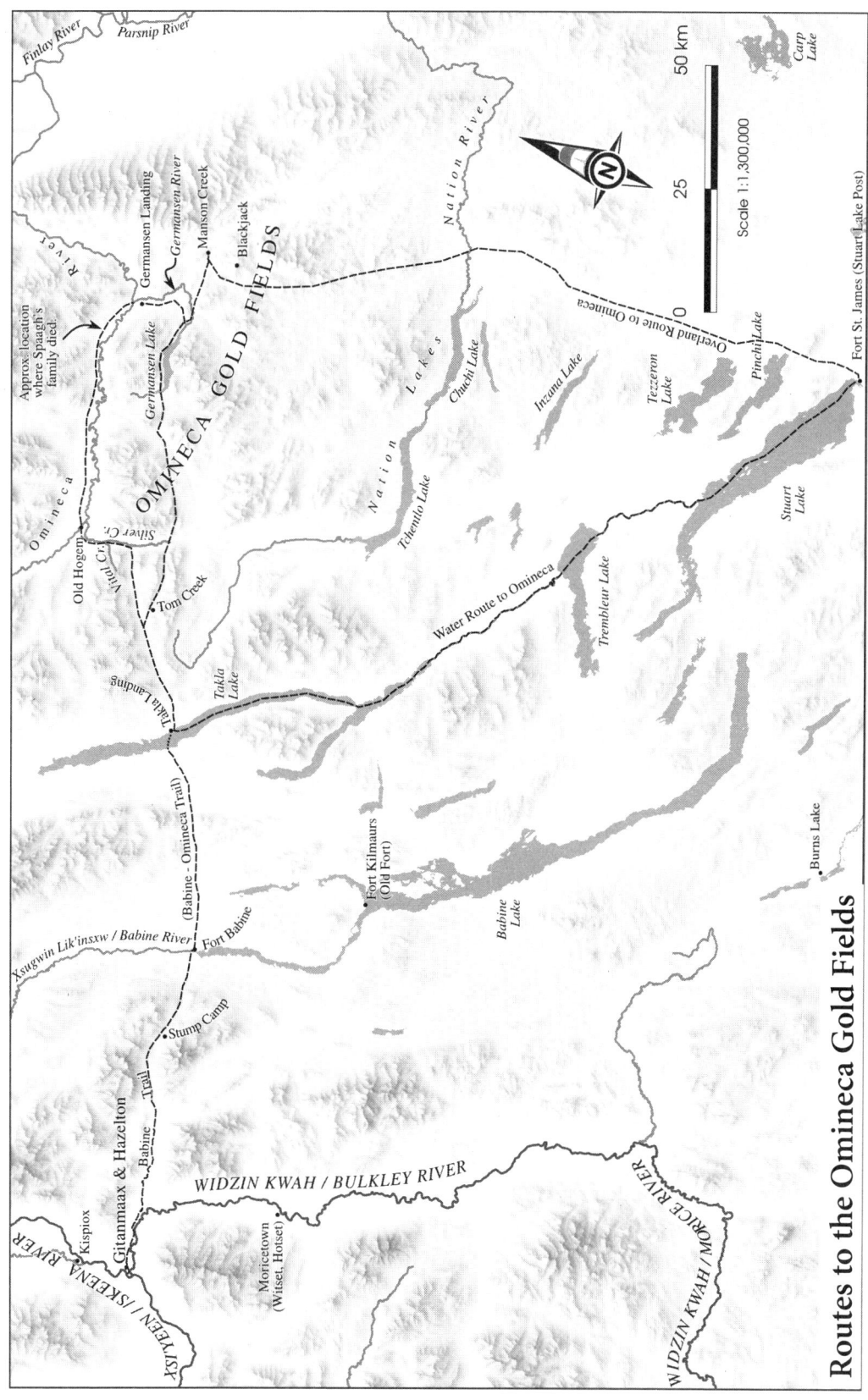

Neil J. Sterritt

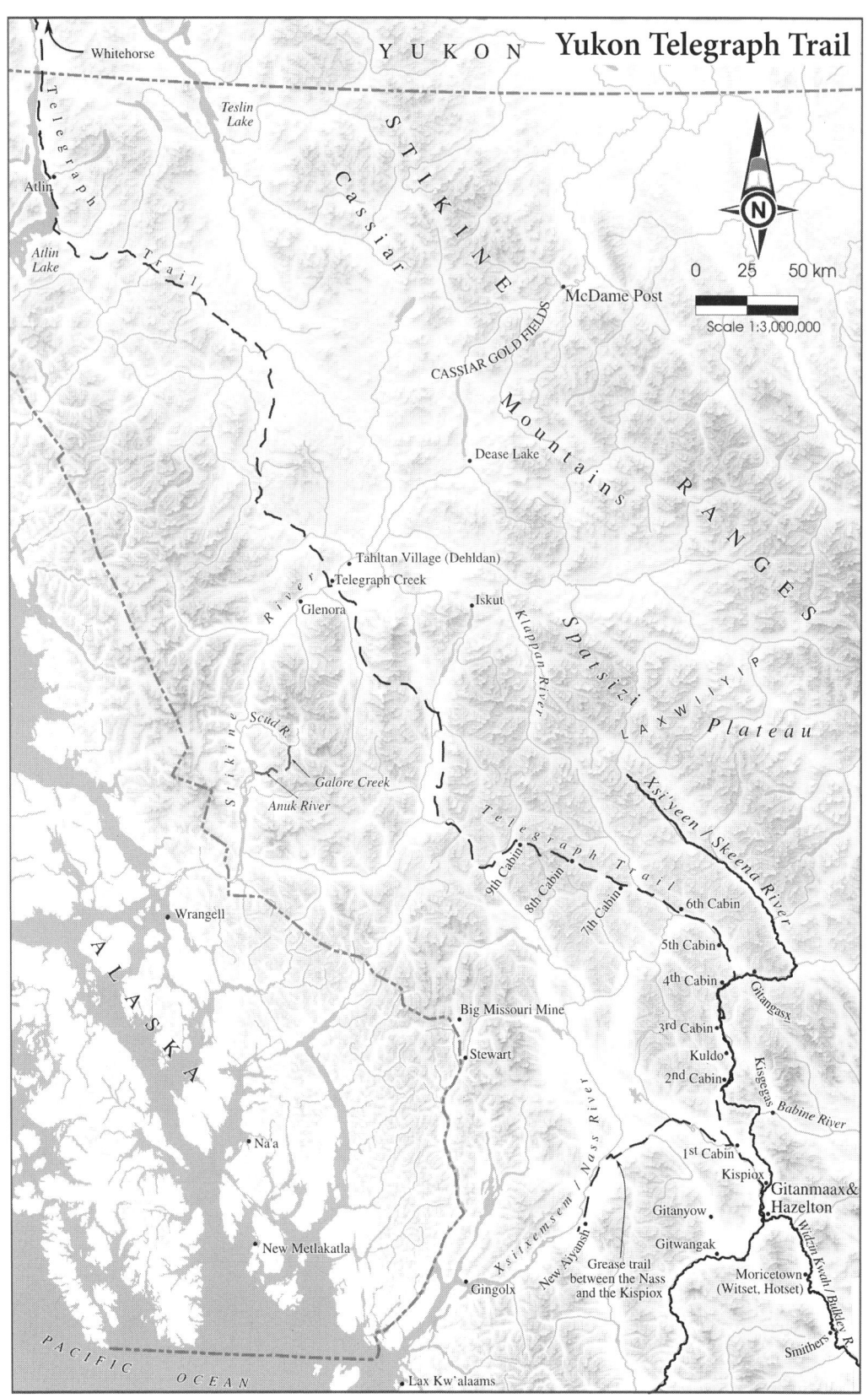

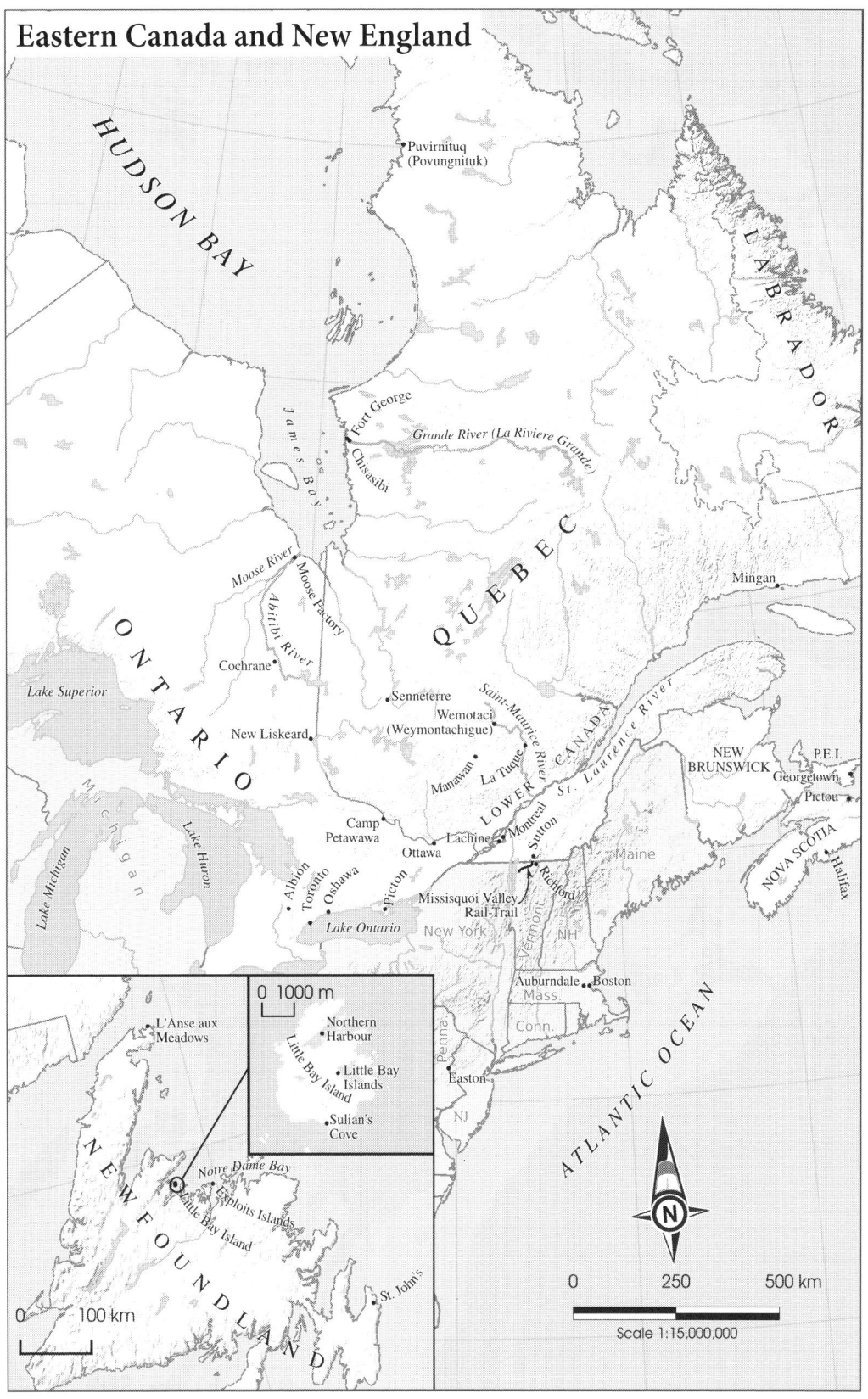

Key to Family Trees

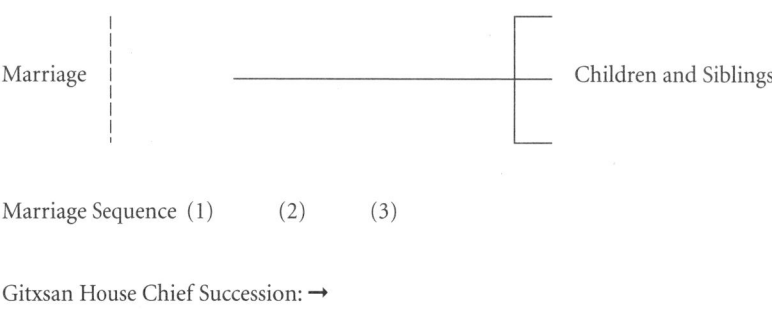

Marriage Sequence (1)   (2)   (3)

Gitxsan House Chief Succession: →

Example:

Charlie Sterritt Family Tree

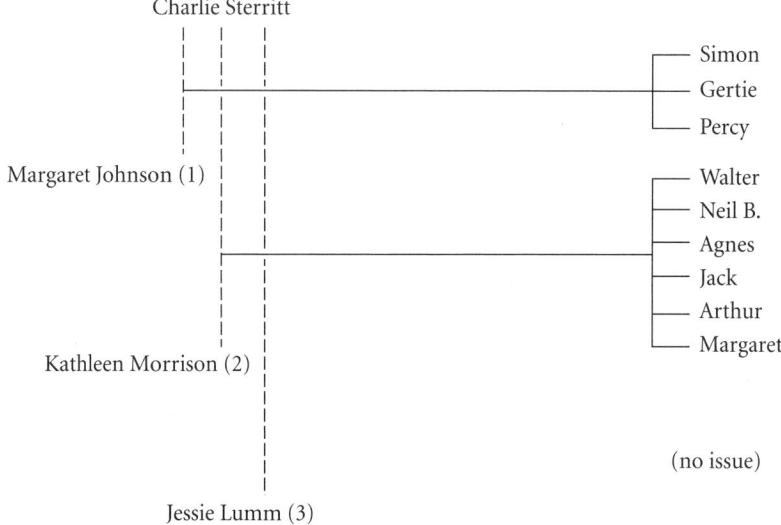

→Hakw→Hahqu→Mark Sampson→Charlie Sterritt→etc.

Please note: Gitxsan descent follows the matriline. Settler descent follows the patriline.

Hankin Family Tree
From 1801

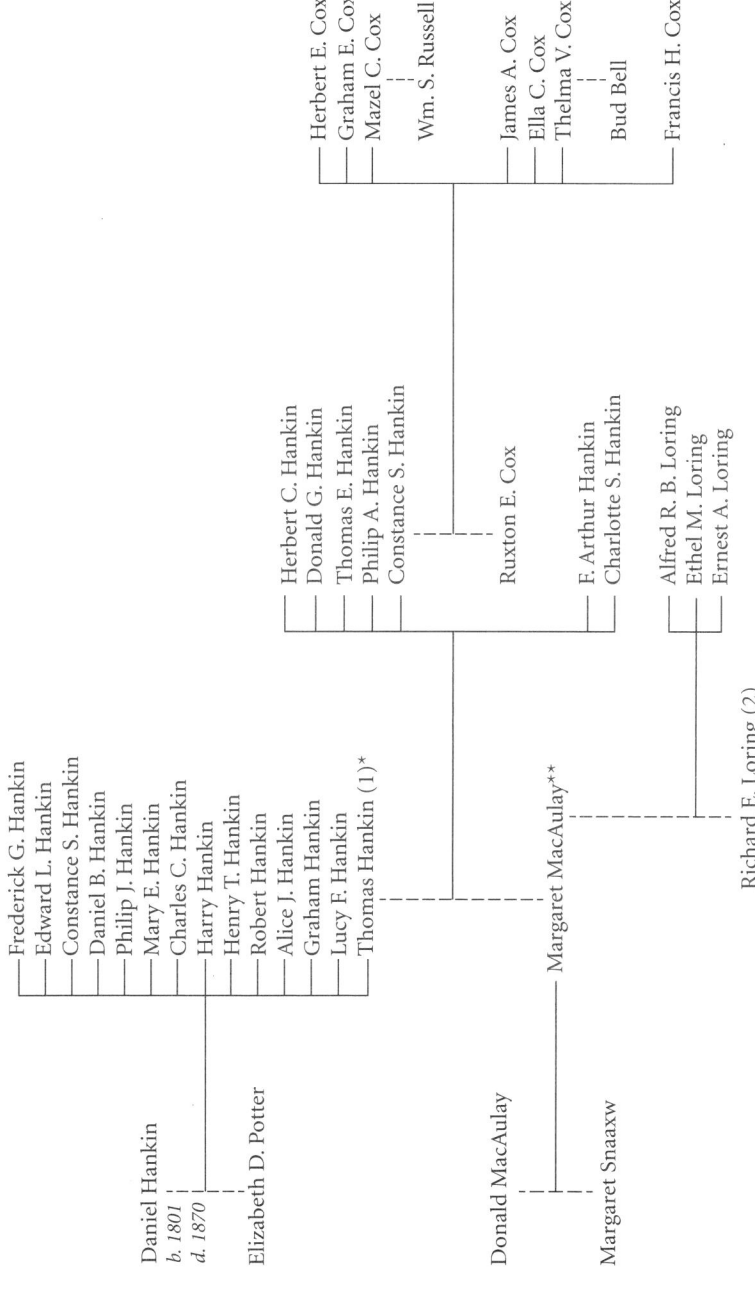

* Thomas (1843 – 1885) was Daniel and Elizabeth's eleventh child.
** Margaret (1855 – 1910) was the MacAulay's fifth daughter.

Neil J. Sterritt

Starrett and Cummins Family Tree
From 1771

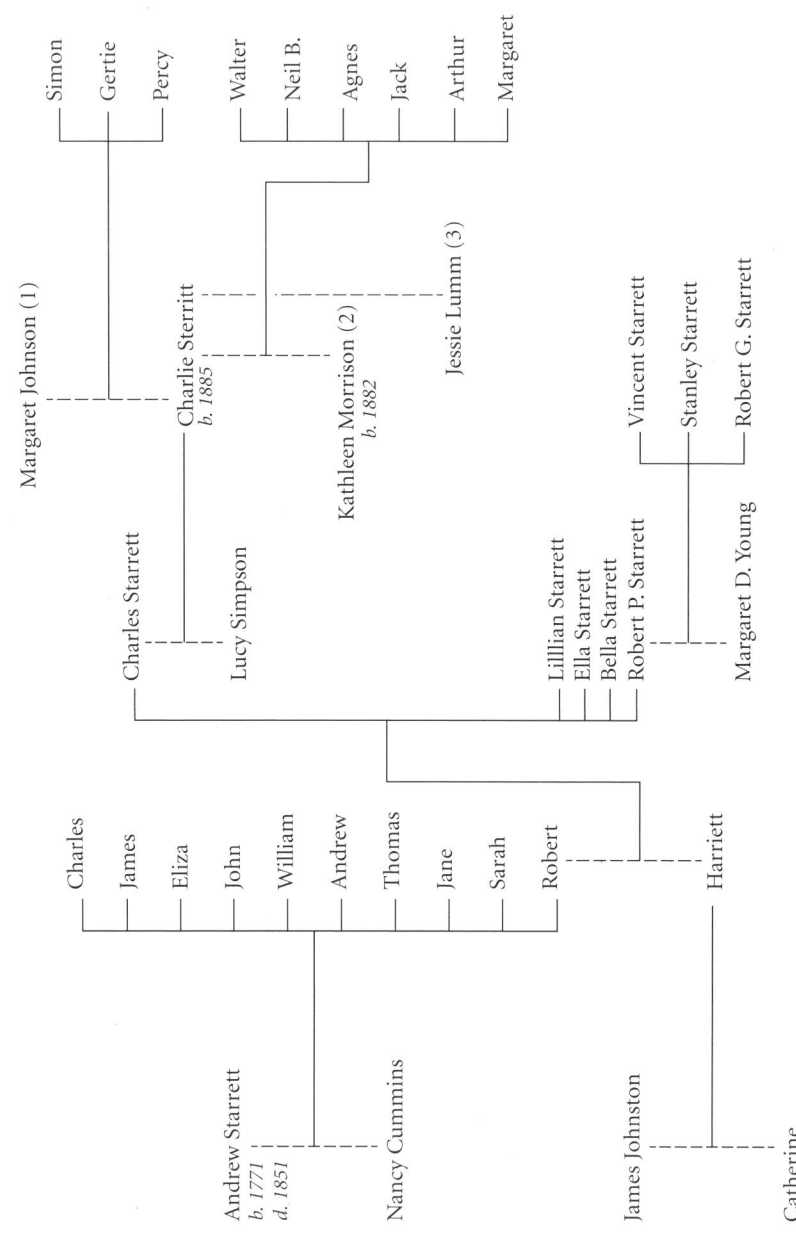

Russell and Weir Family Tree
From 1837

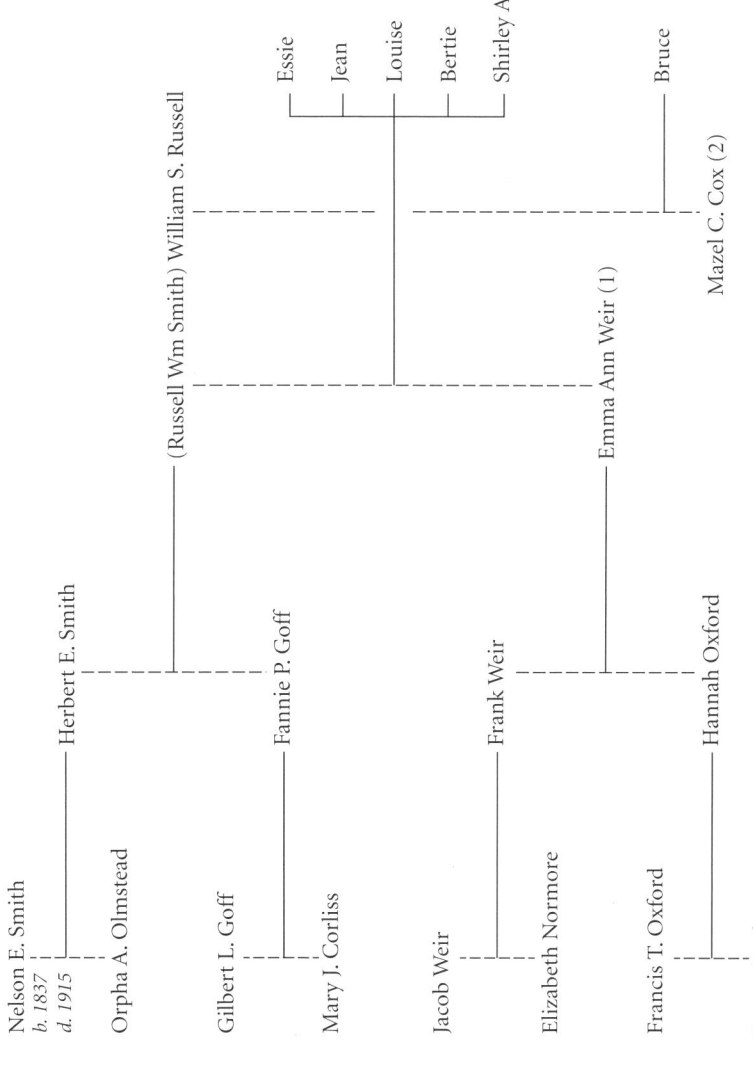

Neil J. Sterritt

Haaxw Family Tree
From 1830

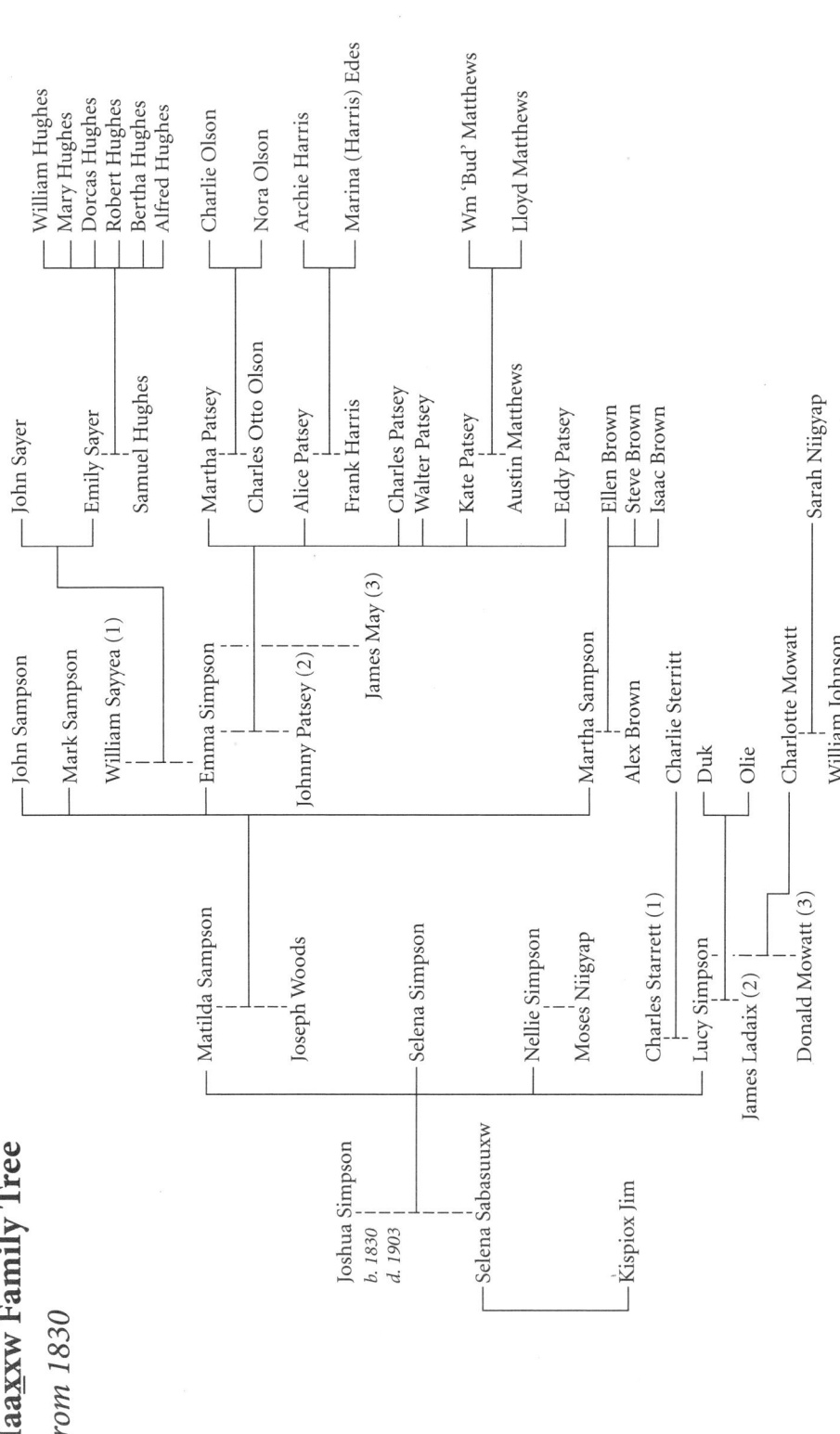

Haaxw Succession 1881 to Present:
→Hakq *(age 60 appears in the 1881 census of Kispiox)*→Hahqu→Mark Sampson→Charlie Sterritt→Marina Edes→Charlie Olson→Wm Matthews→Byron Edes→Shannon Wright

Wiiḵ'aax Family Tree
From 1842

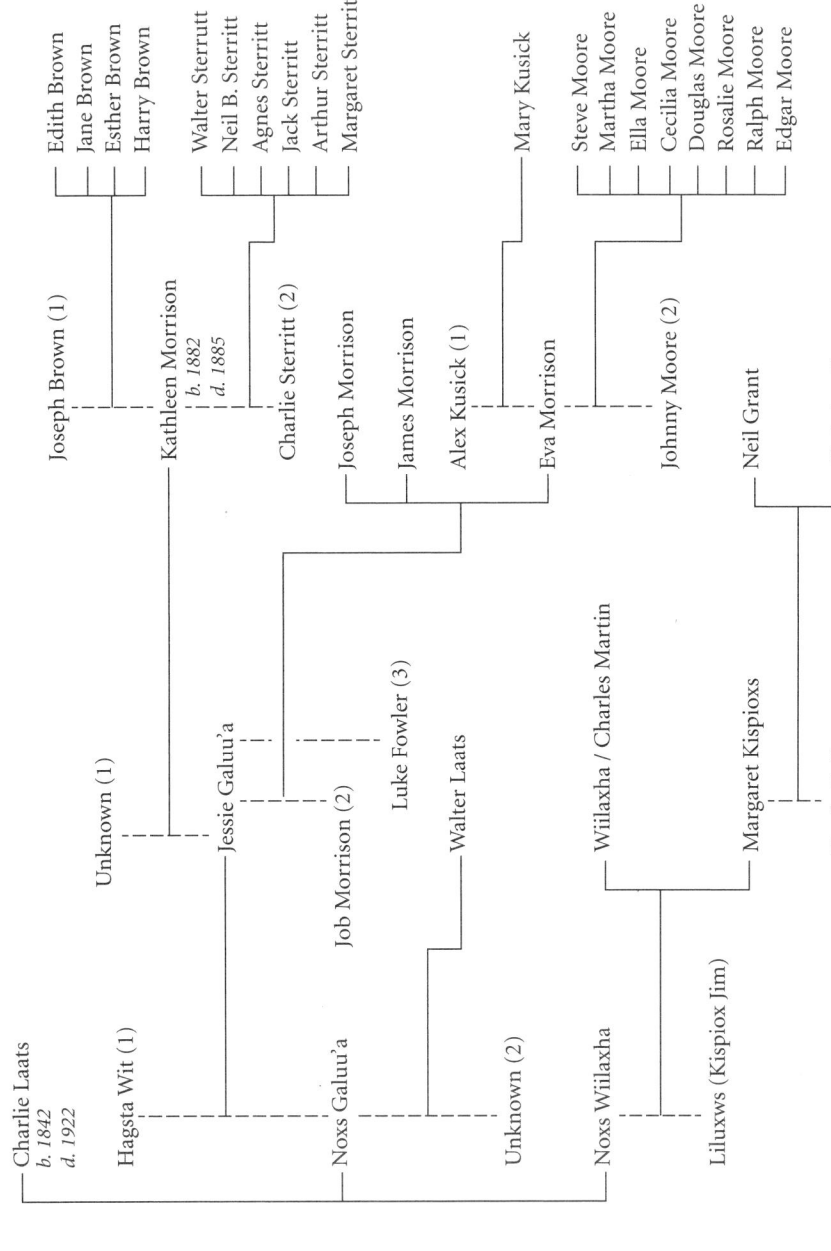

Sterritt Family Tree
From 1882

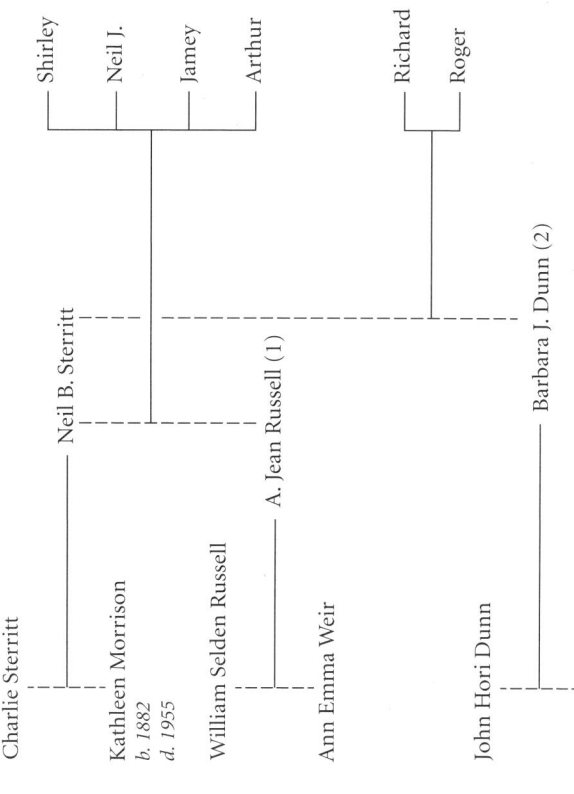

Introduction

My parents and grandparents, aunts and uncles told exciting stories about growing up in northwest British Columbia. They laughed and joked, gossiped and teased. They spoke of amusing, larger than life people and romantic places along winding forest trails, places like Kisgegas, Kuldo, Bear Lake, Manson Creek, Telegraph Creek, the Omineca and Cassiar gold fields and the Yukon. Their stories gave texture and meaning to my mental maps. I longed to travel their trails, to experience those places for myself. Later in my life I did that, and went far beyond the familiar paths of my ancestors. Eventually I realized that maps, both imagined and real, can unite people and define their connection to the land, family, culture, language, history—to home.

But that would come later. I was born and raised in Hazelton in the 1940s. My father was born in a Gitxsan village, Glen Vowell, and my mother was born in a Newfoundland outport village, Little Bay Islands. Whenever we visited my Gitxsan grandparents, the adults spoke Gitxsan† unless my mother was present and then, out of respect, they switched to English.

Hazelton was the white community, and Gitanmaax—the reserve just up the hill from our house—was the Gitxsan community.‡ There were disputes and rivalries between the children of these communities but they were never serious. And when it came to sports and games, we all played together.

Horses and cows wandered the dirt streets and wood plank sidewalks. Because livestock ran free, everyone fenced their yards to protect their gardens. During spring breakup we all played in the melt water that ran down the hill and along Government Street, building dams and making hand-carved boats. We caught (and set free) swallows with simple bolo-like devices as they swooped about looking for nesting material. We played marbles and other children's games along the streets and in the school yard. The only building specifically designated a school was next

---

† There are two dialects of the Gitxsan language, one used by those people living in the villages below Gitanmaax on the Skeena River (the Gyeets) and another by those from Gitanmaax and above (the Gigeenix). Most of the stories in this book involve my family and therefore Gigeenix villages but this is not to downplay the importance of villages such as Gitsegukla, Gitwangak and Gitanyow in Gitxsan history.

‡ See Map 2: Gitanmaax & Hazelton:1946.

Taking a break from lessons at the Hazelton Superior School, ca. 1950. The author is sitting to the left of the girl in the white sweater near the back of the class. (Sterritt Family coll.)

to our house. It had one teacher who taught about twenty pupils in several lower grades. Empty buildings here and there about town provided makeshift classrooms for those in the higher grades. Barrel stoves were lit each cold morning to heat the schools. Our homes were heated the same way, with the addition of a McClary cook stove in the kitchen and a wood or coal heater in the front room. During winter we slid on sleighs, cardboard or tin or skied down Smith Hill and the hill by Gitanmaax Community Hall, near our house.

Hazelton had three general stores, a drug store and confectionary, a hotel, three Chinese cafes and a Chinese laundry. Wong's laundry sat beside the Skeena across the road from our house. There we frequently watched Wong and his Chinese brethren smoke a bamboo water pipe.

There were three churches: Anglican, Catholic and Pentecostal. Although located off reserve, the Anglican church hall also served as the Indian day school for those of our Gitxsan friends who did not attend residential school.[†] Kids from mixed marriages went to the Hazelton Superior School in the lower grades. In the upper grades children of all races from the surrounding villages attended the Hazelton Amalgamated School. The school was opened in 1951 by the Gitanmaax Band Council, the Hazelton Municipal Council, BC provincial officials and local residents and was reputed to be the only school of its kind in Canada.

The Gitxsan children who did go to residential schools in places like Lejac, Lytton, Port Alberni and Edmonton in the fall usually came back in the spring. There is no doubt many Gitxsan children suffered different forms of abuse while attending residential school and some never

---

† My grandparents bought a house and moved from Glen Vowell to Hazelton in 1921 so my father and his siblings could get the education they might not have acquired on reserve.

The Hazelton Amalgamated School for children of all races was opened in 1951 by provincial, municipal and band council officials such as Ray Williston, provincial Minister of Education (far left), and Gitxsan Chief Charlie Clifford (at mic). (Sterritt Family coll.)

came home again. Others benefited from the experience, picking up practical skills and acquiring an education. Some also formed lasting alliances at residential school that benefited both them and their communities as they battled for recognition of aboriginal rights and title to land in subsequent years.

Hazelton's community hall served many purposes: concerts and dances, meetings, recreation such as boxing and wrestling, badminton, basketball and volleyball, and afternoon and evening movies on Saturdays, with my father running the projector.

Government services included the Indian Agent, Forest Service ranger station, public works, the RCMP detachment and a jail. Telegraph services existed from about 1900, a telephone before 1921, and party lines from the late 1940s. A diesel generator, owned by R.S. Sargent & Company and operated by my father when he returned from Europe after World War II, provided electricity to most of the town. Several springs or wells provided fresh water to those fortunate to have them nearby. The rest of us packed water in buckets from the Skeena River year-round. Rainwater sufficed for laundry and bath water during spring, summer and fall. We, and most others, bathed in a galvanized tub in the kitchen for most of the 1940s. Everyone had an outhouse, some with two-seaters for those who didn't mind the company on a freezing winter day. The United Church-sponsored hospital was built one mile from town in 1903 on land that Chief Gidumgaldo designated for that purpose.

Gitanmaax Reserve accommodated the Salvation Army church and the Salvation Army hall that doubled as a school. The Gitanmaax community hall was used for on reserve events such as

Gidumgaldo's pole and longhouse on the banks of the Skeena at Hazelton. The pole, raised in 1881, is called 'Nose Like Coho' and now stands beside the Hazelton Public Library. (Image E-08409 courtesy of RBCM & A)

dances, weddings, funerals and feasts, although feasts had to be held secretly because of federal legislation banning them.[†] The ball field at Totem Park was on reserve, as was our swimming hole on the Bulkley Slough.

Employment along the Skeena was mainly seasonal, based on trapping, selective logging, farming and, for aboriginal people, the commercial fishery in the Skeena estuary near Prince Rupert. Government services, the hospital, several retail stores, the Silver Standard Mine and Marshall Brothers Trucking provided steady employment for some, including the blacksmith because horses were still the main mode of transportation. At the same time, everyone added to their meager incomes with large gardens and by harvesting domestic and wild berries, salmon and wild game. Potatoes and carrots were stored along with canned or jarred fruit and jams in frost-free cellars dug beneath kitchen floors. In summer, homemade root beer put up in beer bottles was kept cool there too, a treat not to be underestimated and almost equaled by Bud Dawson's ice cream which arrived weekly by train in large insulated canvas tubs.

Many Gitxsan families made a living logging spruce and hemlock trees for lumber and western redcedar trees for telephone poles. The BC Forest Service allocated timber limits to those wishing to log. Trees were felled with axes and crosscut saws. I recall my grandmother, Kate Sterritt, working at my grandfather Charlie's pole camp. She might fall and peel a twenty-five or thirty-foot cedar tree between lunch and supper. She was as much a driver of their business as my grandfather. She too was an entrepreneur and managed their rental cabins in Hazelton.

One afternoon she came walking down the hill towards us on her way home. She had a four-gallon cedar bentwood box filled with huckleberries on her back and was followed by two large dogs with packs. She had been away alone for several days picking berries about eight kilometres from town.

Although she had limited writing skills, she knew how to delegate. I recall on two occasions when she needed to convey a message and told me what to say as I printed the letters for her.

[†] The Indian Act abolished all cultural practices, including feasts, in 1880, under the Potlatch Law. An amendment the same year made such practices a criminal offence. This law remained in effect until 1952. In 1918, violation of the Potlatch Ban was made a summary offense triable by the Indian Agent. In the early 1920s, the Department of Indian Affairs instructed the Hazelton agent to enforce the ban, resulting in charges being brought during the next decade against Edward Sexsmith, Robert Wilson, John Morrison, Silas Johnson, Sam Dick, Moses Stevens, John Smith and Tom Campbell. Charges were dropped for some and others received suspended sentences.

Hazelton, ca. 1956. St. Peter's Anglican Church with bell tower is at bottom right. (Image I-28180 courtesy of RBCM & A)

Sawmill owners hauled their lumber to R.S. Sargent's in Hazelton or to the railroad in New Hazelton. Some pole camps hired Marshall Brothers Trucking to haul their poles to the railroad. Others floated their winter's harvest down the Skeena in river drives. This was an annual event when we watched the men break up log jams and send the poles past the village of Hazelton. The poles were gathered in a boom that spanned the Skeena River at Nash Y, about a kilometre below the village of Gitsegukla.‡ There men brought the poles ashore and, using a cable powered by a mechanical donkey, skidded them up a high, steep hill to the railroad on the right bank§ of the Skeena where men loaded them onto flat deck rail cars and shipped them to Minnesota.

We lived in a house at the east end of Government Street near St. Peter's Church. We often played along Government Street which, at that time, was the main road from Hazelton to the world as we knew it—Kispiox, New Hazelton, Prince Rupert, Prince George and Vancouver. My grandparents lived about two blocks southwest of us, also on Government Street. Once, my friends and I were making bows and arrows in my grandparents' yard. I struggled with my bow but managed finally to get the red willow carved, bent and strung. My grandfather, who was chopping wood nearby, summoned me as I began to carve an arrow. He chose a piece of cedar kindling and with his jackknife whittled it expertly until the business end was blunt, the other end notched. He

---

‡ See Map 3: Central Skeena.

§ Throughout the book, the terms 'right bank' and 'left bank' are used to designate the riverside location of villages, homes, etc. The direction is determined by facing downriver.

On Babine Slide Road in 1953 after a goat hunting trip; (L-R): Mickey Smith, Jamey Sterritt, the author, Gary Marshall, Bimbo (dog) and Blaze. (NBS photo)

said, "You can kill a rabbit, squirrel or grouse with this, but you can take someone's eye out with the arrow you are making."

A small Catholic church that my grandmother supported, St. Theresa of the Child Jesus, was built on Hankin Street around the corner from my grandparent's house. She once asked my cousin Johnny and me to accompany her there. She had a child-sized fedora, which we called a *gaytim* (hat) Boston (American), for each of us to wear. We may have been six or seven years old and off we went, two little men wearing our fancy toppers.

Frank Harris and his wife lived above the Bulkley River at the southwest end of Gitanmaax. Frank had an apple tree and four of us snuck into his yard, picked apples and ran off. We ate them down at the slough. A day or so later my grandmother summoned us to her house. She sat us in a row, held court and let us off with a lecture.

In March of 1956, when I was fifteen, I quit school. As with many teenagers, it was obvious to me that I knew far more than my teachers and we weren't getting along. I went to work for my father who had a pole camp along the left bank of the Skeena River north of Hazelton. He put me to work packing boulders from the road he was building with his D4 bulldozer. It took a pretty smart guy to pack boulders.

Dad started his pole business in 1948 using five-foot crosscut saws and work horses. By 1956 he had added a forty-pound power saw, the bulldozer and a team of horses to his outfit. I worked with him that summer, camping in a tent beside Sterritt Creek. I asked Dad how the creek got its name. He said he didn't know. I assumed he was being modest and that it was named for him or his father.

That fall my working days ended. I had been hunting mountain goat with several men who worked for my dad and arrived home on a Saturday evening in late September. When I walked into the house my mother said, "You are going back to school," and the next day I found myself on an airplane flying from Terrace to Vancouver. I might have gone back to school in Hazelton but was having a major dispute with one of the teachers there. Also, my mother knew I would be well cared for in Vancouver by relatives. Thus began my annual treks between Hazelton and Vancouver. My Aunt Margaret, Dad's sister, and her husband, Bill Heath, had just moved to the Lower Mainland with their children† and bought a house in East Vancouver. My mother arranged to have me board with them. I enrolled in Grade Nine at Gladstone, a high school nearby, and spent the next four years there. I returned in the summers to work with my dad but didn't call Hazelton home again until my wife and I moved back in 1973.

But for Gladstone, I might not have met Barbara, the daughter of Bill and Irene Hepplewhite, who was born and raised in Vancouver. In 1960, a friend introduced us and we dated for a few months. In 1963 we again began dating and were married in Port Moody in September. Barbara's Aunt Hazel once read her tea leaves and said, "You are going to marry, have twins, and travel the world." Hazel was right about the marriage and travel, but our sons were born in New Westminster and Winnipeg three years apart.

I graduated from Gladstone in 1960 and went to the University of British Columbia for the next two years, still working summers with my dad. In the spring of 1962 I landed a summer job as a field assistant with Kennco Explorations at their Galore Creek property in northwestern BC. Company geologists taught me about rocks and minerals and I also learned that topographic maps, air photos, compasses and notebooks are basic geologist's tools used to plan field trips and record key features and locations along the way. Later, in 1963, while still working with Kennco, I began to record information in the field that was transferred to working maps.

In the fall of 1964 I enrolled in the British Columbia Institute of Technology's two-year mining technology program which included courses in surveying, mapping and drafting. I worked for Amax Exploration at their Lucky Ship property near Morice Lake during the summers of 1965 and 1966. After I graduated, Amax hired me full time.

But back in 1962, after spending the summer prospecting in the Stikine Mountains near Telegraph Creek in northwestern BC, I visited my grandfather in Hazelton. He was seated at the kitchen table in the house he shared with his third wife, Jessie Lumm. When I told him I'd been to Telegraph Creek, he said he'd been there too, a long time ago:

> I was with some men driving cattle from the Chilcotin to the Yukon. It was a tough trip. The weather was bad. It rained most of that summer. Feed was scarce because other men were driving herds north too. Some of the horses died, and others were weak and lame and we abandoned them. We had to put packs on some

---

† Billy, Linda, Barry (1952-1991) and Brian.

of the cattle. I quit at Telegraph Creek and took a boat down the Stikine River to Wrangell, then to Port Essington and home to Hazelton.

My grandfather was in his mid-teens at the time.

The first lengthy journey I recall making was with my Uncle Walter, Dad's brother, in 1952. He was driving to Chilliwack to get an engine for the sawmill he was building near Hazelton. The drive took more than four days over gravel and dirt roads in my grandfather's one-ton Chevrolet truck. By contrast, the trips my grandparents took by foot, saddle horse, canoe and sternwheeler took weeks and sometimes months. And through my own journeys I have come to appreciate that the distances my grandparents traveled during their lifetimes—both geographically and culturally—began in the mists of time when our aboriginal ancestors first settled the Skeena Valley.

While the village of Gitanmaax is so ancient that its years may be numbered in the thousands, Hazelton has yet to mark its second century. Hazelton is an incorporated municipality a few kilometres off Highway 16 between the 20th century communities of Smithers and Terrace. It was founded in 1871 when the Omineca goldfields proved viable. Soon after, Gitanmaax and Hazelton became the hub of a transportation network along pre-existing aboriginal trails that radiated east to Babine Lake and the Omineca; south to Fort Fraser and the Cariboo; west down the Skeena to Port Essington and Fort Simpson; and north to the Yukon. Another trail running west from the villages of Gitwangak and Gitanyow also linked upper Skeena villages to Nisga'a villages on the lower Nass River.

Although Gitanmaax and Hazelton seem to share the same land base and services, there are significant historic and cultural differences between them. The colonial government surveyed the

Gidumgaldo's pole (L) and St. Peter's Anglican Church (R), Government Street, Hazelton, ca. 1935. (Toby Marshall coll.)

townsite of Hazelton and granted it thirteen acres of land in 1871. Canada imposed a 2,400-acre Indian Reserve on Gitanmaax villagers in the 1890s, although territories belonging to Gitanmaax chiefs run to the height of land of the surrounding mountains and east more than fifty kilometres to the Suskwa River headwaters. Today Gitanmaax falls under the jurisdiction of the federal Indian Act while Hazelton falls under the jurisdiction of the provincial Municipal Act.

A casual visitor could be forgiven for assuming Hazelton is larger than thirteen acres. Gitanmaax and Hazelton appear to be one community with the reserve boundary bordering the town's. On the side of the road by our house stood St. Peter's Anglican Church. Nearby, overlooking Hazelton and the church, stood Gidumgaldo's totem pole.[†] The pole and the church symbolize very different histories, customs, values and beliefs. Gidumgaldo's totem pole was carved and erected in 1881; St. Peter's Church was built twenty years later. Gidumgaldo's long house once stood behind the pole. My grandfather, Charlie Sterritt, was born there, in Gidumgaldo's house, in 1885.[‡]

[†] Jessie (Lumm) Sterritt and the Gidumgaldo family moved the pole ca.1960 to its present location next to the Hazelton Public Library.

[‡] See Sterritt Family Tree.

Part I

The Aluugigat

In 1920, Naalaxha/Abel Oakes told the story of Temlaham:

> *Two thousand years ago, I guess, a few people lived in that community and a few animals too. The water was about halfway up the mountain. That was not quite water but more like soap with clouds. It easily killed a man that water...*
>
> *Quite a great many people lived in Temlaham before, they had only to shout together and there were so many people that the birds fell down when they shouted. That is before the earth was full with water. And they spoke a different language then. Some can talk animals and birds. They understood what the birds sang some people in that time.[1]*

The Gitxsan have several ancestral villages including Temlaham and Gitangasx.[†] The ancestors of Abel Oakes (1879 – 1956) hailed long, long ago from Gitangasx, a now abandoned village on the Skeena River about 150 kilometres north of Hazelton. Nevertheless, Oakes was also knowledgeable about Temlaham, another abandoned village on the right bank of the Skeena River about three kilometres below Hazelton.

Many aboriginal peoples in northwest BC, especially the Gitxsan, Nisga'a and Tsimshian, name Temlaham as their ancestral village. While anthropologists define these three peoples collectively as Tsimshian, they know themselves and all other aboriginal peoples in the western hemisphere as the Aluugigat, those who began to settle the Americas more than 20,000 years ago.

[†] Gitanyow, for example, was a substantial ancient village.

CHAPTER ONE

From Asia by Land

The Skeena River is a mere trickle at Otsi Creek near Gunanoot Mountain, 220 kilometres north of Hazelton, and enters the Pacific Ocean at Port Essington, near Prince Rupert. Its 620-kilometre journey makes the Skeena BC's third longest river. The Gitxsan name for the river is *Xsi'yeen* (river of mist) from which the word 'Skeena' is derived. Three major tributaries flow west into the Skeena between its source and Hazelton.†

Xsuwii Aks (Sustut River) is its first major tributary, and joins the Skeena 160 kilometres north of Hazelton. *Xsugwin Lik'insxw* (Babine River) comes next and joins the Skeena near the village of Kisgegas, about seventy kilometres north of Hazelton. Next is *Xsi'yeen Andoʼo* (Bulkley River),‡ which enters the Skeena at Hazelton.

These rivers are significant salmon producers and contributed to the prosperity of the Gitxsan, Tsimshian, Wet'suwet'en, Nedut'en and other northwest nations for millennia. Each river has a significant lake at its headwaters where sockeye salmon rear: Bear and Sustut lakes for the Sustut River; Babine Lake for Babine River; and Morice Lake for the Bulkley River. Numerous other lesser tributaries not only contribute to the Skeena's volume but also provide feed and spawning grounds for salmon and other fish species.

A spectacular mountain—Stekyawden (Rocher Deboule)—rises majestically from the valley floor directly south of Hazelton. A person standing on its highest point—Hagwilget Peak—on a cloudless day would embrace an awesome vista of mountains and valleys to the north, east and west. To the south are the peaks and valleys that comprise Stekyawden's southward extension. Turning north again and looking down an 1800-metre drop, the viewer would see Gitanmaax and

---

† See Map 5: Skeena River Watershed.
‡ Widzin Kwah to the Wet'suwet'en.

Rocher Deboule Mountain from the slough at the junction of the Skeena and Bulkley rivers. Originally, the Hudson's Bay Company French employees named Hagwilget Village 'Rocher Deboule' because of the boulders that fell into the nearby Bulkley River in 1824. Much later, the mountain, Stekyawden in the Gitxsan language, became known as Rocher Deboule. (Image I-21830 courtesy of RBCM & A)

Hazelton. There the Skeena, which has largely flowed south from its source, trends southwest for the rest of its journey to the ocean.

The bottomland between the Skeena and Bulkley rivers resembles an eagle's beak. The beak, for the most part, is covered by intermittent meadows amid groves of cottonwood trees, jungle-like red willow and hazelnut bushes. Cottonwood trees border the banks of both rivers. Poplar and birch tree forests rise from the valley floor towards the base of the mountains where the deep green of cedar, hemlock and spruce forests prevail, and these give way to light green alpine meadows at the 1400-metre level.

Until about 20,000 years ago, the landscape at Hazelton was not as we know it today. About half of northern North America was enveloped by the kilometres-deep Laurentian and Cordilleran ice sheets.† The Laurentian blanketed much of eastern Canada while the Cordilleran extended from the Rocky Mountains west to the seacoast and from Washington State north beyond the BC-Yukon border.‡ This massive body of ice gouged out the landscape at its base, melted, receded, and left the Skeena Valley much as we know it today.[2]

---

† Geologists believe that some very high mountains, like Rocher Deboule, rose above the Cordilleran Glacier.

‡ The glacier was estimated to be 2000 by 600 kilometres and to have an average depth of two kilometres.

Equally wondrous, while the glaciers were still very large and sea levels much lower—perhaps as many as 23,000 years ago§—our ancestors were slowly finding their way across Beringia, the 2000 kilometre-wide expanse of mixed tundra-like lands between Siberia and Alaska.¶ But as glaciers receded and sea levels rose, the land bridge disappeared beneath the waters, cutting our people off from their Asian kin.

Then our ancestors began to move south along the coast and inland continental routes over a very long period. Small families and groups likely spent generations in a region before moving on to another habitable area. Finally, there is evidence that by 13,000 years ago some aboriginal migrants had settled at the southern tip of South America at Monte Verde, Chile.³ This means that aboriginal people had populated the Americas from the Arctic to the southern tip of South America far earlier than previously thought. By as much as 11,000 years ago, the Cordilleran glacier had finally receded from coastal BC, making it possible for our ancestors to enter the estuaries and lower valleys of the Nass and Skeena rivers.

It is difficult to imagine that such an extensive body of ice—in excess of 1.2 million square kilometres—could melt within a few thousand years. Melt it did, however, and as it receded from the Skeena Valley, it delivered large volumes of water to streams and rivers throughout the area.

Late in this period an ice lobe dammed the valley below the mouth of the Babine River, forcing the Skeena to flow east to Babine Lake, thence through the Nechako River into the Fraser watershed.⁴ In time, the lobe melted and the Skeena and Babine rivers resumed their present course to the Pacific. A similar event occurred near Terrace, and the Skeena then flowed southwest to Kitimat and into tidewater at Douglas Channel.

Glacial melt led to large-scale erosion and the eventual creation of the many terraces found along the Skeena and Bulkley rivers. For example, the field at the entrance to today's 'Ksan Village ('Ksan) is prone to flooding during extremely high water. The terrace next to this field might be entirely the result of river flood deposit.

The next six ascending terraces at Hazelton between the Skeena and Bulkley—including the highest terrace at China Grade hill above the cemetery—are likely created by river deposition and subsequent erosion. The terraces were down cut soon after deposition. As geologist Allen Gottesfeld explained, the sediments in the higher terraces are the ice contact deposits of de-glaciation and the down cutting erosion process. They were formed by 5000 BP and perhaps several thousand years earlier. The lowest terrace at Hazelton and on the left bank of the Bulkley River at Mission Flats, for example, may date from between 1000 and 3000 BP.

Gottesfeld believes that during the early post-glacial period, the Skeena valley bottom was braided and a principal river channel may not have existed. He was puzzled at first by the shallow dry gullies. Based on his observations of another river, the McGregor,** and on the lower Skeena, Gottesfeld suspects the gullies were considerably larger and deeper at one time but, as the channels dried up, they filled in and got narrower and shallower. River terraces three kilometres below

---

§ There is now debate that this could be as much as 40,000 years ago.
¶ See Map 1: Migration Routes to the Gitxsan Ancestral Villages
** A Fraser River tributary near Prince George.

The bottomland between the confluence of the Skeena and Bulkley rivers (the Skeena flows off to the middle right of the picture) is said to resemble an eagle's beak. The ascending terraces at Hazelton are likely created by river deposition and subsequent erosion. (Image D-07305 courtesy of RBCM & A)

Hazelton on the right bank of the Skeena at Temlaham show evidence of a shallow dry gully at the base of a nearby hill, indicating that at one time water flowed through it. Such terraces are likely the product of the process Gottesfeld describes.

Archaeologists have suggested that the first Americans journeyed from Asia to Alaska some 13,000 years ago and followed an ice-free corridor east of the Rocky Mountains south perhaps as far as Texas. But archaeological finds in Oregon at Five Mile Point Caves date human faeces to 14,400 years ago and stone tools at Buttermilk Creek, Texas to 15,500 years ago. These findings suggest there were earlier migrations along the northwest coast of North America.[5]

As the glaciers melted it seems some people, over generations, travelled widely before settling into their current locations. At least two histories speak of such travels, one told by our southern coastal neighbours, and the other by a Gitxsan chief.

Hul'qumi'num history speaks of such a time:

> [They] lived a long way farther south than we their children do now. Northward from the seacoast to the farthest mountains, the whole country as well as the sea was covered with snow and ice, so deep that the summer heat failed to melt it. The old folks tell us that their fathers did not like the land they lived in, but were at a loss where to go…[for] Southward lived a people they feared…After the snow and

ice had all gone, the climate became warmer and the land drier, which enabled the Whull-e-mooch to move northward to where we, their children, now live and our fathers lived before us.[6]

Gitxsan chief Guuhadak/Thomas Wright (1901-1987), explained how his ancestors from the House of Wiik̲'aax had once lived on the lower Skeena, migrated far to the north and finally returned to the upper Skeena:

> Wiik̲'aax came from Skeena City[†]…and then he travelled all the way up to the Yukon…It was long before the white man came to that city… After they came back from the Yukon, they split up. A lot of people stayed at Kisgegas. A lot of people went to Kitwanga [Gitwangak]. A lot of people went to Tsimshian, and they just scattered all over the place…[then] they went [back] to Kisgegas…[7]

There were several periods that led to the four Gitxsan clans we have today: Frog, Fireweed, Wolf and Eagle. During one of the early periods, members of the Frog and Fireweed clans resided beside the Nass River near Kwinamuck Lake.[‡] They later abandoned the villages on the Nass and settled at Temlaham. My paternal grandfather's ancestors from the House of Haax̲xw (Frog Clan) are said to have lived at Temlaham before relocating to Kispiox.[§]

During another period, two other groups—the Wolf and Eagle clans—migrated south along separate routes. Thomas Wright's ancestors and those of my grandmother and father from the House of Wiik̲'aax, for example, returned from the Yukon, south into the Stikine Valley at Tahltan Village. They later journeyed south by land from the Stikine Valley to the upper Skeena, where they settled first at Gitangasx̲, west of Bear Lake, and finally at Kisgegas on the lower Babine River.

By this time—long after the glaciers melted and rising seas had flooded Beringia—Asia faded from our consciousness and from that of all indigenous Americans. Our home—our universe—became the Americas, the seas lapping at their shores and the cosmos above. For at least 14,000 years, the rest of the world did not exist.

---

† According to the 1929 pre-emptor's map, Skeena City was on the right bank of the Skeena near the Khyex River confluence.

‡ Kwinamuck Lake is about eighty kilometres north of Gingolx (Kincolith).

§ Another view is that Haax̲xw and Gwinuu (of Gitanyow) had similar origins on the Nass River (Barbeau, *Totem Poles*, 78).

ENDNOTES

1. "Barbeau and Beynon Fieldnotes", B-F-94.1, 1920: 1+.
2. Stumpf *et al.*
3. Pringle, 73.
4. Cannings *et al*, 73.
5. Pringle, 68-75.
6. Deans, 57.
7. Marsden, 1987: 64-7. Also see *Delgamuukw v. BC*, Thomas Wright, Vol. I, 1986: 16-19.

CHAPTER TWO

Wiigyet: The Essence of Human Frailty

WE WENT TO SUNDAY SCHOOL AT ST PETER'S ANGLICAN CHURCH NEAR OUR HOUSE, BUT NOT REGULARLY. WE WERE AN UNFAITHFUL LOT AND OFTEN ATTENDED SUNDAY SCHOOL elsewhere, sometimes later the same day at the Salvation Army or the Pentecostal Church. At St. Peter's the minister's wife, Mrs. Bird, taught us about God and Jesus and how Jesus was sacrificed on the cross for our sins. She taught us about good and evil, and she certainly let us know that God could punish us if we transgressed.

Our grandmother made sure we attended midnight mass each Christmas at the St. Mary Magdalen Catholic Church in Hagwilget where, with the Sargent family, we joined church members from Hagwilget and New Hazelton. My grandfather may have been a reluctant participant, but sat inside, perhaps because it was warmer there. It has been said merchant fur trader Dick Sargent (1864-1941), the owner of the R.S. Sargent business in Hazelton, always waited outside in his vehicle.

Rather than Bible stories, the tales of Wiigyet (big man) seemed more to my grandfather's liking. Guu Saxtoosw/Freddy Jackson, a member of the House of Niik'yap who lived from 1922 to 2000, told me:

> Your grandfather used to tell us Wiigyet stories after we went to bed. This was at Shewililba Creek (Xsi'an Bin'aast) in the big cabin after we were all in our bunks. He called them 'Adaawgam Ts'iisus' (stories of Jesus), because, as he said, Wiigyet created the world the same as Jesus did.

The Wiigyet/Txemsem stories, shared among the Tsimshian speaking peoples—the Gitxsan, Nisga'a and Tsimshian—have been gathered since the late 19th century by numerous people and organizations: ethnologists Franz Boas, Marius Barbeau and William Beynon, the Book Builders of 'Ksan†, native organizations and many others. There may be as many versions as storytellers, as each adapts his or her story to locale and circumstance.

Nevertheless, for the Gitxsan and other north coast peoples the central theme of all Wiigyet/Txemsem stories remains consistent.

> [Wiigyet] was the essence of all man's frailties exaggerated into gentle humor or ribald laughter. His misjudgments, calculated transgressions always ended in disaster. He thought only of the moment, leaving tomorrow's decisions to tomorrow. Wiigyet was craft without wisdom, power without regard for consequences. He was unheeding and petulant as a spoiled and pampered child and yet often as appealing as an unloved one. Wiigyet's blunders, tricks and falsehoods changed the face of the earth and the shape of many of earth's creatures. Wiigyet closely resembles Raven, the Trickster-Transformer of Haida and Tlingit history but with this difference: our Raven, alias Wiigyet…manipulates, duplicates, instigates and disseminates…[and] was caught between spirit and flesh. He was no man, yet all men.[1]

I have been fortunate to work with many elders over the past four decades who have pointed out place names arising from Wiigyet's adventures, thus connecting the moral map contained within the Wiigyet stories with actual land marks on the physical map of Gitxsan territories. In the following stories I join the tradition by incorporating this knowledge into my versions of the old stories.

Wiigyet brings light to the world

> Long before Temlaham, some of our ancestors lived by the sea near the Skeena estuary. There, benefiting from its bounty, lived a chief and his family. The chief hunted the forests nearby for deer and bear, rabbits and grouse. He snared goats and whistlers (hoary marmots) on nearby mountains, and from tidal waters he took sea otters, salmon, halibut and many other foods. But the world was in near darkness and life was challenging.
>
> One day the chief set out in his canoe to hunt sea otter. As he approached a large kelp bed, he heard what sounded like a baby crying. He wondered what it could be. He was wary, for it might be a *luulak* (ghost) or *similoo'o* (creature). But

---

† The Book Builders of 'Ksan brought together eighty-seven people, mainly Gitxsan, including elders, researchers, writers and administrators who contributed to *We-Gyet: Legends of the Northwest* published in Hazelton by the Kitanmaax School of Northwest Coast Indian Art in 1977.

he was awed by what he saw, for on the kelp lay a naked baby boy. The chief placed the crying baby in his canoe and quickly paddled home to his wife.

The chief had a son the same age as the foundling, and his wife said, "We shall raise them as brothers." As they grew they played games with rocks, bows and spears that provided them with the skills they would need as adults. Once they saw ducks near shore and agreed to a competition. "Let's see if we can kill those ducks," one said. And they picked up stones, threw them and killed two. They swam out to the ducks and brought them to shore. They skinned the ducks, tied the wings to their arms and flew about, practicing until they could fly long distances.

The boys decided to see whether they could swim amongst the ducks unnoticed. Donning their mallard garments, they flew to the flock and landed amidst them. The birds paid no attention to them. Now the boys, who had supernatural powers, were sure they could travel where they wished and do as they pleased.

The chief named his son Lagabuula and made him responsible for Xsi'yeen (Skeena River). He named his adopted son Wiigyet—because he ate so much and had grown so big—and made him responsible for Xsitxemsem (Nass River).

Wiigyet was always scheming and instigating. Although the world was in darkness, on a cloudless night stars twinkled in the sky. Wiigyet recalled that before he descended to earth he had known light. He flew as a raven through the hole to the sky world. There he removed his cloak, placing it next to the hole. A chief lived nearby with his daughter. Wiigyet was thirsty and went to a spring for water. He saw the chief's daughter coming to the spring with her bucket and quickly transformed himself into a pine needle. The girl bailed water from the spring without noticing the pine needle in her bucket. Later she drank water along with the needle. She soon became pregnant and eventually gave birth to a baby boy. But the baby cried continuously, and no one knew what to do. Finally, a very old woman said, "I know what this child wants. It is in your house hanging up."

There in a corner of the chief's dwelling hung a vessel, and it contained light. The chief's daughter gave the vessel to the child and he immediately stopped crying. He played every day with the vessel and dragged it along with him as he crawled about the house. At first he was watched closely but soon was ignored. One day the child darted from the house and too late the people realized he had taken the vessel. They pursued him but he was wily. As he raced off he changed again to a raven and flew down to earth. There he opened the vessel, letting out light. And when he returned light to the vessel, there was darkness. Which is how daylight, not just darkness, came to the world.[2]

Wiigyet brings water to the world

Now that day and night existed, Wiigyet's curiosity and imagination knew no limitations. The seas existed but the small amount of fresh water was controlled by a very selfish chief. Wiigyet reasoned that if he could somehow embarrass the chief he might be able to get the water container.

After many days' travel, Wiigyet arrived at the chief's village. The chief was napping and Wiigyet noticed dog's excrement on the ground. He devised a plan. Gathering it up in birch bark, Wiigyet stole into the chief's house without arousing him. He gently lifted the chief's blankets, put excrement on the mattress near the chief's buttocks and gently placed some on the chief too.

Wiigyet quietly left the house and waited nearby. After a short time, Wiigyet knocked boldly on the door and re-entered the house. "Chief. What have you done? It smells in here and you have soiled yourself. Let me help you." The chief was embarrassed. "Wiigyet. There is water over there and diaper moss. Please bring it to me."

Wiigyet did as he was told. But instead he grabbed the water bag and ran from the house, accidentally spilling water here and there, making lakes, creeks and rivers. As he neared the place where the Kispiox River flowed down to the Skeena, a *luulak* suddenly *gitwinkxw* (whistled) in his face. Startled, Wiigyet spun about, retreating upstream for a short distance before regaining his composure and continuing along to the Skeena where he rested. And now a sharp Z-turn in the Kispiox River above Kispiox Village may be seen. It is known as Gitw'inkxws Wiigyet.[3]

How the lynx got tufted ears

Wiigyet was an opportunist. Once, while visiting a famous chief, Wiigyet saw many swan pelts hanging on the walls of his house. Wiigyet asked, "How did you capture so many swans?"

"I have my own way of capturing them," said the chief. "I have a swan disguise and when I want more swans, I wear it and swim amongst them. I take fine, strong sinew with me, dive below the flock and choose two, maybe three, but no more than that. I tie their legs with the sinew and drag them to shore. But remember, Wiigyet, do not take more than three."

Wiigyet prepared his own swan cloak and put it on. Then, pretending to feed, he slowly swam to the flock. When amongst his prey he dove and tied the legs of several choice birds together. But it was so easy he couldn't help tying more and more birds until he was satisfied that he had enough for his feast. But when he tugged them towards shore, the startled swans took flight. Wiigyet struggled but the swans easily flew off with the hapless Wiigyet pleading as he swung through the air. He did not know what to do for now the swans were far from the lake with Wiigyet dangling helplessly. He threatened the swans, he cajoled them, but to no avail.

Finally, the swans turned towards the Kispiox River with the intention of landing in a meadow (near the present-day Kispiox Valley rodeo grounds). As they descended, Wiigyet was pleased, thinking his flight was about to end. But no, just as his left foot touched a rock outcrop—known to the Gitxsan afterwards as Wilgyehlhetxw See'es Wiigyet—the swans quickly rose and continued south towards Gitanmaax. They flew higher and higher and finally, above Ts'ilaasxwit, Four Mile Canyon near Gitanmaax, Wiigyet let go of the sinew and fell. His great body landed on a large flat rock and he was embedded there. He struggled but could not free himself. Finally, *weex* (a lynx) came by.

"Wiigyet," the lynx said, "what is wrong?"

"Please help me. I am stuck in this rock," Wiigyet pleaded. "I will give you a lovely gift if you can free me." Lynx, with his rasp-like tongue, then began to lick the rock around Wiigyet's body until finally he was set free. Wiigyet stood, but his imprint remained, and became known as Wiluux T'aas Wiigyet (where sat Wiigyet).[†]

"Thank you," Wiigyet said, "and now I will take this hair from my groin and place it on your ears." And from then on, all lynx have had a unique sprig of hair at the tips of their ears. It is also how Wiigyet's large footprint came to be atop a small knoll beside the Kispiox River at Seventeen Mile Bridge, and why the outline of his body is pressed into rock at Ts'ilaasxwit.[‡]

[†] Another version of this story involves Wiigyet's attempt to capture a steelhead for dinner: see Constance Cox, "Wiigyet's chair", 1957.

[‡] The outline of Wiigyet's body at Four Mile was destroyed during bridge re-construction. His footprint at Seventeen Mile Bridge was destroyed during power line installation.

Wiigyet and the abalone

Wiigyet travelled on, walking from the Skeena to the Nass Valley. He canoed down the Nass River, intending to harvest *bilaa* (abalone). Abalone shells were used to adorn the regalia of high chiefs. As usual Wiigyet over-harvested, dangerously filling his canoe with the shells. Then he set out for the Skeena, as he wished to trade his *bilaa* for groundhog skins with the many high chiefs at Temlaham.

Wiigyet was happy to find his brother Lagabuula near the entrance to the Skeena. Lagabuula said, "Wiigyet, where are you going with those abalone shells? You have not changed. Your greedy ways will cause you to swamp your canoe."

Wiigyet laughed, "No, that will not happen. I know how to manage this vessel."

They reminisced about the adventures they had shared as children. And Wiigyet, of course, bragged about his many exploits.

Lagabuula grew tired of Wiigyet's bragging and said, "What shall we do? We can't sit here talking all day. Let's do something."

Wiigyet agreed, "Yes. Let's continue up the Skeena."

They soon arrived at the limit of tidewater and rested on shore near what is known today as Tyee. Wiigyet said, "Why don't we gamble?" He pointed to a nearby mountain and said, "We will shoot our arrows into that crevice and whoever hits it will be the winner."

"Yes," Lagabuula said, "But what is at stake? What will I win if I hit the target and you do not?"

Wiigyet said, "Let us stake the Skeena River against the Nass River."

At this time, salmon came to the Skeena, but were not fat, and oolichans, an important food source, came to the Nass, but not in great numbers. Lagabuula said, "Brother, you shoot first."

"No," said Wiigyet, "We will shoot at the same time."

While preparing to shoot, Wiigyet willed that Lagabuula's arrow fall short and that his hit the mark. The brothers shot. Lagabuula hit the mark and Wiigyet missed.

"I hit it. I hit it." Wiigyet exclaimed.

"No, you didn't," Lagabuula said.

But Wiigyet insisted. Lagabuula knew Wiigyet would never give in and relented, "Yes, brother. You have won. So now oolichans will come to the Nass River in great numbers."

And Wiigyet said, "Now salmon rich in fat will come to the Skeena River. Oolichans will come too, but they won't swim beyond this point."[4]

The brothers parted. Lagabuula paddled back down the Skeena and Wiigyet continued upriver. It was a difficult and treacherous journey but Wiigyet managed to avoid tipping his canoe. Nearing Temlaham, Wiigyet became excited. He believed he could convince the chiefs to give him far more value in groundhog skins than he had in precious abalone shells. He paddled with anticipation but carelessly. Suddenly he struck a rock and tipped his canoe, spilling its contents on the right bank of the Skeena a few kilometres below Temlaham. And large abalone shells have been found there at the base of the hill known to the Gitxsan as Ansa Bilaa.[†]

---

† Ansa Bilaa is a hill on the Kitwanga Backroad at the fifteen-kilometre post.

ENDNOTES

1. Book Builders of 'Ksan, 7.
2. Barbeau and Beynon, 11-12.
3. Barbeau and Beynon, 16; Book Builders of 'Ksan, 62.
4. Boas, 68-70; Beynon, 61-62; Barbeau and Beynon, 25-26.

CHAPTER THREE

Temlaham: The Ancestral Place

In 1973 my wife and I, with our two sons, moved home to Hazelton from Arizona where I had been working for a mining company. Two years later we bought a farm on the right bank of the Skeena River a few kilometres below Hazelton at Temlaham, the prairie place. But it is much more than a prairie place. It is said to have been a village of hundreds of people, the ancestral home of many Tsimshian, Nisga'a and Gitxsan until they abandoned it and scattered throughout the northwest. For the next thirty-five years we lived in this mythic space, envisioning ancient events as depicted in the stories of our peoples. Barbara and I have spent more of our lives at Temlaham than anywhere else—and raised our sons there. Regardless of where we may be, Temlaham is home.

Temlaham Ranch on the right bank of the Skeena River where the author lived from 1975 to 2009. The Madiik (supernatural grizzly) crossed the Skeena here and attacked the people of Temlaham along what Niistahuukw/Walter Wright called 'The Street of Chiefs'. (Jamie Sterritt photo)

Ska'woo

According to our histories, some of our ancestors settled at Temlaham. They settled first in two villages, one on each side of the Nass River about thirty kilometres above Aiyansh, near Kwinamuck Creek.† The forerunners of the Fireweed Clan lived on the right bank of the river in Gitxandakhl, while the Raven Clan lived on the other side of the river in Gitgwinyookhl.

Tension and jealousy between the two villages eventually erupted in violence. The young people of one village burned the other and killed all of the people except for a woman—Ska'woo—and her daughter. They escaped the devastated village and fled upriver, where Ska'woo finally stopped and sat out on a rocky point‡ mourning her loss.

Ska'woo feared for her daughter, who now had no suitors, and repeatedly cried out, "Who will marry my daughter?" Animals came from near and far, offering to marry the young woman, but Ska'woo, who sought a strong warrior to avenge the loss of her people, rejected them.

A brilliant light and the crash of thunder startled Ska'woo. She turned, and before her stood a man whose garment was aflame. He said, "I will marry the daughter of Ska'woo. I have great powers. If any come to battle with me, I have only to wave my hand and the whole earth will roll over and bury those who will harm me."

To further demonstrate his powers, he extended his hands with his palms up, then down, and the trees before him were buried. Ska'woo knew this man had the powers of a supernatural being and would be able to avenge her massacred relatives. She asked, "What will you do when the enemy comes?"

He said, "I can turn the earth over right on top of them." As he spoke, the earth and the whole hillside crashed down. And a hill on the trail from New Aiyansh to Gitanyow near Wiluuks t'aas Ska'woo, is that way still today.[1]

Ska'woo's daughter and her husband ascended into the Sky World where their children were trained to be warriors. The children acquired supernatural powers, names and crests, and were taught how to successfully wage war on their enemies. When they returned to earth, a fog descended over the land.

Tsimshian elder, Joshua Ts'iibaasaa said:

> In the morning the fog cleared away and the people of Gitxandakhl saw before them four houses on the site of the burned village...Each house had a different painting. The first house was that of Dagmwilgyet and had the sun (*gyamk*) as a crest. The second house, that of Andisa'm, had the stars (*bil'ust*). The third house, that of Laxhlmaxai, had the rainbow (*maxmaagay*). The fourth house, that of Ligiyu'en, had sky (*lax'om*) in front of it. All of these paintings were very bright and shining.[2]

---

† 'Kwinamuck' is derived from the Gitxsan word, *gwin ha'mook* (where wild celery).

‡ The point is known today as 'Wiluuks T'aas Ska'woo' (where sat Ska'woo).

These tribes were born of the Sky brothers, in the different nations of the Indians, the Nisga'a, the Gitxsan and the Tsimshian. They all claim their origin from these brothers. Their crests have been handed to them from supernatural beings.[3]

Eventually, the people abandoned the two villages and scattered in all directions. Nisga'a elder, Emma Wright (1883-1959) said:

> Finally they came to the Skeena River where they found a large prairie all clear on a very high bank above the river. Here they made their village, which they called Temlaham…So now Temlaham became a large place and these people were of the [Fireweed] and the [Frog] clans. The houses in which the four brothers were returned to earth had been left on the Nass River. And now, at Temlaham, the brothers built four houses exactly like the houses they had left on the Nass River. As they became larger and more powerful, also the other clans began to grow.[4]

Thus, the original inhabitants of Temlaham belonged to just two clans: the Gisk'aast (Fireweed) and La<u>x</u> See'l or La<u>x</u> <u>G</u>anada (Frog-Raven). And the Fireweed brought with them four important crests that endure to this day: the sun, stars, rainbow and sky.

The principal requirements of all Gitxsan villages included access to food, fuel and other resources and shelter. Our oral histories refer to salmon, bears and mountain goats. Huckleberries, blueberries and other fruits of the forest were abundant. Amid such plenty, the village of Temlaham grew large and stretched for several kilometres along the right bank of the Skeena in three parts: Anwok'esxw (place of digging), Temlaham (the prairie place), and Gwingadal<u>k</u> (where sandhill cranes rest).

Each year the villagers built a weir across the Skeena in anticipation of the first spring salmon. In *lasa 'yanja* (May), new posts were gathered and sharpened if necessary. Then the men used heavy, flat rocks to pound the posts into the riverbed and build platforms upon them.

> They dammed the Skeena River right across…Each man had a small section of his own to build up. Everybody brought roots and slats and reeds to make the fence with. After this was ready, they began to make the [*moohl*] fish basket; each man furnishing thin poles, and women were sent to pull up roots for tying. Other women made the roots pliable by running smooth stones on them, so that they would be easily tied. The work was all divided up between them. The heads of the houses were given a portion of the fence. All those that belonged to the Raven crest took care of one fish basket. Every family had its own part. After it was built, it was divided between the different crests. And, once finished, everybody awaited the arrival of the salmon.[5]

Some villages may have had a *ta'oots'ip* (fortress) where women, children and the elderly could shelter while warriors fended off enemy attacks. Gwits'enxsim Sim'oogit/Philip Turner said Temlaham's *ta'oots'ip* was located on a pyramid-like knoll on the left bank of the Skeena, north of

Sealy Creek. Kaldixgyet and his family chose to live below the *ta'oots'ip* at the mouth of this creek. His being the only family on that side of the river, he built a heavy door hinged at the top, allowing it to open upwards. When ready to retire at night, Kaldixgyet let the door slam shut with a loud bang. "Kaldixgyet is going to bed," the Temlaham villagers said to each other.

The people's histories tell of a mysterious event that once caused the entire river valley to be shrouded in a fine mist-like substance. But as one elder said, it wasn't mist: it was soap-like and cloudy. It was said that this mist could kill a person.[6] Perhaps it was from a major, far-off volcanic eruption. Nevertheless, the term used is *yeen* in the people's language. From that time on, the river was known as 'Xsi'yeen' (Skeena—river of mist).

Run after run of salmon made their way up the river during summer and early fall, with some branching off to go to their spawning grounds at the headwaters of the Bulkley River. More plentiful runs continued up the Skeena to their own particular spawning sites in lakes and streams far away. Throngs of eagles and seagulls from the coast followed the salmon, feeding on their carcasses along the shore. Occasionally seals were seen amid the fish bubbling in the rush of waters where the rivers met.

A winter's supply of salmon for the entire village was captured in weirs at Temlaham and perhaps in barrel traps strategically placed in nearby canyons.

Madiik

A beautiful lake nestled at the base of the mountain across the Skeena opposite Temlaham. Because of its proximity to the splendid mountain, Stekyawden, the lake was named Tam Stekyawden (Sealy Lake). Coho salmon ascended a creek to this lake each fall where they spawned and died.

The villagers not only caught trout in the lake, but salmon as well. Village youth sometimes bathed in the lake and frolicked on its shores. One day some of the village maidens took fish skeletons from the lake's edge and fashioned them into garlands they placed on their heads. They knew that showing disrespect to animals and fish was wrong, but they ignored the elders' warnings. The lake began to churn and, amidst the tumult, a monster arose from the water—Madiigam Ts'uwii Aks—a grizzly bear unlike any ever seen by the people. It was angry, not only with the maidens, but with the villagers for becoming forgetful about their ancient laws.

As Wiiyagadeets/Elijah Turner (1909-1993) said, the Madiigam Ts'uwii Aks (supernatural grizzly of the waters), or Madiik, swept up the girls and, travelling down the lake, uprooted trees, flinging them high in the air. The Madiik struggled to climb over Ansin Gyam, the rock knoll that rises near the lake's west shore. Failing there, the monster started up one small gully and fell back, then up another gully and fell back again. Finally it continued along the lakeshore and down the creek that flowed to the Skeena.

By then the villagers knew a great calamity was about to befall them. The Madiigam Ts'uwii Aks thundered as it made its way down the creek, sending water, trees and boulders before it. It crossed the Skeena and swept into the village, taking up buildings and people. The warriors set out to do battle, but the grizzly flung them aside and created mayhem throughout the village. And then, as quickly as it had come, it returned to the river, swam across and disappeared.†

The village was devastated. They rebuilt Temlaham and were careful to teach their children what would happen if they continued to be disrespectful of the creatures and materials they depended on for food and shelter.

The Dispersal

Yet again some of the youth had become complacent and disrespectful of the laws. When they caught the first spring salmon, a foolish villager, Gyagan, mocked it and the sun which hung high over Stekyawden. "Sun of the blue vault, what will you do when you behold this? Here is the Salmon-prince's own self bare to the bone. Still, what do the chiefs care? They have plenty to eat in deep and brimful trays."[7]

Suddenly an ominous mist blotted the sky, a chill enveloped the valley and snow began to fall on Stekyawden. Now Gyagan mocked the snow. "Snow, winter snow, oh *maadim* (winter), why are you fooling us at this season of the year? It is springtime. Don't you know it? Salmon is here. Don't you see it? The winter is past.…The summer moons must run their course onwards, not backwards, as you would have us believe."[8]

Snow continued to fall, blanketing Stekyawden. Finally the village was buried until only the dimmest of light could be seen through the smoke hole of each *da'ak* (a partially buried house). The villagers already had scarce food following the long winter and could not leave their homes to snare rabbits or grouse. They were starving and, fearing death, some began to pray. The wife of Tawee-welp prayed to the heavens.

Tawee-welp's neighbour, Chief Nola, was also alive. Soon after his neighbour's prayer, a *k'aliidakhl* (Steller's jay) landed at the smoke hole of Nola's dwelling.

The jay had a twig in its beak, a twig of red elderberries, and chirped, "Sa sa sa, wiihloots, wiihloots." Nola saw him, Nola, whose eyes could still see. Nola heard him, Nola, whose ears could still hear. Nola was wise. His was the wisdom of a seer, a man of power over spirits. He cried out, "Our life shall be saved. Summer dwells elsewhere. Our homeland harbors a curse, our homeland alone. Let us take flight. Let us burrow our way out. Let us follow blue jay to the fields of springtime."[9]

Tawee-welp and his family fled downriver. They stopped at Gitsegukla along with Haxbagwootx. Niistahuukw and Gwiiyeehl stopped at Kitselas. Kyeekw and Toq fled to the Nass River. Ts'iibaasaa, Wii Seeks and Niis Nawii went to the coast. Ts'iiyee (the forerunner of the Wolf House of Kliiyeemlaxha) and his family fled downriver to Gitanyow, which already existed.

---

† While gathering evidence for the *Delgamuukw v. BC* case in the 1980s, we retained scientists to conduct surveys of the Sealy Lake area and retrieve sediment samples from the lake bottom. In 1978, a disastrous storm with torrential rains occurred along the Skeena Valley causing catastrophic floods. They washed out many roads, including sections of Highway 16 and the railroad. Flooding along the base of the mountain near Sealy Lake exposed deeply buried trees. Carbon 14 dating of the trees and lake sediments reveal that a major landslide had occurred 3500 years BP (see Gottesfeld *et al*, 1583-93).

Yee'l, the warrior, and his family had already settled at An'spa'yaxw (Kispiox—the hiding place) on the Kispiox River. In time, not only would Ts'iiyee join Yee'l, but also Haaxxw, Delgamuukw and many others. Nola and his family made their way upriver to Ts'ilaasxwit (the canyon at Four Mile bridge) and eventually founded Gitanmaax.† Although Temlaham was abandoned in favour of other villages near and far, it continues to live on in the histories of the Gitxsan and many other coastal nations.

The author's depiction of the first spring salmon was made when he was a student at Kitanmaax School of Northwest Coast Indian Art in 1977.

The agricultural potential of the meadows at Temlaham attracted fur traders and gold miners during the late 19th century, some of whom took up pre-emptions there. Donald McIntosh (1881-1968), for example, pre-empted the properties Barbara and I later owned.‡

Our many years at Temlaham gave us the opportunity to observe the Skeena River and the surrounding terrain throughout the seasons while our sons and grandchildren hunted and trapped in the nearby forest and fished in the river. Sometimes the river near our house became shallow enough that I could have crossed, albeit cautiously, on my saddle horse.

Having lived there for so long without finding artifacts or other evidence to support the existence of a large village leaves a lingering question: Where is the concrete archaeological evidence for Temlaham's existence? The answer to this may lie in Gottesfeld's suggestions that the

---

† Based on our *adaawk* (oral histories), the nature and extent of Temlaham is more complex than one might assume from this book. This is why some consider Nola's family, after moving from Ts'ilaasxwit, to be the last to leave Temlaham.

‡ Son of fur trader Angus McIntosh (ca. 1840-1922) and brother of Alex (ca. 1880-1906), of Simon Gunanoot fame.

gullies running through the fields of our farm represented earlier, deeper and wider river channels.[§] In other words, Temlaham may have been built on what became a floodplain.

Our people settled on the upper Skeena some 6,000 to 8,000 years ago, after the glaciers receded from the valley. Nevertheless, catastrophic floods have occurred since and may easily have flooded the prairie at Temlaham, washing away evidence of the village.

---

§ See Chapter One.

ENDNOTES

1. Marsden, 1996: 7-8.
2. "Barbeau and Beynon Fieldnotes", Tseebasae, #12, 1916.
3. "Barbeau and Beynon Fieldnotes", Nisyaganaat of the Frog Clan, #7, 1915.
4. Marsden, 1996: 11-12.
5. Barbeau and Beynon, 255.
6. "Barbeau and Beynon Fieldnotes", Abel Aoks/Oakes (BF 94.1).
7. Barbeau and Beynon, "Temlarh'am" (n.d.), The Downfall, I No. 8: 72.
8. Barbeau and Beynon, "Temlarh'am" (n.d.), The Downfall, I No. 8: 72.
9. Barbeau and Beynon, "Temlarh'am" (n.d.), The Downfall, I No. 8: 74.

CHAPTER FOUR

Gitanmaax: The Torchlight People

My employment at the 'Ksan Indian Village and Museum began in May 1973. Early one morning, while walking along the gravel path to work, I was struck by the cries of hundreds of crows in the cottonwoods and the humid fragrance of the budding willow and hazelnut leaves beside the slough. The scene took me back to my childhood. In those days, the slough was our only swimming hole. With our mothers present, we children were allowed to wade in the water at its edge and play in the sand and mud. It was too wide and deep for us to wade across, but sometimes a teenager might piggyback us over to the island there.

The slough could be dangerous. A six-year old cousin drowned there in 1936.† I nearly drowned there myself but one of the mothers, Jane Marshall, waded in, grabbed me by the leg, for I was upside down (so I was told), and brought me spluttering to shore. As we grew older we spent hot summer days there on our own, swimming and lying on the sandy beach. Sometimes we jigged for humpback salmon in the Bulkley River shallows near the head of the island or fished for trout at the point.

The point is the pie-shaped gravel bar at the end of the slough where the Bulkley and Skeena rivers meet. Sometimes, when a large tree was left stranded out in the Bulkley by receding floodwaters, the older boys swam out to it and rested. I was always impressed that teenaged Charley Myros had once swum from the slough right across the Bulkley River. I didn't know until recently that it was by accident. Charley got caught in the current, tried valiantly to get to the tree, but was forced to swim for his life across a river that has taken many a life before and since. He was among the lucky few. He made it to the far shore where my aunt and uncle, Edith and Al McDougall, lived. Six-foot Charley borrowed a pair of pants from five-foot-something Al and walked home to Hazelton via the Hagwilget Canyon Bridge.

---

† Willie Bird, son of Billy and Edith Bird (*The Omineca Herald*, 5 August 1936).

The Department of Public Works was building a new road from Hazelton to New Hazelton in the late 1940s. While bulldozing the corner near the slough, the workers exposed small cedar boxes and skeletal remains. While playing in the freshly excavated banks along the side of the road, we saw the boxes. The remains, we were told, were gathered up and buried at the Gitanmaax Cemetery.

After the great snowfall at Temlaham and the dispersal of its inhabitants throughout the northwest, Nola chose to relocate first to Aakts'ilaasxwit at the head of the canyon above today's Four Mile Bridge and later to a bench near the confluence of the Skeena and Bulkley rivers. It was an ideal location. The family had but a short walk to the slough where they could safely beach their canoes, bathe and swim on hot summer days and sometimes catch salmon or trout resting in the backwater. A nearby spring provided clear, fresh water year round. Great tangles of driftwood and brush at the mouth of the slough provided the villagers with firewood. Cottonwood was plentiful on the island across from the slough and smoke from its slow burning kept flies from salmon and game curing on racks in the smokehouses. The people named this tiny summer village Ansi'suuxs—the place of driftwood. It would later become known as today's village of Gitanmaax.

When a chief died, his name survived through the chosen son or daughter of one of his sisters. Thus the leader of this tiny village was also known as Nola.

> Nola's sister had a daughter whose favourite pet was a dog. Its fur was black and grey and it had white legs. It followed her everywhere—when she went to the spring for water, when she picked berries, when she tended fish at her father's smokehouse and when she went to the slough to bathe.

The Bulkley Slough, near the original village of Gitanmaax, was a source of food for the Gitxsan. It also served as a popular, though sometimes dangerous, recreation area for families in more recent years. (Image G-03105 courtesy of RBCM & A.)

As she approached puberty, young men from nearby villages travelled the river to court her. But as a chief's daughter, she should marry only someone who was acceptable to her parents and of interest to her.

Eventually, a young man from a distant village caught her eye. Her parents approved of him. They took long walks together, sometimes along the path that ran north from her home to the Skeena. Or they sat and talked at the edge of the slough on the point where the rivers meet. The chief's daughter wanted her pet to accompany her on these walks, but he was nowhere to be seen and only appeared when the young man returned to his village.

Her pet's puzzling behaviour was on her mind as she fell asleep. She thought she was dreaming for someone seemed to be in her bed, and she felt it was the young man. She fell asleep again, and no one was there in the morning. This happened again, and she decided to find out whether or not she was dreaming. She took red ochre and dabbed it on the edge of her blanket. That night she again woke from her slumber and felt someone with her. It appeared to be her suitor. But when she awoke in the morning, she was alone. As she left her father's house to bathe in the slough, her dog accompanied her. To her horror, she saw that his white legs were stained with ochre. Confused and embarrassed, she told no one.

Soon the young woman realized she was pregnant and told her mother. Her mother, believing the young man to be the father, was happy with the news and began to prepare for the birth of her grandchild. By spring she had made a beautiful white caribou skin blanket to wrap the child.

When the day arrived, the birth was quick. As her mother came to assist, she heard the cry of the newborn. But it was the mewling of a pup, not a child. Her mother said to her daughter, "Open the blanket. Show me your child."

When she refused, her mother tugged the blanket away. She couldn't believe her eyes. Her daughter had given birth to two male puppies and a third male was on its way. In all she had four pups, the last being a female.

"This is a disgrace to our family. Your uncle and father will be humiliated," her mother said. "We will be banished. Give them to me. I will drown them in the river before anyone learns of this."

The young woman refused to give up her pups, and by then it was too late. The pups could be heard and others were curious. Word spread and Nola decided the entire family had to leave Ansi'suuxs except for his niece and her strange offspring.

Nola ordered everyone to gather food and possessions. They were to load their canoes immediately and seek a new home. Being cursed, his niece was left with nothing—neither food nor fire—with which to survive. She and her puppies were left to die.

Her cousin pitied her. He placed live embers in shredded cedar bark and buried the embers at the base of a house post. As he went out the door, he whispered what he had done.

The chief's daughter was grief-stricken and ran crying to the point only to see the canoes pass from sight, one by one, around the bend in the river. She knew they would not return. That evening, she dug up the embers and lit a fire to keep warm, but she had no food. If she and her offspring were to survive, she would have to feed herself.

She knew from her father's stories that at night trout often rested in the shallows along the edge of the Xsi'yeen where they could be seen by torchlight. After a

The Luring of Salmon at Gitanmaax   N.J. Sterritt

The village name of Gitanmaax means 'people who fish by torchlight', from a silkscreen print by the author.

day without food, she made a *maa hixs* (torch) and a spear and left her pups locked in the house.

She followed the short path from Ansi'suuxs to the river where she planted her torch in the sand at the water's edge. Soon she had speared enough trout to feed herself. She returned to her house, stoked the fire, put hot rocks into a water-filled cedar box and cooked the fish. After that, she gathered berries during the day and continued to fish at night, sometimes roasting the fish over a fire.

While fishing one dark night, she thought she heard children's laughter. Curious, she took her torch and spear and went back to the house. As she neared home the noise stopped. When she entered, the pups were asleep in their beds. This happened again the next night, prompting her to develop a plan.

The next time she heard children's laughter she left the torch lit beside the river and silently made her way home in the dark. She crept to the house and, peering through a crack in the logs, spied four children playing. The boys had piled their puppy skins by the fire and the girl had hers wrapped about her waist like a skirt.

One of the boys said to his sister, "Go and see if mother is coming."

She went to the side of the house and, peering through a crack in the logs, said, "Her torch is by the river."

Their mother returned to the river and continued fishing as the children played on. Then she took her fish and the torch to light her way home. As usual, the noise of children stopped as she approached her house. When she entered, the pups were asleep. The next day she decided to put an end to the puppies' games. While they were playing at the slough, she prepared the door of her house so it would open easily and quietly and removed a knot so she could see what her children were doing.

That night she went again to the river to fish. Once again she left the torch by the river and stole back to the house. The children were laughing and singing by the fire. She peered through the door watching the children and, when they were at the back of the house away from the fire, she rushed in, gathered the puppy skins and threw them into the fire. But the little girl was too quick for her mother. She threw her dress over her head and became a puppy again.

The boys were heartbroken, for although they were now human, their sister alone would be a pup. Their mother tried to console them. She said, "I will make bows and arrows for you, and you will learn to hunt. Your sister will be able to find animals and bark, and you will follow her and shoot them. We will call her Oomits."

The brothers were pleased and soon forgot their sorrow. Their mother set about making clothes for her sons. To ensure success, she fasted for four days before making their weapons.

She taught them how to use bows and arrows, snare grouse and rabbits, and how to spear fish by the light of a torch at night. The boys relied on Oomits to find game and, as they grew older, they became very successful, filling their cache with berries and furs and their earthen pits with dry salmon.

Years later, the woman was sitting at the point with her sons, comforted by the pleasant hush of the rivers and enjoying the evening sun. Oomits, lying nearby, suddenly perked up her ears and looked down river. At first the others heard nothing but gradually they began to hear a dirge in the distance. It grew louder until around the bend of the Skeena came a great coastal canoe carrying many people singing a lament.

As the canoe approached, the woman recognized her father's slaves and, seated in the middle of the canoe, her cousin. He had been sent by her father to gather and cremate the bones of his daughter and her pups. Oomits barked and refused to let them come ashore but the woman quieted her. Her cousin was amazed at what he found. Not only had she survived but, with the help of her sons and Oomits, she had thrived. Hers was a wealthy family.

The slaves were sent back downriver to bring the good news to the aged Nola and the woman's parents. The family returned to their former village site. Throughout that fall and winter the chief prepared for a feast with the help of his great-nephews and Oomits. In the spring he invited chiefs from villages up and down the Skeena to the feast. There Nola honoured his niece and her sons with proper names.

The chief's guests, upon hearing her amazing story, began to call the village at the forks and its people, *Git An Maa Hixs* (The People Who Fish With Torches). It is known to this day as Gitanmaax.†

Constance Cox (1880-1963), the daughter of Thomas Hankin and Margaret MacAulay, was born and raised amongst the Gitxsan at Hazelton. She spoke the language fluently.

Cox said that twins or triplets among the Gitxsan were rare and some considered them a bad omen. The mother was not allowed to drink directly from a spring—someone else would have to bring water to her. Only one child, if that, was allowed to survive. And the mother had to wait until the survivor could walk before she could take water from a spring.

---

† There are many versions of this story. In 1920, Marius Barbeau, National Museum ethnologist, recorded at least three versions with Gitxsan elders (Wawsemlarhae Robinson, Isaac Tens and Peter John). Other versions have been recorded since. While details vary, all are consistent in terms of location; the birth of pups to a young woman; her being abandoned; how she survived by spearing trout with the aid of torchlight at night, and the human transformation of three pups. This version is my rendering of the story, expanded from the above versions.

Constance Cox, here in regalia, was the daughter of Hazelton merchant Thomas Hankin and Margaret MacAulay. (Betty Ann Russell coll.)

Paddy Sheehan's wife had twins. After leaving the hospital she stayed with a friend, Mrs. Stanton, who lived near a spring. Cox overheard a Gitxsan man, Jimmy Robinson, say, "I hear that the woman with twins is living in this house here, and the white people don't know anything. They will make her dip water in this spring and it will go dry on us."

On another occasion a Gitxsan woman had triplets. The children, only about six inches long at birth, appeared to be healthy. Anticipating what might happen, Cox's mother asked for and was given one of the children, hoping that the mother would raise the other two. But the family did away with them. One day the mother asked Mrs. Hankin for the third child. She complied, thinking it would now be all right. An aunt later said the child had suddenly died.[1]

It is understandable how a taboo around multiple births could arise within aboriginal families at that time. For most of the year they traveled great distances for food and shelter in rugged terrain and crossed turbulent rivers and creeks. Not only would it have been difficult and dangerous for the mother and her infants, the entire family would have been at risk.

ENDNOTES

1 "Barbeau and Beynon Fieldnotes", Constance Cox (B-F-68.37: 2).

CHAPTER FIVE

Kispiox: The Hiding Place

The village of Kispiox sits on a terrace at the confluence of the Kispiox and Skeena rivers fifteen kilometres above The Forks. Kispiox became one of the largest Gitxsan villages because of the abundance of berries and animals in the valley and on nearby mountains. Equally important was the availability of salmon at fishing stations at Xsan, a five-kilometre canyon on the Skeena above the village. 'Niist/Charles Sampson (1888-1963) said there were so many smokehouses in the canyon the sun was red from smoke during the fishing season.

Yee'l and Ts'iiyee

Ts'iiyee and his family went down the Skeena and turned north to Gitanyow, while Yee'l the warrior went to his hiding place—An'spa'yaxw†—on the Kispiox River and made it his home.

Wii Muugilsxw/Jonathan Johnson (1902-1968) said:

> Late one summer Ts'iiyee set out on a hunting trip. He went alone, for woods and mountains held no fears for him. He hunted eastward, for in that direction lay his hunting grounds. That night he made his camp high in the timber. The weather was good, the country pleasant and on the morrow he went farther to see what lay beyond the mountains.
>
> Toward sundown he made a great discovery. The small creek he had followed joined a river somewhat larger than the river from the lake at Kitwancool [Gitanyow] and in it were more salmon than he had seen in any one place before.‡ They almost

---

† Kispiox is the modern spelling of Git'anspayaxw (people of the hiding place).

‡ See Map 4: Central Skeena.

crowded one another out of the water. Ts'iiyee named the creek Tsihl'nii'din [McCully Creek] because so many fish made him think of fat bubbling in a pot.

Ts'iiyee speared some fish and made ready to stay the night. The next day he would discover more of this fine new country. He gathered some dry wood and was starting to make fire when he looked up and saw a man rushing at him along the narrow bar of gravel. The man was big and strong and angry. Ts'iiyee knew he must fight for his life. He took up his club and charged the stranger.

The two were evenly matched. As the stranger raised his club, Ts'iiyee grabbed his arm and held it. The stranger could not hit him. Nor could Ts'iiyee hit the stranger because his arm was also being held. Then began a mighty wrestling match, each struggling to pull free and strike down the other. Back and forth over the gravel they strained and pulled, until at last the stranger grunted, "I know you. Are you not Ts'iiyee, my neighbour in the days of Temlaham?"

Ts'iiyee's eyes opened wide. "You are Yee'l?"

"I am Yee'l. This is my valley, my hiding place. But let us drop our clubs and talk this over."

They did so, but kept their weapons close to hand because the feeling was still not altogether good between them.

"I do not know how you found Git'anspayaxw, my hiding place," Yee'l said. "I want it all to myself but since we are both strong men nothing will be gained by going to war over it."

So Yee'l made a bargain with Ts'iiyee and this is the way of it. Ts'iiyee was to hold the river on both sides from Ts'ihl'nii'din [McCully Creek] down to Anxya'gen, which is today Seventeen Mile at the head of the canyon. In this canyon Yee'l had a winter fishing place. As he lay on the ice, he dropped mouthfuls of chewed dry salmon to bring the fish, so he named that place Anxya'gen [chew]. Ts'iiyee's grounds went all across the valley, mountain to mountain. Yee'l held the river from the canyon to its mouth.

While all this was being settled, Yee'l, a big-hearted man in many ways, confessed to being lonely all these years. He said it would be good to have a neighbour, and one he had always held in respect. The two camped together for a number of days. At the end of their days together Ts'iiyee went back over the hills to Kitwancool and brought his large family back with him. This valley has been their home ever since.[1]

This is how Yee'l's hiding place became Kispiox.

This 1910 photo by Lt. G.T. Emmons taken at Kispiox shows poles belonging to the following Kispiox chiefs (L-R): (1) and (2) Woosimlaxha's "White Owl" and "Sun Dogs" poles; (3) and (4) Kliiyeemlaxha's "Running Backwards" poles; (5) Woosimlaxha's "Wii Ax" pole; (6) Gwiiyeehl's "Crazy" pole; (7) Gwiiyeehl's "Grizzly Bear of the Sea" (on the platform); (8) Gwiiyeehl's "Prince of Blackfish" pole; (9) appears to be Skabek's "Small Hat" pole. (Image 71-5524 Courtesy of the National Museum of Canada, Viola Garfield coll.)

Meanwhile, other families in other clans settled at Kispiox. While their numbers rose, Yee'l's declined for lack of childbearing women as Woosimlaxha/Jimmy Williams (1849-1924) explained:

> Yee'l hunted along the Kispiox River, and fished nearby at his fish camp on Xsigwinya'a [Shegunia River]. His sister, Gidix'uus, and her family picked berries nearby at Lax Ansi Matsa on Gwin Wijix [Sidina Mountain].† Although Gidix'uus had several children, she had but one daughter who could carry on the Yee'l line.
>
> Gidix'uus's daughter entered puberty while at the fish camp and lived separately in an underground hut. Gidix'uus brought food and water to her daughter from time to time, but when alone, the girl signaled her needs by pulling a rope that rattled hooves at her mother's house.
>
> One day the girl got no response to her signals but could hear children. Fearing the worst she left her hut and went cautiously to the house where she discovered that everyone was dead except for the children. After cremating the deceased, the

---

† *Wijix* means caribou—Sidina Mountain is locally known as Caribou Mountain.

Headstone of Alexander Gitluudaahlxw (ca.1844 – 1910). Descendants of the House of Yee'l comprise today's House of Gitluudaahlxw. (Sheila Peters photo)

young woman and children prepared for the coming winter by fishing, hunting, and picking berries.

Soon afterwards a young man appeared from a distant village and seeing their plight offered to help. The girl accepted and, him being of a Wolf Clan, they married. The following year they had a son whom they named Yee'l after her deceased uncle. By then, the girl had taken her mother's name, Gidix'uus.

One day while fishing, again at Xsigwinya'a, a bear appeared wearing a sun collar.† Gidix'uus's husband killed the bear and gave it to Yee'l to use as a crest. And soon after, the couple had a daughter, Ts'ixs Gibuu.

Gidix'uus's husband taught his son what he knew of warfare and hunting. He tested Yee'l's courage by bathing him in grizzly blood and repeatedly forcing him to endure bee stings. Finally, when Yee'l was old enough for battle, his father made him a war club—a *haxgwi'laax*.‡

The Nisga'a often raided Gitxsan villages and Yee'l sought to bring an end to it. He travelled the grease trail across the mountains to Gitlaxtaamiks on the Nass River where he attacked at dawn, surprising the villagers. Yee'l killed many men with his war club, and then returned home, where he composed his war song.[2]

---

† *Madiigam Gyamk* (supernatural grizzly of the sun).

‡ The war club was still in existence in 1920 and had a war song.

This photograph of a feast at Kispiox ca. 1898 may have been Xsaxgyoo's feast, House of Kliiyeemlaxha. (Image from Haida and Tsimshian: A Photographic History, 1972)

Generations later, the Houses of Yee'l and Ts'iiyee became known as the Houses of Gitluudaahlxw and Kliiyeemlaxha, respectively. While other Houses with many childbearing women flourished, Gitluudaahlxw's declined, so much so that by 1910 the only heir in the Yee'l line was thirteen-year-old Moses Morrison. When his uncle Alexander Gitluudaahlxw (ca.1844-1910) died, Moses assumed the name.

During the next seventy-five years Moses built close relationships with others from the Fireweed Clan and, by applying the Gitxsan adoption law of *ts'imil guut*, he brought women and men into his House, including those who had ancient ties.

The *ts'imil guut* complex is a part of traditional Gitxsan law and custom.§ It is traditional because our ancestors passed *ts'imil guut* down to us. It involves law because it gives the appropriate people the right to sanction wrong-doers, to remedy improper situations, and the power to change people's memberships, or to bring them in as members in the first place.

As Delgamuukw/Earl Muldon said:

> To us, adoption is the white man's way of taking someone away from us. We had welfare people and church people pull our children away, but we take people in. And when we take someone in, it is usually a family member. My mother and father took in nearly fifty children and they were all relatives. Gitluudaahlxw did the same thing in 1971. He took my wife, Shirley (Sterritt), and our children into his House because he needed House members. But he did this because Shirley is Moses and Gertie's niece. *Ts'imil guut* is our word for bringing people in like this.

---

§ Linguist Bruce Rigsby refers to "ts'im wil" as an older pronunciation meaning 'into', and "guut" meaning 'to get, take or bring'.

The Madiigam Gyamk (supernatural grizzly of the sun) pole at Kispiox belongs to the House of Gitluudaahlxw. (Sheila Peters photo)

Moses married Naagahl Banda/Gertie Sterritt in 1931, the daughter of Margaret Johnson (House of Kliiyeemlaxha) and my grandfather, Haaxxw/Charlie Sterritt.† Although of the Wolf Clan herself, Gertie had nephews and nieces whom Moses could bring to his House as described by Earl Muldon.‡ Two years after Barbara and I moved home to Hazelton, Moses brought me into his House and gave me the name Gotsxw'm Gipaiykw.§ Aunt Gertie and Wii Bowax/Uncle Percy (1910-1998) also brought my wife Barbara and our sons into their House and gave them Gitxsan names.

Being a member of a Gitxsan House is a serious matter:

> At the foundation of…Gitxsan…society lies the inalienable and exclusive title of each House to its territories and resources. This title is entrenched in a complex legal system that validates the acquisition and inheritance of House territories and regulates rights of access and resource use.
>
> Membership in a House is inherited through the mother's line, with all members of the House inheriting rights of access and resource use in their House territories. Membership in a House is formalized in a *yukw*, or feast, by the taking of a name. With the name, one acquires rights to use specific areas in the House territories; these areas are allocated by the chief and announced by him in the feast. The chief manages or governs all aspects of the territory and is responsible for ensuring both the well-being of the House and the health of the territory.³

Although rights and obligations flow through the matriline, a father might extend limited privileges to his children through the law of *amnigwoot* (father). *Amnigwoot* privileges expire, however, when the father dies, or if a son or daughter is disrespectful or abuses their privilege. When a new chief is installed he or she can extend or deny privileges.

Moses, along with Dinii/Alvin Weget and Wii Seexs/Peter Muldon, hired master Gitxsan artist Earl Muldon to carve the Madiigam Gyamk pole. The House raised the pole and held a feast in 1971, at which time Moses, Alvin and Pete brought more people into their House, including today's Dinii/Fern Weget, Laa Good/Shirley Muldon, her children and others.

When Moses died, in 1985, Peter Muldon (1911-2007) assumed the name Gitluudaahlxw, as did Alvin Weget when Pete died. The ancient House of Yee'l/Gitluudaahlxw, the founder of the village of Kispiox, survives through the people Moses brought in.

---

† Margaret (Maggie) Johnson and my grandfather were married at Kispiox in 1905.

‡ In recent years, the House of Kliiyeemlaxha has become so large that it has subdivided into a second related House—the House of Xsaxgyoo, Hawaaw and Wii Muugilsxw.

§ When Moses died in 1985, Alvin Weget put the name Madiigam Gyamk on me because I had been kind to one of his sons who experienced a serious illness.

Liluxws/Kispiox Jim

In about 1920, Liluxws's son, Wiilaxhaa/Charles Martin, told the story of his father, but the story begins with the earlier migration of some of Liluxws's relatives from Kisgegas to the Nass River.[†]

> In ancient days, a Frog Clan family migrated from the north to Kisgegas, led by Xsimxsan. Although some of the family married at Kisgegas and remained there,[‡] others felt like intruders and chose to leave. Xsimxsan and his family built a raft and floated downriver, beaching finally on the right bank of the Skeena near Usk. Xsimxsan sent his young hunters out in search of a new home. They walked west up a small creek to its headwaters and across a large plateau where they found a place with many lakes. The area was abundant with berries and beaver and there was no doubt it could sustain the large family. The hunters returned to the Skeena and told what they had found. Xsimxsan made the lakes area his new home, but years later would settle nearby on the Nass River at Gitlaxt'aamiks.[4]

Charles Martin said:

> Liluxws belonged to the House of Haaxxw of Kispiox. He married a woman from the House of Wiik'aax in the mid-1860s and afterwards he and his wife decided to move to Gitlaxt'aamiks to join his maternal uncle, Nigitxw. Nigitxw lived in the House of his relative Xsimxsan, an influential Nisga'a chief who oversaw not only his own House, but also three others in the village.[§]

> Soon after Liluxws and his wife arrived, jealousy over a woman developed between Nigitxw and Naxwan, a Nisga'a man [Eagle Clan]. One day Naxwan approached

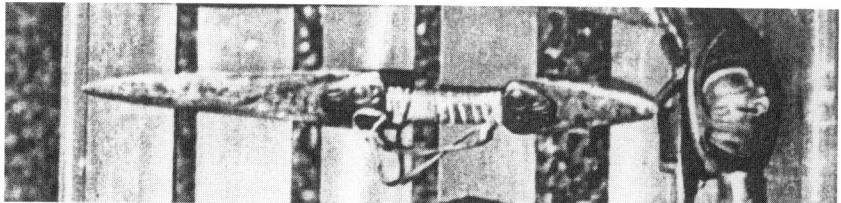

The laax wan (double bladed knife) in this picture may have been the one used by Liluxws to kill Halal. It was part of a collection amassed in the 1930s by a CNR employee at South Hazelton. Both the employee and the collection have since disappeared. (Edward Kindle photo)

---

† See Map 5: Skeena River Watershed.

‡ Galsidipxaat (Xsimxsan's younger brother), Axtiiwuluugoodii and Gudeex.

§ Liluxws's uncle, Nigitxw, belonged to the House of Xsimxsan. This may explain why Kispiox Jim considered Xsimxsan a close relative, although of different origins.

Nigitxw and said, "Did you get the woman that I want?" Nigitxw said, "Yes. I got her already."

Without warning, Naxwan stabbed Nigitxw in the neck with a dagger, killing him. Naxwan fled and hid. Liluxws and his allies retaliated. They shot at Naxwan's house for several days, preventing the occupants from getting water and wood. It was fall and the Eagle Clan occupants were cold and starving. Eventually Liluxws and his allies ended their siege, after which Liluxws and his wife returned to Kispiox.

The following year, Naxwan invited his Kispiox foes to a peace ceremony at Gitlaxt'aamiks where Naxwan and [the Eagle Clan] gave them a whole lot of goods and blankets, which they called *xsiisxw* (consolation), in compensation for murder.

Afterwards, Liluxws and his family returned to Kispiox with their gifts. But Liluxws was not satisfied. He returned to Gitlaxt'aamiks two years later and held a meeting with his kin while the rest of the village was asleep. Liluxws said, "I am going to kill Naxwan. If I do not run across him, I will kill any one of his brothers." Xsimxsan's family agreed but warned Liluxws not to do anything until they said so.

Liluxws purchased a *laax wan*.¶ It was very expensive, costing the equivalent of six marten pelts. He sought out Naxwan but Naxwan evaded him. Liluxws pursued Naxwan's brothers but they evaded him too. It was winter and the young people whiled away their time gambling. Liluxws noticed that Naxwan's younger brother Halal was playing as well.

Liluxws retrieved his *laax wan*, put on his blanket and hid the knife under his left arm. He entered the house singing and dancing with the blanket draped over his head so he would not be recognized. He danced beside Naxwan's brother and whispered, "I will show you what to do so you will win." Halal wanted to win, and said, "Alright, do it."

Everyone ignored what Liluxws was doing. Suddenly, he draped his blanket over Halal, grabbed his hair and pulled his head back. He intended to stab Halal in the stomach, but Halal moved and Liluxws stabbed him under the chin. Halal was killed, but his head fell to his chest, and Liluxws could not withdraw the knife. Blood gushed from Halal, and everyone scrambled for the door. Liluxws finally freed the knife, forced his way out the door and ran to Xsimxsan's house where he explained what he had done. The four Lax See'l houses in the village prepared to defend themselves.

Xsimxsan had a cellar in his house where the women and children could hide because the Lax Skiik would shoot at his house. Liluxws retrieved a gun and hid

---

¶ A *laax wan* is a double-bladed fifteen-inch knife with a handle between the blades.

outside the village where he could see what was happening. Xsimxsan told Liluxws to watch the smoke hole of his house. If a Lax̱ See'l was killed, someone would climb up to the smoke hole and give a raven's cry three times: "gaak, gaak, gaak". That would mean Liluxws should go to Kispiox and return with warriors. The Eagle Clan attacked Xsimxsan's house for two days but no one was killed.

Finally, Bagayt 'Neexhl shouted, "You had no right to kill Halal, Naxwan's brother. Many years ago, the Indians of Gitlax̱t'aamiks went up to Kuldo…and I fought against the Kuldo Indians. And they killed Haax̱xw's nephew. They did not intend to kill him but they did it by mistake as they thought he belonged to Kuldo. As soon as Haax̱xw got the news he came down [here] to fight on account of the killing of his nephew at Kuldo. And he found T'ax̱xw'm Waax. And Haax̱xw found T'ax̱xw'm Waax's fishing camp, Gwanks Ts'ak, and killed T'ax̱xw'm Waax. He killed his wife and all his children. That was the reason Naxwan killed Nigitxw, your uncle, and now [you have] killed Halal again. That was not right."

Liluxws immediately left for Kispiox to determine the truth of this story. He arrived at Gyahl T'in† at midnight when everyone was asleep. He took a pair of snowshoes and continued travelling. The next day he met with many Indians on their way to get oolichans, including his mother, sister and uncle. Upon hearing Liluxws's story, they returned with him to Kispiox. Liluxws expected the Nisga'a to be on the warpath, but they did not show up that winter.‡

Liluxws went to Haax̱xw and asked him about the T'ax̱xw'm Waax story. Haax̱xw said, "The Nass River Indians came and fought against Kuldo all right, they did that. But they did not kill his nephew. And Haax̱xw (a predecessor) did not go to the Nass River to fight. He did not kill T'ax̱xw'm Waax and his wife and children."

Anticipating a Nisga'a retaliation, Liluxws and his brother, and the spouses of their sisters built a fort about a mile above Kispiox on the Kispiox River at Ts'im'ansi'mal.§ They shot at the fort to see if the bullets would penetrate it, cut holes to shoot through, and armored the walls with flat stones. Liluxws also dug deep pits in the ground on both sides of the Kispiox River.

Liluxws made himself a wooden *laax wan*, and told one of his warriors to challenge him from outside the fort. When the warrior said, "Come out. We will fight," Liluxws ran from the fort with his wooden *laax wan*, and the two men wrestled. Liluxws was ready for the Nisga'a.

---

† A Gitanyow fishing camp located at the Kiteen River confluence with the Nass River.

‡ At this time, Liluxws took a third name—Hla'aksim Maaxws (like melted snow water)—which he used from then on. However, Liluxws will continue to be used so as not to confuse the reader.

§ Where Yee'l made his canoes. It may also have been a cremation site.

When Liluxws heard that the Nisga'a were about to arrive on the opposite side of the river, he sent a messenger to tell the Nisga'a, "I don't want Nass River to fight against Kispiox...but Naxwan and my uncle...are against one another."

Naxwan heard the message, but was afraid. The Nisga'a went to Naxwan and said, "What is the matter? You are supposed to be the brave man. Now Liluxws is...the brave man, he wants you to fight with him." Naxwan did not answer, and another Nisga'a man pulled his hair, "Get up," he said. The Nisga'a mocked him, "You had better put on a woman's dress. You are not a man..."

The Nisga'a walked towards the river. Liluxws's warriors, concealed in pits on the near shore, shot at the Nisga'a, forcing them to take cover. Liluxws walked from the fort, with his real *laax wan* in his hand, and said, "Where are you Naxwan, the bravest man on the Nass River? He had better come if he wants to see me." Liluxws held up his knife. "Where is the knife that you used when you killed my uncle? You had better bring it now, and we will fight right here."

Naxwan didn't respond, and Liluxws called again. Finally, Xsimxsan took Naxwan [by] the shoulders...lifted him from the ground and said, "Go...go and fight him." But he wouldn't, even though they were coaxing him to do so. The Nisga'a applauded as one of them shot at Liluxws, who suddenly pitched face down on the ground. Thinking Liluxws had been shot, the Kispiox and Gitanmaax warriors opened fire.

The Nisga'a continued towards the riverbank, but Liluxws had warriors concealed in pits there too, and as they began firing, the Nisga'a stopped firing, lay down, and rolled into depressions in the ground. Liluxws crossed the river but the Nisga'a remained concealed for about an hour. Finally, a Nisga'a warrior with a *s'id'axt* (a top-knot tied with a weasel pelt) looked up to see what was happening. Liluxws took aim and shot the *s'id'axt* from the man's head.

Liluxws thought he had killed the man, but the man stood and said, "I am Xsimxsan. What is the matter? You should not kill me...don't you know me?" Xsimxsan walked to Liluxws, spreading his arms, "I am your relative, you had better kill me now. You have killed me already but you had better finish it." But Liluxws couldn't do it. Liluxws went into his fort and hid, and the Nisga'a followed. The Kispiox warriors entered as well, with their guns and spears. Nigitxw's sister, who was very old, was there too. Naxwan and his brother sat down before the Nisga'a warriors.

Liluxws's mother stood, "What are you doing here now? And what do you want? You call yourself a brave man. Why don't you come and meet Liluxws, my son, who wants to fight with you?[5] My son is not a brave man at all. You killed my brother Nigitxw and mocked him on account of he does not belong to the Nass River, and now my son Liluxws killed your brother so we are all even. Why are you fleeing after my son killed your brother? Do you feel good or not?"

Naxwan did not answer, nor did anyone else. Liluxws suddenly appeared before Naxwan, with his knife in hand. He asked Naxwan, "What do you want me to do? Do you want me to stick this knife in you?" Everyone was afraid.

Xsimxsan stood and spoke to Liluxws, "Brother, [you] cannot kill Naxwan. He came here for peace, to make peace. We don't want anyone to kill him. We want to make friends with everybody. Put the knife away."

Naxwan had put his knife away, but Liluxws intended to kill him. They both stood, but Woosimlaxha† intervened, "Indeed, we intended to kill…but the Nass Indian wanted to kill [an] Indian belonging to the Skeena River right from the beginning. Now, if you people intend to be a friend of us, according to what Xsimxsan said, let us be friends together, and no more murder one another."

The peace ceremony—a *gawaganii*—was held.‡ Liluxws's mother retrieved goods from storage boxes, laid them before Naxwan and his brothers, and gave a woman to the Nisga'a as well, but Liluxws wouldn't allow this.[6]

This was the successful conclusion of negotiations between the two parties.

Liluxws later gave the *laax wan* to his maternal uncle, Haaxxw. The 1881 census for Kispiox includes the following entry: "Hakq, male, 60, married", and a fifty-five-year-old female—Nox Lubathl—presumably Hakq's wife. Several entries on the same page include names from the House of Haaxxw.[7] A monument in Glen Vowell cemetery reads, "Hahqu/Died April 20, 1911/Age 70 Years". When he died, Mark Sampson (aka Mark Simpson), my grandfather's first cousin, became Haaxxw.

The word *gawaganii* originated with the Tlingit in Alaska. They say it may have originated long ago in the south—with the Coast Salish in or around the lower Fraser River—and later moved northward, much as the Whull-e-mooch had during their ancient migration to Vancouver Island. The Gitxsan word, *gawaganii,* is derived from the Tlingit word, *guwakaan,* meaning deer.

As MA candidate Kenneth Austin wrote:

> Since a *guwakaan* is perceived as a gentle animal that does not prey on other animals, it seems that in ancient times the Pacific Northwest Coast Indians chose it to be a symbol of peace. Ultimately it assumed a central role during the deer ritual practiced along the coastal lands of BC to the southern end of the Gulf of Alaska.[8]

---

† Woosimlaxha Robinson (1841-1923), said to be 103 when he died, but was age 40 on the 1881 Canada census.
‡ Kispiox Jim told his son Charles about the above events. Charles said the peace ceremony took place when he was three years old.

Austin explained:

> Although all offenses were negotiable, Drucker (1965:72, 73) mentions two basic courses of action that were open to an offended group. One was to seek revenge by slaying a member of the offenders' [side], usually not the one [that] did the killing but rather someone from his group of equal social standing as the slain person. At times a relative came forth to be slain. In Peck's account (1986:63), an uncle must take the place of his nephew if it was the nephew who killed a person of high class standing.[9]

The offended side expected prompt action, or warfare could resume. According to Austin, sometimes the "disputants…exchanged hostages who, before the deer ritual began, became *guwakaan* (deer)."[10] Sometimes the *guwakaan* were held by each side during an eight-day ceremony and then returned. Under other circumstances, they might be sacrificed.

The author's Aunt Margaret stands beside her father's pole—Gans'Niigyamks (pole the sun shines on) from the House of Haaxxw—ca. 1947. (Bill Heath photo)

Austin explained elsewhere in his thesis that the ritual might include the building of a fort, a mock battle, and the staging of rituals. Although not expressly stated, there are many aspects of the process at Ts'im'ansi'mal that suggest this may have been the case: the building of the fort; Liluxws pitching to the ground when the first shot was fired; the fusillade of shots without injury to either side; Xsimxsan stating the Nisga'a came to make peace, and Liluxws's mother having food and gifts available before hostilities began.

There were fifteen people living in Haaxxw's house at Kispiox in 1881. Haaxxw, sixty, was the oldest person in the house while the youngest was a boy of twelve. The rest of the occupants were eighteen years of age or older.[11] This Haaxxw commemorated his predecessor by erecting a totem pole—*Gans' Niigyamks* ('the sun shines on' pole)—at about this time.

Marius Barbeau spoke of the pole, which was carved by Gitanyow artist Gai'nim with the help of Ts'ugyet/James Green of Kispiox:

> It counts among the best carvings of the Skeena. It is treated with vivid power and definiteness. Although its style conforms to the current conventions, it is remarkably ingenious and original. The figure of the Frog-Woman, 'Niigyamks, with the tiny frogs creeping out of her mouth, over her eyes, and on her body, is certainly one of the most artistic and impressive illustrations ever made of a native myth on the whole of the North West Coast.[12]

My grandfather, Haaxxw/Charlie Sterritt, established himself in Gitanmaax and moved his pole there in the mid-1940s. The Niigyamks pole is among the last of the 1880s Kispiox poles still standing.

ENDNOTES

1. Evans, 16-18.
2. Barbeau and Beynon, "Temlarh'am" (n.d.), The Downfall, II No's. 98 - 100: 776-782. My rendering of this story is also based on other stories I have heard.
3. Sterritt, Marsden *et al*, 11.
4. Sterritt, Marsden *et al*, 26-7, fn 24.
5. "Barbeau and Beynon Fieldnotes", (B-F-89.26).
6. "Barbeau and Beynon Fieldnotes", Charles Martin (B-F-89.26).
7. Canada: 1881 Census of BC, Coast of Mainland Indians, Kispiox, p. 1, family 2, house 2, lines 4 - 7.
8. Austin, 97.
9. Austin, 20.
10. Austin, 97.
11. Canada: 1881 Census of BC, Coast of Mainland Indians, Kispiox, p. 1, families 2 – 5, house 2, lines 4 - 18.
12. Barbeau, *Totem Poles*, 79.

CHAPTER SIX

Gitanga̱sx̱, Kisgegas and Bear Lake

The House of Wiiḵ'aax comes from La̱xgitanga̱sx̱ (on people of wild rice). An old village on the river Skeena, up the river. At this place we still see some [fish] caches…in the ground. The flat is still open there. They were there at Gitanga̱sx̱ thousands of years ago, even before they came to Temlaham. This family never went to Temlaham.

—Wiila̱x̱haa/Charles Martin ca.1920[†]

In October 1984, Delgamuukw/Albert Tait (1902-1987) and Gisday Wa/Alfred Joseph (1928-2014) filed a Writ and Statement of Claim against the BC government. This was our attempt to have the provincial and federal governments recognize aboriginal rights and title to Gitxsan and Wet'suwet'en territories in northwest BC. Competing territorial claims were an issue, and we wished to meet with our neighbours from Takla Lake, some of whom were Gitxsan, to discuss our eastern border. It was a historic event, and some fifty elders, leaders, and families of four peoples—the Dakelh (Carrier)[†], Sekani[‡], Wet'suwet'en and Gitxsan—camped at Bear Lake in July 1985 to meet, exchange stories and renew acquaintances. We traveled to Bear Lake by road, rail and plane, and hired a helicopter and pilot to fly us to the territories. The old village of Bear Lake is at the centre of the territories we were there to discuss.

---

† French fur traders named them *Carriere* because Dakelh widows carried bits of their husband's cremated remains in a satchel until the family could hold a feast (Morice, 6).

‡ A branch of the Dunne-za, the so-called Beaver Indians who were once centered on the Peace River and its various tributaries, two of which—the Omineca and Ingenika—gave them relatively easy access to Bear Lake.

Bear Lake, site of a four-nation meeting in 1985 to discuss ancient boundaries, is at the eastern edge of Gitxsan territory. (Image G-06636 courtesy of RBCM & A)

Because Bear Lake was a spawning ground for salmon, it had no doubt been of interest to aboriginal people hunting in the area for generations. After James Douglas established Fort Connolly there in 1826, inter-tribal conflict among those seeking to trade furs—the Gitxsan, Sekani and Dakelh—was inevitable.

Gitangasx is a short helicopter ride west of Bear Lake. On July 17, four of us—my father, William Charlie, Edward John and I—flew to Gitangasx.† Later, Alec Bob and Peter Abraham flew with me and Edward to Wisanskit, a mountain north of Bear Lake where Tsetsaut warriors had killed a Gitxsan hunting party early in the 19th century.‡ Some of the elders with us were descendants of those in the Gitxsan hunting party (Wiik̲'aax for example), and some of the Sekani participants may have been descendants of those our people encountered there. We spent our time flying with elders throughout the area and exchanging histories and views.

The Gitxsan and Dakelh elders knew each other, all having trapped in the area until about forty years earlier. Some of the younger people from Takla, however, were surprised and perturbed that Gitxsan people they had never met were claiming land in the area. The Takla women were very much concerned about—and engaged in—the discussions, all the while keeping everyone well fed. The youth drummed and sang each evening. It was apparent from our meetings, however, that settling our differences might be as emotional as the circumstances leading to the Gitxsan migration from Gitangasx to Kisgegas.

---

† Wosi'midiik/William Charlie (1918- ?) was born and raised at Bear Lake. Akile Ch'oh/Edward John was then the leader of the Carrier-Sekani Tribal Council.

‡ Haatix Lax Nok/Alec Bob and Miinhl Gan/Peter Abraham (b.1932).

Thomas Wright spoke of Wiik̲'aax's long ago journey north to the Yukon and back to the headwaters of the Skeena. Wright too was a member of the House of Wiik̲'aax. Those ancient Wolf Clan members—ancestors of Thomas Wright, Charles Martin and my father—ended this journey by settling at Gitangas̲x. But they weren't alone. Others joined them and Gitangas̲x became a village of three clans: Lax̲ Gibuu (Wolf), Gisk'aast (Fireweed) and Lax G̲anada (Raven-Frog).

Members of four aboriginal groups—Carrier, Sekani, Wet'suwet'en and Gitxsan—met at Bear Lake in 1985 to discuss tribal boundaries. Pictured here (L – R) at Gitangas̲x are William Charlie (who was raised in the area and a Wiik̲'aax House relative), Neil B. Sterritt (author's father), and Ed John, Grand Chief of the Carrier-Sekani Tribal Council. (NJS photo)

The Tsetsaut

Gitangas̲x was a frontier village because its territories comprised the northern and eastern limit of Gitxsan territories. Gitxsan families hunting and trapping on or beyond their territories were vulnerable to attack by other nations. In relatively recent times—during the mid- to late-1700s—a domino effect arose from the westward progression of the fur trade.§

Fur traders relied on aboriginal allies such as the Iroquois and the Cree of James Bay as they established trading posts westward. These allies, armed with guns, traveled ahead of the traders

---

§ The events are said to have occurred before the Gitxsan and their northern neighbours had guns and before the abandonment of the village of Gitangas̲x. It may have occurred as a result of indirect contact by pushing the eastern tribes further west. David Gunanoot dated the events as "About three or four of those, my grandfathers, that's all." *Delgamuukw v. BC*, David Gunanoot, Vol. 1, 68.

The site of the ancient village of Gitangasx̱, along the right bank of the Skeena River east from Fourth Cabin on the trail to Bear Lake. (NJS photo)

forcing vulnerable western tribes to flee into and beyond the Rocky Mountains. The identity of the displaced tribes is uncertain but the Gitxsan referred to such intruders as Tsetsaut.[2]

One group affected by this western progression was the Luu Ts'abim Tsimyip, who lived in underground houses. They began to hunt *gwiikw* (hoary marmots or groundhogs) on territories owned by Gitangasx̱ chiefs. Groundhogs were a valuable resource as they were relatively easy to snare, their meat was rich in fat and their pelts made warm, light blankets and clothing. The Tsetsaut came upon a chief from the House of Wiik̲'aax and his family, killing all, except for an infant boy. This is the story of how the boy avenged his parents' deaths, as told by Smax/Arthur P. Sampson (1911-1981).[3]

> Wiik̲'aax had a brother, Laats, who was hunting groundhog on his territory northwest of Gitangasx̱. The Tsetsaut killed Laats and his family, except for the baby, whom they left for dead. Two days later another Gitxsan family traveled through the area and found the bodies. One of the women noticed a cradle, turned it over, and discovered a baby, alive, but barely.
>
> They returned to Gitangasx̱ with the baby and raised him as their own. Growing up, he quarreled with other children. The children taunted him, saying, "What's the matter with this up-side-down-child? Why is he so cranky?" The boy was puzzled by this and asked his parents why the children said such things. His mother said, "Maybe they don't know what to say to you." The boy left it at that, but a few days later he went to his mother crying and said, "You must tell me why

they are saying such things to me. I don't understand why they call me the up-side-down-boy."

His mother relented. She told her adopted son that the Tsetsaut had murdered his parents and all their companions on their hunting grounds. She said, "These people came from Lax Wii Yip. They killed them because of their hunting grounds. Perhaps your father made a mistake and was using some of their hunting grounds. This is the reason for the killings. But we found you, maybe because they didn't want to kill you. So they just laid you down, face down in the snow. This is why we have taken care of you, even until now." This was the first time the young boy knew what had happened. Laats's son never forgot what his adopted mother told him, and he vowed to one day avenge the deaths of his parents.

Hostilities continued for many years until the brother and nephew of Suuwiiguus, a chief in the House of Kyoluget, failed to return from a hunting trip. Suuwiiguus put together a search party and found them as well as many dead Tsetsaut. They cremated the bodies and returned to Gitangasx.

By this time, Laats's son was a grown man with the name Gwilagantxw. Suuwiiguus was preparing for war and Gwilagantxw was eager to join the party of 100 warriors. He proposed that they kill a grizzly and use it as a decoy to fool the Tsetsaut. He said, "We will dry the hide, smear jack-pine pitch all over it, and then spread sand over the pitch. We will use it for a target with bows and arrows." The warriors killed the biggest grizzly they could find and skinned it carefully, leaving the front paws, the hind paws and the bear's head on. They prepared the hide until they thought it was ready. But when they shot arrows at it, some pierced the hide. They added more layers of pitch and sand until finally the arrows and spears of the best warriors would not pierce it. By then the grizzly bear hide was so heavy only the strongest of warriors could pack it.

The war party led by Suuwiiguus set out on their journey. One warrior carried the grizzly hide but he could only go for a short distance and then another warrior would pack it. They crossed rivers and creeks, went by lakes and on beyond the head of the Skeena until they reached Lax Wii Yip, a large prairie with small hills here and there and a few jack pines.

Gwilagantxw spoke. "When the sun starts to rise very early in the morning, I will wear the grizzly bear armour, and I will walk along the hillside where the grass grows."

As the sun rose, the warriors could see down into the valley as smoke came out of the ground. The Tsetsaut lived like groundhogs and used ladders to get in and out of their homes. The warriors remained hidden while Gwilagantxw donned the hide and crawled to and fro across the meadow, imitating a grizzly eating grass and digging at groundhog burrows. After a while a man emerged and spotted the

Artha Smiak's headstone in the Gitanmaax cemetery shows the bear between two mountains. Artha Smiak was the uncle of Arthur P. Sampson, who told the story about the Gitxsan defeating the Luu Tsabim Tsim Yip (Tsetsaut). (Sheila Peters photo)

grizzly high on the hillside. He rushed back into his house and then many people came out and looked towards the grizzly.

Finally, Tsetsaut men with bows, arrows, and spears began to stalk the grizzly. Gwilagantxw knew they were coming but continued to imitate a feeding grizzly. As the Tsetsaut neared, they began to shoot at the bear. Suddenly, Gwilagantxw threw off the hide and ran to his weapons, while the hidden warriors leapt from hiding and attacked the Tsetsaut. Gwilagantxw grabbed his bow and arrows, shooting the Tsetsaut and killing many.

Other Tsetsaut warriors fled down the hill shouting, "This is not a grizzly. Warriors are shooting us. Take down your ladders and prepare to defend yourselves."

Gwilagantxw ran out of arrows and took up his war club made of bone with sharp spikes and raced after the Tsetsaut. He jumped down into the Tsetsaut home, clubbing people and killing many. Some tried to escape but other Gitxsan warriors killed them as they emerged. The battle lasted nearly all day.

When the battle ended the warriors found boxes with hides—caribou, moose, fox and martins—along with food and other treasures. They gathered these treasures and began their journey home but they had so much to carry they had to relay their packs.

After they got home they held a feast and adopted crests to commemorate their victory. Gwilagantxw said of his exploits with the grizzly bear hide, "We will erect a totem pole with the grizzly bear hide hanging between two mountains, because we travelled so far."[4]

Years later, after the move from Gitangasx to Kisgegas, the family of Gwilagantxw had grown and had their own House at Anlagasimdeex led by Ts'iiwus, Ts'abax and Smax.

Hostilities continued, however, as the Tsetsaut continued to be pressured from the north and east by the fur traders and their aboriginal allies. Finally, Gitangasx leaders decided to relocate their village and move south. Miluulak, Wiiminoosikx, Niik'yap and Wiik'aax set out together. They had heard about the canyon at Kisgegas and made that their destination. The family of Kyoluget and Suuwiiguus eventually made Kuldo its home, as did 'Niist and Wa'a and Xsim'gwneekxw.[5]

Wiik'aax had a large family and had two houses in Kisgegas, one directly behind the other, named Ts'im Gaak and Sk'alaa'nt, which was reached through the first house.[6] The chiefs found Kisgegas to be an ideal village. Berry patches abounded nearby and salmon gathered in astounding numbers in the canyon below the village. Groundhog, mountain goats, caribou, bear, rabbits and grouse were abundant and provided variety to their diet. Many chiefs in addition to Wiik'aax—Miluulak, Wiiminoosikx, Ts'abax, Niik'yap and others—continued to hold territories north of the Sustut River.

Bear Lake

And there was a new danger. Many years after the Gitxsan had fought the Tsetsaut at Lax Wii Yip, some Tsetsaut obtained guns from fur traders and threatened Gitxsan chiefs north of Bear Lake. This finally came to a head when Miluulak and Gits'abixw[†] were hunting on Wisanskit, a good groundhog mountain north of Bear Lake.[‡]

The grandmother of Gwiiyeehl/John Brown witnessed what happened and told him the story:

> At five walks from Bear Lake another territory belonged to Miluulak, the name of which was Wilgawsuuk (where-you-keep-silent). He went there accompanied by his relatives and Gits'abixw. They camped there and stayed some time.
>
> While Miluulak was at his groundhog traps, the Tsetsaut arrived at Wilgawsuuk. Gits'abixw then invited these visitors and sat them down around the house on furs, any furs at all: mountain goat and caribou or anything.
>
> Then one of the Tsetsaut wanted to test the strength of Gits'abixw wrestling in play. This they did. And each Tsetsaut in turn tried to test the strength of Gits'abixw, but

---

† Gits'abixw is a chief's name in the House of Wiik'aax.

‡ Wisanskit is the bald mountain east of Bird Hill. A boundary between Wiik'aax and Miluulak runs along Wisanskit.

none was able to throw him over. The Tsetsaut man was so incensed at not being able to overcome the Wolf clansman that he shot him with a gun. This happened at the time when the first gun was received in the country. Then the Tsetsaut destroyed all the rest of the inmates of the house.

Miluulak returned and saw that many of his company…were killed. But he did not take flight, although his people were lying dead. He was a great *halayt* (shaman). As the Tsetsaut saw him coming towards them they noticed that his mouth was foaming with a green fluid. This was from his power as a *halayt* which he was going to exercise over the *hayuux* (spirits). This green fluid kept issuing from his mouth. They killed him.

After Miluulak's death, the Tsetsaut became attracted to one of Miluulak's nieces because of her good looks. They now went back home. Before they had traveled five miles, the Tsetsaut who had killed Miluulak fell down, because of the manner the fluid came out of Miluulak's mouth. That fluid also oozed out of this man's mouth when he fell. The niece of Miluulak who was with them noticed it…. They kept going eastward until half of the company had fallen dead.

The Tsetsaut later returned with their captive to where the white people were living at Bear Lake…The white people observed that the woman was a stranger, so they took her into their care, into their house. They did not want her to go out again because they were afraid the Tsetsaut would molest her.

The men at the fort took good care of Miluulak's niece. She spent the summer there, putting up berries for herself and the people at the fort. The following spring servants from the fort accompanied her as far as Xsigwin Gyila'a (Squingula River) and from there she made her way home to Kisgegas.

The Kisgegas warriors decided to retaliate.

They prepared themselves to go out on a raid…The raiding party included the Lax See'l (Raven-Frog), Gisk'aast (Fireweeds) and the Lax Gibuu (Wolves). Waiget (Fireweed) was the chief of the Kisgegas group. His name meant 'A [dead] fall'—a type of trap, a *naxnok* (spirit) name. Niik'yap was the leader of the Wolves and Wiiminoosikx of the Raven-Frogs. They all travelled together. They went to where the white people lived.

When they arrived at Bear Lake they were undecided. Should they take revenge on the Tsetsaut or attack the white people for giving the Tsetsaut firearms. They captured a Tsetsaut man they found at the fort, but when he offered half of a nearby mountain to the war party, they let him go unharmed.

As Gwiiyeehl said, seeing the white men and their fort was a unique experience:

This was the first time that they had seen a white man's dog. The Gitxsan's dogs' ears stand up, the white man's hang down. So then they decided that they should adopt as a crest the white man's dog's head with dropping ears. They called this, *osii midoo*—white-man's-dog.

They asked among themselves, "Who will take this as a crest?" The Fireweeds decided to take it, and it was theirs, in the House of Waiget. Then they said, "What will Niik'yap take? He shall take half of the mountain that was given by the Tsetsaut." Then, "What will the House of Miluulak have?" they asked. They said, "We will own the *yees* (palisade) as a fortress," [which] had been surrounding the white man's house. And it became the crest of Miluulak.

Next they inquired as to the white man's name. And the white man said, "Mr. Ross [Misa'loos to Gitxsan ears]. He shall take this name as his property. So they agreed that the man that had taken the dog as his crest should also take the name of *Misa'loos*. There was another Wolf clansman who had no crest—that is, Y'ool. Then they agreed upon him taking 'Sunbeams-Feet-of-the-Sun' (Hl'sise'e Hloxs). Still another man had no crest. They allotted to him the white person's name of Malii (Mary), and he gave it to his sister. This name has become his property. After they had agreed to all that they left this place. They received many gifts from the white people, including axes, knives and many other objects.

(L – R) Alec Bob, Ed John and Peter Abraham at Wisanskit where a Gitxsan hunting party perished at the hands of the Tsetsaut. Bob and Abraham were with the Carrier-Sekani Tribal Council and were raised in the Bear Lake area. (NJS photo)

The war party returned to Kisgegas and decided to hold feasts to commemorate their adventure. "Waiget must give the first white feast," they said, and "he will exhibit the 'Dog of Misa'loos.'" They invited all the Gitxsan villages to their feast: Kuldo, Kispiox, Gitanmaax, Gitsegukla, Gitwangak and Gitanyow.[7]

The killing of the Gitxsan at Wisanskit was described in the Hudson's Bay Company (HBC) journals of Charles Ross who succeeded James Douglas at Fort Connolly in 1827. In January 1829 Ross wrote:

> There is here an Atnah woman whom I purchased from the last Indians I saw with the intention of sending her to her friends in the spring. Our Indians had her as a slave, and she's the only survivor of the party of her people, which they cut off last summer.[8]

Miluulak's niece spent the winter at Bear Lake. The following spring, Ross had some of his men accompany her part of the way to Kisgegas and she made the rest of the journey on her own.

By 1830 the Gitxsan of Gitangasx were well established at Kuldo and Kisgegas, and would also make Bear Lake their home. Nevertheless, warfare with the Tsetsaut continued until Gaidaxgyet decided to bring hostilities to an end. Arthur Hankin (1882-1968), who was born and raised in Hazelton, spoke fluent Gitxsan and spent much of his life trapping and hunting with the Gitxsan throughout their territories, told how our eastern boundary was confirmed, bringing peace between the Gitxsan and the Sekani. This is when the Sekani adopted the Gitxsan crest and clan system:

> Gaidaxgyet[†] called all the tribes together. That cost him $7,000.[‡] And the boundary was shown to the Interior Indians, the Tsetsaut. Arrows made of bone were shot into a crevasse of rock at Takla Lake. This was to show how far the Gitxsan territory went. And this was mapped in Indian paint on some moose skins. And a potlatch was held. The map was kept.
>
> As to exactly what took place, Abraham Gaidaxgyet knows the whole narrative, a very long story. After this, Gaidaxgyet lived at Babine. Bear Lake was his headquarters. It is a moose hunting territory. During the feast the Indians joined their crests. The Lax See'l [Raven-Frog] of the Tsetsaut became relatives of the Kisgegas Lax See'l, and the Lax Gibuu [Wolf of the Tsetsaut], of the [Kisgegas] Lax Gibuu. They made a settlement in that way. Before they had become linked together, there were always murders and treachery. This happened not so long ago, after the Hudson's Bay came to that country [1823 at Fort Babine, 1827 at Bear Lake]. The man who brought about this settlement is living still.[9]

---

† Bear Lake Abraham (aka 'Old Abraham') died at Babine May 16, 1925, age eighty. He was the father of Haspaiyets/Michell Abraham (1892-1973), who belonged to the House of Wiik̲'aax.

‡ In food, moose and caribou, by today's economic standards. Cash was not used during the 19th century.

Members of the Gitxsan nation discuss territorial boundaries with the Carrier-Sekani Tribal Council at Burns Lake in 1987. From left are Ralph Michell, Mary McKenzie, David Gunanoot and the author. (NJS coll.)

John Brown confirmed our eastern boundary when he said:

> It is near Miluulak's hunting ground, Giletuhl'hamook, the home of Ha'mook [wild celery]. And there is a big rock [there]. I was a very small boy when my uncle told me about this. But he showed me this big rock and said, "This is a sign that we won't fight with the Sekani anymore because [they] have driven [their] arrows and the Kisgegas 20 arrows. This is the way they put them in the crack. When you see arrows with the points down it means peace, with the points up, it means war. And the arrows were pointed downward in the rocks…. This must have taken place about one hundred years ago.[10]

This was an important event. It took place at Red Bluff on the east side of Takla Lake. After the peace ceremony many Kisgegas chiefs and their families resumed hunting and trapping on their territories north and south of Bear Lake, and continued to do so well into the 20th century.§ Another fifty or so—many of whom were Gitxsan—married Sekani and Dakelh persons and lived there year round.¶

---

§ In 1915, there were 231 people in Kisgegas, of which three-quarters lived "principally…at Bear Lake…" (Loring to Royal Commission, Victoria, BC, 1915: 131).

¶ Canada Census, BC, Yale-Cariboo, Cariboo, 1911: 20. Also see Fort Connelly [sic] births, marriages and deaths (Catholic Church records, ca. 1890 to 1930: 112-137).

ENDNOTES

1. "Barbeau and Beynon Fieldnotes", Charles Martin (B-F-81.1).
2. Sterritt, Marsden *et al*, 19.
3. "Interview with Smax/Arthur P. Sampson," 1972. Here I have paraphrased Sampson's history. With so many warriors involved, other Gitxsan Houses have similar accounts emphasizing their involvement.
4. Sampson, 1972.
5. Barbeau and Beynon, "Wolf-Clan Invaders", No. 75: 1-7.
6. "Barbeau and Beynon Fieldnotes", Mrs. Jimmy Williams.
7. Barbeau and Beynon, "Raven Clan Outlaws", 1-7.
8. HBCA: Ross to Connolly, Bear Lake, Jan. 1829 #116 (B 188/b/4).
9. Barbeau and Beynon, "Raven Clan Outlaws", No. 84: 1.
10. "Barbeau and Beynon Fieldnotes", John Brown and Mrs. Cox (B-F-68.5).

CHAPTER SEVEN

Hagwilget: The Gentle People

There have always been harmonious relations between the Gitxsan and the Wet'suwet'en peoples. Although the territorial boundary between the Gitxsan and Wet'suwet'en is about halfway between Gitanmaax and Moricetown,† many Wet'suwet'en have lived at Hagwilget on Gitxsan territory since 1824. Before that, the Wet'suwet'en's main village was at Witset, near today's Moricetown.

As mentioned earlier, an 1824 rockslide dammed the Bulkley River a few kilometres above The Forks, preventing salmon from swimming any further up the river. The Wet'suwet'en became concerned and went to Gitanmaax to get permission to fish in the canyon below the rock fall. A very old woman from the House of Guuxwo'ot later told Guuxwo'ot/Peter John (1864-1926) what happened:

> The chief of the [Wet'suwet'en] was Sedzan [Satsan]. Satsan took a present to each of the chiefs, a reindeer skin. And these he presented before [asking] them for permission to come and move at the canyon as the fish was gone from where they were. They were living then at [Witset] Moricetown. Gitomgaldo [Gidumgaldo] then presented Satsan with much dried salmon.

> This was seen and told by an old grandmother…a big chief woman in our house. She had seen this in her own time. [Peter John] thinks it was over 100 years ago, because she was very old. She herself was in four battles…[with Nisga'a] raiders coming here. So upon that Satsan returned to his people. He told them…that there was much fish on the other side of the canyon and that he had…Gidumgaldo's

---

† Sophia Mowatt (ca. 1902-2002) said, "Xsi Gwits'iik/Boulder Creek and Sta'gapsit/Porphyry Creek is our land. It belongs to my uncle, Sam Jones (1987)." Donald Grey (1877-1970) said, "Porphyry Creek, Sta'gapsit was the old line between Gitxsan and Moricetown. It belonged to Gitanmaax" (Wilson Duff files Bdc Art 35 V.12 c.b., ca.1965).

permission to move near the canyon and fish on the other [side]. That is why they are there today. Before that the Gitxsan used both sides of the canyon.

Gidumgaldo has still the right and the La̱x Gibuu chief has still the right to fish on the Hagwelgate [side] and they still have their House there in many instances selling the fish to the Hagwelgate or they have the privilege to fish for themselves.[1]

Gidumgaldo and Satsan made an agreement that led to many Wet'suwet'en abandoning Witset.

The new village came to have three names: Hagwilget (Gitxsan), Tsë Cakh (Wet'suwet'en) and Rocher Deboule (French).

As a child, Arthur Mowatt (1907-1991) lived with his grandfather, Anda Ap/Johnny Muldoe (1846-1928). Johnny's father was a former Gidumgaldo, and his mother was Tu Etisht from the House of Gutgwinuxs in Kispiox. Each spring they moved to Muldoe's smokehouse in a field just above the Bulkley River. Arthur said his grandfather used a *moohl* (dip net) to catch spring salmon on the Hazelton side of the Bulkley and when "spring salmon season was over, we used to move to Hagwilget Canyon, below the bridge to catch fish. This is where he and I used to live all summer catching fish."[2]

Arthur explained what he saw as a child and what his grandfather told him:

> When I was quite a little boy I saw Hagwilget people build a fish trap dam below the bridge. They staked posts right across the canyon, then [hung] fish traps—*'din*—between these posts…They split the river in half. What fish was caught on this side, the people that lived on the same side took the catch. The fish caught on the other side [the people there] took the catch…This is what my grandfather told me. They only use to come there to fish, then they made their home there now. They really did not own Hagwilget. It belongs to Gitanmaax.
>
> I don't really know how the Indian made fish traps (*'din*). I didn't see…any ropes at all, such as the ropes the white people use today. They used *maa k'okhl* (cedar bark rope). They pound it until it looks like cotton batten, then they twist it and it will never rot. And once it burns, it will not burn out easily. I might as well say that it's just as good as nylon. It will never rot. You could keep it for many years. And it will never rot, so this is what they use when they build fish traps across the Canyon.
>
> The Government blasted off the big rock in the Canyon not so long ago [1959], so the falls no longer exist anymore. The fish used to jump these falls, where the fish barrels use to hang underneath them. The fish use to fall back into the trap. One type of trap they call *ploo'ah* some of the big fish barrels, fish fall into them traps.
>
> Early each morning, the young men would string a rope across the river, where the fish barrels [were]. Take the fish from the barrels and hang them on poles tied on the ropes that was strung across the river, and the other men would pull the fish to shore. Then they used to start packing the fish to the smokehouse, and the people

that lived across the river would be doing the same thing. They would work at this all day long.

The old road used to cross the Bulkley River just about where the Larsons at Two Mile live today; this end of the bridge crossed just at the mouth of Two Mile Creek long ago. It was just a wagon road. We used to cross this old bridge, my grandfather and I.

They started to build the steel bridge, where it is now, while they were still using the old bridge at the mouth of Two Mile Creek. I was still a small boy when they started to build the first steel bridge at Hagwilget.[†] I watched them build it. I was quite a little boy at that time.

I used to fish for trout at the back eddy, and watched the bridge builders at the same time. And yet the people down below crossed the whole canyon with their fish traps, and caught all the fish they want. And all those years they still fished; they came every summer. There were no Fisheries [Department] or nobody that ever say about fishery. And right today they still fish. This is as far as I have seen.

It's surprising what the Indians can do. I sure would like to know how to make 'wee da wo'ga—another type of fish trap. Some of those racks were still there when I was small. They were there in front of Bill and Dan Skawill's smokehouse. Maybe they were destroyed when the government blasted up there. You see below Hagwilget, where the big circle [the eddy] is. There's a clearing above it, just where the clearing is, that's where my grandfather's smokehouse used to be. This is where he and I used to live early in the spring. That is when he used to prepare his fish trap equipment, and I used to sit with him. He used to make a big dip net, with a long handle on it. They use to dip this and catch fish with it. When the fish got in there they would pull the string or a rope [to] let the handle go, then they pulled the fish out. This is all I know about this.[3]

My father, Neil B. Sterritt, said his parents fished at Hagwilget. Once, when he was about ten years old, they lived in a tent on the left bank of the Bulkley River near the smokehouses. He spoke well of the Wet'suwet'en:

We always called them *hagwilget* because *hagwil* means 'good' or 'gentle' people who never broke the law. The opposite of *hagwilget* is *lax wilget*, a person who's suffered a real hardship and doesn't seem to observe the laws.

They used to go out to their own territories and bring in dried moose meat and other food that we didn't have. Then they put up a feast and invited the people

---

† The first wood and steel bridge over the Bulkley at Hagwilget was known as the Craddock Bridge and built in 1912 when Arthur Mowatt was five years old. The current all-steel bridge was built in 1932 and is known as the Carruthers Bridge or the Hagwilget Canyon Bridge.

from Gitanmaax. This was their way of thanking the Gitxsan for being on their land and at their fishery. Felix George was one of them. He was a really fine man and always showed his respect to the people.

One time I was at the canyon with my mother. Beal and Tommy Muldoe were fishing there on the [left] bank They were only there because their father was Gidumgaldo and he was chief of Gitanmaax and owned the fishing site there. My dad [Charlie Sterritt] came down and he talked to me. He said, "You watch those people. They will come down and sit on the rocks above the fishing sites. Then when one of our people is through, he will wave them down and that's when they'll get their fish."

These stories by Peter John, Arthur Mowatt, my father and others reveal that the Gitxsan and Wet'suwet'en lived together on both sides of the canyon, some for part of the year, and others who intermarried lived there permanently.

Summer salmon migration up the Bulkley River was blocked by huge rocks which fell into the water in 1824. Note gaffing poles on the right bank of the river below the rocks. The blockage was removed in 1959. (Image B-00702 courtesy of RBCM & A)

My earliest memories of Hagwilget include watching Gitxsan and Wet'suwet'en fishermen gaff salmon on each side of the canyon below the village. My father fished there after he returned from the war in 1945. Sometimes, while he was busy, we fished for trout and Dolly Varden in the eddy downriver. The largest of the boulders that tumbled into the river in 1824 sat mid-river directly

Totem poles, houses and fish drying buildings in Hagwilget Canyon. Artifacts found here date human habitation back 4,000 years. By 1904 the Wet'suwet'en had established a large village and built a new church on the bench above the canyon. (Image A-06052 courtesy of RBCM & A)

under the suspension bridge. The salmon gathered in great numbers below the boulder, resting before they made the effort to leap through and over the torrent.

The canyon was dangerous. Fishermen perched on rocks or wood platforms above the river felt for salmon with their gaff poles deep in the turbulent water. Some secured themselves with a safety rope and some didn't. A fourteen-year-old friend didn't bother with his safety line. He gaffed a spring salmon that weighed as much as he did and was never seen again.

The Gitxsan were fortunate. They relied mainly on the huge salmon runs that swam up the Skeena, Babine and other Skeena drainage tributaries like the Kispiox and Sustut to spawn each year as well as those travelling up the Meziadin, Bowser, Kwinageese and Blackwater rivers in the Nass watershed. The Wet'suwet'en, on the other hand, were dependent on a single river, the Bulkley, as their main salmon source. Some Wet'suwet'en, whose territories included the headwaters of the Fraser River near Burns Lake, supplemented their salmon supply there when the Bulkley River run failed. In any event, the main salmon fishery for the Wet'suwet'en was originally at the waterfall in the canyon at Moricetown.

Although there is no obvious physical evidence of it today, a village sat in Hagwilget Canyon for nearly a century with Gitxsan and Wet'suwet'en totem poles. The residents relocated to the bench above the canyon by 1904. Ward Marshall said that two totem poles remained down in the canyon, one of which belonged to Spookxw/Johnny Patsey†. Ward's company, Marshall Brothers Trucking, was hired to remove the other pole from the canyon and take it to Hazelton where it was crated and sent to France.‡

National Museum archaeologist George MacDonald and grad student Kenneth Ames conducted excavations in Hagwilget Canyon in 1966 and 1970. They determined the site had been abandoned for 3,500 to 4,000 years.[4] MacDonald's three-metre test pit yielded some sixty artifacts, including both prehistoric and historic items. At 1.8 metres MacDonald obtained a carbon date of about 3,400 years BP.[5] Ames recovered 160 artifacts that included lithic points, knives, a bone barb, a drill, some teeth from the prehistoric period, along with broken pottery from the recent period.[6] Ames's carbon dates cluster between 3600 BP to 4200 BP.[7]

MacDonald and Ames did not identify the tribal group that occupied Hagwilget Canyon at that time. However, given that an event nearby at Sealy Lake dates to 3600 BP (the Madiigam Tsu'wii'aks *adaawk*, or history), it is likely that the Gitxsan built weirs and fish traps along the Bulkley River throughout the millennia.

---

† The pole of Anklawrh (Gidimt'en/Bear/Wolf Clan). "Anklawrh" is "Anhlo'o" (avalanche area) in Gitxsan. Johnny Patsey and his sister, Christine, were closely related to Anklawrh, and Christine's second marriage was to Gyaedem-Skanees (Burns Lake Tom).

‡ The pole belonged to Gyaedem-Skanees of the Wet'suwet'en Likhsilyu (Small Frog) Clan.

ENDNOTES

1. "Barbeau and Beynon Fieldnotes", Peter John 1920 (B-F-89.22).
2. "Interview with Arthur Mowatt".
3. "Interview with Arthur Mowatt".
4. Ames, 208.
5. Ames, 183.
6. Ames, 194-202.
7. Ames, 214, Table 4.

CHAPTER EIGHT

The Halayt

THE FIRST FAMILIES TO LIVE AT GITANMAAX BUILT SMOKEHOUSES ON THE ISLAND AT THE SLOUGH AND HARVESTED SALMON FROM THE NEARBY RIVERS. THE CHILDREN WADED AND swam in the slough, and along its shore they hunted with bows and blunt-headed arrows and snared grouse, rabbits and squirrels.

While the people thrived on the bounty of the river for many years, a major change was coming, a change first sensed when some of the children once again became careless. They did not heed their parents' warnings to be respectful of fish and animals.

Early one spring, before the main salmon runs began, a child joked about a steelhead he had caught and told his friends there were so many fish in the river it didn't matter what happened to one fish. Laughing, he flung it into the bush. Some warned the child, but he ignored them.

The *halayt* was fearful of such behavior. He was a keeper of the laws and a healer. The parents had grown equally thoughtless and said, "They are children, what harm can there be in this?" The *halayt* was troubled.

Late one evening, while the villagers slept, the *halayt* gathered the few possessions he would need for his journey: his rattle and drum, regalia, blanket, a bit of food, an ember container and his medicine bundle. Well before dawn he quietly left the village. As he paddled his canoe across the Skeena, a *naxnok* whistle pierced the air high on the hill above the village. Then, from the hill opposite the village, came another. The eerie sounds echoed throughout the valley. *Naxnok* whistles, four in all, each from a different direction, signaled the *halayt*'s departure from the village.

He beached his canoe, secured it to a tree and set off upstream along the trail beside the river. Below Xsi'gwin Hu'ums (Hazelton Creek) the Skeena divides and flows around Lixs Ta'at.† *Halayts*

---

† An island just below the confluence of Hazelton Creek with the Skeena. The *halayts* used to go there. They boiled devil's club and bathed themselves before going hunting. Mary McKenzie's grandmother, when young, saw rocks there they used for their sweat lodge.

Imbued with supernatural powers, a halayt, or shaman, like John Larahnitz [Laga<u>x</u>nits] of Kitwanga (pictured here), was both healer and prophet. (Image C-05304 courtesy of RBCM & A)

had used the island for centuries. In another canoe, he crossed to the island and made his way to a small clearing at the island's centre.

Before dawn he built a fire and began to prepare his *anguuxw'uutx* (sweat lodge) in which to purify himself before proceeding to the next stage of his journey. He placed rocks in the fire and while they were heating, he took his *galdim aks* (water pail) and fetched water from the river. When satisfied the rocks were ready, he used deer antlers to place the rocks in the centre of the lodge. He stripped, entered the lodge and, with a small wood dipper, dripped water on the rocks to begin the cleansing ceremony. Afterwards, the *halayt* went to the river and bathed. He then returned to the glade and rested for the day. He ate sparingly that evening.

He arose early the next morning and, with the fire flickering in the pre-dawn darkness, he chanted, drum in hand, striking it slowly and softly. Walking about the fire, almost floating, he became transfixed. Rising through different levels of consciousness, he suddenly was struck by intense pain—a pain like the sting of hundreds of bees. Then he lost consciousness, awakening, exhausted, after the sun had risen.† Now he was ready to go to the mountain.

He returned to the mainland and climbed to a sheltered glade and a spring near timberline on a nearby mountain, Andamixw (Hazelton Peak). Here he made his camp as he had many times before. Soft mountain balsam branches provided bedding and dry branches for fuel to make his fire. He gathered an extra bundle of dry twigs and wrapped them with cedar rope so they would be

---

† Ts'igwii/Isaac Tens, a Gitxsan *halayt*, reported such an experience in the 1920s. He spontaneously fell into a trance, spoke in tongues, and said, "The bee-hive's spirit stings my body…In my vision, I went round a strange land which cannot be described. There I saw huge beehives, out of which the bees darted and stung me all over my body (Lewis-Williams).

easy to carry the next day. Exhausted from his climb and his ceremony the day before, he bathed in the spring, prepared his bed and slept.

The *halayt* awoke well before dawn. The moon was high in the sky, a full moon, and it flooded the mountains and valley in a silvery, radiant light. The *halayt* gathered his medicine bundle, his ember container, his dry wood, a small water container and, by the light of the moon, made his way out of the forest and across an alpine meadow to a special knoll, one among alders. The *halayt* would use this knoll for ceremonies in the spring before the salmon began to arrive in the estuaries. It provided him with a clear view of the mountains at Uuxs Bahlit (near French Peak), the eastern limit of Gitanmaax territory. More importantly, it might provide him with insight into his concerns.

Andamixw/Moonlight Mountain or Hazelton Peak. (NJS photo)

Now the *halayt* carefully placed shredded birch bark among dry twigs on the bare rock. He set embers from his container among the kindling. Then he took the *gwalgwa hon* (dried salmon) from his medicine bundle. As the moon set behind him, he began to see the light of dawn beyond the eastern mountains. He blew softly into the kindling, lighting a small fire.

Sitting with his back to Andamixw and with his fire before him, he could see a notch in the mountain at Uuxs Bahlit. He waited and, knowing the time was near, put the *gwalgwa hon* into his mouth and chewed it. He was tense with anticipation, for he knew the people of Gitanmaax relied on the outcome of this ceremony.

In the instant before the sun appeared, the *halayt* swept the fire from the rock, spat the *gwalgwa hon* into his hand and spread it on the hot rock. He poured water over the fish. Chanting, he peered through the rising steam at the sun's first flash in the distant cleft.† At that precise moment he discerned what he already suspected.

When the *halayt* returned to his people, he invited the village leaders to join him. They knew he had been on a quest but were uncertain why. They were worried about what he might have determined. After eating, the *halayt* told them what he had done:

> I have been to Andamixw. There I performed the salmon ceremony. I am sad to say that the answer was not good. I advise you to speak to your children. They need to respect the laws and values of our ancestors. I fear this will be a bad year. When the salmon season arrives, it will be poor. Hopefully the berry crop will be bountiful. Hopefully we can get enough caribou, bear, groundhog, rabbits and grouse to supplement our salmon stores and carry us through the winter. If not, we will starve and some will die.
>
> But this is not the only message I was given. My heart is heavy. I sense a change coming to our people. Not just for those in this village, but for everyone near and far. I sense this change but barely comprehend it. I must confer with others and will do so over the coming year. In the meantime, speak with your children. Remind them of the lessons of Madiigam Ts'uwii Aks and of Temlaham's snowfall. They need to be respectful of our laws, as will their children and their children's children.

---

† In 2009, Perry Sampson told me he had been told about a ceremony like this having been held near timberline on Andamixw (Hazelton Mountain).

CHAPTER NINE

Gitxsan Time, Territory and Technology

In the early spring of 1964, with snow still on the ground, I decided to make a day hike up Nine Mile Mountain. Sammy Gunanoot (1919-1986), Simon Gunanoot's youngest son, lent me a pair of snowshoes that were hanging in his woodshed. I set off early in the morning and snowshoed north from the Babine Trail, through the huckleberry patch and beyond to the sub-alpine. At noon I decided to have lunch and enjoy the panorama before me: the Bulkley Valley to the south, the Skeena Valley to the southwest and the Suskwa Valley to the east. The air was clear and I could see vehicles travelling along the roads to and from Hazelton. The Catholic church at Hagwilget stood radiant in the noonday sun.

Soon after my father returned from World War II, we picked huckleberries not far from where I ate lunch. Back then berry picking was an annual event that included many families from surrounding towns and villages. While adults picked berries we played nearby and ate berries. My father said the Gitxsan had relied on this and other berry patches for centuries. When he was growing up, they picked all they could get. The whole valley was full of berries on both sides of the Kispiox and Skeena rivers.

Berry patches were gardens in every sense of the word for they were as vital to the Gitxsan diet as vegetables are to the European diet today. Berry crops on Nine Mile Mountain and elsewhere were in decline mainly because government legislation prevented the aboriginal practice of intentional burns and allowed competing vegetation to take over. Regulations didn't stop Bella Green (1891-1967); she was a one-person flame-thrower and diligently went about her business throughout the spring and summer, attempting to re-invigorate berry patches she had worked throughout her life. The BC Forest Service hired men to follow her and put out the fires.

When I started down the mountain I broke through the old and fragile snowshoe webbing and sank to my thighs. Suddenly Hazelton was a long way off. But I was able to retie the foot webbing and, with careful steps, got to the valley bottom without further incident.

After my family and I returned to Hazelton in 1973, my Uncle Percy (1910-1998) taught me how to make snowshoes. Along with the teaching came stories about his life trapping, hunting, fishing and packing throughout Gitxsan territory. His continuous use of Gitxsan place names to describe where he traveled made me worry. Might this legacy vanish with the passing of Percy and those like him? Since then I have talked to dozens of elders—most of them now gone—mapping and documenting where they travelled and what they knew.

The Seasonal Cycle

The Gitxsan adapted to their environment year round through the mastery of snowshoes, fish traps, weirs and important food processing techniques.

Percy, his sister Gertie and my father explained how berries were processed and how fish baskets were made. This made me wonder what life was like for the people of Gitanmaax before Europeans arrived in Gitxsan territory. We know enough from the legacy left by our elders and the historical record to say how our people lived as Christopher Columbus sailed west to his 'East Indies'.

Gitanmaax in Nola's day had perhaps two or three longhouses in which he and his extended family lived. It had likely grown by Columbus's time, but not by much compared to Kispiox and Kisgegas which were much larger, likely because they were each located near long, narrow canyons with excellent fisheries.

There were two clans: the Lax See'l (Frog-Raven) and Lax Gibuu (Wolf). Nola not only led the Frog-Ravens, he was the village's *xsgoogam sim'oogit* (leading chief). Generations of his predecessors had held the name since relocating from Temlaham. Nola's closest relatives in this line were Luutkuts'iiwus and Ts'iin.

Two other Lax See'l chiefs at Gitanmaax (not of the Nola line) were Nikateen (aka 'Tens) and Sa'noos. Spookxw, who originated at Gitangasx or further north, led the Wolves.[1]

Each Gitxsan House has two names: that of the leading chief (Wilps Nola or Wilps Spookxw for example), and that of a significant house crest. Nola and Luutkutsiiwus's house crest was the *Ts'im Gipaiygim Ganao* (Flying Frog), while Tsiin's was a *Ts'im Getim Gawax* (human being); Nikateen's was the *Ts'im 'Moot'ixs* (barn owl), and Spookxw's was the *Ts'im Da'ak* (graded house).[†] On the assumption that there were four houses (and forty people per house) at Gitanmaax by the year 1500, its population may have been 160.[‡]

Gitanmaax was then located on the second river bench between the two rivers, safe beyond the reach of extreme floods. Fresh water was available nearby in a spring, and driftwood for their fires washed up at the entrance to the Bulkley Slough. Salmon and trout swam in nearby sloughs, creeks and lakes, but to get the quantities needed to sustain themselves through long, cold winters meant travelling several kilometres to their fishing stations at nearby canyons on the Skeena and Bulkley rivers. Moreover, to secure the resources (berries, meat, fur and hides) needed to survive and thrive

---

† A partially buried house with excavated dirt sloped part way up the outside walls as insulation.

‡ The 1881 Canada Census recorded forty-one people living in one longhouse in Kispiox.

in this challenging environment, they journeyed up to fifty kilometres to their most distant berry grounds and hunting territories at the headwaters of the Suskwa River.

In 1826, the first Europeans to Gitxsan territory found that the Gitxsan lived only part of the year at their main villages. This practice continued into the early 20th century.

> In the spring they moved to their salmon fishing villages and [caught and dried] salmon…After they had dried all the salmon, the berries were then ripe…[and] they went to the mountains to gather berries. They would split up in parties, the men going after…*matx* [mountain goats] and the groundhog…the women after the berries. And after this they would return again to Gitanmaax….The fall months, until the cold weather set in, were given over to festivities. When the cold weather came they went to their winter houses so as to be closer to wood. They hunted and got skins to trade with the Tsimshian, and during this season made fur garments, which they also traded to the Tsimshian.[2]

Winters were often so difficult that food resources had dwindled by early spring. But trout were plentiful in nearby lakes and steelhead swam in the rivers. Some families set their *moohl* (barrel traps) at the outlet of Tam Stekyawden (Sealy Lake) and others joined their Kispiox relatives at Tam Lax'antaahl (Robinson Lake). At times, so many trout were taken in these traps that it took strong men to pack the fish to their camp or village.

Nola's family had a steelhead site at Anx Milit on the Suskwa River, about thirty kilometres east of Gitanmaax. There the men cut holes through the ice at three-metre intervals. Using poles, they pulled cedar rope from hole to hole beneath the ice, dragging a *ts'ogom beehl* (fine cedar net) across the river.

At the same time, other family members made the long journey to the lower Nass River to trade hides and other products with the Nisga'a and Tsimshian and to participate in the remarkable oolichan fishery. Men and women returned to Gitanmaax carrying heavy packs of oolichan oil in cedar bentwood boxes.

By April or May, when the sap began to flow, families returned to the forest to work with two important tree species: *am hat'al* (cedar, good inner bark) and *am giikw* (hemlock, good bark). Cedar is incredibly versatile and every part of the tree was used from the roots to the small, pliable branches. The Gitxsan made waterproof, cedar bentwood boxes of various sizes and shapes. The most common boxes were used for packing or storing goods and to hold red-hot rocks that would boil water for cooking.

When the sap was running, the bark of young, standing cedar trees was easily removed in strips of up to nine metres.[3] It was braided into rope to snare large animals, especially mountain goats and bears, and for lashing together bridges, river weirs and large basket traps. Strong fishing lines were made of inner cedar bark as well as from nettle fiber.[4]

Hemlock trees also had multiple uses: the needles were used as tea; branch tips as bedding; wood for carving dishes, pots and spoons;[5] and the cambium layer for food.

The sophisticated process of converting the cambium layer into food was described by the Book Builders of 'Ksan:

> First the people make a special [scraper or *hagehlast*, which is a long pole with one end shaped like a wedge or chisel]…. [It] is used to scrape off the inside sapwood from the bark. Sometimes if May is warm, the bark is ready. On a cold year the bark may be good right through July. They prepare to…[be away] a week or longer, and go off to a place known to be good for hemlock bark.
>
> When they get there, one of the wise ladies tries the taste of the sapwood. She chews it herself and scrapes some off for her partner to taste. If the sapwood tastes sour and tough, they try another tree and go on testing until they find a tree to their liking—it tastes good, sweet and tender.…They cut off the bark while the tree is still standing, a strip of about six feet long and three inches wide, or more. The ladies start right in scraping the inner sapwood as fast as they can. They don't let the inner bark dry [and]…keep on working until they have about one hundred pounds of sapwood.
>
> The men make a barbecue pit. They dig out the ground about four feet deep and six feet in diameter. They build a fire inside the hole until it is very dry and hot. Then they gather stones (not too big) and line the pit. Now they build a fire on top of the rocks until the rocks are very hot.
>
> Now they gather clean moss and line the hot pit; they dampen this and place skunk cabbage leaves on top. On this they put the hemlock sapwood, spreading it very carefully. They repeat the layers of skunk cabbage and sapwood until the pit is nearly full, then they put on more skunk cabbage and then moss. When they have a good covering of moss and skunk cabbage leaves, they put on about one foot of dirt and build a fire on top of which they let burn overnight. Next morning they remove the wood [from the] barbecue pit and uncover it immediately to avoid souring. If it is well cooked and tender and smells fresh, not sour, they remove the sapwood from the pit. While it is still hot they crush it….
>
> To crush the bark they make a four-pound hammer from a young hemlock tree. They call the younger boys and girls with strong arms to do the crushing. This is done on a crushing board [a kind of v-shaped trough] made of oblong pieces of hemlock.…When the sapwood is all crushed, they pack it in large bentwood boxes and return home with a heavy load.
>
> To dry the hemlock bark they prepare wooden trays one inch deep by fourteen inches by fourteen inches. They spread broad thimbleberry leaves in the trays to prevent the sapwood from sticking to the trays. They make syrup from the fireweed by scraping the sticky syrup from inside the wood stem. They mix the

syrup with a little water and then sprinkle it on the thimbleberry leaves, then put on a layer of crushed hemlock, sprinkle it with fireweed syrup [which holds it together]. Continue this until the tray is full. Now turn the tray upside down on the wooden rack and remove the thimbleberry leaves. Build a fire underneath the dryer and keep a low fire going until each cake is dry; store the dried hemlock cakes [*xsuu'w*] in a wooden storage box.

When it is to be eaten, soak it in warm water until soft. Pour oolichan grease or bear oil on the hemlock bark. Another way to serve it is to crush the cake and pour crumbs over berries.[6]

When the families returned to Gitanmaax in the late spring, *ya'a* (spring salmon) were in the Skeena and Bulkley rivers. Nola had two main fishing camps along the right bank of the Skeena River at what we know today as Four Mile Canyon: the first at the lower end of the canyon at Xsigwin Hu'ums (Hazelton Creek), the other at the top end at Aakts'ilaasxwit. Nikateen and Sa'noos had fishing camps nearby on the opposite side of the river. Spookxw's fishing camp was located at Hagwilget Canyon on the right bank of the Bulkley River.

Salmon was a critical component of the Gitxsan diet. The villagers were fortunate because each year millions of fish swam up the Skeena and Bulkley rivers on their way to their spawning beds. Three important species swam by Gitanmaax, beginning with spring salmon in *lasa ya'a* (April), *miso'o* (sockeye) in *lasa 'wiihun* (July) and *eek* (coho) in *xwsit* (the fall). And because the run was richer in oil, the Gitxsan favoured *hl'hunhl gitgwooyim*—sockeye bound for Babine Lake. Other fish species were also harvested but when the major runs failed—which they sometimes did when people became careless and disrespectful—everyone faced the prospect of starvation the following winter.

Elders handed down fishing technology over the generations. My Uncle Percy witnessed the building of a *wo'o* (large fish trap) by his grandparents and other Kispiox elders.

> I was about ten years old when my grandparents decided to build a fish trap. My grandmother and I got some of the spruce material they needed on Sigit'ox Mountain.† We searched for two small u-shaped pieces of spruce that they needed for the *hlam'gan*.‡ We spent all day going back and forth on the hillside to find the two pieces they needed.
>
> The *wo'o* was about seven feet high and five or six feet long. They built the *wo'o* with one-inch diameter spruce. The *hlam'gan* was about sixteen feet long, thirty inches deep and thirty inches wide. Joshua Johnson (1876-1948), Samuel Johnson (1856-1934), Solomon Johnson (1851-1931) and Isaac Skulsh (1856-1951) built the *wo'o* and *hlam'gan*. It was hard work. The women of the village also worked hard tying

---

† Locally known as Elephant Mountain.

‡ A *hlam'gan* is a rectangular-shaped wooden box, open at the top. Fish swam through the *wo'o* and into the *hlam'gan*, where men stood, tossing the fish into a pond. Women dressed the salmon at the edge of the pond.

Fish traps were used to catch salmon as they tried to leap past the fallen rocks in the Bulkley River at Hagwilget. (Image A-06010 courtesy of RBCM & A)

the *wo'o* with spruce bark. My grandmother and her sister worked steadily on this for over two weeks.

There was no bottom on the *wo'o*. The top front of the *wo'o* was fancy and they spent a lot of time making sure it was done right. They made hoops (*gelpgasw*) with the spruce material my grandmother and I got so the *hlam'gan* would slide up and down on two of the posts they had pounded into the river.

The men built the *wo'o and hlam'gan* beside Robert Wilson's house, and then they took them to Ana'bisxw, a fishing site on the Skeena River owned by Samuel

Johnson (a member of Albert Tait's House). Robert Tomlinson (1870-1959)† hauled the *wo'o* with his horses and wagon and Albert Tait (1902-1987) hauled the *hlam'gan* with his.

The men chose a site near shore where the *wo'o* and *hlam'gan* were set up in slow-moving water. They used big rocks to pound six-inch posts into the riverbed. The river was shallow, perhaps between four and six feet deep. They stood on a platform laid on the posts as they worked their way onto the river. They also built a holding pool with rocks beside the beach for the fish they would catch. There were so many fish the men in the *hlam'gan* had difficulty keeping up, and Albert Tait hauled wagonloads of salmon to Kispiox for the families there.

I sat on the beach, watching the men fish. My grandmother cooked fish heads which I ate as I watched. The women prepared a big dinner for everyone.

The harvesting of salmon continued throughout the summer and fall, but the people of Gitanmaax were also busy preserving other food, especially berries, which were more than a garnish or dessert. All berries—black huckleberries especially—were as important to the Gitxsan diet as vegetables are today. All Gitxsan people managed their *ansin maa'y* (berry patches) along the valley bottoms and at timberline by burning the undergrowth when it began to choke out the berry bushes. The Gitxsan ate fresh or dried *gam* (Saskatoon), *gapk'ooyp* (bunchberry), *is* (soapberry), *'miiyahl* (low bush blueberry), *simmaa'y* (black huckleberry), and *ts'idipxs* (high bush cranberry).

The people of Gitanmaax had several important huckleberry harvesting areas less than a day's walking distance from their village. The nearest patch was at timberline a few kilometres from Tam Miinhl Stekyawden (Sealy Lake). And the most significant berry patch was located on the south slope of Lax Antaahl (Nine Mile Mountain), about ten kilometres east of Gitanmaax. This patch provided immense quantities of berries each summer. There, each family made between ten and twenty *daganasxw* (cakes) depending on the size of the family. Low bush blueberries were prepared in much the same way.

The process of making *gwalgwa maa'y* (dried berries) is called *nii'a gatsa* (from *nii gats*—to pour). The berries were gathered in large cedar bentwood boxes, four or five boxes at a time. Each box made about two dried berry cakes. The berries were squeezed or *'witxsw* (mashed) into a froth then ladled onto berry racks covered with *'nisgo'o* (thimbleberry leaves).

The berry racks were made of several two-metre cedar poles spaced a centimetre apart and tied to cross bars with spruce or cedar bark. Each rack was about half a metre wide and stood a metre off the ground. Women and children collected many thimbleberry leaves, taking care not to pick leaves with holes. The women placed three layers of leaves on the racks, each layer in opposite directions so the berries would not drip through.

---

† Robert Tomlinson Jr., the son of Robert Sr. & his wife, Alice.

Women drying fish at Hagwilget ca. 1890. (Image A-06051 courtesy of RBCM & A)

They built a fire beneath the racks at a temperature that would dry and brown the bottom layer of leaves. When the bottom half of the cakes had dried, the women placed another leaf layer and cedar rack on top of the crushed berries, and turned the racks upside down.

It took a day to dry each cake, which measured about forty centimetres wide, two metres long and a centimetre thick.

The men built a *wilp haniits'ok* (lean-to) over the racks to protect the berries from rain or sun. Children (and adults too) clamored for the leaves when the women removed the cakes from the racks. It was called '*moogan nisgoo* (sucking the thimbleberry leaves), and children's faces would be covered with berry stains.

After returning to the village, the women further cured the cakes by rolling them loosely and hanging them from the rafters of their longhouse or smokehouse. Afterwards, they tightly rolled and stored the cakes in a cedar box. From time to time they inspected the cakes to ensure they weren't getting mouldy. If they were, they were aired and repacked.

Adults usually soaked the dry cakes in water and ate them with salmon. Children often tore what they wanted directly from the cake. The women rationed the berries to ensure they would last until spring.

T'imi'yt (kinnikinnik) was also picked, but was stored in a shallow hole lined with birch bark. They poured the kinnikinnik berries onto the bark, covered the berries with another layer of bark and one of dirt. Saskatoon berries, *lan* (fish eggs) and *logo lan* (fermented fish eggs) were stored in the same way. The pits were shallow because these foods were retrieved during the winter.

In early fall, animals were fat and their winter fur was nearly ready. Nola and others hunted *matx* (mountain goats) and *wijix* (caribou) in the mountains surrounding Uuxs Bahlit, the headwaters of the Suskwa River at the eastern limits of their territory. They understood the habits of the animals and set snares for them along narrow mountain paths. For caribou, they built fences and herded the animals to areas where they could be snared or killed with bows and arrows.

A chief whose territory was abundant in *gwiikw* (hoary marmot or whistler) was considered wealthy: the meat was rich in fat, and the fur made warm blankets and clothing. Nola and his men set snares along the marmots' paths between their dens and feeding sites.

A snare consisted of a willow or alder pole sharpened at one end, with strong, fine sinew tied to the other end. Nola drove the sharpened end of the pole into the ground on the downhill side of the path setting an anchor and trip device in the ground above the trail. The willow was bent and tied to the trip device with a loop to snare the whistler's head as it ran along its trail. When sprung, the willow swung out and away from the path, leaving the animal hanging helplessly in the air.

The women dried the meat and prepared the hides and fur. Goat hides made good blankets and mattresses, while caribou hides were tanned and made into clothing. Warm waterproof boots were made with the hide from a caribou's hind leg, peeled from hock to thigh without cutting it lengthwise.

Sometimes, when Nola and his family had taken more meat than they could carry in one trip, they resorted to a relay system known as *gimdiiyee'asxw* to convey the meat to Gitanmaax. By the time they had relayed the meat from Uuxs Bahlit to Gitanmaax, they would have walked three times the distance, nearly 150 kilometres.

Now, with their salmon, berries, meat and other needs put away for the coming winter, the people of Gitanmaax were ready for fall festivities before they headed back out on their territories.

Fall festivities consisted of various kinds of feasts, gambling, and sporting events. If a person had died during the year, a feast would be held in that person's honour, especially if the deceased was a *sim'oogit* (leading village chief). If the house had acquired all the food and goods needed to compensate witnesses, the deceased's name would be passed on to a sibling, nephew or niece within the house. If more time was needed to prepare, the family would announce its plans to hold the *sim'oogit*'s succession feast a year or two later.

Other feasts were held to validate boundary issues, to celebrate pole raisings, marriages, house openings, to show appreciation for kind acts, and to mark a divorce. In the case of a divorce feast, the aggrieved person put up the feast and composed a *limx bitx* (divorce song), which he or she sang during the feast. On occasion the aggrieved might enact the offender's amorous preferences to his or her embarrassment and the witnesses' amusement.

Sporting events included gambling, races and feats of strength. *Xsan* (gambling) was a favourite activity amongst the Gitxsan. Gamblers played throughout the year but especially in the fall. The game, called by the Chinook word *lahaal* today, was played with four bones (two marked, two unmarked) and ten counting sticks. It was a team game with five players to a side. Each team began with five counting sticks and aimed to win all ten.

To begin, one team held the four bones. They concealed their hands under a blanket and passed the bones from hand to hand and to and from each other. When they stopped, the other team used special hand signals to indicate who they thought had the bones, and in which hand. The game went from side to side until one side has won all the counting sticks. Meanwhile, each side's supporters sang and drummed to cheer on their team and taunted or distracted the opposing team.

In 1977 I saw *lahaal* played for the first time at 'Ksan near the site of the original Gitanmaax village when two indigenous groups visited from Mexico and Hokkaido, Japan. A number of older Gitxsan women were present, all with strong Christian ties. I naively doubted that they knew the game. It was a remarkable eye-opener for they had undoubtedly seen *lahaal* played over and over and participated when they were younger. They sang, they drummed, and they flirted shamelessly with songs and moves that would have distracted a blind man. It was hilarious. Since then I have watched the game in the Yukon many times, but nowhere have I seen older women perform as those Gitxsan women did.

In earlier times, the Gitxsan gambled year around, and the drumming and singing would have reverberated throughout the valley as they entertained and competed with neighbouring peoples. But Gordon Smith (1923-1984) told me this was the downfall of some Tsetsaut.

> There is a deep hollow on the west side of Kispiox Road, near Yaga'yansit (China Grade Hill) where drumming during *lahaal* was amplified as though in an amphitheatre. The Tsetsaut stopped there to gamble, and the Gitxsan ambushed them. That is why we call it Lax An'xsan Tsetsaut (on/where gambled/the Tsetsaut).

Games of strength and skill were played too. For example, men made staffs that they glided along the surface of calm water on the Skeena, Bulkley or in the slough to see how far they would go. As Perry Sampson said, "This was called *ts'ogo guuxdit gan lax aks (*floating a wood staff on the river)." They also shot-putted heavy rocks and ran endurance races.

It was also the time to tell *ant'imahlasxw* (stories) to younger children—Wiigyet stories for example—that instilled values necessary to guide them later in life.

These are but a few of the activities that occupied our people's time in the late fall, before they moved to their winter villages or went out onto the land to hunt and harvest fur-bearing animals.

Bridges

In order to move to and from their different fishing spots, berry patches and hunting grounds, the Gitxsan became expert bridge builders. The early suspension bridges over the Bulkley River at Hagwilget are perhaps the best-known examples but there were many others. The Gitxsan built bridges across the Babine River at Kisgegas, the Skeena at Kuldo, the Sustut near Bear Lake, the Kispiox at Gitangwalkw and the Cranberry at Anxhon. When Europeans, including engineers, saw these bridges they marveled at aboriginal ingenuity. The bridge at Hagwilget was well documented.

Xsemgitgiigeenix/Johnny Moore (1902-1987) described the bridge at Kuldo. He also saw the old Hagwilget Canyon Bridge and described the Hagwilget fishery:

Now I am going to tell you about what I have seen when I was just a little boy. Not so long ago, one of my uncles brought me out there, Joseph Wilson. This is when I saw where the Indians had built a bridge across the river at Kuldo. The rocks were still there but the rotten remains of the old bridge was all I saw. We used to cross this bridge when we still lived at Kisgegas a long time ago. One of these bridges was built at Kisgegas.

There was not a nail in these bridges. They used what we call *k'okhl* (cedar bark rope). There were no cedar trees around Kisgegas, so they travelled back maybe half way [to Gitanmaax] on the trail, where the cedar trees stand. I did not see a nail in the bridge I saw; they said that the cedar tree branches lasted a long time, and red willows, and high bush cranberry sticks or branches, this was all they used that I know, but the rest of any kind [of wood] was no good, because they rotted faster, they said.

I crossed the bridge, and they made a good job of it, they made a good job of what they called *gan'il* [the guard rail]. This is what I remember—they were many places, where these bridges were built across rivers and creeks up on the Kisgegas

A Gitxsan suspension bridge over the Babine River at Kisgegas. (NBS photo)

trail. This was all they used a long time ago. This was what I saw about bridge building.

I also crossed the bridge that they built across the Bulkley River at the canyon. I still see the pictures around it. It stood across there for a long time. They built that bridge across there because some people from here used to live down below Hagwilget, at the canyon.

I used to watch there and saw three places where they had *'din* (fish traps). One belonged to [Guuxwo'ot] Peter John, one was Wiigoobil's and one was Skawats'eekx's [Gidumgaldo]: these were across the river, and there were two that were on this side of the river. Everyone was taking fish from there, when the fish were running in the summer…until they were satisfied with whatever fish they wanted to put up. Whenever fishing season was over, they used to all help one another, pulling these fish traps out. This is what I saw. There's another way of catching fish they call *anyuusxw*, on this side of the canyon. This they set whenever the river is down in the springtime. I remember this because my father used to stay there too; they used what they call *banna*. When the fish hits this *banna* they would pull it out right away. [A] *banna* had ropes tied to it, something like a dip net. They would catch about three big springs in this *banna*. The Indians had many ways of doing things their own way. Not so long ago, maybe around sixty years I think. I don't

The first cantilevered suspension bridge over the Bulkley River at Hagwilget. Large rock piles anchored the upper poles to the shore. (Image A-06048 courtesy of RBCM & A)

know what date of the year it was. This is all I remember of how they fished long ago."[7]

In 1878, geologist George M. Dawson provided a detailed description of how the old Hagwilget suspension bridge was built:

> The Indians in this part of the country construct bridges across streams too rapid to be crossed in canoes with safety, when not too wide for the means at disposal.
>
> These have been called suspension bridges, and are ingenious in plan. The Watsonkwa [Bulkley] is spanned by one of these about five miles above The Forks. The river is here about fifty feet wide, rushing between rocky cliffs of about fifty feet in height. At each side two beams are placed, projecting at an angle of twenty or thirty degrees, their butt-ends being firmly planted in a rude crib-work of logs weighted with stones. The ends of the projecting beams from opposite sides are then joined by a pair of light but strong horizontal pieces, which are lashed to them. The footway or floor of the bridge may consist of a single large flatted beam or of several lengths of poles spliced together and laid parallel. The footway is suspended to the superstructure above described by a series of vertical poles with hooked ends, withes being used as lashing, or, as in the instance now described, telegraph wire, being a portion of that left by the Western Union Company at the time of abandonment of their enterprise.[8]

Dawson left The Forks on June 23, 1878 and about six miles beyond where the Suskwa joins the Bulkley, he discovered a second "…newly constructed Indian bridge like that previously described…a very rapid stream fifty-seven feet wide, and two feet deep."[9]

Fish weirs and fish traps, along with bridges, weren't the only technological achievements of the Gitxsan. There were two Kuldo villages: Ts'ilasxwm Gansxwit (New Kuldo) and Gowal Mihl (Old Kuldo). Gowal Mihl is located in a meadow along the right bank of the Skeena about ten kilometres north of the reserve at New Kuldo. The village was so-named because the Nisga'a often raided the village and once burned it down.

In September 1986, four of us—Albert Tait, Walter and David Blackwater and I—landed at Gowal Mihl. There were no roads to the area at the time and we were travelling by helicopter, mapping features in preparation for the *Delgamuukw* case. Tait, who was Delgamuukw at the time, and the Blackwaters described the location of houses that were once in the village and who lived in them.

The elders mentioned a trench the villagers once dug to bring water to the village. They explained that, "Where the trench begins, it's very narrow, about thirty inches deep. The whole village went out to dig it."

A road was built to the area several years later and in 2005, my son and I were moose hunting north of Gowal Mihl. On our way home we decided to walk to the old village. Near the village, someone had built a small bridge across a dip in the trail. The dip had been dug by hand and was about one metre deep and one metre across. I thought it might be a remnant of the trench I had been told about in 1986. We had a GPS with us and decided to follow the trench to its source.

Gitxsan chiefs (L-R) Walter Blackwater, Albert Tait and David Blackwater mapping Gitxsan territory at Old Kuldo, 1986. (NJS photo)

We walked the length of the trench through the trees, which had grown up in and around it. The trench was 330 metres long and wound through the forest up the hill away from the village and ended at the road. Across the road was the creek at the trench's source which had long ago resumed its original course and now flowed south of the village. We measured the trench at several points. Its width varied but at most places the walls were a metre deep, with the greatest depth being two metres. The villagers had moved an incredible amount of earth and dug a canal—a *xsigis ba'anasxw*—not a trench.†

I thought perhaps the canal had been dug after non-natives brought shovels to the area. Niist/Bill Blackwater, who was born in 1933, corrected me:

> No, it is very old and they dug it with a *hagemgansxw*. That's something they pry up with. They find a strong, burnt two-inch pole to make it. They sharpen the business end of the pole and drive it into the dirt and rocks and twist it to loosen the dirt. Afterwards, they can scoop the dirt. Maybe they could use a *galenx* [box]

---

† Assuming the 330-metre long trench averaged one metre square, the villagers moved 530,000 kilograms (530 tons) of soil.

or something to scoop the loose dirt. It really works. They used a *hagemgansxw* to dig their gardens too.

The area along the Skeena near the two Kuldo villages has always been known for its deep snow. When the Gitxsan traveled through the area, they carried a *ts'in duuhl*, a two-metre staff with an eighteen centimetre blade at the bottom. Bill said his mother always carried a *ts'in duuhl* for shoveling snow when they made camp. Bill thought they might also have been used when digging the Gowal Mihl canal.

In addition to the *ts'in duuhl,* which made it easier to build camp in winter, snowshoes were critical because they allowed the Gitxsan to travel throughout their territories despite snow that might be three to six metres deep. Bill said his father, Wiiminoosikx/Jimmy Blackwater—who had his home base at Tamtuuts'whl'aks (Blackwater Lake) in the Nass watershed and a cabin on one of his territories east of there in the Skeena watershed—made snowshoes for the entire family, perhaps a dozen pairs each year.

Bill told me an interesting story about John Nole, a member of the Iskut First Nation, a small village on Highway 37 just south of Dease Lake. The Iskut people often drive up the abandoned BC Rail grade past Spatsizi Park, over the height of land and down to the Skeena headwaters. This is Bill's story:

> John approached me one day and said, "Who are you, Jimmy Blackwater or David?" I said, "I'm Billy, Jimmy's son and David's brother." John said he had once found an abandoned trapper's cabin on the west side of the Skeena south of Groundhog Mountain. He went into the cabin and found a large galvanized washtub with a hole in the middle. He asked me, "Why would someone cut a hole in the middle of a tub?"
>
> I laughed and said, "One time we went to my dad's territory on the Skeena in March. I was about twelve years old, and the snow was deep. We went up Xsi'ansix Moohl (Sansixmor Creek). At the top of the mountain, another creek goes down the other side to the Skeena named Xsi'ansix Moohl Ando'o (Cutfoot Creek).‡ We followed that creek down to the valley bottom and there was snow everywhere, but no cabin.
>
> My dad looked around and said, "There it is." He went over to a little mound of snow, brushed it away, and there was the top of the stovepipe. Then we went to work, digging our way down to the doorway with our snowshoes and *ts'in duuhl* (wooden snow shovel). It was lots of work. Finally we got into the cabin. It was beautiful in there. My dad went to a tub he had brought in years before. It had a hole in the middle and a stick in the hole. My dad blew up. He must have hit the ceiling twelve times. He was mad at Axmoogasxw/Jack Wright. Jack had punched

---

‡ The Gitxsan sometimes have one name for two creeks flowing in opposite directions from the same mountain. Thus, Xsi'ansix Moohl Ando'o: *ando'o* meaning 'the other side' or 'over there'.

a hole in my dad's bathtub and made a bass fiddle out of it. Jimmy had packed it all that way and Jack had destroyed it.

ENDNOTES

1. "Barbeau and Beynon Fieldnotes", Isaac Tens and Edward Clarke (B-F-72).
2. "Barbeau and Beynon Fieldnotes", Isaac Tens (B-F-110.1).
3. Turner, 88.
4. Stewart, 26.
5. GWES, Part 12, 1.
6. 'Ksan, 83.85.
7. "Interview with Johnny Moore" by A'yawasxw/Martha Brown, 1972.
8. Dawson, 21b-22b.
9. Dawson, 22b.

Part II

The K'amksi'waa

Temlaham & Gitangasx

The first successful migrations of Homo sapiens out of Africa began about 125,000 years ago. By 75,000 years ago they had spread across Asia and by 50,000 years ago they had entered Europe. From France and Austria, people moved southwest into Spain and Portugal and some went east towards eastern Siberia and Beringia, a place of little snowfall and thus a refuge during the last ice age. Populations already in Asia also migrated northeast to Beringia.

As the continental ice sheets melted between 18,000 and 10,000 years ago, people moved into northern Europe and also crossed the channel to populate the British Isles. People from the areas north of the Caspian and Aral seas moved further north to populate northern European Russia.

Exploration of the Americas by Europeans began with the Vikings 1000 years ago. It would be another 700 years until the first Europeans arrived on the northwest coast of North America to encounter the Aluugigat who had come to this continent, indeed to Gitanmaax itself, many thousands of years earlier.

Each spring the Skeena and its many tributaries gather debris—brush, sticks, and trees—and deposit it as driftwood—k'amksi'waa as we know it—at the estuary. There it comes and goes with the tide. Because the first Europeans to appear on our shores—Russians, Spaniards and British—were bleached as white as the driftwood and came and left with the tides, they too came to be known as K'amksi'waa and are so called to this day.

CHAPTER TEN

From Europe by Sea

From at least the time of Alexander the Great in 330 BCE until late in the 15th century, European armies, merchants and religious orders made forays eastward along well-established trade routes to Asia seeking spices, textiles, silk and other luxury goods. Venetian Marco Polo (1254-1324) recorded the events of the twenty-four-year journey he made with his father and uncle along the Silk Road through to India, China and Japan.

Most of these trade routes, including those travelled by Marco Polo, converged on Istanbul, which straddles the Bosporus Strait, long considered part of the boundary between Europe and Asia.† He who controlled the city controlled the trade route to the east.

The Greeks founded Byzantium ca. 660 BCE. It became known as Constantinople in 330 CE when Constantine the Great made it the capital of the Roman Empire. It remained the capital until halfway through the 15th century. In 1451 Sultan Mehmed II ascended to the Ottoman throne and two years later besieged, attacked and conquered the city.

But another force contributed to the Ottoman's success. During the siege the city was struck by "thunder storms, hail, and drenching rains, and, on May 22, experienced a terrifying lunar eclipse." The eclipse in particular demoralized the citizens, and "four days after the eclipse, on May 26, fog enveloped the besieged city."¹ Constantinople fell to the Turks on May 29 and thereafter became known as Istanbul.‡

The Ottoman victory allowed Mehmed II to control trade traffic to the east. With that route cut off, European nations sought another route to Asia. At that time no one from Europe had sailed

---

† The Bosporus Strait is thirty-two kilometres long and ranges in width from 700 to 3,400 metres. Istanbul is today one of the largest cities in the world with a population of almost fourteen million.

‡ Kevin Pang, a scientist at the Jet Propulsion Laboratory in California, attributed the climactic phenomena to a cataclysmic volcanic eruption in the South Pacific at Kuwae that has been dated to 1453.

south and east around the southern tip of Africa, nor had anyone sailed west. Apart from Viking legends about Vinland, the Americas simply did not exist. Thus the fall of Constantinople in 1453 led to the next great exploration era: the search for a maritime route westward from Europe to Asia.

Within half a century, eastern aboriginal nations encountered white strangers sailing along the Atlantic coast of North America in huge sea-going vessels. But it wasn't until almost two centuries later that stories of similar peoples began to circulate among aboriginal nations along the Pacific coast. Some of the stories originated with the Tlingit and filtered south from Russian Alaska. And some Gitxsan had seen white strangers in large ships while visiting Nisga'a and Tsimshian friends and relatives at the Nass and Skeena estuaries.

Not only were the aboriginal peoples of the Americas startled to learn of such beings and their world, western Europeans were equally surprised to discover that an unknown continent inhabited by thriving civilizations stood between them and the riches of Asia. Life for each would never be the same.

Christopher Columbus (1451-1506) was two years old when Constantinople fell. He was born in Genoa and claims to have gone to sea at age ten, spending much of the rest of his life there. A seafarer with considerable navigation skills, he was also an ambitious man. By his early twenties, he was an apprentice business agent and, over the next several years, sailed to England, Ireland, Portugal and traded along the coast of Africa as far south as the Guinea coast. Inspired by Marco Polo's life story, he was extremely interested in history and exploration.

In 1488, Bartolomeu Dias, sponsored by King John II of Portugal, sailed south and rounded the Cape of Good Hope, opening a new route to Asia from Europe. Ten years later Vasco de Gama followed Dias but continued further east to India. Columbus concluded there was a safer, shorter route to Asia sailing west from the Canary Islands to Japan. He was correct—the straight-line distance from the Canaries to Japan is shorter—but unbeknownst to Columbus, the Americas were in the way.[2]

Columbus, too, sought support for his venture from King John II of Portugal (twice), and from Henry VII of England and Queen Isabella of Spain but was rebuffed. Finally, in 1492, Queen Isabella agreed to his request.

He left Spain August 3, 1492 with three ships: the *Nina*, *Pinta* and *Santa Maria*. He led the convoy south to the Canary Islands and from there, on September 6, began his five-week voyage westward. He first sighted land, an island in the Caribbean, on October 12.

> At the hour of vespers, he entered the harbor, and gave it the name Puerto San Nicholas, because it was the feast of St. Nicholas....He considered it his right and responsibility to confer names wherever he went, regardless of the site's traditional designation, and in many instances, the name has stuck, erasing history in the process. There was a power in naming, almost as if he were converting his surroundings to Christendom; naming was claiming.[3]

Columbus spent the next two and a half months exploring the islands and making contact with indigenous peoples. He is believed to have spent time at the present-day Bahamas, Cuba and Espanola (Hispaniola), all the while thinking he had reached the East Indies.

Columbus made three subsequent voyages to the Caribbean. One of his tasks was to take measurements to determine how far Asia was from the Caribbean and help define accurate locations for the boundaries of a proposed territorial treaty between Portugal and Spain.

He was to accomplish this by recording the time of a lunar eclipse in the Caribbean while others recorded the same eclipse in Europe. Columbus knew he had a problem when his lunar calculations revealed that Espanola was much farther from Japan than he believed; nonplussed, he simply ignored his findings.

Queen Isabella also expected Columbus to establish a trading community in the Indies. Engineers would be required, and some speculate that John Cabot may have joined Columbus's second voyage as an engineer. Columbus had obtained fame and fortune through his discoveries, and Cabot was an opportunist with powerful connections.

Cabot was born about 1450, also in Genoa. By 1476, he was engaged in the maritime trade in Venice. Later, he built houses and began to promote himself as an engineer. In 1488, he left Venice for Spain with creditors in pursuit. In Valencia, he developed plans for improving its harbour and later, in Seville, he worked on the construction of a bridge. There are, however, many gaps in Cabot's life, one of which may have occurred during Columbus's second voyage.

By the mid-1490s, Cabot sought support in Spain for an expedition westward to Cathay (China). Failing there, he turned to England. Because the distance between lines of longitude narrows towards the poles, he argued that sailing from a more northerly point would shorten the distance to Cathay. Bristol was then the second largest port in England and a natural point of departure for his expedition.

Through his connections, Cabot gained the sponsorship of King Henry VII. In 1496, the king issued Cabot letters of patent by which he was "to find, discover and investigate whatsoever islands, countries, regions or provinces of heathens and infidels, in whatsoever part of the world placed, which before this time were unknown to all Christians."

Cabot made three voyages from Bristol. His first voyage, during the summer of 1496, was unsuccessful. He departed Bristol with a single ship, encountered bad weather and other problems and returned to England. During his second voyage on the Matthew of Bristol, Cabot sailed west beyond Ireland and sighted land on June 24, 1497. Cabot believed he had found Asia.

He wasn't in the habit of keeping accurate records of his voyages, but it was believed he had sailed west from Dursey Head in Ireland and arrived at a place he called 'new founde land' near today's L'Anse Aux Meadows.

In May 1498, his third voyage left Bristol with a fleet of five ships. Cabot and his fleet disappeared, presumed lost at sea.

By the mid-1560s, the lands encountered by Cabot and Columbus had become more broadly known as 'America.'† Their discoveries established the existence of land to the west between Europe and Asia. Others, many others, followed in the wake of these early explorers when they realized that the land might be a continent (or continents) and the search for routes across and around the Americas to Asia began in earnest.

---

† After Amerigo Vespucci (1454-1512), an Italian explorer. After several voyages, Vespucci proved that Brazil and the West Indies were separate landmasses and not connected to Asia.

ENDNOTES

1 Pang, 14.
2 Hunter, 64.
3 Bergreen, 81.

CHAPTER ELEVEN

Ayton's River

On the 1st of June I got in amongst Princess Royal's Isles, and not finding anchorage, made fast to trees, head and stern; boomed the vessel off from the rocks, and on the 2nd of June in the evening anchored in the mouth of Ayton's river about six leagues north-east off where I had stopt the night before…

—Captain Charles Duncan to George Dixon 1790[1]

Columbus's and Cabot's discoveries eventually demonstrated that not only islands, but whole continents blocked any direct route to Asia. Subsequent expeditions were forced to sail south around the southern tip of South America and far beyond to reach their destination. This quest for Asia's riches brought Europeans into the world of the Gitxsan and their neighbors, although given the vast distances westward by sea and land, it took close to three hundred years.

Between the mid-1770s and 1800 the Spanish made several voyages to the north Pacific coast and the Russians, too, reached the Pacific as early as the mid-1600s. British explorer George Vancouver (1757-1798) was the first to map in detail the BC coast during his 1791-95 expedition. It wasn't his first visit. In 1778, at age twenty-one, he served as a midshipman during Captain

Cook's voyage along the Pacific coast.† But other Europeans had been to the Skeena estuary before Vancouver.

James Colnett (1753-1806) had also sailed with Cook during his third expedition and became a skilled navigator in his own right. After leaving the navy, he led a commercial venture to the northwest coast‡ with two ships: the *Prince of Wales*, which he captained, and the *Princess Royal*, captained by Charles Duncan. They left London in 1786 and reached Nootka Sound in July 1787 where they made contact with native groups and then wintered in Hawaii.

Returning to the northwest coast in 1788, Colnett sailed north to Prince William Sound, while Duncan sailed to Haida Gwaii and on to Princess Royal Island, where he anchored overnight on June 1, 1788. The next evening he sailed northeast and anchored in what came to be known as the Skeena estuary. Duncan realized he was at the mouth of a significant river and named it Ayton's River after George Ayton who had sailed with him in 1782-83.§ This reveals that the Skeena River was known to English free traders five years before Captain Vancouver surveyed the area in 1793.

In 1791 Vancouver left from England as captain on a voyage of discovery along the Pacific coast with two ships, HMS *Discovery* and HMS *Chatham*. Vancouver and his men explored and mapped northwards along the west coast in impressive and accurate detail, eventually arriving in the vicinity of the Skeena estuary in 1793.

Using dinghies, Vancouver's men charted inlets and bays along the coast. In early July, he described what Lt. Joseph Whidby, in a dinghy, had done:

> [He] directed his course towards the entrance into the extensive sound he had seen on the 9th. During their late researches in this branch, which I have called Port Essington, after Captain Essington of the navy, the flood tide was observed to run up at the rate of four, and the ebb tide down at the rate of five knots per hour… Many sea otters were seen playing about, and diverting themselves amongst the rocks at all times of tide.[2]

Neither Vancouver nor Whidby realized they were at the mouth of BC's third longest river and second most significant salmon producer. Nor could they know, of course, that for millennia the Gitzaxhlaahl had been using the Port Essington area at the confluence of the Ecstall and Skeena rivers as their autumn village, which they called Spaksuut (Spokeshute).

Continuing north, Vancouver explored and mapped the Nass River estuary, again failing to appreciate that he was near the mouth of another important west coast waterway. Here Vancouver met a fur-buyer, Commander Brown of the *Butterworth of London*, who told him more about the river:

---

† This was during Cook's third and final voyage between 1776 and his death at Hawaii in 1779. Vancouver, at fifteen, also sailed with Cook in 1772 during his second voyage to the South Pacific. For more about Cook, see Chapter 22.

‡ Richard Cadman Etches & Co. hired Colnett to lead the expedition.

§ The Skeena River appears on Arrowsmith's 1790 map as Ayton's River.

> ...a small branch extended to the south-eastward, up which he [had] proceeded with his sloop and schooner about six miles, where they anchored before a village⁋ of the natives, whose improper conduct made it necessary to fire upon them from the vessels, which was attended with some slaughter.³

Vancouver wrote:

> ...some of Mr. Brown's gentlemen considered the opening meant by those people to be further to the westward, it is called by them Ewen Nass. The word Ewen we understood to signify great, or powerful; as, Ewen Smoket, a great chief; the word Nass was completely unknown to Mr. Brown, and all of his party.⁴

Although Vancouver dismissed the streams flowing into Port Essington and Ewen Nass as insignificant, he was nevertheless the first explorer to accurately map the Skeena estuary, and with regard to the Nass estuary, used Nisga'a/Gitxsan names, 'Ewen' being *wii* (big or large) and 'Smoket' being *sim'oogit* (chief).

Five weeks before Captain Vancouver mapped Port Essington at the mouth of the Skeena, Alexander Mackenzie approached the Skeena watershed from the east. In October 1792, on behalf of the North West Company, he set out by land on his exploratory journey from Fort Chipewyan to the Pacific Ocean.** On May 31, 1793 he arrived at the forks of the Finlay and Parsnip rivers. There he was faced with a choice: paddle, pole and hike north and west up the Finlay or turn south up the Parsnip.⁵ His guide, a Sekani man who had been on war parties up the Finlay, perhaps in battles against the Gitxsan of Gitangasx, advised Mackenzie to turn south. Although far northeast of the Skeena estuary when he chose the Parsnip, had Mackenzie chosen the Finlay route to Thutade Lake and beyond, he and Vancouver might have been in the Skeena system—albeit 500 kilometres apart diagonally—within days of each other.

Daniel Harmon (1778-1843) may have been the first fur trader travelling overland from the east to enter the Skeena watershed. Harmon was born in Vermont during the American Revolutionary War.⁶ In April 1800, as an employee of the North West Company, he set out for the west from Lachine, Lower Canada (Quebec). His journey ended sixteen years later with his return to Fort William (Thunder Bay), Upper Canada.

In the summer of 1810, Harmon was assigned to New Caledonia, "a huge ill-defined area corresponding roughly to the Cariboo country and the central interior of what is now British Columbia."⁷ There, Harmon spent over seven years at Fort St. James on Stuart Lake and over two years at Fort Fraser on Fraser Lake.

On June 6, 1811, a party of Indians from Babine Lake arrived at Fort St. James in six canoes. Among the group were a father and son who belonged "...to a Tribe who call themselves Nate-ote-tains [Nedut'ens] and are the first of that nation ever saw here. But they say they are a numerous Tribe who are scattered over a large tract of Country almost west of this, and that it is not more

---

⁋ The place referred to by Vancouver may be today's Gingolx at the mouth of the Nass.

** See Map 6: The Fur Trade in Western Canada

Fort St. James on the shores of Stuart Lake (ca.1900), headquarters of the Hudson's Bay Company New Caledonia District from the early 1800s. (Image D-06382 courtesy of RBCM & A)

than eight or ten Days march to their first village."[8] The two men also described a large river (today's Babine and Skeena rivers) that passed through their country and flowed into the Pacific Ocean, saying that, "…every Autumn a number of White People come up that River in barges to traffic with the Indians who live along its banks…"[9]

Trade was by this time taking place in the large meadow known today as Mission Flats at the junction of the Skeena and Bulkley rivers near the village of Gitanmaax. Thus Harmon is referring to the Skeena River proper, and the "Indians who live along its banks" were, on its upper reaches, the Gitxsan. The Wet'suwet'en of Witset (Moricetown) also participated in this trade.

To Harmon and other fur traders of the day, the geography of northern New Caledonia and the upper Skeena River was largely guesswork. They had yet to explore and properly map the area and, until that was done, the Skeena, Babine and Bulkley rivers and some of their major tributaries had a confusing array of names. Harmon, for example, wrote that the "other large river of New Caledonia, rises near Great Bear's Lake; and after passing through several considerable lakes, it enters the Pacific Ocean, several hundred miles north of Fraser's River."[10]

This other large river is no doubt the Skeena; Great Bear's Lake is likely Thutade (in the Mackenzie system), rather than Bear Lake (in the Skeena system); and Harmon's Nedut'en River is certainly today's Babine.[†]

In January 1812 Harmon, along with James McDougall and fourteen men, set out for "the Nedut'en Lands and Tribe who never had any intercourse with White People…"[11] His party arrived at the first village on January 24 after seven days travel. The villagers met them anticipating war but Harmon convinced them he was there to establish trade.

The next day the Harmon party visited four more villages and found in the second village the two men who had come to Fort St. James the previous year. The Nedut'en men explained that

---

† See Map 5: Skeena River Watershed

"…their Neighbors the Atenas [Gitxsan]‡… purchase directly from the white people…Guns, Cloth, Blankets, Axes and cast Iron Pots &c."[12] There he obtained "a Blanket or Rug which was manufactured by the Atenas, of the wool of the Sheep§ that are numerous on the Mountains in their country."[13]

The Nisga'a, Tsimshian, Kitselas, Gitxsan, Wet'suwet'en and Nedut'en were known to have gathered each year for many years, perhaps centuries, at Mission Flats to trade. With the advent of Europeans, axes, knives, guns and huge quantities of tanned leather were bartered in exchange for furs. European explorers and the North West Company were slowly but surely pressing in on the Gitxsan people by land and sea. And free traders with aboriginal coastal allies were trading with the Gitxsan and Wet'suwet'en at Mission Flats.¶

Harmon estimated that two thousand people lived in the five Nedut'en villages he visited, people "who are well made and appeared healthy, but they like the Carriers subsist principally on Salmon & other small Fish."[14]

He described their land tenure system:

> The people of every village have a certain extent of country, which they consider their own, and in which they may hunt and fish; but they may not transcend these bounds, without purchasing the privilege of those who claim the land. Mountains and rivers serve them as boundaries, and they are not often broken over.[15]

As William Brown, an HBC trader, would later find, this land tenure system also existed among the Atnahs of Kisgegas and Anlagasimdeex, another Gitxsan village about four kilometres below Kisgegas on the Babine River.

---

‡ According to Lamb, the Nedut'en term, 'Atena' or 'Atnah' means 'neighbour' (Lamb 1957:199, fn 70). Alaskan linguist James Kari gives several meanings, including 'people, human, man', but nowhere defines it as 'neighbour' (see Kari, 476).

§ The wool is that of a mountain goat.

¶ American free traders, known to aboriginal peoples as 'Boston Men', had been sailing to the northwest coast since at least 1787.

ENDNOTES

1. Galois, *Colnett Journals*. 401, fn 11.
2. Vancouver, 99.
3. Vancouver, 114.
4. Vancouver, 118.
5. Lamb, *Journals and Letters*, 278.
6. Lamb, *Sixteen Years in Indian Country*, ix-x.
7. Lamb, *Sixteen Years in Indian Country*, xii.
8. Lamb, *Sixteen Years in Indian Country*, 140.
9. Lamb, *Sixteen Years in Indian Country*, 140.
10. Lamb, *Sixteen Years in Indian Country*, 241.
11. Lamb, *Sixteen Years in Indian Country*, 149.
12. Lamb, *Sixteen Years in Indian Country*, 150.
13. Lamb, *Sixteen Years in Indian Country*, 150.
14. Lamb, *Sixteen Years in Indian Country*, 150.
15. Lamb, *Sixteen Years in Indian Country*, 250.

CHAPTER TWELVE

Voyages of Discovery (1822-1885)

William Brown

There are two Atnah Villages† situated on the Banks of McDougall's River‡, about forty miles below where it falls out of this Lake, which according to my information contain two hundred and thirty one grown-up men. The manner I received this account was as follows: The Indians of this place [Fort Kilmaurs] having gone there on a visit in the beginning of March I desired one of them to go into the first Lodge, and cut a small piece of wood, for every man that was in it, then proceed to another and do the same.[1]

—William Brown 1823

WILLIAM BROWN WAS BORN IN KILMAURS, AYRSHIRE, SCOTLAND IN 1790. HE ENTERED THE HUDSON'S BAY COMPANY (HBC) SERVICE IN 1811 AND WORKED AT SEVERAL COMPANY posts before 1821 when the North West Company amalgamated with the HBC. The next year Brown and thirteen men built Fort Kilmaurs (Old Fort) on Babine Lake. Kilmaurs, an outpost of the HBC headquarters for New Caledonia at Fort St. James, was the first trading post established

---

† Kisgegas and Anlagasimdeex.
‡ The Babine River.

Fort Kilmaurs, known today as Old Fort, was constructed on the east shore of Babine Lake by the Hudson's Bay Company in 1822. (Sheila Peters photo)

in the Skeena watershed. The firm wished to trade with the Nedut'en and Wet'suwet'en but was also interested in trade with the Atnahs (Gitxsan) to the north and west of Fort Kilmaurs.

The Wet'suwet'en were based at Witset on Simpson's River (the Bulkley) about 130 kilometres southwest of Fort Kilmaurs. Brown considered Witset to be "…the most populous of all the Babine Villages, it being the principal resort of all the Indians of that quarter."[2]

In 1822, Brown learned that Indian traders were ascending McDougall's River (the Skeena) and trading with the Wet'suwet'en at the confluence of the Bulkley and Skeena rivers, known then as The Forks (now Mission Flats). Brown was concerned because his overhead was significantly higher than that of Russian and American traders on the coast.

In January, 1823, a large Wet'suwet'en delegation arrived at Fort Kilmaurs seeking salmon as the 1822 run had failed on the Bulkley River. Brown learned from the Wet'suwet'en that they had already taken their furs to The Forks "…and sold them to the Indians of the seacoast who mounted the river to there."[3] After Brown learned that the Nedut'en at Fort Kilmaurs were also going to take their furs to The Forks the next year, he made plans to visit the Wet'suwet'en at Witset.

Witset was located near Moricetown Canyon where the Wet'suwet'en harvested great quantities of salmon each summer. Their territories extended south from Witset into lakes and creeks at the headwaters of the Fraser River. Brown estimated the Witset population to be about 750. In an exchange with Fort St. James Chief Factor John Stuart, he wrote:

> From the account of the Indians, and from what is still more to be depended upon, the number of European utensils the Babines are possessed of, these are Russians or other traders on the seacoast who supply them. To ascertain the number of these people, their means of furnishing the articles of trade, etc. I would suppose to be an object of some importance to the Concern, as these points being known, measures might be adopted to oppose their views, either by forming establishments in their vicinity, or by drawing the Indians to the Interior with their furs.[4]

Brown was concerned that coastal traders with Tsimshian allies were making inroads on the interior fur trade, and that an outpost at The Forks might be needed:

> …if they are allowed quietly to collect their Furs along the seacoast, they will ere long extend their views to the Interior, and if we do not go to meet them they will come to meet us. The consequence of which will be the Ruin of the whole trade of this quarter. In fact, if any reliance is to be placed on Indian Reports, they have already establishments in the Interior, and every year ascend the Babine or McDougall's River† to a considerable distance for the furs.[5]

Seeking cheaper goods, the Wet'suwet'en told Brown that traders already had establishments at the coast and at The Forks. Brown found "by questioning several at different times and unknown to each other, I ascertained there are no European settlements either there or at the seacoast."[6] But traders were cruising the coast, firing their guns when they approached land and wanted to trade.

> The Natives on hearing this push off in Canoes and barter such Furs as they have, with the property they receive in this traffic, they mount the River and trade the furs of the Indians of the Interior, by which means they derive handsome profits themselves…The Arms they trade are mostly Old muskets and Pistols. Their leather is what the people here speak most of, as being good and cheap … the distance from the Forks to the sea being so short that they make three trips in the course of the summer. This with the spirit of trafficking which exists amongst all the Carrier Tribes, would render the thing perfectly easy, were they not to come higher than the entrance of the Lake, or even the Forks where they now come to.

In January 1823, Brown gave presents to a leading Witset chief, Quilt No:

> [He subsequently]…assembled his people and made a long harangue to them, stating that he forbids any of them from carrying their Furs below, and hopes that they would all exert themselves to make good spring hunts. And go to the Fort and

---

† As stated before, the early fur traders did not have a good understanding of northwest BC geography. During the 1820s, the Babine River to the Skeena and the Skeena down to The Forks were considered to be one river and known as both McDougall's River and Babine River. The Bulkley from its source to the Skeena and down to the coast was also thought to be a single river and was known as Simpson's River. When Brown says Indian traders were ascending McDougall's River he was wrong; it was what was known then as Simpson's River.

> trade the whole of their Furs in the summer. An Indian there named Kill Kiss has 50 Beaver but he will not part with them till we go there next fall, when he means to make a present of them. It appears all the Chiefs talk of making us a present if we go there, as it will be the first time such white men were in their Country.

Brown intended to visit Witset in the spring of 1823, but did not get there until fall.

> These Indians have much more the appearance of hunters than any of the other Carrier tribes—they being in general tall and clean made—which may in a great measure arise from their being more accustomed to hunt, and to live upon animal food—From their manner of working the salmon with the scoop net or spear…[7]

Brown suggested the Wet'suwet'en consider barring the river with fish weirs instead of using nets and spears as they had to supplement their salmon harvest with extensive hunting. However, nature intervened in 1824 when several huge boulders tumbled into the Bulkley a few kilometres upstream of The Forks. This event led to the creation of Hagwilget, a new Wet'suwet'en village within Gitxsan territory.[‡]

Brown found that the Wet'suwet'en chiefs, as with the Gitxsan, were almost exclusively interested in trading their fur for leather, and wouldn't accept anything less. He also found that two-thirds of the Wet'suwet'en furs were being traded to the coast, which led him to seriously consider building at The Forks and supplying it, as well as Fort Kilmaurs and Fort Fraser, from the coast.[8]

This was logical. Brown was finally instructed to embark on 'voyages of discovery' down the Babine River to the seacoast for the purpose of trading with tribes to the north and west of the Gitxsan.

Brown set out down the Babine headed for the coast in 1825.[§] Unfortunately, river conditions and the onset of rheumatism forced him to abandon his journey at Kisgegas. This was the least of his worries, for in June, after returning to Fort Kilmaurs, Brown found the Wet'suwet'en—who discovered they could get superior leather and other goods for better prices from coastal traders—to be extremely uncooperative.

On March 1, 1826, Brown again set out from Fort Kilmaurs to determine the fur trade potential of the Gitxsan. With good weather, Brown, six men and a guide set out on foot along Babine Lake and down its river, estimating the distance from Fort Kilmaurs to Kisgegas to be 170 kilometres. He was pleasantly surprised to find the river was navigable to Kisgegas, and mistakenly assumed it would continue that way to the sea.

Encountering snow and ice along the Babine River, Brown arrived March 7 at Needchip's (Niik'yap) village on the right bank of the Babine River ten kilometres upstream of Kisgegas.

---

‡ The new village came to have three names: Hagwilget (Gitxsan), Tsë Cakh (Wet'suwet'en), and Rocher Deboule (French). Today Stekyawden, the impressive mountain directly south of the canyon, has taken the Rocher Deboule name. See Chapter 7.

§ By this time, the river from Babine Lake to the Bulkley confluence was known as the Babine, and the Bulkley from its source to the coast was known as Simpson's River.

There was no one to be seen when he arrived, but he was surely being watched, as Niik'yap and forty armed men arrived shortly afterwards. Brown missed out again, for Niik'yap, as with the Wet'suwet'en, had traded all his furs to coastal traders in the fall.

The next day Brown arrived at Kisgegas, which he identified as the village of Sojick (Miluulak). There he learned that several Kisgegas chiefs were away hunting marmots an eleven-day walk northeast of Kisgegas† along the Sustut River.[9]

Brown also learned of another Atnah village—Kuldo—about three days travel up the Skeena.[10] On March 9 he visited Quo em (xGwoimtxw) at Anlagasimdeex, about an hour's walk below Kisgegas.

After having spent three days in the area, Brown estimated that there were at least 1000 people living in this part of the Gitxsan nation.[11] His Atnah sources described five further Gitxsan villages downriver:

> [They are] large and populous—The first is two days march below Kisgegas—and the second is at the Forks which is two days march further. The other three are below the Forks and are each two days journey asunder. From the upper of which there is a track over Land to another Large River, where the Nation called the Ute sin nah‡ reside.[12]

Although Brown did not provide the names of the Gitxsan villages he intended to visit, they were, no doubt, Kispiox, Gitanmaax, Gitsegukla, Gitwangak and Gitanyow.

With regard to the potential for furs, Brown concluded that xGwoimtxw's country in general was too mountainous for beaver. However, the upstream territories of the Gitxsan, which bordered Sekani lands, had an abundance of beaver and marten.

Brown recognized, however, that his challenge would be in securing all the furs the Kisgegas trappers harvested. Not only were the Gitxsan travelling to the coast to trade, but a powerful Tsimshian chief from Fort Simpson, Legaic, had been purchasing furs at The Forks for many years.

In order for the HBC to compete with the existing trade, Brown had some doubts about trading for pelts provided by the Gitxsan:

> [They would] cost higher than those traded from the Carriers [and] it will be necessary to make a Voyage to them late in the spring, to collect what they may have killed in the winter, to prevent the traders from the Coast securing it in the summer. And another voyage in the fall, this last should be in a canoe. And on reaching the Forks go up in Simpson's River [as the Bulkley was then known] as far as it may be practicable by water, & from there overland to Hotset [Witset]§ and

---

† Miluulak, Ts'abax, Niik'yap and Wiik̲'aax all had, and still have, territories along the Sustut River.

‡ Ute sin nah, or Utseni is the Wet'suwet'en name for the Nisga'a people (Morin, 346).

§ Witset was an ancient Wet'suwet'en village located near Moricetown Canyon (Morin, 346).

trade the fall hunts of those Indians after which the party might go as far down the River as it may be deemed prudent or anything to procure.[13]

Brown estimated a three-day trip to Kisgegas, three more to the Skeena/Bulkley Forks and six days from there to the sea. Allowing five days return against the current for each day travelling downstream, Brown estimated it would take two and a half months to travel from Fort Kilmaurs to the sea and back.

Brown's Atnah hosts advised that the river between Kisgegas and The Forks was barely navigable and, being ill, Brown decided to return to Fort Kilmaurs on March 10. Eventually he became bedridden and in 1826 was given a leave of absence and went to Europe to convalesce. He died there in 1827.

Simon McGillivray

The next HBC trader to find his way into Gitxsan territory was Simon McGillivray. Born in Indian Country (probably Manitoba) in 1791 to William McGillivray and Susan, a Cree woman from Flin Flon, Simon joined the HBC in 1822, serving in the Rainy Lake District at Lac La Pluie, Fort Resolution at Great Slave Lake and Fort Nez Perces in the Columbia District before being assigned to the New Caledonia District ca. 1833.¶ He continued the work of William Brown in terms of extending the trade to the north and west of Fort St. James.

The HBC established Fort Simpson** at the mouth of the Nass River in 1831. The geography of northwestern BC was poorly known and HBC men in New Caledonia believed Fort Simpson was at the mouth of the Skeena River.†† However, free traders and their Tsimshian allies continued to trade at The Forks, much to the consternation of the company. The HBC needed to act, and chose chief trader Simon McGillivray to determine whether Babine and Simpson's rivers were navigable.

McGillivray left Fort St. James with seven men on June 8, 1833. He was to make his way from Stuart Lake to Fort Kilmaurs on Babine Lake, descend Babine River to The Forks and then descend Simpson's River to Fort Simpson. He enlisted a Babine chief, Chilchowan, to guide him during his journey because he had made the journey several years earlier.[14]

> [Chilchowan advised]…that the post of Nass was not at the mouth of Simpson's River, but far to the left, and that we had a long traverse to make to reach it, and that near the seacoast Simpson's River was as broad as we are here [on Babine Lake], about 1½ mile. The information surprised my men very much as well as my interpreter, for they had an idea that Nass was at the entrance of Simpson's River. Chilchowan pronounced the navigation of Babine River impracticable, owing to a

---

¶ Simon McGillivray was well placed: his godfathers were Joseph Frobisher and Alexander Mackenzie. His father was the last chief partner of the North West Company before it merged with the HBC in 1821.

** Named after HBC employee Aemilius Simpson who died there.

†† Then known as Simpson's River after Sir George Simpson, governor of the HBC.

succession of strong rapids, occasioned by high precipices, he also says there is no difficulty reaching the sea in 1½ days from The Forks of Simpson's River.[15]

After ferrying his men and goods across Babine Lake by canoe, McGillivray and his men set out by foot for Simpson's River on June 17. The trail crossed the summit west of Babine Lake and followed the Suskwa River down much of its length. En route McGillivray realized the "natives must be very persevering to carry heavy loads of oil all the way from Simpson's River to Babine Lake on their backs, and with these heavy loads the journey is performed with ease in 5 days."[16]

Averaging about twenty-five kilometres a day, McGillivray arrived on the bluff opposite Hagwilget in a downpour on Thursday evening, June 20. He counted three houses nearby and fifteen houses in the village, and saw men fishing at the river.[17] The men crossed the bridge and entered the village where they were given salmon and a house to stay in. The house next to McGillivray's had the "…most hideous large figures carved on the posts and on the sides a 3-masted ship under full sail with 2 tiers of cannon, there were also two armed brigs. These vessels were very well depicted."[18]

McGillivray described the village:

> The Roche Deboulez or fallen rocks in Simpson's River is a remarkable place. [Two] immense large rocks have fallen from a high precipice on the south side of the River which has almost blocked up the passage leaving a small channel open when the water is low the salmon cannot go beyond this spot, which accounts for the number of houses and inhabitants resorting here in summer and winter. It was in 1824 these rocks fell into the river. When the late Mr. Brown on Derouines† to visit the Babine Indians of Simpson's River he found them about 20 miles above this spot [at Witset], these rocks had not then fallen. From what I saw of Simpson's River above the Fallen Rocks I should pronounce it rather hazardous to navigate with the boats or canoes owing to the strong rapids and eddies.[19]

The next day, McGillivray learned of a letter held by the Atnahs in one of the villages nearby. He sent a runner for the letter and made a day-trip to The Forks, "…to see where the Babine River falls into Simpson's River."[20]

> We again saw Simpson's River, here it is broad, and my men could not but remark all with one voice "Un grande Riviere". I was as much astonished as themselves… It is broader than Fraser's River, and may be compared with Athabasca River in its greatest breadth. I cannot but call it a noble stream, followed the beach a short distance till we reached a channel, the natives went out for a small wooden canoe, and having brought it, I embarked and visited Babine River[;] it is as broad as Simpson's River.[21]

---

† A voyageur expression meaning the traders visited the Indians instead of the Indians taking their furs to a fort or trading post.

As it was June, the Skeena and Bulkley were probably in full flood, which would have been an impressive sight. The channel McGillivray refers to above may have been the slough at 'Ksan. However McGillivray's map depicts a 'small poplar island' in the Babine (Skeena) River, opposite the mouth of Simpson's (Bulkley) River. McGillivray canoed to the island and named it Smith's Island in honour of a friend.[22]

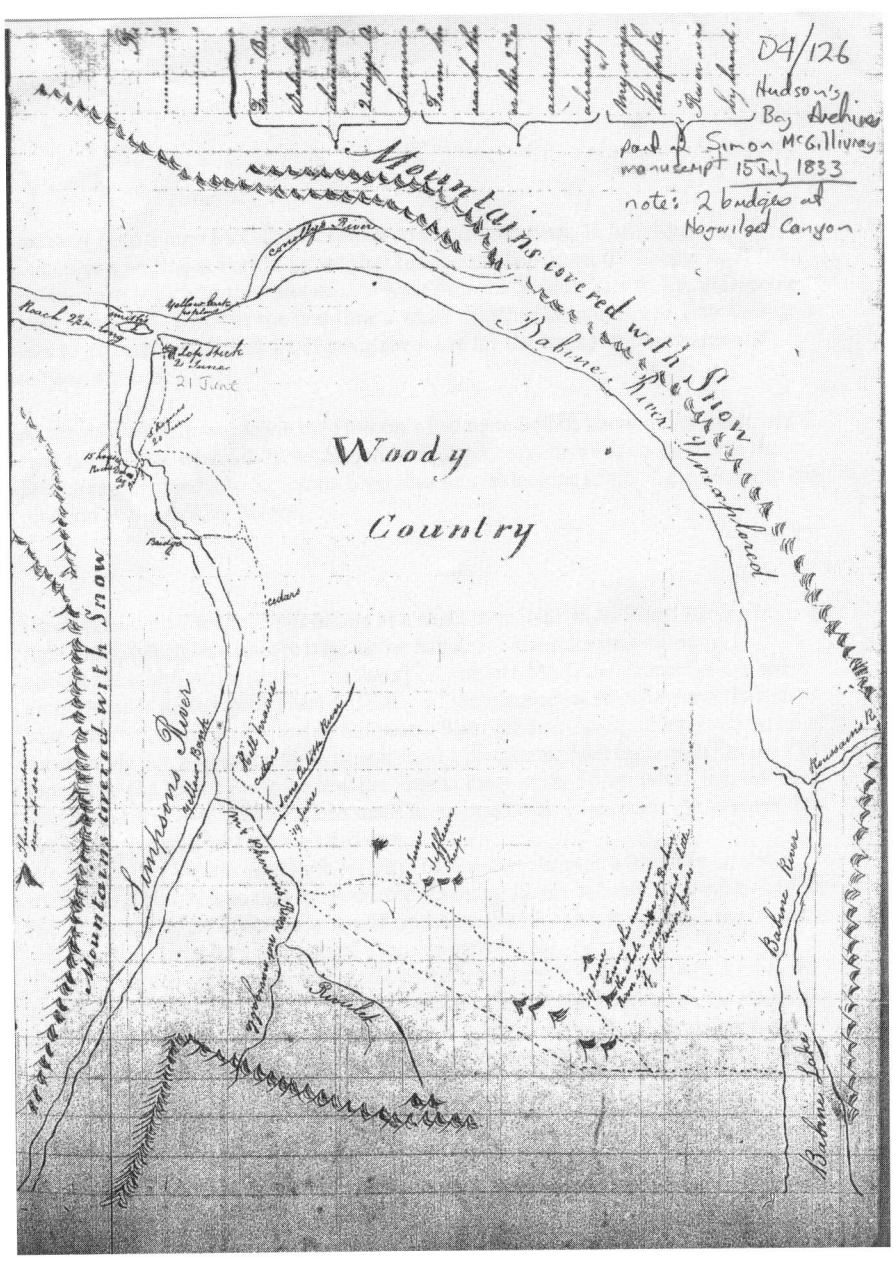

McGillivray's map was drawn in 1833 as part of the report on his trip from Fort St. James to the confluence of the Skeena and Bulkley rivers. (Image courtesy of Hudson's Bay Archive, D. 4-126, P. 35/63 to P. 36/65)

McGillivray learned that the Atnahs had three more villages below The Forks and that beyond them was "another tribe of Indians" who had traded at Hagwilget a few days before he arrived. This tribe was likely the Tsimshian of Kitselas or those of Chief Legaic and his people from the coast.

On his return to Hagwilget, McGillivray found that ten men armed with muskets from the first village (Gitanmaax) had arrived. Another twenty men from the second village (Kispiox), also armed with muskets, arrived in the evening. They had the note McGillivray was seeking, which read: "Reports are in circulation here that a party of whites [McGillivray's company] are in quest of this place, if so I shall be happy to see them. Fort Simpson, 23rd February, Observatory Inlet, Peter Skene Ogden."†

McGillivray believed that many of these Atnahs (the Gitxsan) had never seen whites because they seemed much surprised to see his company.

> [I] never saw Indians so destitute of European manufacture, they had 3 Blankets, some cheese cloth as brayets [breechclouts], and one of them a cloth capot [hooded cloak]. One of the blankets was dyed all in crimson colour. It is American property—they were pleased with everything we gave them. They demanded balls from us which I would not give, in fact we had no more than what we carried in our shot pouches.[23]

During his 1825 journey to Kisgegas, William Brown provided our first written account of Niik'yap's fishing village at Xsigwitselasgwit (Shenismike Creek), along with Kisgegas and Anlagasimdeex. Simon McGillivray provided us with similar insights into the Wet'suwet'en of Witset and Tse Cakh (Hagwilget) and the Gitxsan of Gitanmaax and Kispiox. Before he departed on his return journey, McGillivray found further evidence of interaction between traders and the Gitxsan:

> [I met an] Indian [who] talked broken English, but not sufficiently to carry on a conversation. He had been taken prisoner when a child by Indians of the Coast, who had come to war on the Atnahs in Babine River. He last year came up the river with the Indians of The Coast and, on seeing his countrymen, deserted them[.] [H]e traded me with a small cedar mat, and on my presenting him with a piece of tobacco and 7 brass rings he said, "it was very small" and counted the rings from 1 to 7 in the English language.[24]

McGillivray observed Stekyawden, noting that it was "...a remarkable high rock bearing SSW by compass" from the house he used at Hagwilget. He also noted that "Boats come up from the Sea as far as Roche Deboulez, and from this place to where we left our canoe in Babine Lake the distance is about 74 miles by land. The Indians are quiet, we received some fine fresh Salmon, 3 men on watch."[25]

---

† Ogden and Aemilius Simpson established Fort Simpson on the Nass River in 1831. Ogden was fort manager in 1833.

McGillivray set out for Fort St. James on June 22, his mission largely accomplished without actually descending Simpson's River to the sea. On Sunday June 23, before descending to Babine Lake, McGillivray noted that from there to the fallen rocks in Simpson's River horses could be pastured, and a road could be constructed so as to avoid most hills.[26]

McGillivray recommended that the best route to the sea from Fort Babine would be by land from Babine Lake to The Forks, then to the coast by canoe. He arrived back at Fort St. James July 3, 1833. Simon McGillivray appears to have been the first Euro-Canadian to visit and write about The Forks.

While Brown and McGillivray initiated their 'voyages of discovery' on behalf of the Hudson's Bay Company from east to west without ever getting below The Forks, the company was also looking inland from the coast with an eye to increasing trade.

Not only had the HBC employees Aemilius Simpson, Peter Skene Ogden and John Work built a fort at the mouth of the Nass in 1831, company trader Donald Manson canoed from the mouth of the Skeena fifty miles upriver looking for an appropriate site to build another trading post.

He didn't find one, but in 1834 the company moved Fort Simpson from the mouth of the Nass to the tip of the Tsimshian Peninsula at the camp site of Lax Kw'alaams (Port Simpson) where it was accessible not only to the Nisga'a but also other Tsimshian communities.

For the next thirty-plus years, despite the success of Fort Simpson in garnering coastal trade, the HBC continued losing furs to the free traders who roamed the coast and ventured inland. In January 1866, chief trader William Manson (son of Donald Manson) took charge of Fort Simpson. Manson recommended that the HBC expand its trade to the Nass and Skeena rivers and the chief factor of New Caledonia, Roderick Finlayson, agreed.[27]

Manson established an outpost in the home of Neshaki on the Nass River. Neshaki was the daughter of a Nisga'a chief and a successful entrepreneur in her own right. She was married to Captain McNeill‡ who since 1863 had piloted the fort's sloop, the *Petrel*,§ successfully acquiring furs for the HBC in opposition to free-trading ships like the *Nanaimo Packet*.[28] In the spring of 1866, "When [Neshaki's] trade was well established…[the HBC] sent a man named Thomas Hankin to take it over from her."[29] Hankin, who a few years later established the first trading post on the Skeena at The Forks, remained on the Nass River until July, when former missionary Robert Cunningham took his place.[30]

While the fur trade of northwest BC had dominated business interests in the area for decades, a second major economic enterprise was about to evolve thanks, in part, to a decision by Governor James Douglas to send a Scottish gold seeker, William Downie, on another voyage of discovery.

---

‡ Neshaki was Captain McNeill's second wife.

§ Since a sloop is a sailboat, large canoes would have been necessary above tidewater.

William Downie

William Downie (1820-1893) was born in Glasgow and died in San Francisco. He was an adventurer and world traveler, having visited Australia, the East Indies, Canada and the USA. He apparently spent most of his life seeking gold and is said to have found and lost a fortune. He first arrived in San Francisco in 1849 bound for the California gold fields. He arrived in Victoria in 1858, perhaps en route to the Cariboo gold fields.

Within the year, Governor James Douglas employed Downie to determine the mineral potential of the colonies of Vancouver Island and BC. On July 27, 1859 Downie set out from Victoria on the *Island Queen*, bound for Gold Harbour on the west coast of Moresby, one of the Queen Charlotte Islands; The Forks of the Skeena; and Fort St. James. In the execution of this project, Downie appears to have been the first white visitor to document the Gitxsan name—Gitanmaax—for the village at The Forks.

Downie arrived on Moresby Island on August 6. There he spent considerable time searching for gold in the hills, bays and inlets of Gold Harbour but found little of interest. Many of his men wanted to return to Victoria, but Downie "did not like the idea" as Douglas wanted him "to explore the Inlets on the main land, so I formed one of a party of fifteen in a canoe, bid goodbye to Gold Harbour and started for Fort Simpson where we arrived eight days after leaving Gold Harbour."[31]

At Fort Simpson, Downie exchanged his Haida canoe for one more suited to ascending the Skeena River. On August 31, he and his men departed on the sixty-four kilometre journey to Port Essington and "the Skinnas River…Indian name Lee An."[32] According to a chart in Downie's possession, "the salt water runs up about thirty miles from the mouth…and vessels drawing over four feet of water cannot come up Lee An more than twenty miles."[33]

Despite his inability to write exactly what was said by his aboriginal sources, Downie made a valiant effort to record their place names: "Lee An Indian names will be best for me to use hereafter as they are best adapted for an Indian country, in fact I cannot get along with any other."[34]

Although Downie was conscientious about documenting the terrain, mineral prospects and place names, he was less rigorous about dating his journal entries. After an unstated period of time, Downie was 120 kilometres up the Skeena from Port Essington, likely near Kitsumkalum. He noted, "[B]elow this a short distance on the North side of the river is an Indian trail to Fort Simpson, it is a low pass and the Indian says it is not far to go that way." This is likely the trail that ran up the Kitsumkalum Valley to the Nass River.

The Kitimat Valley runs south of Kitsumkalum to Douglas Channel. Downie noted:

> …On the South side here is an Indian trail to what they call Kittlop, on the Salmon River the South branch of Salmon River is called Kittama [and] with regard to the harbour and depth of water on Salmon River I cannot say anything as I have not been there yet.[35]

The villagers also told Downie that a "large stream comes in from the North called Kittchumsala [Kitsumkalum] where the Indians grows plenty of potatoes the land is good and well adapted for farming [and]…coming in from the South is a small stream called Chimhoatch [Xsim Hayetsxw or Copper River]."[36]

Downie then turned his attention to the rest of his journey up the Skeena, noting, "We are now fairly over the coast range and the mountains ahead don't look so high, the current is strong and it is hard work getting the canoe along but we are strong too, and we get ashore with a good long rope and pull her along."[37]

Downie thought the country ahead "looked very much like gold country [with] fine bars and flats and more clay in the bars as we get up."[38] He camped that day near the village of Kitselas and, with the aid of a Kitselas man "who spoke good Chinook", explored the river above the village. The villagers advised Downie he could get to the HBC at Fort Fraser in two days from The Forks.

> From here up to the village of Kittcoma [Gitwangak] the land gets better all the way, the mountains is further back from the river fine flats common away back four or five miles to the base of the mountains up on the sides of which can be seen the smoke rising from the Indian fires where they are gathering berries and preparing for winter…here I went over to the fishing ground over fine land to a small river, the Indians most kind and gave me bear meat, invited me to build a house, on their land and live with them as they said it was all the same as Victoria.[39]

Downie considered this to be the best looking land for gold prospecting and coal he had seen in BC. However the river itself presented problems:

> From this place to the village of Kittsagathala [Gitsegukla] the river is rocky and dangerous the Indian canoe I was in came near getting smashed and our own canoe got split from stem to stern, our goods was saved and I felt thankful that none of our men was drowned.[40]

The Gitsegukla chiefs confronted Downie, informing him he was on their territory.

> [We]…sat down beside them on the bank without assuming any alarm, gave them a small piece of tobacco and looked as if we did not care for them, I find it best to take things cool when the Indians is in for a fight and this is the way I get along— look as if I did not care for them and not afraid.[41]

Downie wrote that after Gitsegukla, "The land gets regular to North…until we get up to The Forks or the village of Kittamarks [Gitanmaax, where] the canoe will stop."[42] Although Downie mentioned Gitanmaax, he did not visit it, and camped instead on the left bank of the Bulkley River at The Forks. Downie was anxious to get to Fort Fraser and sent a messenger ahead to the village of "Augelgeth" [Hagwilget] to hire guides for the trip.

Much had changed since Simon McGillivray's visit twenty-six years earlier, for not only had the villages of Gitanmaax and Hagwilget become common names and destinations, but 'Simpson's' River had given way to 'Skinnas' [Skeena] River.

For thousands of years, The Forks has been a focal point for residents and explorers of the Skeena watershed. This 2009 photo shows the sweep of the Skeena flowing around Hazelton with the Bulkley coming in from the right. The author's home at Temlaham is just outside the photo at the lower left corner. The large cleared area across the Bulkley on the right has been called Ackwelget, Fort Finlayson, Skeena Post and Mission Flats. (NJS photo)

In his haste, Downie's instructions to his guides must have been unclear. There were two routes to Fort Fraser from Hagwilget or Gitanmaax, the shortest being south up the Bulkley River and into the Fraser watershed. The longer route went east to Babine and Stuart lakes, then west to Fort Fraser. On September 21, Downie left his canoe and five men at The Forks and set out with two men and two guides. They stopped at Hagwilget for lunch. He recognized the development potential of the area and, when leaving, erected a sign that read, *NOTICE—September 22, 1859.—I have this day located and claimed this pass, as the route of the Great Canadian and Pacific Railroad.*† *William Downie.*[43]

His description of the subsequent journey is as tortuous as the trip itself seemed to be:

> [We] started on a fine trail through a beautiful country for Fort Fraser crossed over an Indian suspension bridge and the land is what may be called first rate we came across plenty of Indians loaded with berries and the trouble is we have to get to eat berries with them all for which they expect a small bit of tobacco our course today has been about East came about twelve miles…the second day it rained our course about NorEast got along about twelve miles still in as fine a country as man could desire for farming…[44]

---

† Downie was right—the Grand Trunk Pacific railroad came through the valley from Prince Rupert not far from his sign.

On the above leg of his trip, Downie shared berries with the Gitxsan near Nine Mile Creek and continued east, probably camping that night at or near the confluence of Natlan Creek with the Suskwa River. By this time, Downie was well east of the shorter Bulkley Valley route to Fort Fraser:‡

> [T]he Indians say we are going [to Fort Fraser] and will be there in two days more so I let them go ahead when I take an Indian for a guide or Pilot I let him have his way until I tell him to go…fine weather third day the trail has not been so good the Indians came the worse trail over fallen pine…along the base of a mountain instead of keeping down in the bottom where the trail is good, and the grass in abundance, our Indian started away after a goat up the mountain but three bears made him come back in double quick time.[45]

Now Downie was approaching the headwaters of the Suskwa River at Xsu Uuxs Bahlit and was probably at or near French Peak. From there he could see north towards Fort Connolly at Bear Lake, and northwest towards Kisgegas and Anlagasimdeex, but not Kispiox, which was a few miles from Gitanmaax.

> Fourth day came over what is called rocky pass by keeping down in the bottom, this can be avoided, our course to day has been N N East the land looks low to the East. North of us is a chain of mountains covered with snow distant thirty miles in this chain of mountains the HBC have a trading post called Bear Fort [Fort Connolly] in the bottom south of this is the Indian Village Kisspiyacks [Kispiox] along the bottom runs Lee An, past the Indian village Allagasomdaa [Anlagasimdeex], further up is the Indian village Kitthathraths [Kisgegas]. Still [farther] on [we] see a river the Indian says we have not far to go now.[46]

By the fifth day out from Gitanmaax, Downie was seriously concerned and sought to get to Babine Lake as soon as possible. He met "four hard looking Indians" who said, "Mr. Manson was not there where we were going."[47]

Shortly afterwards, Downie arrived at Nass Glee, a Nedut'en village at the outlet of Babine Lake, fifty miles north of Fort Kilmaurs. He then realized he had spent five days travelling in the wrong direction, and he set out down Babine Lake and on to Fort St. James and Fort Fraser.

Downie's journey was significant. His survey set the groundwork for miners later coming up the Skeena River to discover gold at Lorne Creek; he identified a route to the Omineca and its gold; and he recognized the potential of the area for what became the Grand Trunk Pacific Railway.

Charles Morison

Less than ten years later, large numbers of men and animals and tons of equipment and supplies would stream into the area as eastern industrialists sought to establish a reliable telegraph

---

‡ See Map 4: Skeena River Watershed

link between North America and Europe. Efforts to lay a trans-Atlantic cable had failed several times and an overland link west across North America to the Bering Sea, to Asia and on to Europe began in the mid-1860s. Among the work crews arriving at The Forks during the summer of 1866 was a young man from England, Charles Morison. As Morison later wrote:

> The first white who resided on Mission Point for any time was your humble servant. I passed several months there in charge of a Large Depot of material, provisions etc. of the old Yukon Telegraph line (never completed). The Freight came up Skeena river by canoes manned by Indians and some 35 white Boat men and captain James L. Butler. This was in 1866 and during that summer I was the only White man in that part of the World. There was no Hazelton then…It is a mistake to say that Hazelton was an old Hudson Bay Post: other men started stores there first. T. Hankin, Nelson, Youmans and a man named Welsh who having made money sold out to The Hudson Bay Co, then they started in his premises. The Anglican (church) started a mission under Bishop Ridley and (it) is flourishing today. The other storekeepers retired leaving the H.B.Co and R. Cunningham & Sons in Business. The writer ran the Cunningham business for 15 years & also acted as Church Warden & Treasurer for that period. Incidentally I was the first to ascend the Ackwelget Canyon in a canoe, a rather perilous undertaking.[48]

Charles Frederic Morison was born March 29, 1844 in London, England and died at Metlakatla on March 19, 1933. In September 1861, lured by glowing reports of the opportunities to be had in BC, Morison set sail for Canada. The seventeen-year-old stopped over in Antigua, West Indies to visit his eldest brother at his sugar plantation, then sailed in April 1862 for Victoria, crossing the Isthmus of Panama by rail.

Charles found "…the 1862 population of Victoria decidedly a mixture [of characters], all the way from the 'One-eye-glass' English dude to the toughest of humanity from Montana; but all under well-enforced laws and police regulations: the dude restrained in the use of his monocle, and the tough in the use of his six-shooter."[49]

Morison also had a brother, William, in New Westminster who was deputy registrar in the colonial government. He found work for Charles with the Royal Engineers as a clerk on the trunk wagon road to the Cariboo. Travelling first by sternwheeler on the *Colonel Moody*, then by canoe as the Fraser River was in flood, Charles arrived in Yale. That night he camped with Joseph Trutch and Edgar Dewdney who later became lieutenant-governors of BC.

It was perhaps a testament to his brother's connections, but equally likely to the small population of the period, that during the next few years young Morison was to become acquainted with the pioneer personalities of the day: Trutch and Dewdney of course, but also Governor James Douglas, Chief Justice Matthew Bailey Begbie, editor John Robson (later premier), Judges Crease, McCreight, Walkem, and Peter O'Reilly and many others.

Morison's work took him to the Boston Bar–Lytton road section and later back downriver to the Sailor's Bar–Chapman's Bar section. When the work ended in the fall of 1862, Charles returned to New Westminster where he worked as a clerk and at other odd jobs for the next four years. But he wanted more exciting work and found it with the Collins Overland Telegraph (COT).

Cyrus W. Field's Atlantic Telegraph Company laid the first undersea cable across the Atlantic in 1858. The cable had broken within three weeks and efforts to reconnect it repeatedly failed. Meanwhile, the Russians were building an overland line east from Moscow to Siberia. Perry Collins, a California gold rush veteran and well-connected business promoter, had visited Russia and on his return recommended that a landline be built from San Francisco north through BC, the Yukon and Russian Alaska to link with the Siberian line.

Collins and Hiram Sibley, the head of the Western Union Telegraph Company, joined forces. On July 1, 1864, with American, British and Russian support, President Abraham Lincoln granted Sibley and Collins a right-of-way from San Francisco to the BC border. With full support of the colony, the COT established a BC terminal in New Westminster.† The line reached there in the spring of 1865 and its first message was of Abraham Lincoln's assassination on April 15.

Construction crews continued north through Yale and the Cariboo until they stopped work at Quesnel with the onset of winter. In the spring of 1866, a crew of 150 men resumed work at Quesnel with the Skeena Forks as their destination. However, transporting tons of wire and insulators by pack train from New Westminster up the Fraser and northwest to The Forks of the Skeena and 'Hagwilget' rivers would be a costly and herculean task. A viable alternative was needed.

Paddlewheel vessels had not yet ascended the Skeena, but that was about to change and twenty-two-year-old Charles Morison would have a part in the historic venture. Morison, as commissary clerk, joined Ed Conway (engineer in charge), Charles Burrage (paymaster), a Mr. Lugenbeel (chief bookkeeper), Dr. George Chismore (chief surgeon), Captain James Butler (party chief), R.W. Brown (accountant) and forty construction and utility men.

In 1864 Captain Tom Coffin "…investigated the turbulent waters of the Skeena in a small sternwheeler, the *Union*." Apparently the *Union* was "…the first steam powered vessel to enter that river."[50] Coffin, one of the most experienced swift-water men in the province, had designed a craft suitable for the shallow, fast-moving Skeena, but the COT rejected Coffin's plans and designed and built a vessel in Victoria—the *Mumford*—that turned out to be unsuitable to the task.

The *Mumford* arrived in New Westminster on July 2, 1866 and was loaded and ready to sail late the following day. Captain Coffin was in charge of the boat, but Captain Butler managed the project and, given the *Mumford*'s limitations, ultimately took charge of the effort to convey the men and supplies up the Skeena River. Apart from Coffin, the men had no idea where they were headed nor the challenges they faced. As they steamed across Queen Charlotte Sound in a vessel suited neither to the open sea nor the Skeena River, Butler remarked, "It was very [much] like going to sea in a wheel barrow!"[51]

At the north end of Grenville Channel the ship turned east into the murky waters of the Skeena River and continued to the head of tidewater, about sixty-five kilometres above Port Essington.

---

† See Map 7: Pacific Northwest

Haida canoes and later paddlewheel steamboats, like the SS Omineca, seen here in Kitselas Canyon, plied the Skeena from the coast to Hazelton from the mid-1860s until the arrival of the railroad in 1912. (Image D-09562 courtesy of RBCM & A)

Here they encountered "…the full current of the river. We could make no headway so tied up to the riverbank. The men built a rough warehouse in which half the cargo was stored."[52]

They made a second valiant try:

> The *Mumford* made one more effort to surmount a riffle, Captain Coffin wedged the safety valve down. We had a line ahead fastened to a tree, which was heaved on by a hand-power windlass. I was busy with a bucksaw sawing short lengths of wood to feed the furnace. They heaved a five-gallon tin of tar into the furnace, all the cook's slush and several sides of fat bacon. The steam gauge had gone to 'no man's land'. The line ahead parted and we gave up, dropped down stream several yards and tied up. The Chief Engineer knocked away the throttle lever, threw the fire overboard, and we were at peace.[53]

As Coffin expected, the *Mumford* was ill-suited for the Skeena. He and Butler took it as far as Fort Simpson where Butler obtained large canoes with which to freight their equipment up the Skeena River.[54] Meanwhile, Captain Coffin set out for New Westminster for further supplies. This and future cargo was off-loaded at Port Essington and paddled, poled and lined 160 kilometres up the river to The Forks by canoe.

> [The canoes] were magnificent craft hewed out of the body of a single red cedar tree by the Haida Indians of the Queen Charlotte Islands. Most of them had a capacity of over two tons deadweight cargo, manned by a crew of five: the Captain

who steered with a long sweep balanced over the stern, a bow man equipped with a pole and paddle, whom the crew tabbed 'Captain Bow', three other men who toggled on to a cotton rope towline to haul her through the swift rushing current. The larger canoes had space for three or four passengers, marvelous craft.[55]

The men and canoes continued to fight their way up the Skeena, through Kitselas Canyon and beyond.

They finally beached their canoes in late July on the left bank of the Skeena at the large meadow immediately below The Forks, which later became known as Mission Flats. Here Butler's men built a second depot to store their supplies. Additional trips had to be made downriver and Butler invited volunteers to stay at the depot and safeguard the COT equipment. None would, fearing the Hagwilgets who lived nearby on the same side of the Bulkley. Butler finally asked Morison and he agreed. Morison would be alone for the next two to three weeks, while the rest of the men made the return trip to the mouth of the Skeena.

After he finished breakfast the next morning, Morison had unexpected visitors:

> …down came about a hundred Hagwilget Indians to survey the white boy and his camp. They were a fierce looking lot, not a pair of trousers among them, their faces painted red and black, and each carrying a Hudson's Bay Company flintlock musket and long knife. I think they were more curious than warlike.[56]

Meanwhile the overland work party from Quesnel was nearing The Forks with a herd of cattle, and sent Indian packers ahead with freshly butchered beef, a welcome change from "beans and bacon", as Morison said.

To meet the crew from Quesnel, the COT hoped to move telegraph wire and insulators up the Bulkley River by canoe past the fallen rocks that made the river almost impassable. After the coastal freighting Indians refused to attempt the feat, Captain Butler asked Charles whether he would attempt it. Morison agreed and persuaded "…three 'dare devil' young Coast Indians to accompany [him]."

The four men took three-quarters of a day to line an empty canoe up the canyon and past the fallen rocks at Hagwilget to a small bay above the bridge. After resting, it took little more than three-quarters of an hour to make the dangerous run past the fallen rock in the canyon and back down to The Forks. This ended any further thought of trying to ascend the Bulkley in loaded freight canoes.

The main Quesnel work party finally arrived on the left bank of the river at Hagwilget. It was a massive undertaking with a herd of beef cattle, 200 pack animals, 105 white men, numerous Chinese cooks, and Indians—Haida, Tsimshian, Bella Bella and Bella Coola—and their baggage.

Although the COT workmen marveled at the bridge spanning Hagwilget Canyon, and all agreed it was an impressive engineering feat, Steve Decker, the general foreman, chose to build a new bridge rather than reinforce the existing one. When the Hagwilget Indians objected, Decker relented and reinforced the bridge with rawhide lashing and a new deck atop the old.

Although some might have been startled when the COT men arrived at Hagwilget, Gitanmaax and Kispiox in the summer of 1866, they weren't completely taken by surprise. Advance exploration parties traveled throughout the territory in 1865 with men who had interpreters and could converse with the Gitxsan. The Gitxsan would have known that a "talking wire" hanging on trees would soon be built through their land. It's not hard to imagine the Gitxsan—with some among them who could foresee the future and read others' minds—sitting at night by a campfire, or in a dimly lit long house, teasing each other about what this might portend.

As Gwiiyeehl/John Brown said:

> The people heard of the news that a *mahlasxwm duutsw* (talking metal) was coming through here. The impression they had of this…was that if a person wanted information on another man all he had to do was to attach this wire. And this wire would give all the information they wanted, and tell all of the bad things he had done, and all the good things, and all the things he kept hidden and all the secrets.

Leftover wire from the Collins Overland Telegraph was sometimes used to strengthen and repair suspension bridges, as in this span over the Suskwa River. (Sheila Peters photo)

Many of the people were troubled when they heard of the approach of this new thing. Many men were frightened that their secrets regarding other men's wives would come out and be exposed in public through the influence of this wire. And they thought that this wire would tell it in public so that everybody [would] hear it. [Among] the people that were coming with this wire were "Jayn" [Chinese]. And they heard that these Jayn were going to take all the women away from [them] and massacre them. And then they heard also that these Jayn had their wives with them and the women Jayn would take the men and exterminate them off. So they were troubled when they heard of the approach of the wire. "What will we do?" said many of them.

So then it was planned that the women should blacken themselves in order that they may go in mourning and this would scare the Jayn away. So when this wire did come everyone was afraid to go in the vicinity of this wire, as they did not want this wire to expose their secrets. They had all planned to keep away from it. They saw the pole on which the wire was but they were frightened again to come in contact with the pole because they were frightened that…the wire would speak in person. And they went on with this wire about forty miles from here, and [they] stopped and abandoned a lot of wire in huge bundles and reels [there].

But these the people did not touch. They were still frightened of the wire. Then Yen of Kispayaks said that he did not care if this wire exposed all his secrets. If you kill me afterwards it must not be frightening. I am going to touch the wire first. So he touched one hand on the wire and the wire never spoke, and he cut off a piece of the wire. Even though he hurt the wire it never spoke when cutting it off. And when the people found out that this will never kill anybody, and never speak, they all came and gathered up wire for their own use.[57]

The COT had more trouble with the chiefs at Kispiox who believed if the wire crossed the Skeena "…no more salmon would ascend the river… and furthermore, all birds and animals crossing under or over the wire would instantly die."[58]

The COT men were well armed. Conway strategically located them in the bush on the left bank of the Skeena opposite Kispiox and returned to the depot at The Forks for a council of war. He decided to send two men, Charles Burrage and Morison, to negotiate a settlement. Burrage was able to convince the chiefs that the project would be a source of revenue. When they relented, Burrage and Morison shared tobacco with them.

Construction continued another forty miles beyond Kispiox to a point near the confluence of the Nangeese and Kispiox rivers. There, with winter fast approaching, a telegrapher "… attached his equipment to the end of the wire, and presto! [They] had the latest news from New York."[59]

One evening the usual things were going on when Mr. Conway called a halt, then turning to the listening crowd announced: "Boys, the Atlantic Cable has been successfully laid by the steamship *Great Eastern* and messages are now crossing from London to New York via the Atlantic Ocean, so I expect our work is over!" This news came to us in September 1866 towards the end of the month, I cannot recall the exact date.[60]

The trans-Atlantic cable was successfully connected on July 28, 1866, but Conway's party did not learn about it until almost two months later.

…all construction was stopped, and all hands, with the exception of a few, were ordered to the coast and thence to Victoria to be paid off. The depot at Mission Point[†] was empty, all the stores having been shipped to the end of the telegraph line.[61]

Captain Butler sent orders to The Forks that his bookkeeper, R. W. Brown, and Morison were to travel to Wrangell in Russian Alaska where another COT depot had to be de-commissioned. The Tsimshian chief, Legaic, happened to be at The Forks, having delivered the last load of COT supplies. He invited Brown and Morison to accompany him and his crew to Fort Simpson. They travelled non-stop in Legaic's great canoe throughout the night, past Port Essington at the mouth of the Skeena and on to the village of Metlakatla.

At that time, Port Essington was much the same as Captain Vancouver found it in 1793. It was, Morison said, "…a perfect solitude; the location only being used by the Indians as their last camp on their return from their hunting and salmon drying up river; from this camp they proceeded and gathered into their winter quarters at Metlakatla and Fort Simpson."[62]

The next day, Brown and Morison found passage from Metlakatla to the HBC establishment at Fort Simpson, twenty-two kilometres away. It consisted of a seventy-five-metre-square stockade with seven metre-high walls and a metre-wide, elevated platform around the inside, on which sentries kept watch. Bastions were built at each corner, and a huge gate sat in the centre of the stockade, facing the sea. On Sunday, the two men relaxed and explored the village. They were impressed:

The large Indian Long Houses with huge totem poles in front of them, the Indian men and women promenading in their bright colored blankets, their faces touched up with vermillion, the beach lined with magnificent canoes—some sixty feet in length, the largest canoe in most cases traded from the Haidas of the Queen Charlotte Islands. Altogether it was a most picturesque and colorful sight.[63]

While in Port Simpson, Morison met a man—Robert Cunningham, the HBC postmaster in charge—with whom he would later work for many years.

Charles Morison spent most of the rest of his life in the northwest. He worked for the HBC on the Stikine and was manager at Fort Simpson where he married Odile Dubois in 1872. They

---

† The meadow became known as 'Mission Point' after the Church Missionary Society acquired it ca. 1900.

An 1862 drawing of Fort Simpson, with the Hudson's Bay Company stockade and Tsimshian longhouses. (Image PDP00089 courtesy of RBCM & A)

went on to have seven children. Morison and his family lived in Victoria for about three years, after which he started a sawmill business at Georgetown (between Prince Rupert and Port Simpson). From 1887 until about 1910, he was the Cunningham's business manager in Hazelton. Charles Morison died at Metlakatla, BC in 1933, 110 years after William Brown visited Witset (Moricetown).

The adventures and records of these four men—Brown, McGillivray, Downie and Morison—provide important insights into European settlement along the upper Skeena. Two other men—Thomas Hankin and Robert Cunningham—had equally significant roles. Their 1870 decision to leave the HBC and build a business at The Forks led to the founding of Hazelton at Gitanmaax.

ENDNOTES

1. Brown, "Fort Kilmaurs".
2. Brown, "Babine Report".
3. Brown, "Fort Kilmaurs", 50.
4. Brown, "Fort Kilmaurs", 34.
5. Brown, "Fort Kilmaurs", 34.
6. Brown, "Fort Kilmaurs", 55.
7. Brown, "Babine Report", 9.
8. Brown, "Babine Report", 22-23.
9. Brown, "Babine Report", 3, 5.
10. Brown, "Babine Report", 5.
11. Brown, "Babine Report", 7.
12. Brown, "Babine Report", 7-8.
13. Brown, "Babine Report", 7.
14. McGillivray, 68.

15 McGillivray, 69.
16 McGillivray, 74.
17 McGillivray, 76.
18 McGillivray, 77.
19 McGillivray, 82.
20 McGillivray, 77.
21 McGillivray, 77.
22 McGillivray, 78.
23 McGillivray, 78-9.
24 McGillivray, 79.
25 McGillivray, 79.
26 McGillivray, 80.
27 Finlayson.
28 Meilleur, 122-23.
29 Meilleur, 123.
30 Meilleur, 123.
31 Downie, *Journal*, 10-11.
32 Downie, *Journal*, 12.
33 Downie, *Journal*, 13.
34 Downie, *Journal*, 13.
35 Downie, *Journal*, 14.
36 Downie, *Journal*, 15.
37 Downie, *Journal*, 14.
38 Downie, *Journal*, 15.
39 Downie, *Journal*, 16.
40 Downie, *Journal*, 16.
41 Downie, *Journal*, 17.
42 Downie, *Journal*, 17.
43 Downie, *Hunting for Gold*, 225.
44 Downie, *Journal*, 18.
45 Downie, *Journal*, 18.
46 Downie, *Journal*, 19.
47 Downie, *Journal*, 19.
48 Morison to Pound.
49 Morison, *A Brief Narrative*, 3.
50 Morison, *A Brief Narrative*, 26.
51 Morison, *A Brief Narrative*, 28.
52 Morison, *A Brief Narrative*, 28.
53 Morison, *A Brief Narrative*, 28-29.
54 Morison, *A Brief Narrative*, 29.
55 Morison, *A Brief Narrative*, 29.
56 Morison, *A Brief Narrative*, 35-36.
57 "Barbeau and Beynon Fieldnotes", John G. Brown ca.1920 (B-F-90.15).
58 "Barbeau and Beynon Fieldnotes", John G. Brown ca.1920 (B-F-90.15), 43.
59 "Barbeau and Beynon Fieldnotes", John G. Brown ca.1920 (B-F-90.15), 43.
60 "Barbeau and Beynon Fieldnotes", John G. Brown ca.1920 (B-F-90.15), 44.
61 "Barbeau and Beynon Fieldnotes", John G. Brown ca.1920 (B-F-90.15), 44.
62 "Barbeau and Beynon Fieldnotes", John G. Brown ca.1920 (B-F-90.15), 45.
63 "Barbeau and Beynon Fieldnotes", John G. Brown ca.1920 (B-F-90.15), 47.

CHAPTER THIRTEEN

Thomas Hankin: Skeena Merchant

The arrival of Thomas Hankin and his bride, Margaret MacAulay, at Gitanmaax in July 1871 heralded a new era on the upper Skeena. That was the year Edgar Dewdney laid out the lots and streets of the village that became Hazelton, and the Hankins became the first mixed-race couple to settle and build there.† During the next twenty years many others would join them.

Several Hankin family brothers arrived in BC in the late 1850s. Philip joined the navy at age thirteen in 1849 and "…first arrived on this coast as mate of HMS *Plumper* [in] 1857."¹ Correspondence between Governor James Douglas and another brother, Charles, indicates that Charles and his younger brother Graham had arrived by 1858. Thomas Hankin applied for a 320-acre pre-emption in the Cariboo District in 1863, which may have been the year of his arrival. This fits with Constance Cox's belief that her father "…came out via Cape Horn in 1862."²

Constance Cox was an historian, translator, storyteller, court interpreter and advocate on behalf of BC's aboriginal peoples. Having heard about Connie for years, I finally saw her when she attended a Native Brotherhood of BC convention at Hazelton in 1953. "That's Connie Cox and Maisie Hurley," my dad said, as they walked past our house on their way to Gitanmaax Hall.‡

---

† They married June 20, 1871 at Fort Rupert on Vancouver Island. It would have taken two weeks or more for the couple to make the journey by ship and canoe (and perhaps overland from the Nass River). Margaret was the daughter of Donald MacAulay and Margaret Snaaxw, who was of Tlingit or Tsimshian heritage. See Hankin Family Tree.

‡ Maisie Hurley (1887-1964) founded *The Native Voice* newspaper in 1946. Tom Berger, in a tribute to Maisie, said she was a lifelong advocate of aboriginal people (Dec. 2010). Maisie married Thomas Hurley (1884-1961), a Vancouver lawyer who also advocated on behalf of minority groups. Gitxsan chief, Guuxsan, adopted Maisie in a ceremony at Gitsegukla in 1949 (Cox, Constance. "White Woman Honoured." *The Native Voice* III 05 1949: 2.). Ronald Campbell-Johnston (1844-1929), Maisie's father, conducted a significant geological examination of the Groundhog Coalfield at the headwaters of the Skeena River in 1910 and 1912.

Taken in the fall of 1910, this photo shows (L-R) Connie (Hankin) Cox's son Herbert; Connie with her daughter, Mazel; Connie's sister Charlotte (Hankin) Boyd; her son, John Wm. Boyd; Margaret MacAulay/ Hankin/Loring; and her grandson, Howard H. Boyd. Margaret died in December. (Lorraine O'Leary coll.)

Three years later I met Connie and over the next few years got to know her well. As mentioned earlier, my mother sent me to school in Vancouver in the fall of 1956, where I boarded with my father's sister, Margaret, and her husband, Bill Heath.

Later that fall I was invited to an aunt's wedding reception in the Legion Hall on West Broadway. By then I was familiar with the Vancouver bus system and able to get around on my own. At the hall, my aunt sat me with an elderly couple, but amid the noise and excitement I didn't catch their names. They were friendly and the man startled me when he asked, "How is the grouse hunting up at the graveyard?"

"You know Hazelton?" I asked. "Oh yes," he said, "I lived there for many years. Connie was born there." To my surprise and delight, for I knew few in the room and was terribly homesick, Ruxton and Connie Cox were my seatmates. This was the beginning of a close friendship that lasted until each of them passed on, Connie in 1960 and Ruxton in 1971.[†]

My grandfather and step-grandmother were also at the reception. Bill Russell left Hazelton in 1936 after his marriage with my grandmother failed. In 1940 he married Mazel, Ruxton and Connie's daughter. The Coxes, along with my grandfather and his new family, had retired to White Rock. During the next few years, I sometimes spent weekends visiting my grandfather there, but

---

† Ruxton's parents, Emmanuel Cox (1832-1894) and Mary (1838-1911) emigrated from County Cork, Ireland to the USA ca. 1870 and to Canada in 1873.

spent most of my time visiting the Coxes and listening to their stories. They were both interesting, but Mr. Cox tended to take a backseat to his wife.

After Connie died, Barbara and I discovered that Ruxton had led an equally exciting life. He was born on Vancouver Island in 1880 and at age twenty-two walked from the Lower Mainland to Hazelton to work as a telegrapher. There he met, courted and married Constance Hankin in 1905.

He loved birds and kept many species in a rookery beside his house. My work in minerals exploration took me to remote areas of Canada. I often wrote letters to Ruxton describing where I was and what animals and birds I encountered. In 1967, I wrote to him from Bamfield, a tiny community on the west coast of Vancouver Island near Cape Beale. He immediately replied and with great excitement wrote that he was born at Bamfield and that his father, Emmanuel Cox, was the Cape Beale lighthouse keeper from 1877 to 1894. He was extremely interested in wolves and asked—if I happened to come across it—to get him a copy of Adolf Murie's seminal work, *The Wolves of Mount McKinley*. Eventually I found it but Ruxton died before I could give it to him.

Connie spoke fluent Gitxsan and often translated for Marius Barbeau during his expeditions to the upper Skeena. In 1958, the British Columbia Provincial Museum was concerned about preserving the totem poles at Gitanyow which were, and still are, among the oldest and finest in North America.

Provincial ethnologist Wilson Duff had approached several Gitanyow chiefs to see if they were interested in the project. Historically the Gitanyow had fought strenuously to keep the government and settlers out of their territory and did not trust provincial representatives. Surprisingly, they were open to Duff's proposal and negotiations ensued.‡

Duff proposed that the Gitanyow chiefs store several of their finer poles at the museum in Victoria; the museum would replace them with copies made by skilled carvers. The chiefs agreed but added that they wanted the museum to record and publish their histories. Although Duff had a limited budget he agreed to the terms which included the chiefs choosing a person capable of translating to English the elders' histories. Thus it was that Constance Cox travelled from White Rock to Gitanyow in the fall of 1958, where she worked with a committee of six chiefs to produce what became *The Histories, Territories, and Laws of the Kitwancool*.§ The book was published in December 1959, a legacy not only for future generations of Gitanyow children, but for British Columbians too.[3]

During my visits, Connie told many stories about her life growing up in Hazelton. Her stories about her father, Thomas Hankin, and her many Gitxsan experiences—both humorous and tragic—brought to life the time when European fur traders and gold miners made their way into and through Gitxsan territory. She liked to write and showed me her essays, sometimes allowing me to copy them. I have carried them with me since. They include a brief Hazelton history and

---

‡ The Kitwancool (now Gitanyow) have opposed European encroachment into their territories for a century and a half. As recently as the mid- to late 1950s, provincial employees (BC Forest Service in particular) have discovered cottonwood trees fallen by the Gitanyow blocking their way as they drove home from work in the Kitwancool Valley.

§ The committee included Ernest Smith, Walter Douse, Fred Good, Solomon Good, Maggie Good and Peter Williams. B.W. and Ann McKilvington were very helpful to Connie and the elders.

several Gitxsan stories and legends. I realize now that some of Connie's efforts were based on assumptions, for she was just five years old when her father died. Nevertheless, she got most of the story right when she wrote, "Thomas Hankin decided to branch out for himself, and started a…trading post one mile up the Skeena [from The Forks] at a spot overburdened with hazel nut bushes. This he fittingly named Hazelton."[4]

Thomas Hankin and Robert Cunningham were both employed by the HBC, but had become disenchanted and left in 1870 to take advantage of the opportunities created by miners travelling the Skeena River route to the Omineca gold fields.

In the spring of 1871, Hankin built a log cabin on the left bank of the Skeena River a kilometre above the Skeena-Bulkley confluence. His store was the first of several buildings built that year as hundreds of miners made their way to the Omineca.

Of the four Hankin brothers who came to the northwest coast, only Thomas was important in Gitxsan territory, but all played a significant role in colonial BC.

By age thirteen, Philip had entered the navy, passed his exams and begun a career that included several postings to BC, the first in 1857. Later, after having resigned the navy, he returned to BC where he married and held several significant positions in the colonial government including colonial secretary-designate and administrator of the colony.

Hankin was one of the first settlers to pre-empt land along the Skeena River in the 1870s. By the 1890s about forty others had followed suit. The only photograph of Hankin that's come to light is this one from the 1958 special edition of the Native Voice.

> [He] was elected speaker of British Columbia's first representative legislature in January 1871….[and] had the distinction of being the colony's last, and informally the province's first, governing official, having served as administrator or acting governor between Governor Musgrave's departure in July 1871 and Trutch's installation as Lieutenant-Governor the following August.[5]

In May of 1858, we find Thomas's brother Charles at Hudson's Bay House in London meeting with Governor Henry Hulse Berens.† Berens wrote to James Douglas:

> Mr. Hankin [intends to] visit your Island with a view of engaging in some pursuits which may become profitable to him and I am sure he cannot apply to any person more able to assist him with advice than yourself—I shall feel much obliged to you for any kindness or civility which you may be able to show to Mr. Hankin…[6]

---

† Henry Hulse Berens, a Bank of England director (1849/50), deputy governor (1858), and governor (1858/63).

Charles came to Vancouver Island with his twelve-year-old brother, Graham. Together they made their way to the Cariboo district on the mainland where, in 1862, they and four other men struck gold with their partner, William 'Billy' Barker.

Fort Alexandria, a former HBC post in the Cariboo District, began operations as a fur trading supply depot in 1821. There we find Thomas Hankin in 1863 when he and Charles T. Seymour[‡] sought to pre-empt "Three hundred and twenty acres of land…on the East bank of Fraser River situated about 9 miles from Fort Alexander [sic] on a creek known as the 9 mile[§]…"[7] Three years later Hankin showed up on the northwest coast at Fort Simpson working for the HBC.

Hankin's timing couldn't have been better. The construction of the Collins Overland Telegraph made the mid-Skeena region more accessible to coastal fur buyers. And here, in the northwest, Hankin's career path joined with that of Robert Cunningham's.

Robert Cunningham (1837-1905) was born in County Tyrone, Northern Ireland. In 1862 the Anglican Church Missionary Society (CMS) sent Cunningham to the northwest coast on missionary work. He married Elizabeth Ryan (ca. 1846-1888) at Metlakatla in 1864. Cunningham found missionary work was not his calling and resigned, taking work with the HBC in 1866. He was a shrewd businessman and served the company well as postmaster at Fort Simpson from 1866 to 1871. From the outset the HBC appears to have been impressed with Cunningham's and Hankin's ability to work with the aboriginal peoples along the Nass and Skeena rivers.

In August 1866, HBC chief factor Roderick Finlayson wrote to chief trader William Manson:

> …The establishment of small trading Posts up the Skeena and Naas from Fort Simpson is very desirable, to prevent the furs getting to the Coast—and we trust to your making some arrangement without going to much expense, in keeping Mr. Cunningham trading up the Naas River for the Winter, and Mr. Hankin up the Skeena, and to be supplied with the necessary Outfits for the purpose…As the cost of sending supplies by the Frasers River route to New Caledonia is very high, and bears heavily on the trade, we are of the opinion, that we can get supplies in cheaper to that district by the Skeena River route. You will therefore please as early as possible, after receipt of this, organize a party at Fort Simpson and proceed up that river, and examine it well, to the head of Navigation for a small stern wheel steamer, drawing from two to 3 feet of water, and from that point explore the Country to Lac de Francois[¶]…Examine also the river as far as Roche de Bouillet, where the telegraph line intersects it, and see, which is the best way to get our supplies in, either to Babine Lake or Lac de Francois…Now that the telegraph line is cut through to Skeena and will be finished this Autumn to the Stekine River, we must make arrangements shortly for opening trading stations, where it intersects those rivers…[8]

[‡] A Charles Theobald Seymour was living in Victoria in 1874 (BCGS Heads of Households 1874: 93).

[§] Nine Mile Creek may be today's Australian Creek, south of Quesnel.

[¶] Today's Francois Lake.

On September 12, 1866, William Manson and Hankin embarked on an expedition up the Skeena River "...to Explore a New Road to convey supplies from the coast into the Interior Posts & Forts."[9] Manson and Hankin separated at Kispiox, with Manson bound for Fort Fraser[†] on Fraser Lake via Babine Lake and Stuart Lake. This was a longer route than Hankin's. He was tasked with finding "a suitable pass from the Skeena to Francois Lake...and successfully completed his explorations [via the Bulkley Valley] and returned to Fort Simpson on November 6, 1866, five days earlier than Manson."[10]

After he returned to Fort Simpson, Manson sent Hankin, James Otley and an assistant, Kiona, to The Forks. They traveled by sloop (the *Petrel*) and canoe and were told to "put up a small house to winter in for trading purposes."[11] The HBC expected to compete successfully against the coastal fur traders who were not only paying higher prices but also providing liquor to aboriginal trappers. The HBC believed an outpost on the upper Skeena would attract interior trappers, especially some of the Nedut'en and Wet'suwet'en who understandably preferred the higher prices paid by the competition. The HBC sought to intervene with an outpost at 'Hacwillgate'.[‡]

R.G. Cunningham trade dollar from the late 1800s. Cunningham, and partner Thomas Hankin, ran a store in Hazelton and a salmon cannery at the mouth of the Skeena.
(Image B-00450 courtesy of the RBCM & A)

For years, perhaps centuries, the Gitxsan and other nations had gathered at Gwin Ts'ihl (The Forks) for feasts and, after 1800, to trade with Tsimshian middlemen and 'Boston' free traders. In 1866 the COT beached their canoes at both The Forks and Kispiox, off-loaded equipment and supplies, and built living quarters and a warehouse at each site. The large blockhouse the COT built at Kispiox was named Fort Stager.

The HBC was interested primarily in trading with the Wet'suwet'en and may have intended to establish its outpost at Hagwilget. On November 20, 1866, Hankin obtained canoes from Legaic at Metlakatla to ferry his supplies up the Skeena to The Forks. Winter had set in when Hankin arrived. He established the first Skeena outpost in a COT building at The Forks—"Ackwellget Station" as chief trader W.F. Tolmie later described it. Hankin spent a year and a half there gaining him the distinction of being the first European to have spent more than a few months at The Forks.[§]

The outpost failed from the outset. Furs from the area were found to be inferior to those from colder climates farther inland and local trappers tended to hold out for the higher prices they could get at the coast.[12] Hankin, who was just twenty-four years old, was blamed in part for the

---

† See Map 8: Northern British Columbia.

‡ Many confuse Hankin's 1866-68 business location. He operated from a COT building at The Forks variously known as 'Mission Flats', 'Skeena Post', 'Ackwelget' and 'Fort Finlayson.' For example, on Dec. 20, 1867, Tsimshian entrepreneur Arthur Wellington Clah wrote, "I got Fort Finlayson HBC Ackwelget Mr. Hankin."

§ Two COT men, John McCutcheon and William McNeill (son of Captain McNeill and his first wife, Matilda, also a Nisga'a woman) spent almost exactly the same period of time at Fort Stager in Kispiox as caretakers of the fort (a large warehouse) containing tons of wire, supplies and other equipment (Fitzgerald, 61).

outpost's problems. Nevertheless, on August 14, 1867 the HBC reappointed Hankin as the Skeena postmaster until they closed the post for lack of business the following year.

Although some gold had been found in the Omineca during the 1860s, a significant find was not made until 1869. Six men known as 'The Peace River Prospecting Party' set out that spring from Quesnel, travelling what was known as the water route (up the Fraser River to the Nechako, then up the Stuart River to Fort St. James and on to Takla Lake via Stuart Lake and the Middle and Tachie rivers) as opposed to the overland route from The Forks.¶ Peter Dunlevy, Edgar Dewdney and Gustavus Blin-Wright grubstaked the party, which included former COT men, Vital Laforce, William Humphrey and Mike Byrnes. On June 21, Laforce discovered gold on a tributary of Silver Creek.

Laforce's discovery rekindled the HBC's interest in provisioning New Caledonia from the Skeena and, with the potential of hundreds of miners flocking to the Omineca, triggered the development in 1870 of two new settlements at the mouth of the Skeena: Woodcock's Landing and Port Essington. Meanwhile, Thomas Hankin and Robert Cunningham envisioned business opportunities for themselves in a partnership and resigned from the HBC.** They were clearly focused on an area they were familiar with—the Skeena Valley—with establishments at the mouth of the Skeena and 275 kilometres upriver at The Forks.

They moved quickly. In December 1870, Cunningham and Hankin wrote to the Chief Commissioner of Lands and Works in Victoria seeking to pre-empt 160 acres of land at The Forks and at Woodcock's Landing, also known as Skeena Mouth.†† It later became the site of the Inverness Salmon Cannery. Hankin also offered his services as "Postmaster…without remuneration…on the Skeena."[13] Hankin may have been in Victoria, for the governor accepted Hankin's offer the same day.[14] When the partners ran into problems with William Woodcock at Woodcock's Landing, they moved across the Skeena to Spokeshute, where Cunningham would build and create the town of Port Essington, while Hankin would build upriver at The Forks.[15]

In 1871 Hankin was courting Margaret MacAulay, the sixteen year-old daughter of veteran HBC employee Donald MacAulay (1805-1868). While at Fort Simpson, Donald MacAulay married Margaret Snaaxw (ca. 1819-1869), who was "…possibly from the Tlingit tribe on the Tongass River, Alaska."[16] MacAulay resigned from the HBC in September 1850. The family moved to Victoria where Donald worked in various capacities until he drowned in Esquimalt Harbour in 1868. The MacAulays had at least six children, all daughters. Their fifth, Margaret, was born at Victoria in 1855.

Thomas Hankin left Victoria for the upper Skeena in February or March 1871. He traveled via Fort Simpson and the Nass River to Gitlaxt'aamiks and hiked across the grease trail to The Forks of the Skeena.[17] The post office was probably located at Port Essington, but may have been at Hazelton.[18] Meanwhile, Cunningham and Hankin's first business advertisement appeared in

---

¶ See Map 9: Routes to the Omineca Gold Fields.

** Robert Cunningham resigned from the HBC during the 1871 outfit year (HBCA Arch. B.226/g/14-18). Because an outfit year ran from June 1 to May 31, it is possible he resigned late in the fall of 1870.

†† See Map 5: Skeena River Watershed.

a Victoria newspaper on May 4, 1871, located their operations at "Skeena Mouth and Forks of Skeena, BC" with no mention of Hazelton.

The partners must have realized that the COT site at The Forks, while suitable for conducting business with trappers, would be less convenient for miners bound for the Omineca. Hankin therefore built his store and house along the left bank of the Skeena about a kilometre north at a location that had practical advantages over The Forks.

The trail from The Forks to Fort Babine required men and animals loaded with equipment to cross the Bulkley River at the Hagwilget Canyon Bridge or swim the river farther up at Mosquito Flats. At Hankin's new location, freight canoes and eventually larger vessels could easily off load, eliminating the need to cross the Bulkley River. The influx of men was expected to be large. In 1870 ninety-one gold seekers had taken the Skeena River route to the Omineca and hundreds more were expected in 1871.[19]

The partners hired the Tsimshian entrepreneur Arthur Wellington Clah to convey their cargo by canoe.[20] Clah was a student of and mentor to William Duncan—Duncan taught Clah to write and Clah taught Duncan Tsimshian. Clah traveled widely throughout northwest BC on fur trading, prospecting and freighting ventures between 1859 and 1881.[21] He kept a diary that is now an important record of the villages he visited and the business he conducted. Through his diary, we learn much about the man:

> During his long life Clah witnessed and grappled with the consequences of the imposition of colonial structures on the Tsimshian world. Rooted initially in the fur trade, his colonial encounters were later shaped by wage labour, industrial technology, missionary activity, and the apparatus of the modern state.[22]

It took Clah and his men twenty-five days to ferry Cunningham & Hankin's freight to the upper Skeena. Clah left Skeena Mouth May 11, 1871 with four Haida canoes and eight tons of freight. He said his destination was 'Hazelton', which may be the first written record of the newly built town's name.[23] Clah made two more trips to Hazelton during 1871, carrying miners and supplies bound for the Omineca.

Hankin and Cunningham were so busy that Hankin could not take the time to return to Victoria. Instead he met Margaret at the north end of Vancouver Island at Fort Rupert where they married June 20, 1871. They then left for Hazelton and prepared for the increase in business the miners would bring.

The colonial government was supportive of mineral development and took a keen interest in the Omineca mines. Civil engineer Edgar Dewdney (1835-1916) emigrated from England to BC in 1859. He became the sixth lieutenant governor of the Northwest Territories (1881-1888), and the fifth lieutenant governor of BC (1892-1897). In the fall of 1870, he was on the upper Fraser River:

> I was determined to go...to the mines and prospected for myself and located some mining grounds. Then I returned to Tatla Lake landing and had returned there only a few days when the lakes froze and I was able to get back on snowshoes. I

came down to Victoria. The Government asked me to make a report of the mines, which I did, and the following spring they were anxious to get easy access into the mines to furnish supplies to the miners, and they asked me to explore a route from the mouth of the Skeena, which falls into the Pacific about the north end of Queen Charlotte Islands.[24]

In the spring of 1871, Dewdney set out for the Omineca, travelling by ship from Victoria to Port Essington and by canoe up the Skeena. At the Forks, Dewdney "…laid out a town called Hazelton…and [the 190 mile] road from there into the Omineca Mines."[25] The thirteen-acre townsite was situated along the left bank of the Skeena, less than a kilometre above the Bulkley confluence, and grew quickly. When Charles Horetzky arrived in 1872, about twenty log cabins of various sizes and shapes had been built within the townsite.

Business was booming for Cunningham & Hankin (C&H). Nearly 500 miners passed through Hazelton on their way to the Omineca (another 400 took the Fraser River route) in 1871.[26] Twenty miners are known to have wintered at Hazelton in 1872. The next fall, about 100 miners left the Omineca, wintered at Hazelton and went north to the Cassiar in the spring.[27] But interest in the Omineca dwindled. By 1881 the number of men working there had fallen to about 100, some of whom had pre-empted land and built homes at Hazelton but continued to work their Omineca diggings over the next thirty years or more.[28]

Hankin built his house and store at the north end of Hazelton where St. Peter's Church now stands. A 'Mr. McK' (presumably Omineca gold miner, Charles McKinnon) built next to Hankin. The town boasted a saloon "…which formed the favourite resort of the residents during their hours of leisure, when 'poker', 'euchre' and 'forty-five' absorbed the attention of the jovial and reckless population."[29]

A friendly man, Hankin often welcomed travellers into his home. For example, when photographer Charles Horetzky† showed up in Hazelton at midnight on December 18 he was greeted by Thomas Hankin who poured him a "homeopathic dose of hot-scotch…." The next morning Hankin introduced Horetzky to Margaret, whom he found, "…a very nice, agreeable person, who seconded her husband's endeavors towards my comfort."[30]

Hankin convinced Horetzky that he should spend Christmas and New Years at Hazelton, as celebrations had begun and guides would not travel until the New Year. Horetzky spent the next two weeks visiting nearby villages. His photographs and notes of the area provide an important record about Hazelton and the Gitxsan and Wet'suwet'en peoples.

Horetzky mentioned Gitanmaax as being "A little below Hazelton…but of small extent, and, like that of the Achwylget, it was also abandoned by its usual denizens [for the winter]. Those were the first really large and well-built dwellings of Indians I had yet met with…."[31]

---

† Horetsky was the official photographer for Sir Sandford Fleming during the Canadian Pacific Survey. Departing Fort Edmonton in September 1872, he walked west through the Omineca and on to the Pacific coast, arriving at Fort Simpson in January 1873.

An 1890s sketch of the Hagwilget suspension bridge by Indian Agent R. E. Loring. (Image A-04018 courtesy of the RBCM & A)

Horetzky, with Hankin, McKinnon and an Indian helper, toured the area for several days. At Kispiox they examined the stores of telegraph wire the COT had abandoned in Fort Stager. On their return, they visited Hagwilget:

> Several bands of Indians live and hunt in the vicinity of The Forks. They are generally of a peaceable disposition, and work for the whites with alacrity and goodwill. About three miles from Hazelton and three hundred feet down in the rocky bed of the Watsonqua, there is a large Indian ranche, or village, of some twenty houses, called the 'Achwylget.'
>
> Immediately in front of it the Indians have thrown a suspension bridge across the rocky chasm, through which the waters of the Watsonqua rush with impetuous haste towards the Skeena.…Several very elaborately carved and lofty crest poles stand in front of the principal houses of this ranche. Those are generally hewn out of large pines, often sixty feet in height, and from base to top are carved many curious figures, representing bears, toads, fish and creatures of mystical origin. Some of the carving is so well done as to equal the best work I have ever seen executed by the New Zealanders, who excel in that art. The carvers of those poles often spend many months in their construction, and the amount of ingenuity displayed and labour expended varies directly as the rank and wealth of the chief whose motto or crest they are intended to represent.…The houses are of great size, but with few pretensions to comfort, and always have a large fire-place in the middle, round which from fifty to one hundred persons can find accommodation…These large ranches are generally deserted during the winter months, when the Indians retire

to the shelter of the woods, where fuel is more easily obtained, and the trapping of different furred animals can be prosecuted with advantage.[32]

Sometime between Horeztky's visit in 1872 and George Dawson's visit in 1878, the Gitxsan rebuilt their village on the bench above Thomas Hankin's store. The move may have begun in 1875, as "George Dorsey states that the old village of Gitanmaax just above the junction of the Skeena and Bulkley River was destroyed by fire in 1876, though shortly before the people had started to build a little further above the river on a low bluff overlooking the Skeena."[33]

This photo, taken sometime after 1900, shows St. Peter's Anglican Church and the rebuilt village of Gitanmaax on the bench just above. (Image A-06053 courtesy of RBCM & A)

George Dawson was born in Pictou, Nova Scotia. His father, a geologist, was appointed principal of Montreal's McGill College in 1855. By age ten, Dawson suffered from tuberculosis of the spine. Despite the stunted growth this produced, Dawson became a geologist and led remarkable field surveys throughout much of Canada. In 1879, he conducted a topographical and geological survey from Fort Simpson to the Peace River and Edmonton. He arrived at The Forks of the Skeena in June, spent several days in the area and described Hazelton as he found it then:

> The Forks, or Hazelton, is situated on the left bank of the Skeena, a short distance above the junction of the Watsonkwa. It stands on an extensive flat elevated ten

or fifteen feet above the river, and at the base of a higher terrace, which rises very steeply to a height of 170 feet. Two or three traders live here, and there is an Indian village of about half-a-dozen barn-like buildings, each accommodating several families. The Indian village is quite new, and there are no carved posts, though the people speak of erecting some soon. The old village, where carved posts are still standing, is about a quarter of a mile further down stream.[34]

The summer temperature of the region about The Forks is often high. According to Mr. Hankin, a trader who has resided many years at this place, snow generally falls in October, but melts again, the winter snow not coming till about the middle of December. The winter is in general steadily cold, though there is almost always a thaw in February. The thermometer has been known to reach forty degrees below zero of Fahrenheit, and to remain for days at a time below -30°.…A few cattle and horses have been wintered here, the former requiring to be fed for five months, the latter have been kept by clearing away the snow to a certain depth in strips to allow them to scrape for grass.…The Skeena usually opens during the last week of April or the first week of May. Ice begins to run in the river early in November, but the river does not generally freeze till the end of December .… In 1867 the river closed on the 13th of November, which was exceptionally early. The river is generally highest in July, deriving most of its water from the melting snow of the mountains. It is lowest immediately after the ice goes.[35]

Of the Watsonkwa River, which joins the Skeena from the southeastward at The Forks, Mr. Cambie reports that the valley throughout its entire length is in part prairie and sustains a magnificent growth of grass, but is subject to frequent frosts and unsuited to agriculture.[36]

Gamayam/Charles Mark was five or six years old in 1873 when he first met Thomas Hankin. Charles and his parents were returning to Gitsegukla. They had been on the Nass River making grease:

[We]…were returning by the Kitwancool [Gitanyow] road…I was but a small boy and as I was going along, I had come across a great pile of manure and I could not make out what it was. I asked if it was a bear's, but [my mother] said, "No, it is white man's *gyuwadan* [horse]. There are white men ahead of us." There was a nice particular place and the white man had camped there, so the horses might feed.[37]

This was the first time Charles had seen horses. He could not understand why their backs looked strange. He thought they were "gouged out" but was told the horses had saddles on. One of the white men came up to Charles's father, spoke to him in Tsimshian and gave him tobacco. Charles was surprised that the white man understood his father and asked if he knew him. His father said, "Yes. His name is Tom."[38] Charles and his parents continued on to Gitanyow and

Gitsegukla, while Hankin and his party took the trail across country to Hazelton via the Kispiox River at Gitangwalkw (near the Sweetin River confluence).

Charles had more stories to tell about Hankin:

> My grandfather and this man were very good friends. In fact, they called themselves brothers. Each spring the white man would take his canoe and would go in his canoe sometime right to Victoria and get goods. And…on the way down he would camp at Guxsan's house. He always made a point of camping, when going and coming, at Guxsan's house. He was the white man that started the freight canoes up and down the river. Years afterwards, the white men came and there was another white man named Yeoman. He also had a store. There was another white man. His name was Welsh. He had a store. Then there was another white man. He had a saloon. His name was Slater. Tom Hankin always had his freight canoe and Indians to freight for him. And Charles Yeoman had his canoe and Indians freighting for him.[39]

Hankin lacked feed for his horses and was ill prepared for Hazelton winters. The horses died during the winter and in the spring, Hankin went to "Gitgalaxan on Fraser Lake", where he bought four more horses. These he intended to winter at Madii Lii, about thirty kilometres east of Hazelton on the Babine Trail. Meanwhile, as Charles said, "[Hankin] went up to Gisgamaawin and staked land for his own."[40]

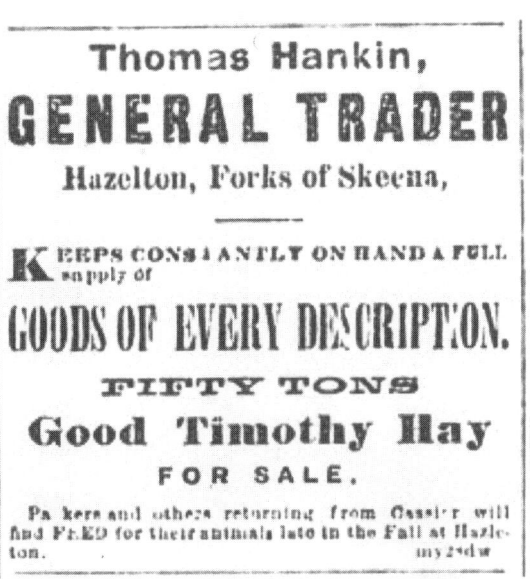

An ad placed by Thomas Hankin in a Victoria newspaper. He lacked feed for his horses in his second Hazelton winter and lost them; subsequently he and others began to grow hay locally.

After losing his horses, Hankin must have realized that livestock would need locally grown hay to survive Hazelton winters. Perhaps he foresaw that pack animals would also be needed for the Omineca mines. Some bottomland along the Skeena had great agricultural potential, especially in the vicinity of today's Glen Vowell. In 1870, Gisgamaawin was a large meadow along the left bank of the Skeena opposite Glen Vowell. By clearing away brush and trees, Gisgamaawin would have hay potential. On July 17, 1874, Hankin applied for 320 acres at Gisgamaawin.

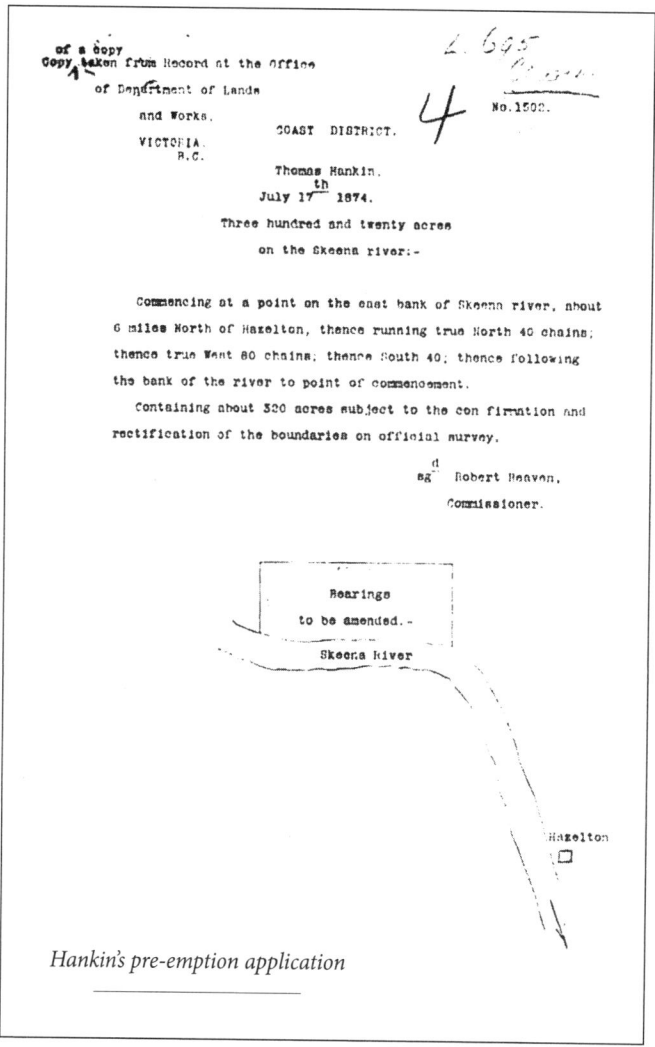

Hankin's pre-emption application

It would have been difficult for Hankin to stake land without the permission or knowledge of the Gitxsan who owned it. According to Woosimlaxha/Jimmy Williams, "He never bought that place. Old Robinson [a former Woosimlaxha, ca. 1841-1923] is the one who placed...the Hankins there."[41]

According to Charles Mark, Hankin hired young men from Kispiox and had them clear his land at Gisgamaawin. Afterwards, he moved his horses to the ranch.[42]

Hankin also got involved in the management of a salmon cannery at Woodcock's Landing (aka Inverness), as Charles Mark explained:

> Tom had another history at Gwinax'hlo'otw [Inverness], the place of sliding earth at the mouth of the River. He would close the store up here for the [summer] season and he went there for his other store.† That was where he died…down at the cannery. And his place up here and horses and store was sold to the Church of England.
>
> And they used the store for the Church. Bishop Ridley bought it from the mother. He never once all the time he was here, had to fight or to row with the Indians. And his wife came back and took the land at Gisgamaawin. This is the story of the first white man that they saw.[43]

By 1880, Hankin divided his time between Hazelton and Inverness. However, his days among the Gitxsan were not exactly as Charles Mark described. Perhaps the presence of Hankin's daughter influenced what Mark had to say and, in any event, it should be kept in mind that Constance Cox translated and perhaps recorded at least some of Mark's interviews and may have influenced the narrative.

Hankin was no doubt a friend of the Gitxsan and Wet'suwet'en peoples, but as a man with business interests in the area, he did experience some difficulties as an 1878 petition signed by him and four Hazelton businessmen reveals:

> Hazelton Forks Skeena 12 July 1878
>
> To the Honourable Albert Norton Richards
> Lieut. Govr of British Columbia
>
> Your Honour
>
> This petition shewith that whereas the petitioners have for some years past been constantly annoyed by the depredations committed by the Indians of this place and the surrounding villages, and have frequently written to the authorities concerning the same; and having received no satisfaction
>
> We now petition your Honour to grant us redress by the [r]esidence of some competent authority who can punish the Indians or "others" when the law is violated—
>
> And in duty bound we will ever pray—
>
> Some of the acts of violence that have been committed are as follows:
>
> The killing of Cattle, breaking into stores, Stealing from packs entrusted to their care having been open and their contents stolen, on two occasions to the amount of several hundred dollars—

---

† A cannery according to Constance Cox.

We Further Beg, that notice is taken of this petition, because if not it will compel us to abandon our Homes and property and the government then (we feel sure) will see that one dollar spent now will save twenty that will have to be expended on a future day—

We would also mention that the Indians numbering some 300 at this place alone are now building their houses on land owned by us and we have no power to help ourselves and in fact we are powerless from the absence of all law to hold our legal rights.

And Further, that This is a Government Townsite "laid" off by a Gov'mt surveyor in 1871 and Licences and Taxes are very carefully collected from us every year.

We feel confident that this petition will [be] duly answered before trouble increases.

Also, that the Indians in this place would if a resident authority where [sic] here, would willingly submit to that power and consequently save a great deal of future trouble and expense—

Thomas Hankin
Amos C. Youmans
William J. Walker
A. Hawin
Duncan McDermid[44]

Margaret O'Neill (Boss) painted this scene of Hankin's ranch ca. 1900 likely from the right bank of the Skeena at Glen Vowell, looking east across the river. (Lorraine O'Leary coll.)

Thomas Hankin died without leaving a will in 1885. Four years after his death and little more than a month after Margaret's subsequent marriage to the Babine Agency Indian Agent, Richard Loring, an October 1889 certificate listed improvements to the Hankin property at Gisgamaawin: "4 Dwelling Houses, 1 School House, 1 Barn, 2 underground cellars, and 100 acres under fence and cleared and under cultivation."[†]

---

† Margaret, along with Thomas's sons and daughters were heirs to the property. Margaret (Hankin) Loring and several local men signed and witnessed a declaration of improvements in October 1889. Constance Cox may have held title after Margaret's death in 1910. In 1920 Constance sold the property to her brother, Arthur Hankin.

ENDNOTES

1. Walbran, 227.
2. "Barbeau and Beynon Fieldnotes", Constance Cox (B-F-79.10).
3. Duff, 3.
4. Cox, 1954, 4.
5. Smith, 37.
6. PABC: Colonial Correspondence 1857-1872, H.H. Berens letter to Gov. Douglas May 1858, GR1372, F704.
7. PABC. Thomas Hankin and C.T. Seymour. Pre-emption application 1863 GR 1182, file 1, p. 22.
8. HBCA. Finlayson to Manson, Victoria 1866 B.226/b/35.
9. HBCA. Fort Simpson Journal, B.201/a/9.
10. HBCA. Fort Simpson Journal, B.201/a/9.
11. HBCA. Fort Simpson Journal, B.201/a/9.
12. HBCA. Finlayson to Tolmie 1868.
13. PABC, Colonial Correspondence, Hankin to Governor Feb. 1871, B1332/708.
14. PABC. Colonial Correspondence, Governor to Hankin Feb. 1871, B1332/708.
15. Large, 36.
16. Hanna, 16.
17. Large, 34.
18. Deaville, 146.
19. Trueman, 182.
20. Galois, "Colonial Encounters".
21. Galois, "Colonial Encounters". Also see Brock.
22. Galois, "Colonial Encounters".
23. Galois, "Colonial Encounters", 125, Table 3.
24. Canada. Select Senate Committee Report, 123.
25. Canada. Select Senate Committee Report, 123.
26. Trueman, 183.
27. Trueman, 184.
28. Canada: 1881 Census, BC, Cariboo Division 188, F2, S.D. Omineca.
29. Horetzky, 105-6.
30. Horetzky, 99.
31. Horetzky, 105.
32. Horetzky, 103-5.
33. MacDonald, 42.
34. Dawson, 16b.
35. Dawson, 18b–19b.
36. Dawson, 19b.
37. "Barbeau and Beynon Fieldnotes", Charles Mark and Mrs. Cox 1923, B-F-658.1.
38. "Barbeau and Beynon Fieldnotes", Charles Mark and Mrs. Cox 1923, B-F-658.1.
39. "Barbeau and Beynon Fieldnotes", Charles Mark and Mrs. Cox 1923, B-F-658.1.
40. "Barbeau and Beynon Fieldnotes", Charles Mark and Mrs. Cox 1923, B-F-658.1.
41. "Barbeau and Beynon Fieldnotes", Jimmy Williams n.d. B-F-78.4; A-VII-67a (iv) a.
42. "Barbeau and Beynon Fieldnotes", Charles Mark B-F-658.1.
43. "Barbeau and Beynon Fieldnotes", Charles Mark B-F-658.1.
44. PABC. Correspondence Inward, 1878.

Part III

The Confluence

Raymattja Marika (ca. 1959-2008), a native of Yirkalla in Australia's Northern Territory, was an aboriginal leader, scholar, educator, translator, linguist and grandmother. Aptly described as a bridge between cultures in Australia, Marika said:

Some of our ideas for our [teachings] come from theory related to the Ganma Lagoon. Ganma is firstly a place; it is an area within the mangroves where the salt water coming in from the sea meets the stream of fresh water coming down from the land. Ganma is a still lagoon. The water circulates silently underneath, and there are lines of foam circulating across the surface. The swelling and retreating of the tides and the wet season floods can be seen in the two bodies of water.

Water is often taken to represent knowledge in Yolngu philosophy. What we see happening…is a process of knowledge production where we have two different cultures, Balanda (European) and Yolngu, working together. Both cultures need to be presented in a way where each one is preserved and respected.[1]

Like Marika's analogy, the Gitxsan confluence of river and sea—of K'amksi'wa and Aluugigat—brings an inevitable cultural mingling, but does not bring an inevitable drowning of Gitxsan history, land, culture and values.

The Gitxsan people faced seemingly insurmountable obstacles for over a century, yet we prevailed legally and can do so socially, economically and politically. We are at a turning point and should make the right and proper choices about how we want the Gitxsan nation and territory to look fifty years from now; choices about what we want to change, create, protect and sustain. This we owe to future Gitxsan generations.

CHAPTER FOURTEEN

Missionaries, Merchants and Miners

By 1881 the old village of Gitanmaax had been vacated by the Gitxsan in favour of the new village they built on the first bench northeast of the townsite of Hazelton. In that same year the first Canada Census was conducted in BC. It included the enumeration of aboriginal people and therefore is the first written record of the Gitxsan nation which numbered 1451 citizens as follows:

- Kitwanga (Gitwangak)   199
- Kitwancool (Gitanyow)   212
- Kitseguecla (Gitsegukla) 196
- Gitanmaax   183
- Kispiox   334
- Kisgegas   270
- Kuldo   57

Rev. Robert Tomlinson conducted the upper Skeena census.† He was living with his family at the mission village of Ankitlas, a short distance up the Kispiox River from its junction with the Skeena. Having spent twelve years among the Nisga'a and Gitxsan, he was fluent in the language and had developed his own orthography.

Tomlinson's work made the 1881 census unique: he recorded the aboriginal names and occupations of 1451 Gitxsan men, women and children then living in seven Gitxsan villages.

---

† It appears that Tomlinson's job was to enumerate only the Gitxsan population in 1881, which he did very well. Unfortunately, the 1891 enumerator did a very bad job of the upper Skeena aboriginal census, making it impossible to determine who was who, or to compare it with the 1881 census.

Robert Tomlinson worked for the Anglican Church Missionary Society beginning in 1867, first with William Duncan in Metlakatla and then at Gingolx (Kincolith) for nine years before starting the mission community of Ankitlas near Kispiox. He also started the mission village of Meanskinisht near Cedarvale. (Image B-07583 courtesy of RBCM & A)

The table below is an example of Tomlinson's work at Gitanmaax. The village had twenty houses with 183 people in forty-six families.† As their contemporary names reveal, many of these individuals played significant roles individually and collectively throughout the next three-quarters of a century, as did leaders in the other six Gitxsan communities.

1881 Gitanmaax Village Census[2]

Building Number	No. of Families / Occupants	Occupants	Contemporary Spelling & Remarks
1	One/3	Niguis Wellis, M, 25	Niguis (father of) "Wellis"
		Nox Wellis, F, 25	Nox (mother of) "Wellis"
2	Two/9	Eeq, M, 45	
3	Three/9	Caldayn, M, 50	

---

† Some of the families relocated to Gitanmaax from other Gitxsan villages, notably Kuldo and Kisgegas. I have added relational and lifespan information where possible.

1881 Gitanmaax Village Census[2]

Building Number	No. of Families / Occupants	Occupants	Contemporary Spelling & Remarks
4	One/6	Weilacha[§], M, 40	Kispiox Jim: "Packer & Miner."
		Nox Zahan, F, 20	Second wife of Kispiox Jim
		Weilacha, M, 16	Wiilaxhaa, Charles Martin.[¶]
		Minskoks, F, 11	Minhl Ts'uusx, later Margaret Kispiox
5	One/3	Illegible	
6	One/3	Illegible	
7	Three/12	Nikadayn	Nikateen
8	Five/17	Lootquezewast, F, 50	Luutkuts'iiwus
9	One/5	Weehatach, F, 80	
10	One/4	Negwaon, M, 50	Nagwa'uun
11	Six/22	Benix, M, 40	Biinix
		Getumcauldalth, M, 70	Gidumgaldo, formerly Skawats'eekx
		Nox Ladai, F, 45	Nox Ladaix
		Ladai, M, 20	Ladaix, James Lattie (1861-1908)
		Maikt, M, 10	Probably Beal Muldoe (1871-1954)
		Caskai, M, 6	Possibly Billy Muldon (1875-1919)
		Bilshaylack, M, 4	Tommy Muldoe (1877-1955)
		Lacktathl, M, 2	
12	Three/10	Squehatach, M, 35	Guuhadak
13	Two/12	Actezaich	Axtiits'eek
14	Four/17	Spauk, M, 35	Spookxw
15	Two/6	Shanaush, M, 30	Shanoss, possibly Moses Shanoss.
16	Two/8	Weeauble, M, 50	Wiigoobil, possibly Charles Oop
		Nox Daow, F, 45	Nox Doo
		Nox Jacksh, F, 25	?
		Daow, F, 10	Doo
		Ishnotux, M, 8	Ishnotux
17	One/8	Medeekumget, M, 50	Madiigam Gyat
18	One/4	Illegible	

1881 Gitanmaax Village Census[2]

Building Number	No. of Families / Occupants	Occupants	Contemporary Spelling & Remarks
19	One/5	John Thomas Wade, M, 35	Episcopalian
20	Five/20	Zeen, M, 65	Ts'iin
		Nox Quishskan, F, 20	Nox Gwis Sgan
		Haatq, M, 50	Haa'atxw, father of Billy Owen and Abel Oakes
		Nox Day, F, 35	Nox Dee, mother of Abel Oakes
		Deadix, M, 2	Dii'atix, child name of Abel Oakes

The village of Gitanmaax with twenty houses, forty-six families and 183 persons

FOOTNOTES

§ Should probably read, "Niguis (father of) Weilacha".

¶ Charles Martin was probably fifteen in 1881 for in 1920 he told Marius Barbeau that he "…was born at the time of the building of the Great N. Telegraph (B-F-89.26, p. 14). The year of his birth, 1866, is relevant as Chapter 15 is devoted to a chronology of Martin's life experiences.

Tomlinson (1842-1913) was born into a well-to-do family in Dublin. He was Roman Catholic, but "…for some reason disagreed with the church and defied his enraged father to become a protestant, an Anglican rector."[3] After his father disinherited him, Tomlinson studied medicine and took jobs to support himself while he comforted families during the Irish famine. He graduated from Dublin's Trinity College and "…was ordained a deacon but never received his full priestly orders."[4] Tomlinson volunteered as a medical missionary and was ordered "…by the Church Missionary Society (CMS) to assist William Duncan in northern BC."[5]

The CMS sent Duncan to Fort Simpson in 1858, and within a few years he had many aboriginal followers. He played an important but controversial role for the church in colonial BC.[†] Although Tomlinson and Duncan had very different backgrounds, they had much in common when it came to their evangelical philosophies, and they both came into conflict with William Ridley when the CMS appointed him bishop of the Diocese of Caledonia in 1879.

Tomlinson arrived in BC in 1867. He was anxious to get on with his work at Metlakatla but met sixteen-year-old Irish-born Alice Woods in Victoria with whom he promptly fell in love. Robert wished to marry Alice but her father, Reverend Charles Woods, said they should wait until

---

† See Chapter Fifteen.

they had spent some time apart. Robert went off to Duncan's Metlakatla where he came to know the Tsimshian and Nisga'a peoples and became fluent in their languages.

Tomlinson married Alice at Victoria in 1869. By then the CMS wished to establish missions among the aboriginal peoples along the Nass and Skeena rivers. Robert and Alice were chosen to begin their work in Gingolx (Kincolith) at the mouth of the Nass River. Robert Jr. was born there in February 1870, the first of their several children born in that village.

The family spent nine years at Gingolx before relocating to Kispiox on the Skeena River with the intent of establishing a mission there. Soon after they arrived, Tomlinson's horse kicked and broke the leg of a dog that belonged to one of Tomlinson's detractors. The owner created a ruckus and the villagers wanted to know why Tomlinson was there. Robert Tomlinson Jr. said:

> The people gathered for an open-air meeting to hear what father had to tell them and why he had come. He explained that he wished to start a mission, and he asked for a place to build a home for his family and later a church, hospital, etc. There was no satisfaction in the answers he received. There was a great deal of powowing among themselves. It was quite evident that the heathen elements were the stronger voices in the discussion. They wanted no interference in their affairs.[6]

Tomlinson retreated about seven kilometres up the Kispiox River where he founded the missionary village of Ankitlas. It became a thriving community. On Dominion Day,‡ Bishop Ridley, Thomas Hankin and others visited Ankitlas to participate in the festivities.

> The Bishop seemed to be very pleased with the progress that had been made at the Mission site. Everyone was in good spirits, and soon a game of rounders was in full swing.§ Father and Mr. Hankin on one side and the Bishop and Uncle Edward on the other. I was kept busy chasing after the batted ball. The Indians too played very well and seemed to enjoy seeing the good Bishop as he ran around the bases. It was great fun and a very welcome change for us all. After the picnic our visitors returned to The Forks.¶

Bishop Ridley, who had purchased Thomas Hankin's store for the CMS in 1880, liked visiting Hazelton, perhaps because it was a reprieve from conflicts he was having with William Duncan at Metlakatla. He remained in Hazelton after the picnic celebration and wrote Tomlinson a letter. He asked Tomlinson to "…abandon the work he was doing and move to The Forks to start a mission there among the Indians."[7] Tomlinson was distraught. He decided to appeal to the CMS and went to England where he was pleased with the reception he got and spent the balance of the winter promoting his Ankitlas mission throughout England and Ireland.

---

‡ There is confusion about the year this occurred. Robert Jr.'s notes give Dominion Day 1884, but elsewhere he gives 1883 as the year they left Ankitlas (Tomlinson, 15).

§ Rounders is a form of baseball using a hard rubber ball. When hit, it goes a great distance.

¶ Tomlinson, 10.

A CMS letter was waiting for Tomlinson when he returned to Ankitlas. It contained the news that Duncan had been let go by the CMS. Tomlinson was shocked. Although he may not have agreed with everything William Duncan was doing in Metlakatla, he respected his accomplishments. To make matters worse Bishop Ridley appointed a layperson, Mr. Falconer, to Hazelton and ordered Falconer "…to oppose [Tomlinson] in every way possible."[8]

When Falconer said he would follow the Bishop's orders, Tomlinson returned to Ankitlas and resigned from the CMS.[9] The family then moved to Metlakatla to work with Duncan and helped when Duncan and his followers relocated to Alaska in 1887. Tomlinson and his family later returned to the Skeena, where they built the mission village of Meanskinisht near Cedarvale.

By 1881, Tomlinson Sr. had spent twelve years among the Nisga'a and Gitxsan. Although he was fluent in the language, it was his second language.[10] On the other hand, Sim'algyax (the Nisga'a/Gitxsan language) could be thought of as Robert Jr.'s first language as he was born and raised among the Nisga'a at Gingolx and spent his teen and adult years among the Gitxsan. My Uncle Percy said that the Tomlinson and Hankin children, having learned the language forty years earlier than he did, spoke an earlier form of Gitxsan.

Although European values and customs were making inroads, the Gitxsan held to their traditions. Gidumgaldo had moved from Kuldo in the early 1800s to Gitanmaax where he was the leading chief.[11] In 1881 he and his house members erected the first of many totem poles at their new village on the bench above Hazelton. Marius Barbeau wrote, "Nola, also of the Lax See'l (Frog) phratry, was the earlier head chief of Gitanmaax, whom Gidumgaldo supplanted through his ability and success in the [feast]. Sanaw's household came into existence not long ago as a subdivision of the family of Gidumgaldo."[12]

Skawats'eekx was a member of the House of Gidumgaldo. He married a woman from the House of Wiik'aax and lived at Kisgegas during the 1870s.[†] The House wanted Skawats'eekx to move to Gitanmaax and assume the name 'Gidumgaldo' at their pole-raising feast. Skawats'eekx agreed and he and his relatives hired workers to secure an appropriate cedar tree and a Nisga'a man—Laxwillamuut—to carve the pole.[13]

The men felled the tree at Skanii'mahl'hoohl'gan (where the pole got stuck), near Gisgamaawin on the Kisgegas trail. They dragged the tree through the forest to the brow of the hill above the Skeena. The hill was steep and the tree got away on them, digging deep into the earth at the bottom of the hill, giving the place its Gitxsan name. The men shortened the tree and floated it down the river.[‡] This was the first pole erected at the new Gitanmaax village site on the bench above St. Peter's Church. Its name is *Ts'akim Eek* (Nose-like-Coho).[§]

Gwa'gayee/Mark Holland (1852-1922) was present during the feast when the pole was raised at the new Gitanmaax in 1881:

---

† Skawats'eekx was the father of Jimmy Ladaix and his brothers, Tommy, Beal and Billy Muldoe.

‡ Gidumgaldo/Charlie Clifford (1881-1953) said the tree dug into the ground, and the top was cut off to free it. He said the tree was floated down the Skeena to Hazelton (Ward and Toby Marshall, 1997).

§ The pole now stands beside the Hazelton Public Library on Government Street.

The raising of Gidumgaldo's pole on the banks of the Skeena at Gitanmaax in 1881 was captured in a sketch by Helen Woods, Robert Tomlinson's sister-in-law. The hill behind the longhouses is where the Gitanmaax cemetery is located. (Image B-00047 courtesy of RBCM & A)

Before this name [Gidumgaldo] was assumed, [Skawats'eek$\underline{x}$] invited five villages: Hagwilgate, Kispayaks, Kitwanga [Gitwangak], Kitwancool [Gitanyow], and Kitsegukla. At this time, they did not come all to the village of Gitanmaax at one time, but kept outside of the village. We were…across the river on the point at Gwints'ihl [Mission Flats].

The people of Git'anmaks came over and distributed food to us. They gave us salmon…After this the *Halaiyt* came out and went among all of the camp houses. After this was over the Gitanmaax returned to their village. And then the Gitanmaax people took and distributed the guests among the different houses of Gitanmaax. After all the belongings had been transported the people themselves came over and stayed on the beach as guests in front of the houses.

And then a *na$\underline{x}$no$\underline{k}$* came out of the house of Gidumgaldo. He was accompanied by all the other performers…and they came out where all the people were gathered on the beach. And there were also a number of women *Halaiyt* to come. They also stayed in front of all the guests. They were about one hour to perform before the guests. They dramatized each of the *naxnoks*.

Gidumgaldo had in his hand a bow and arrow and made mock shooting into the crowd. And then a person came out and shouted he will take [put up] Geel and Kliiyeemlaxha. And then Mool'xan and Wiiget came up, from Kitseguecla; and 'Qoq and Hlengwax (Ganada) of Gitwangax came after. And then Wiixa' (La$\underline{x}$ Gibuu) and Gamlaxyeltxw (Ganada) of Kitwancool. They were all called out and accepted in different houses. And they were called in by Gidumgaldo, who was getting to show them all his *naxnoks*…and of Axtii'am and Bil'amwi'ltxw. There was three in one group.[14]

This Gidumgaldo (formerly Skawats'eek<u>x</u>) died in 1914. He was perhaps ninety years old. Alexander Mowatt (1855-1915) succeeded him and James White (1871-1941) succeeded Mowatt.

After a twelve-year hiatus, the HBC finally returned to the upper Skeena in 1880. By then, not only was it more economical to provision its posts throughout New Caledonia from Hazelton, the company could also benefit by supplying miners in the Omineca gold fields. As Charles Mark said, "Then the Hudson Bay came. When Mrs. Welch [Walsh] left, the Hudson Bay bought them out and they had their store right in Mr. [Walsh's] store."[15] Alfred Sampare was a clerk at Babine Post in 1879 and was transferred to manage the Hazelton post in 1880.

Sampare, who was born in Quebec, had been in the northwest for many years. He and his wife, Bonita of Gitwangak, had a son, Robert, who was born in 1874.[16] In 1884 William Sinclair replaced Sampare who died before he could be appointed to another charge.[17] Charles W. D. Clifford (C.W.D) took charge of the Hazelton post in 1885. He served there until 1891 when J. H. Lyons was appointed.

Clifford was born in Leitrim, Ireland in 1842, one of six children.[18] His family later moved to London where Charles was educated and worked as a clerk in a London insurance office. But in 1862 gold lured him to the Cariboo.[19] By 1874, he was mining in the Omineca at Germansen Creek and at Vital Creek in 1882, where he appears to have remained until taking work with the HBC in Hazelton in 1885.[20]

By the 1870s some of the Omineca miners, including C.W.D, chose to spend their winters at Hazelton rather than make the longer journey south. While there, he met a woman from the House of Gidumgaldo who bore him a son—Charles Jr.—in 1881.† After Charles Jr.'s mother died, her sister Fanny raised him. Fanny's husband—John Thomas Wade—was aboriginal and worked with the CMS. They adopted Charles Jr. in June 1886.[21]

C.W.D later married Lucy Margaret McNeill,‡ the daughter of William McNeill and Mary MacAulay, on May 24, 1888 in Hazelton.[22] They had one child, Harriett Mary, born in 1890. In 1891, C.W.D was transferred to Fort Simpson and placed in charge of the Port Simpson District, which included Hazelton and the posts in New Caledonia.

When Dick Sargent arrived in Hazelton in 1891 to do the bookkeeping at the post, he found Joe Lyons, an old placer miner, in charge of the place. Sargent said, "He was a fine old man with a long white beard, well-liked by everyone."[23]

Joseph H. Lyons was born in the USA in 1830. He arrived in BC in 1858 during the Cariboo gold rush. Afterwards he mined in the Omineca for many years and wintered in Hazelton. He was still mining in the Omineca in August of 1891.[24] The HBC hired him as clerk-in-charge when he returned to Hazelton for the winter.

---

† Charles Clifford Jr.'s mother and Fanny were the sisters of Gidumgaldo/Alexander Mowatt.
‡ Lucy Margaret McNeill was a niece of Margaret MacAulay/Hankin/Loring.

He continued working for the HBC until the end of May 1896, when Dick Sargent took over. According to Sargent, Lyons immediately resumed gold mining and was still in the Omineca in 1901.[25]

Richard 'Dick' Sargent was born in Georgetown, PEI in 1873, the son of a clergyman who moved his family to the Qu'Appelle area of Saskatchewan during the late 1870s. In 1891 the HBC hired young Sargent, and he headed west by train to Victoria, where he received orders to go to Hazelton.

When he arrived, C.W.D, who was in charge of the district, was in Hazelton. He "remained for a few days," said Sargent, "and gave me instructions as to what I had to do and how it was to be done."[26]

Sargent found himself in a new community made up of a few recent settlers surrounded by aboriginal people. He was obviously adaptable for within a few years he was able to communicate fluently with the Gitxsan and Wet'suwet'en people in their languages.

The 1891 census enumerated on August 3 lists a total of eighteen Hazelton residents, including two families: Richard and Margaret (Hankin) Loring with their blended family of eight and John Field and his wife.[27] Other Hazelton residents—James May, Ezra Evans and Charles Rolls to name a few—were in the Omineca and would return to Hazelton in the fall.

On January 1, 1895 the HBC Hazelton diary listed the following residents in the upper Skeena area, perhaps forty in total:

> Hazelton: R.E. Loring, Esq., Indian Agent and Mrs. Loring and three children, Master Arthur Hankin; Rev. E. C. Stephenson; J. J. May, C. Rolls, Ezra Evans, W. K. Speer, W. B. Forrest, E. O. DeLong, O. M. Dutton, Enos Willman, George Nash, James Wells; Gabriel LaCroix and wife; Joe LaCroix, wife and two children; Master Joe Gardner; J. H. Lyon (HB Co); R.S. Sargent (HB Co)
>
> Kispiox: Rev. J.C. Spencer & wife
>
> Mouth of Haguelget [Mission Flats]: R. H. Cole
>
> 4 Mile Below Hazelton: A. McIntosh & family: Wm. Keynton & family
>
> Old Kitzeguecla: Rev. T. Neville
>
> Kitwangah: Rev. A. E. Price & family[28]

Dick Sargent knew all these people and spoke of them fondly.

One of the Hazelton pioneers missed in the HBC list was Ah Lumm, an early Omineca gold miner. He held a mining claim—Ah Lumm Company, Manson River 390—between June 1, 1870 and October 6, 1877. He spent his winters in Hazelton and was living with Noxs Oop/Esther Joseph in 1892. They had four children: Peter (1893), Thomas (1895), Donald (1899) and Jessie (1901), all with the surname Lumm.[29] Noxs Oop died in 1909, and her sister, Noxs Doo, raised the children.

Charlotte Sullivan, wing chief of Gidumgaldo and Ah Lumm's granddaughter (Jessie's daughter), told some of her family's story to Lily Chow in *Chasing Their Dreams*:

"[Ah Lumm] had claims in the Manson Creek area. But my mother and grandma always stayed in Hazelton. We assume that grandpa traveled back and forth between Manson Creek and Hazelton all the time."

Ah Lum was born in Guangdong, China, on October 13, 1843, and came to Canada in 1868. In the census he was listed as a Buddhist who spoke Chinese [presumably Cantonese]. On the Hudson's Bay Company records, Ah Lum is listed as having earned about $300 in six months. Perhaps Ah Lum, like other Chinese miners of his time, also trapped animals and sold the fur to the Hudson's Bay Company.

R.S. (Dick) Sargent worked for the Hudson's Bay Company for several years before opening his own store in the late 1890s. (Image E-06566 courtesy of RBCM & A)

The Ah Lum family did not speak Chinese but Chinook…Sullivan said her mother often talked about Ah Lum coming home with gold. [Jessie] remembered Ah Lum once giving her a good size gold nugget when he returned from the gold field. He made a piece of jewelry out of it and tied it to a silk handkerchief for his little daughter. [Jessie] loved the gift and always carried it with her.

Unfortunately, Esther Joseph died when [Jessie] was only nine years old. After his wife passed away, Ah Lum wanted to take [Jessie] and the youngest brother to China. The young boy did not want to go. Ah Lum, realizing that [Jessie] would be lonely and miserable without her brother in an unfamiliar country, decided against the plan. Finally he returned to China without his children, but maintained communication with them.

"Whenever my mother and uncles received a letter from their dad, they were excited and eager to know what he wrote. But they could not read Chinese characters, so they usually took the letter to grandpa's Chinese friends in Hazelton or in Smithers who would translate for them," said Sullivan. After Ah Lum went back to China, an aunt raised the children on reserve.

"My mother [Jessie] did not have a very pleasant life in the native community," said Sullivan. "She was often looked down on because she had mixed blood in her veins. Regardless, she was a very strong person and held her head up high. All of us children love and respect her. She has been a very good mom to us."[30]

Jessie lived to ninety-three. She married four times: first to Simon Wright in an arranged marriage; then Thomas Danes, Gus Wahlstrom, and finally, to my grandfather, Charlie Sterritt in 1956.

Bronwen Patenaude researched the Cariboo gold rush and its participants extensively and wrote several excellent books about Barkerville and the Cariboo District.[†] One of her books, *The Gold Miner's Journal* (2004), was written as historical fiction. Her account of James J. May's family and his travels matches my research:

James May was born in Tennessee in 1832, the son of William and Elizabeth May. The family moved to Iowa in 1847…"because Tennessee was getting too crowded…By 1848 we had settled on another farm…where I helped to clear the land, and planted corn. The next spring we heard about gold in California and I left home to get some," said Jim.

"When we finally reached California it was hard to find a claim, the country was so overcrowded with prospectors. Later we managed to get mining on a worthwhile claim, and made lots of money. Following that I travelled back home, and gave my family a fair share of my earnings, well, at least they would never again want for anything….Then my buddies and I heard about gold on the Frazer River, in Canada, British Columbia. We travelled by way of the Columbia River, and reached Thompson River in the spring of 1859."

Jim made his way to Lillooett where he "…met John Rose, Ranald McDonald, and an Englishman named Billy Barker, who were all mining there."[31]

Jim and a party of five prospectors (Rose, McDonald, Doc Keithley, John McLean and Bill Cunningham) headed north to Quesnelle Forks where they built a cabin and settled in for the winter. In the spring, they travelled east prospecting. Doc Keithley struck it rich not far from Quesnelle Forks, and George Weaver did the

---

† In June 2014, I phoned Mrs. Patenaude's home and reached a relative, who said Patenaude had spent endless hours researching Barkerville pioneers, and her house was full of old Barkerville newspapers and miners' journals. Patenaude's account is supported by the 1840 and 1850 USA federal census.

A Sterritt family outing to Vancouver. (L – R) Margaret Heath, the author's aunt, Jessie (Lumm) Sterritt and Charlie Sterritt. (Bill Heath photo)

same further on. The rest of us "…kept climbing and prospecting, over French Snowshoe and Little Snowshoe Mountain until we discovered Antler Creek.…It was late fall when we came across the sun burned nuggets sticking out of the dirt on the side of the creek. We couldn't believe it at first, the gold was so plentiful.… There was also lots of antlers of 'Caribou' on the ground near the creek, and for want of a better name, we called our rich find 'Antler Creek.'"[32]

By 1863, May was in the Omineca. Ezra Evans and Pete Toy were considered outstanding prospectors. These two men, along with William Cust and Edward Cary, had found a gold-bearing gravel bar on the Finlay River—named Toy's Bar—in 1862, and by "1863 more than 150 men were in the Peace River area, among them such notables as 'Twelve-foot' Davis and James May."[33] In August 1870, May, with T. Germansen, D. McMartin and W. Smith established the Discovery Bench Company to work their claim on Germansen Creek.

May began wintering in Hazelton as soon as the town was established and, apart from his annual treks to the Omineca, Hazelton was his home. He lived with Mary McKenzie (1869-1918) and Mary Ann, her daughter.[†] The family was in the Omineca in 1901. A few years later he retired, dying in Hazelton in 1917.

The alienation of Gitxsan land began when Edgar Dewdney surveyed the Hazelton townsite in 1871 and continued, albeit slowly at first, when Thomas Hankin sought to pre-empt 320 acres of land at Gisgamaawin in 1874. Others began to squat along the Skeena and Kispiox rivers and by about 1900, some pre-empted the land they were living on. Meanwhile, during the summer of

---

† Mary Ann (Molly) May (1895-1962) married Walter Bob Robinson and was the mother of Louise, Margaret (Maggie), Steve, Bill, Ronny, Perry and Joyce.

1891, Peter O'Reilly, on behalf of the Indian Reserve Commission, began laying out reserves on the upper Skeena.

O'Reilly arrived in BC from Ireland in 1858 and worked as a stipendiary magistrate at Fort Langley and Fort Hope as well as in the Cariboo during the gold rush years. He was appointed to the Indian Reserve Commission in 1880 and served in that capacity until 1898.[34] He allocated over 600 reserves during his tenure, including twelve on the upper Skeena in the Babine Agency during the summer of 1891 (See table below).

These were the first reserves within Gitxsan territory and eventually, with additional reserves laid out for timber and fishing stations, the gross acreage would nearly double. The reserve at the village of Gitanmaax was "…only separated from the Hazelton townsite by a space of thirty-eight feet. The latter is practically environed by the Get-an-max Reserve, the waterfront excepted. The area of the reserve is [3,367] acres."[35]

Gitxsan Reserves and Population 1891[36]

Name of Band	No. of Reserves	Population	Gross Acreages
Kis py oux	1	236	2,252
Hazelton [Gitanmaax]	4	233	3,367
Kit se guec la	3	83	3,103
Kit wan gar	4	141	2,994
Total	12	693	11,716

The 1893 annual report not only listed the size of reserves, but also included population counts. Gitanmaax had a total population of 233, but all who lived there weren't necessarily counted:

> The band proper only counts sixty-five, the remainder of the population being composed of other bands settled here on account of intermarriage and the inducement of the facility in finding employment. There are sixty-eight log and nine frame houses…[and] twenty acres of land under cultivation and broken up …They follow packing into the interior, boating, mining, sawing lumber, getting out cordwood and working about the canneries of the coast, also hunting and trapping.[37]

Peter O'Reilly retired in 1898 and Arthur Wellesley Vowell, also from Ireland, was appointed Indian Reserve Commissioner. As historian Cole Harris pointed out:

> When Vowell took over, relations between Ottawa and Victoria over Native matters had become, if anything, more sour than ever. The reversionary issue

(federal versus provincial control of lands removed from reserves) was much in the air, also the province's view that reserves were already too ample. An early request from Vowell to the chief commissioner of lands and works not to alienate land in part of the Babine agency until he could lay out reserves there, drew the response that the province was entirely opposed to "locking up" public lands.[38]

Nevertheless, by 1905 (with the exception of Gitanyow, a total of 19,918 acres of reserve land had been laid out for the Gitxsan on the upper Skeena River (See table below).

Population of Gitxsan Reserves, including Roche Deboule, July 1901

Village	Population	Area (acres 1905)
Kitwanga [Gitwangak]	153	4,275
Kitwancool§ [Gitanyow]	69	—
Kitseguecla (old & new) [Gitsegukla]	92	2,732
Gitanmaax	244	3,791
Glen Vowell	80	900
Kispiox	214	4,916
Kisgegas	239	2,415
Kuldoe	39	446
Rocher Deboule†	159	443
Total	1,197	19,918[39]

Between late 1892 and early 1893, there was a flurry of lot purchases in Hazelton, beginning with Rev. John Field. He bought thirteen lots for $140 on December 21, 1892; John Bryant bought one lot for $10 on December 22; the Hudson's Bay Company bought ten and a half lots for $110 on January 9, 1893; Robert and George Cunningham purchased seventeen and a half lots for $190 on January 17, and Charles W. D. Clifford bought five lots for $310 on January 31, 1893.[40]

The impetus for this activity may have been the successful ascent of the Skeena River by the HBC's *Caledonia*. Other sternwheelers had ascended the Skeena, but with difficulty. In 1889, the HBC decided to build the *Caledonia* to carry freight to its post in Hazelton. "[It] was launched on February 28, 1891 at New Westminster and made her first trip to Hazelton that May, taking nine

---

§ Another 115 members living at Aiyansh, Gingolx (Kincolith) and Fishery Bay.

† Hagwilget. "The reserve comprises both sides of the [Bulkley River]…which is assigned to the Getanmax (Hazelton) band, for reasons minutely given in my report of 1899" (Loring, NAC, Indian Affairs Annual Reports, Babine Agency 1901).

days to make that trip. The *Caledonia* was considered a success and began serving not only the Skeena River, but also the northern coastal regions."[41]

Meanwhile, crown land was also being taken up by settlers. Although Thomas Hankin had applied to pre-empt 320 acres of land at Gisgamaawin on the Skeena above Hazelton in 1874, the family took nearly thirty years to secure title after he died in 1885. It seems, therefore, that the first successful application to pre-empt crown land on the upper Skeena was made by Rev. Thomas Crosby in January 1889, when he applied for Lot Nine at The Forks, which was becoming known as Mission Flats. The 320-acre property was crown granted to Crosby eight years later. Others followed suit, in particular, Robert Tomlinson and his son. They applied for land on opposite sides of the Skeena ten miles above Lorne Creek in April 1890. The province granted Robert Jr. eighty-one acres on the right bank of the Skeena in April 1897 (Lot 8). Robert Sr. was granted 382 acres on the left bank in November (Lot 7). The cost per acre was one dollar.[42]

As early as the late 1890s, Angus McIntosh and William Keynton recognized the agricultural potential along the right bank of the Skeena below Hazelton at Temlaham. The McIntoshes were among the first settlers to pre-empt land there, with Alex and Johnny on Lot 44, Angus on Lot 149, and Donald on Lots 216 and 217.§ William Keynton pre-empted Lot 733 at about the same time.

Boats regularly stopped there to load wood to fuel their engines and drop off supplies, and the farm became known as McIntosh Landing.

As Polly Sargent (ca.1913 -1993), the daughter-in-law of Dick Sargent, said:

> The…busy time on the river was between 1892 and 1912. During that twenty year period the Hazelton wharfs saw most of the traffic, both human and material, that came into the country; traffic which brought nineteenth century European culture to a people only decades away from [first contact].

---

§ Donald McIntosh later subdivided his lots, which Barbara and I bought in the mid-1970s (i.e. Block A of Lot 217 and Block 1 of Lot 217).

ENDNOTES

1. Marika, Raymattja. "Wentworth Lecture 1998." Dec. 18, 2014.
2. Canada: 1881 Census of BC, Coast of Mainland, Indians, [Gitanmaax], 15 – 25.
3. Tomlinson, 3.
4. Tomlinson, 4-5.
5. Tomlinson, 5.
6. Tomlinson, R. 1968: 1.
7. Tomlinson, R. 1968: 10.
8. Tomlinson, R. 1968: 13.
9. Tomlinson, R. 1968: 14.
10. Tomlinson, R. 1968: 10.
11. "Barbeau and Beynon Fieldnotes", Isaac Tens 1920, B-F-89.23.
12. Barbeau, *Totem Poles,* 66-7.
13. Jessie Sterritt, April 10, 1972, with Martha (Brown) Ridsdale.
14. "Barbeau and Beynon Fieldnotes", Mark Holland 1920, B-F-71.3.
15. "Barbeau and Beynon Fieldnotes", Charles Mark 1923, B-F-90.13.
16. PABC, Sampare marriages and deaths.
17. Large. 46.

18 Ancestry.com. 1861 Census of England (db on-line). Class: RG 9; Piece: 153; Folio: 121; P. 26; GSU roll: 542582.

19 Ancestry.com. 1911 Census of BC, Comox-Atlin, Kitselas, p. 5, Family No. 80.

20 Vibert, 17.

21 Baptism record for Charles Clifford, Jr., June 27, 1886, St. Peter's Anglican Church, Hazelton, BC.

22 Marriage record for C.W.D. Clifford and Lucy M. McNeill, May 24, 1888, St. Peter's Anglican Church, Hazelton, BC.

23 PABC, Sargent Notes 1929.

24 Ancestry.com: 1891 Census of BC, New Westminster, Skeena-Cassiar, Omineca, Family No. 307.

25 Ancestry.com: 1901 Census of BC, Cariboo, Yale & Cariboo, BC, p.7, Family No. 6.

26 PABC, Sargent Notes 1929.

27 Ancestry.com: 1891 Census of BC, Skeena-Cassiar, New Westminster, Hazelton, p. 54, Family No. 306.

28 HBC Diary, Hazelton, 1894-97.

29 Baptism record for Lumm Family, 1904-05, St. Peter's Anglican Church, Hazelton, BC.

30 Chow, 4-5.

31 Patenaude, 171.

32 Patenaude, 171-2.

33 Hall, 12.

34 Harris, 172.

35 NAC, Indian Affairs Annual Report, Hazelton, 1899.

36 PABC, GR 2982, Box 5, File 4.

37 NAC, Indian Affairs Annual Reports, Babine Agency 1893.

38 Harris, 219.

39 NAC, Indian Affairs Annual Reports, Babine Agency 1905.

40 PABC, Crown Land Registry Services.

41 "Steamboats of the Skeena River".

42 PABC, Crown Grand Land Registry Services.

CHAPTER FIFTEEN

Wiila*x*haa/Charles Martin

On my hunting ground Xsuwii Aks, about six years ago, I found stakes for the land. Carman was the name of the staker. And I took my axe and chopped it down. I cut a tree near that place and I write: 'I am Charles Martin who owns this hunting ground from my forefathers. If you want to see me come to Hazelton where I live and I will see you about it. And if you are not careful, to take my hunting ground away from me, I am going to kill you in that line.' And he never showed up since. If an Indian find another Indian on his hunting ground, he will kill him right there. It does not matter if he belongs to the same village because they don't want him there.

—Wiila*x*haa/Charles Martin 1920[1]

CHARLES MARTIN'S LIFE, RECORDED HERE FROM BIRTH TO DEATH, IS IMPORTANT BECAUSE OF ITS COMPLETENESS AND BECAUSE IT REFLECTS THE EXPERIENCE OF SO MANY OTHER GITXSAN whose lives bridged two cultures. Not only did Wiila*x*haa know Gitxsan history and customs, he was born on the cusp of immense change within Gitxsan territory and experienced that change in ways few could imagine possible for an aboriginal person. Until 1866, the Gitxsan lived much as they had for millennia, but this changed during Wiila*x*haa's lifetime.

Wiila*x*haa was born the year the Collins Overland Telegraph (COT) came to Kispiox, and his sister, Minhl Ts'uusx, was born four years later.[2] Their parents were from the Houses of Wii*k*'aax and Haa*xx*w, as were my father's parents a generation later. When prospectors found gold in the

Omineca in the late 1860s, hundreds of wealth-seekers traveled up the Skeena on their way to Manson Creek. Like many of his fellow Gitxsan, Wiilaxhaa was a player in this and other historic events.

Two important developments were about to impact Gitanmaax and Kispiox: the telegraph line, of course, and the Omineca gold rush. American businessmen sought to build an overland telegraph connection westward from New York to London, crossing to Asia at the Bering Strait. Colonel Charles Bulkley[†] oversaw the building of the line and assistant engineer Ed Conway supervised its construction from Quesnel to north of Kispiox in 1866. Conway arrived in Gitxsan territory from the east with about 150 men while another two dozen men with tons of supplies made their way up the Skeena in freight canoes.

In September, the COT built a blockhouse they called Fort Stager beside the Kispiox River at its confluence with the Skeena. Conway suspended work near the confluence of the Nangeese and Kispiox rivers on October 2, 1866 when it was learned a trans-Atlantic cable had been laid. Two men—John McCutcheon and William McNeill[‡]—stayed at Fort Stager for two years until it was certain that the Atlantic cable would work. Soon after their departure, Fort Stager was burned down.

A few years later, in 1871, hundreds of miners made their way through Gitxsan territory bound for the Omineca gold fields. Many Gitxsan people—complete families—found employment packing food, supplies and equipment to the mines. Later, some Gitxsan men bought mules and horses and ferried equipment to the mines. The miners often gave nicknames to the Gitxsan, and Liluxws, Wiilaxhaa's father and key player in the mock battle with the Nisga'a near Kispiox in 1869,[§] became known as 'Kispiox Jim'.

Kispiox Jim worked in the Omineca for a number of years. Wiilaxhaa said, "I was a small child when my father took me to Manson Creek. And as we were travelling there…my father said to me, 'Would you be willing if I sent you to Metlakatla to learn to read out of books?'"[3]

William Duncan of the Church Missionary Society (CMS) moved with his followers to the Tsimshian village of Metlakatla in 1862 and developed an exceptional educational program. Duncan (1832-1918) was born in Stokes Burton, England, the illegitimate son of Maria Donkin. He was raised by Maria's parents, but was never very close to them or his mother. He found mentors among others and was, from a very young age, interested in religious matters. He attended Church of England bible classes for young men: "…his religious and spiritual life was formed in the atmosphere of evangelical Protestantism under the direction of his minister, the Reverend A. T. Carr."[4]

Duncan had another mentor who provided him with skills that would complement his religious side. George Cussons was an alderman and businessman. Duncan joined his business as an errand boy and worked his way up to travelling salesman. Cussons introduced Duncan to a life beyond his expectations, as his journal entry reveals:

[†] Thereafter, Bulkley's name came to be used instead of Simpson's for the river that joined the Skeena at The Forks.

[‡] The same William McNeill (1832-1889) who married Mary MacAulay (1839-1911), Margaret Hankin's sister.

[§] See Chapter Five.

> Travelling also threw me among a class of society which were above what I had been used to, and when seated in a beautiful room surrounded with comforts and at a table covered with the good things of this world, when all my wants were readily and eagerly supplied and I mixed among a class of men far my superiors in education, rank and abilities and treated respectfully by them, Oh! I used to feel my heart overflow in gratitude, for God's wonderful love in thus elevating me from the dunghill and raising my head thus in so little time and so graciously and greatly surpassing my every expectation.[5]

As one of his biographers wrote, "As the example of Cussons, the successful entrepreneur, was a model for Duncan, so too did the devoutness of Carr become a model for his religious life."[6]

Duncan continued his religious training and eventually volunteered his services to the CMS. In 1857, the CMS chose him to head up the first Protestant mission on the Pacific northwest coast at Fort Simpson. After four successful years at Fort Simpson, Duncan and his Tsimshian adherents decided to relocate to a "Model Village…For Good Indians", because some of the aboriginal people at Fort Simpson continued to drink and follow "heathen ways". In May 1862, Duncan and his followers canoed to Metlakatla. That year smallpox broke out in Victoria and swept up the coast with distraught Indians making their way home. Many in Fort Simpson died and others fled to Metlakatla significantly increasing the population of that community. Duncan was able to obtain a shipment of vaccine from Victoria, thereby saving many. Not only did this enhance his stature among those at Metlakatla, it undermined Tsimshian healers who had failed in their efforts.[7]

William Ridley, the son of a Devon stonemason, was appointed Bishop of New Caledonia in 1879. He was an unlikely and surprising choice as he "…had never been considered a man of exceptional ability, and some of his fellow CMS missionaries were skeptical about the appointment."[8] After completing his training at the CMS Islington Training School, Ridley's first assignment was to India in 1866. It was a demanding assignment and Ridley, like three others before him, returned to England "broken in health and spirit."[9]

He worked in English parishes as a vicar, but his health made even these postings demanding. He understood his limitations and sought a lesser charge. The CMS, nevertheless, declared Ridley bishop of New Caledonia on July 25, 1879 and promptly sent him off to Metlakatla. He and his wife arrived in Victoria in October, and William Duncan accompanied them to Metlakatla. By this time Metlakatla was a thriving religious community of some 1,000 members. The two men got along for a couple of years, but eventually their religious differences outweighed their common sense. Ridley, for example, adhered to "High Anglican Church" traditions while Duncan, who was "pious, intelligent and laborious,"[10] was considerably less rigid.

Bishop Ridley, wishing to establish missions along the coast and on the Skeena and Nass Rivers, arrived in Hazelton "…in October 1880 to establish [a] Church…where travelers and prospectors might gather for spiritual strength and upliftment before entering their rough life in the wilds."[11] Ridley purchased Thomas Hankin's log store on behalf of the CMS and held a Thanksgiving service there on October 7, 1880.

A Man of the Cloth

Wiilaxhaa was fourteen years old when he and his father returned from the Omineca gold fields to Hazelton that fall. They visited the Ridleys in Hankin's log cabin. Kispiox Jim explained his purpose, and Ridley asked, "Is this your child?"

Jim said, "Yes, he is my own child."

Ridley said, "Do you really want to give him to me?"

Kispiox Jim said, "Yes, I do," and it was settled.

Wiilaxhaa retrieved his clothes and blankets and moved in with the Ridleys. The bishop left for England shortly afterwards, and Wiilaxhaa and Mrs. Ridley spent the winter in Hazelton.

In May 1881, Wiilaxhaa and Mrs. Ridley set out for Metlakatla by canoe. To their surprise Bishop Ridley, returning from England, met them at Gitwangak where they spent the night. The next day, they continued their journey, with the Ridleys in one canoe and Wiilaxhaa and others in the second canoe.

They camped Saturday night below Kitselas at Xsiphetxw. The next day Ridley held three services. Rising early Monday morning, they made good time to Port Essington and, with a sail and a good tail wind, arrived at Metlakatla at 11 p.m.

Wiilaxhaa lived with the Ridleys. He said, "It was my first experience in a house with rooms, so I wandered in and out of the holes in the house."[12] Three other boys were there: Peter Haldane, Willy Leighton and Charles Peter Ryan. Wiilaxhaa spent the rest of the year in Metlakatla and found the teachers and visiting clergymen, as well as the Ridleys, very kind.

He was a good student:

> I was so keen on learning that I never played a single time, but I took my books and went off by myself and studied as much as I could. And there was another boy who use to stay with me and his knowledge of the books was better than mine. I was very pleased and satisfied with myself.[13]

Chief Legaic's wife invited Wiilaxhaa to visit her. She spent the day telling him that he should study hard and not play like the other boys. She said, "You will become a benefit to your people." Wiilaxhaa promised he would take her advice, but soon became tired of constant learning.

Off Wiilaxhaa went on a hot summer day. He and the other boys failed to return at lesson time and made up stories about why they had missed their lessons. Bishop Ridley learned of this and stomped to the boys' rooms. Everyone ran away except Wiilaxhaa. He jumped into bed and hid under the blankets. Bishop Ridley found Wiilaxhaa and grabbed a pillow:

> And the pillow went thud, thud on my head. And I was not in a hurry to get up, but I got quietly out of my bed and as I was leaving the room, he kept pounding me on the back, sending me to the storeroom. And [when] I got to the storeroom… lo and behold there were the other boys all sitting in a row. And the Bishop came in with me and started to lecture us. "I have you here in my house to learn and not

William Ridley (far left) was named Bishop of New Caledonia for the Anglican Church Missionary Society in 1879 and spent the next twenty-five years at Metlakatla, BC. Ridley Island was named after him. (Image A-02434 courtesy of RBCM & A)

---

to be lazy. And if this thing happens again I will not stop but I will beat [you] with a stick, and fling you all with a stick." And he left us. Then we went on with our lessons. Not one of us feeling hurt at all. We knew that we had done wrong, and that we had escaped luckily.[14]

Wiilaxhaa was fifteen years old when he arrived at Metlakatla. The school took care of all his needs: food, bedding, clothes. He was "warm and comfortable and well fed, and there, for the first time, he ate pie and cake."[15]

One day Ridley asked Wiilaxhaa to meet with him. He asked, "Do you ever pray to yourself in your own room?" Wiilaxhaa said "No!" and the Bishop said, "I think you had better begin, and every evening and morning you pray, you pray all the time when you are alone." Wiilaxhaa promised he would, and so "I went near the water where there were lots of nice bushes, and I was well hid among the leaves and I knelt down and prayed. I did what the Bishop said: I [prayed] all summer."[16]

Wiilaxhaa continued to pray throughout the fall and into winter but by then there were no leaves to hide him, so he prayed in the attic. One day Wiilaxhaa asked Ridley to baptize him.[17] The Bishop obliged him, and on October 25, 1885, Wiilaxhaa became 'Charles Martin'.[†]

---

† Charles's baptism certificate reads, "…[Fa / Mo] unknown, St. Paul's, Metlakatla, C of E, birthdate 1868, tribal affiliation, Kilikshan, name, Wilaka" (PABC July 7, 2008). The Canada Census and DIA records from 1921, along with Charles 1938 death registration, give Charles's birth year as 1866.

Reverend John Field (1846-1918) and his wife Amelia Jane were posted from Ireland to Hazelton in 1886. The Fields stopped at Metlakatla to visit. While there, and before resuming their journey to Hazelton, they took Martin as their servant.†

Martin wanted to continue his studies but had no choice in the matter. In Hazelton, Mrs. Field kept Martin busy cutting wood, packing water, washing dishes, and being her assistant cook. Later in the year, longing to continue his studies, he asked Mrs. Field if he could return to Metlakatla. She said, "No! You are our servant, you cannot go back."[18]

When the next flotilla of canoes left for the coast, Martin fled with his bedding. They camped that night at Xsi'anskeexs (Lorne Creek) and Charlie Rolls, a miner Martin knew from Manson Creek, offered Martin work for $2.50 a day (the Fields paid five dollars a month). Rolls grubstaked Martin with clothes, food and other needs. At summer's end, Martin returned to Hazelton with sixty dollars in his pocket. He spent the winter with his father and in the late spring of 1887 they went to the Omineca.

However, Martin and his father were not getting along and Martin soon left for Hazelton and Metlakatla. By this time Ridley and Duncan were at loggerheads. Not only was Ridley trying to take control of the mission, the federal government was in the process of laying out Indian reserves. Martin said this "…riled the Indians, so it did not take much coaxing for them to follow Mr. Duncan and go to the [American] side. There was a village called New Metlakatla in Alaska and I stayed there for two months."[19]

Their differences also showed themselves in symbolic ways:

> Bishop Ridley wanted Mr. Duncan to wear a surplice when he preached. This Duncan refused to do. It led to a quarrel and Duncan was ordered out of the Mission House. And he went and told the people in the village that he had been ordered out…[20]

Of the 850 people at Old Metlakatla, about ninety percent followed Duncan to New Metlakatla in August 1887, with Charles Martin among them.

After two months, Martin set out for Hazelton, travelling up the Nass River as winter set in with very deep snow. He stopped at the Christian village of Aiyansh, where he met Reverend James B. McCullagh. McCullagh was born near Newry, in County Down, Ireland, in 1854. He and his wife arrived in the Nass Valley in 1883 and he ministered among the Nisga'a for the rest of his life. McCullagh died at New Aiyansh on May 1, 1921 at age 68.[21]

Martin felt welcome at Aiyansh:

> [McCullagh]…was very kind to me and he gave me one of the Mission houses to live in. In fact, the whole village was kind to me. All winter I stayed there. I had nothing to do, there was no real work, but I cut [wood] for want of something to

---

† The Fields remained in Hazelton for thirty-two years, until Reverend Field took ill. He was hospitalized in Duncan and died there in August 1918.

do. I made plenty of wood and anybody who had no wood could come and take it from my pile.[22]

Martin spent the next two winters in the Nass Valley. One day, Reverend McCullagh suggested that Martin get married and "…named a young girl that I should marry." Martin said, "I'll have to think about it first, and I helped the missionary in the school and taught the very small children classes." Martin also conducted church services.[23]

During his third winter, Martin moved to Gitlaxt'aamiks (now New Aiyansh, about five kilometres from the original village of Aiyansh) to preach. He wore a surplice provided by McCullagh and earned fifteen dollars a month for his missionary work. In 1891 he married sixteen year-old Marianne Hans, the girl McCullagh had suggested.[24] Marianne's mother was Lax Skiik from Gitlaxt'aamiks, and her father was "a white man" from Seattle.[25]

McCullagh continued giving Martin lessons "on how to become a religious man." He wanted Martin to become a deacon and learn Greek and Latin. The Bishop was to ordain Martin in the fall, but after several years of married life, there was trouble on the home front.[26]

> …at my home things were very short…because [my wages were] so very small. And of course it caused family trouble of my own. Anything my wife wanted I could not get for her, I could not do what she wanted, and she got very angry with me…I told her to have patience, but she did not listen to me and she got worse and worse with her temper.[27]

Martin was in a quandary because he was afraid he might hurt Marianne when she became so angry with him. He was "celebrated all along the coast" for his work as a clergyman but worried that his marital problems could tarnish his reputation. He decided to leave before things got out of hand. He went to Mrs. McCullagh and told her he was leaving church work, his wife and the country.[28] Mrs. McCullagh didn't say a word. He went home and gathered his belongings. When he told Marianne he was leaving, she took their baby and fled to the McCullagh's house.

Reverend McCullagh sent for Martin and asked if he was leaving. Martin said, "Yes…Nobody has a right to stop me. I am ready and I am going."[29] Martin was about five foot seven but stocky and very strong. As he stood to leave, McCullagh—who was also the magistrate and had Indian policemen standing by—ordered Martin's arrest because he was leaving his wife. As Martin walked to the door a policeman stood in his way.

> And then I got angry and I lost my temper. I took the Indian policeman and flung him across the room, and I went through the door. And I stood at the door and said, "Why have you no strength when you are a policeman." Then the policeman reached up and came toward me and I hit him and he fell.

> Then the missionary ran between me and I did not see him coming…and in his hand he held…a piece of iron about arm's length and three pounds in weight. And he hit me with all his strength over the forehead, and here is the scar. Down I went.

I was knocked out…I don't know how long I was unconscious. When I came to… six men grabbed me…And I said, "Let go of me. I'll have a fight coming with the clergyman, we will have a fight now." And they would not let go of me…It was a lucky thing for the clergyman that several men held me. If I had not been held there would not have been anything left of the clergyman. I was a strong man at that time.[30]

Another missionary, a Methodist, Mr. Osterhout of Lax Galts'ap, was also a magistrate. He held court. As Martin said, "Of course I lost the case as McCullagh had his witnesses tell lies for him." Osterhout sentenced Martin to seven years in jail. The Nisga'a from several villages learned of Martin's sentence, petitioned on his behalf, and had the sentence reduced to two months. Martin traveled alone to Victoria to serve his sentence.[31]

Alice Tomlinson, Robert Tomlinson's wife, visited Martin at the prison. She wanted to know what happened. Martin told her and said:

When I get out of here, I will write a piece and put it in the newspaper that the clergyman has spilt blood. Mrs. Tomlinson pleaded, "Don't do that, Charles. A disgrace will go on the Church of England."

And I said, "I will do it. McCullagh did not think of the Church when he hit me and spilt my blood." Mrs. Tomlinson said, "No, Charles. Be patient. God saw what has happened and He is a just jury and at the last day when He will have to account for all our sins, McCullagh will have to account for all he has done to you."[32]

Martin relented, promising not to publish what happened.† He returned to Hazelton after serving his sentence.

On the Yukon Telegraph

In 1896, prospectors discovered gold in the Klondike. The next year, a stampede of miners and hangers-on made their way there by various means and routes. The demand for news was huge, but took weeks to get to and from Dawson City because "the mail service was chaotic and disorganized."[33] During the long cold winter, little or no news came in for those who worked their claims.

The federal government had taken over the old Collins Overland Telegraph line lease in 1871.[34] The line lay dormant until 1899 when pressure from the Dawson City Board of Trade[35] spurred construction of a line between Atlin and Quesnel which was completed in the fall of 1901.

For the most part, the line followed the original COT route, until it changed course about thirty miles north of Kispiox. From there the trail ran northwards to the Skeena River at Kuldo and on to Galaanhl Giist (Slamgeesh Lake) and Damdochax (Blackwater Lake). It crossed the

---

† My father said that McCullagh, upon hearing that Charles intended to go to the press and sue him, asked the Tomlinsons to intervene.

Nass River northwest of Blackwater Lake, rejoining the original route at the Bell Irving River.‡ J. B. Charleson, a well-connected Ottawa Liberal, obtained the contract to build the line which packer Charles Barrett of Hazelton serviced during and after its construction. J. B.'s son, Edward Ebbs 'Ned' Charleson, managed the line north and south of Hazelton on his father's behalf. Ned married 'Gussie' Cummings. Two of their children, Helen and Jack were born in Hazelton.§

Charles Martin found employment as a linesman on the Yukon Telegraph Line, probably in October 1901. Some of the line cabins between Hazelton and Atlin required an operator and a linesman. However, the operators did not have a lot to do and, where possible, Charleson cut costs by having operators patrol and service their section of the line. Men signed up for three-year contracts at $110 per month for operators and ninety dollars per month for linesmen, room and board included.[36]

Service was often interrupted when fallen trees, avalanches and animals brought down the line. Maintenance was challenging work and men were expected to repair the line regardless of weather conditions. For example, an avalanche in the mountains near Ninth Cabin about 270 kilometres from Hazelton broke the line in November 1901.

Three men were dispatched from Hazelton to repair it while the storm continued unabated. One of the men—Jim Wiggins—developed a serious case of boils on his neck:

> Fortunately, they were near where the Native lineman, Charlie Martin, was known to be a wizard with herb poultices. Assessing Wiggin's condition, Martin diagnosed the poultices would work, but they would take time.
>
> Had there been no occasion for haste, no broken wire ahead, Wiggins would unquestionably have taken the slower treatment. But Dawson City was "hollering" for communications with the outside world, and so he chose the quicker if more painful cure. Martin drew the boils out after applying hot water bottles. There were 11 in all.[37]

Martin worked with a succession of men during his first year: Harry Martin (no relation), Fred Powers, Ed Holley and Thomas Hankin Jr. Holley was an experienced operator and taught Martin the telegraph alphabet.[38]

> I stayed at Fifth Cabin and I learned the telegraph. The first I learned was 'yes' and 'no' on the wire. Of course, I learn a little more each time. And then I was sent back to the Second Cabin with a man named John Angus Morrison. And I stayed there a whole summer, and I learned the telegraph quite well. And I also learned to box. And when I was quite a good interpreter, I could send a message, and I paid a bit [to] the white man Angus [for his lessons].[39]

---

‡ See Map 10: Yukon Telegraph Trail.
§ In 1990, Helen (Charleson) Suggett said that my grandfather had worked for her father as a packer.

Ninth cabin, about 270 kilometres north of Hazelton, on the Yukon Telegraph Line. Heavy snowfalls in the area made the lineman's job a tough one. (Image B-01324 courtesy of the RBCM & A)

Martin became so proficient as a telegrapher that Charleson hired him to operate at First Cabin.

Joseph St. Pierre was Martin's linesman:

> He was a very bad Frenchman. Every day he wanted to pound me. He wanted me to do all the work and I wanted to sit down and do nothing. When I use to say to him: "Pack the water and I will do the cooking," he stood up and hit me. Then of course, I had to leave him alone. Every time he was asked to go and get water there was a fight. He would make to reach to me, to hit me, and call me dirty names. He was a very powerful man.
>
> One evening an Indian, Xantxw, on whose territory First Cabin sat, was passing by from Kispiox. He put his head in the door and said, "I see that your telegraph line is broken just a mile down the road."
>
> I had been there four weeks, and every day St. Pierre and I had a quarrel. I said to St. Pierre, "You will have to leave early in the morning and fix the line." He was the linesman, and I had just returned myself from the upper [line] where I had mended the wires. I had arrived an hour before I heard of this new break. He said, "I won't do anything of the kind. You can go and mend it yourself." And I said, "If you don't mend that wire you shall leave and not be my linesman anymore."

> I was all prepared for a good fight. I had taken off my coat and shirt. And I had no sooner uttered a word [and] he was flying at me. Every time he tried to hit me, I waved off his blows, and would run back to the other side of the cabin, and the fellow several times aimed a blow at me, but missed, so I doubled my fist and hit him right below the eye, and he went flying across the floor.[40]

St. Pierre cut his head badly on a tobacco box. Martin told St. Pierre to get up and fight but he wouldn't. Martin picked him up, banged him around and said, "You have been wanting to fight me for four weeks and now we are having the fight at last," and Martin banged his head on the floor. St. Pierre was in a bad way, and when Martin pulled his whiskers, he began to cry. Martin picked him up and threw him out the door.[41]

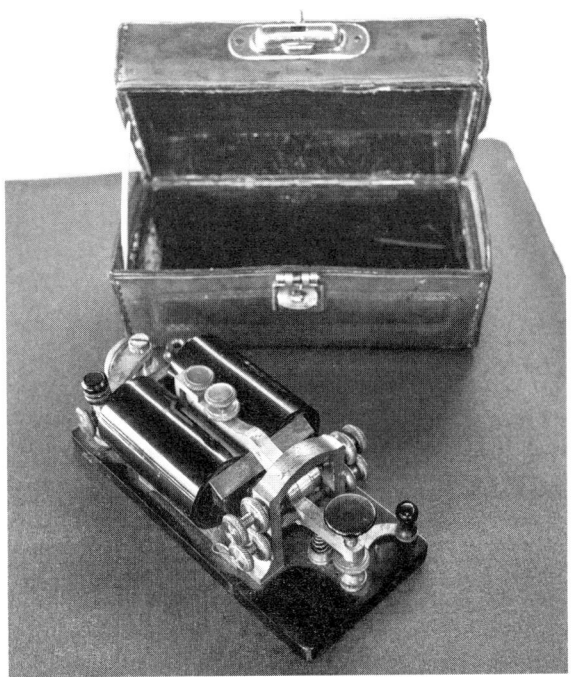

Both a linesman and an operator on the Yukon Telegraph, Charles Martin often had to carry his telegraph key with him to test repairs on the line. His key, pictured here, is now in the possession of Bill Heath, the author's uncle, who came to Hazelton as a telegrapher in 1947. (Jamie Sterritt photo)

St. Pierre lay in the snow for a while, then returned to the cabin pleading for help. Martin cleaned his wounds, bandaged his head, and put him to bed. He sat by the bed and said:

> You have been wanting to fight with me now for four weeks, and every time I [said], 'You might be able to fight with me, but it will do you no good, it will make us no better.' And now that it has happened you are no better…look at the condition you are in.

Martin had his 'spree' (mug up) and went to bed.[42]

The next day, St. Pierre went to Kispiox and had Dr. Wrinch stitch his wounds.† Wrinch then sent him to Hazelton where telegrapher George Swan further attended to him. St. Pierre spent a month in Hazelton convalescing before returning to First Cabin. Meanwhile, everyone along the line knew of the fight, including Ned Charleson who was inspecting the line.

St. Pierre hid in the woods when Charleson arrived and asked what had happened. After hearing Martin's story, Charleson said, "When he comes back in, send him to me in Hazelton." St. Pierre returned to the cabin after Charleson left the next day. Martin sent him to Hazelton and he was fired.

Hartley Cullon worked as Martin's linesman until fall when Martin was sent to Third Cabin, probably in 1902.‡ Martin spent the next six years working alone. In 1906 on July 9, a North West Mounted Police patrol of three men with eight horses left Whitehorse for Hazelton. On August 31, they passed through Third Cabin, noting that, "An Indian named Chas. Martin is the operator there. Camped for night at Indian village Old Kuldo."[43] The patrol arrived in Hazelton on September 6, where they wintered their horses with Charles Barrett, of Barrett & Co.

Although she hoped to reconcile with him, Martin never again saw his wife after he left the Nass. She traveled to Hazelton and inquired about him. When she learned that he was at Third Cabin she wanted to go there but was finally persuaded that he didn't want to see her.§ She returned to Aiyansh and died about five years later.[44]

In 1909, Charleson ordered Martin to relieve the operator at Lorne Creek (just below Cedarvale on the Skeena) who was taking summer leave. There were people at Lorne Creek and having spent so much time alone, Martin welcomed the assignment. However, when the man on summer leave returned, and Charleson told Martin to resume his duties at Third Cabin, he resigned. Now he was at loose ends.

However, his missionary work in the Nass Valley hadn't gone unnoticed. Reverend William H. Pierce of Kispiox sought to recruit him. Pierce's Tsimshian mother died when he was a baby; his Scots father, Edward Pierce, worked for the HBC at Fort Simpson.

The Methodist missionary, Thomas Crosby, converted William to Christianity during a visit to Victoria. Pierce later interpreted for Crosby at Fort Simpson. He served informally as a missionary before being ordained in 1886. He served in various aboriginal villages from Alert Bay to Wrangell until 1895, when he was posted to Kispiox. When he was transferred to Port Essington in 1910,[45] he thought Martin would be a suitable person to replace him since he was Gitxsan and had extensive training at Aiyansh. Martin would have none of it. "I had had enough experience with missionary [life]…It was all on account of a missionary that we would have family trouble. And that was the reason I refused him."[46]

Next, Salvation Army Adjutant, J. P. Thorkildson, asked Martin to assist him at Glen Vowell. Thorkildson immigrated to the northwest coast in 1898 and served at Port Essington before

---

† Dr. Horace Wrinch and his wife Elizabeth arrived on the upper Skeena in 1901. He spent three years at Kispiox and moved to Hazelton when a hospital was built there at his request.

‡ Cullon Creek at First Cabin was named after Hartley Cullon (1867-1951).

§ In 1910 Charles married Maria Smith of Kispiox. They had many children and were together until his death.

arriving in Glen Vowell, near Kispiox, in 1901. The Salvation Army funded the Indian Day School at Glen Vowell and taught twenty to thirty pupils until school buses brought students to and from Hazelton in the 1950s. Thorkildson was Danish, became conversant in the Gitxsan language, and was considered to be "meeting with a large measure of success" by the Department of Indian Affairs.[47]

Hazelton Merchant

Martin declined Thorkildson's offer and made plans to open a store in Hazelton. After so many years working alone on the telegraph line, and being a teetotaller, Martin had money in the bank. He hired men to make shingles for the building, bought lumber from the Kispiox sawmill at Glen Vowell and rafted his materials to Hazelton. Martin found the lumber and windows expensive, and the five men he hired as carpenters "…took a long time to make it."[48] Martin then went to Victoria to buy food for his store.

While strolling about the city, Martin was startled by a woman he encountered:

> She was as black as my coat. She was a colored woman. And her hair was very peculiar. It stayed all close to her head and I thought it was very strange…The ones I had seen never looked as fierce as this one…Having no hair made her look so fierce.[49]

Martin bought ten tons of groceries and supplies and ferried his material up the Skeena to Hazelton on the HBC's steamboat, the *Mount Royal*. He bought a merchant's retail license from the government agent and began business in 1909. As he said, "I did very well. I had many customers. I was kept very busy. I did not have even much time to sleep as there was always knocking at my door, somebody wanting something."[50]

The Gitxsan and Wet'suwet'en came from far and near to trade with Martin. He said, "I always gave them food to eat which I did not charge them for." But he overextended himself on 'jaw bone' (my dad's word for credit), not only to his aboriginal customers, but whites too, "and of course that spoiled my business, the business was impossible, as [everything] was going out and nothing coming in."[51]

Without intending to, Martin's credit policy likely cut into the business of other local merchants, especially that of the HBC and Dick Sargent. Before Martin built his store, Sargent had a thriving merchant, fur trade and hotel business.

In 1910 Martin was again going to contract with the HBC's *Mount Royal* to haul his freight up the Skeena to Hazelton. However, Sargent and other Hazelton men were building "… the sternwheeler, *Inlander*…for freight and passenger service on the Skeena. The freight rates were $50, $60 and $70 per ton, and the passenger fares were $25 and meals extra."[52] Two Prince Rupert businessmen, Morrow and Frizzell, who may have been part of the *Inlander* consortium, wrote to Martin and offered him a gift in return for his freight business. Frizzell promised to haul Martin's freight to Hazelton when it arrived at the coast.† The *Inlander* made its maiden voyage up the Skeena in June that year.‡

Martin's freight arrived on schedule at Port Essington but the entire ten-ton shipment was still sitting on the dock in August. Martin traveled by boat to Port Essington to talk to Frizzell. Frizzell promised Martin his freight would be loaded on the next boat. It was an empty promise for Martin's freight was still sitting on the dock at Port Essington when the river froze over in the fall.[53]

Built in 1910, the Inlander was the last passenger/freight sternwheeler on the Skeena. She sailed for two years before construction of the Grand Trunk Pacific railway made such boats redundant. (Image B-01268 courtesy of the RBCM & A)

Martin hired a Hazelton lawyer to assess his deal with Frizzell. The lawyer thought Martin had a good case and retained the Prince Rupert firm, Williams and Manson, to take the matter to court there. Williams and Manson asked Martin to come to Prince Rupert in July 1911. After the hearing Frizzell confronted Martin outside the court and accused him of being, "A very bad man."

"You made me a bad man, you did not make me a good man," Martin said.

"It was the others in the Company that told me to leave the freight behind," Frizzell said.

"Why don't you use the law on them the same as I used on you," Martin said.

"I had, but I have no written settlements against them as you have against me," Frizzell said.[54]

---

† Merchant George John Frizzell died in Prince Rupert August 10, 1950, age 60 years.

‡ The *Inlander*'s working life didn't last long. In August 1912, the rail line was finished as far inland as Hazelton; in September the *Inlander* left Hazelton for the final time. It was hauled out at Port Essington and left to rot.

Martin returned to Hazelton but his business collapsed with no possibility of his creditors paying him.

Land Rights Advocate

Unlike much of the rest of Canada, the province of British Columbia had no intention of negotiating treaties with its aboriginal citizens. And given that settlers were eyeing agricultural lands everywhere, the federal government was in a bind; it was willing to consider a few aboriginal demands but the provincial government refused to compromise.

In June 1909, Frank Oliver, the federal Minister of the Interior responsible for Indian Affairs, said:

> The question [of agricultural lands] is…of much greater importance in the province of British Columbia, than in any of the other provinces, because though the area of that province is very great, the amount of agricultural land is comparatively small, and of that land, scattered all through the province, the Indians have taken their pick, with the result that the development of the province is very seriously retarded.[55]

Aboriginal leaders along the Skeena were among those at the forefront of the land question issue; conflict was inevitable, and federal politicians knew it. In July 1909 the Dominion government dispatched the Stewart-Vowell Commission to Hazelton to meet with delegations "…from all of the villages up and down the river for forty miles."[56]

The Omineca Herald summarized the chiefs' position:

> [T]heir ancient tribal lands still belonged to them; …the title to these lands could only have passed from the Indians to the provincial government by treaty, purchase or conquest. Having never been paid for, treated with or conquered, the land must still belong to them. They claim that the matter of the reservations was carried out without their consent and that they do not want reservations. They also deem that the time has come when they should be allowed a voice in the affairs of the province and that they should be allowed to vote.[57]

The commissioners spent two days in the area, meeting separately with Gitxsan and Wet'suwet'en delegations. The commissioners had little to offer and departed saying that "they had no power to comply with their demands and that they would make a report to headquarters in Ottawa."[58]

Trouble was indeed brewing. In 1904, there were twenty-two settlers in the Kispiox Valley and competition for good agricultural land was growing.[59] By 1909, work was being rushed on the Grand Trunk Pacific railway and the settlers were demanding a road link so they could get their produce to market. Charles Martin said, "I don't know how early that trouble about the reservation began; [but] it was about a wagon [road] through Kispayaks."[60] In June 1909, without consulting the Gitxsan people, the settlers began building a road from Hazelton.† Their schedule would bring them to Kispiox at the end of October. A notice was posted there "forbidding whites from crossing the river."[61] Martin said no one, not even Indian Agent Loring, spoke to Kispiox leaders.

Fearing an outbreak of violence, the government sent twenty North West Mounted Policemen from Dawson City and Edmonton to work with the BC Provincial Police at Hazelton.‡ Chief Constable G. Maitland-Dougall was in charge.

Hoping to resolve the situation, the *simgiiget* (chief) asked Martin to write a letter that read, "Please do not come through our town. If you are willing to build a road through our town the land here is reservation and we want to get paid for the land."[62] Gutgwinuxs/Billy Williams delivered the letter to the road foreman.

Martin said, "And their boss looked at the letter. He never said a word. He never paid any attention. So the Kispayaks Indians did not try to speak to them anymore."[63]

Road building continued and, in early November, the builders arrived at the right bank of the Kispiox River, where they stored their equipment and supplies. Martin said:

> [The] Kispayaks Indians caught all the road outfit, tools and food and kept them in one house, and [Gamgisti'ltxw] George Robinson, he started to talk to the boss. So the boss strike him without a word. And they fought there. And several of them fought there, but they did not hurt one another. And all the road gang turned back to Hazelton.

My grandfather witnessed the fight. He said the road foreman beached his canoe on the village side, jumped from his canoe and attacked one of the chiefs. No shots were fired, but one chief had a rifle and paced back and forth along the top of the riverbank. The villagers were definitely upset, not so much with the construction of the road and a bridge—Hazelton was the economic centre of the northwest and the Gitxsan would benefit from the construction—but with the fact there had been no consultation and no offer of compensation.

After the fight, the road gang retreated to Hazelton and planned their next move. Martin said:

> I don't remember who was…Government agent…They made everybody in Hazelton as a special police. And sent them to Kispayaks by night. Before the daylight came they reached Kispayaks.

> And they knocked at the Mission house. W.H. Pierce was the missionary at Kispayaks. And they got Mr. Pierce to show the house where the Indian was. And Pierce went around with them. And at first they knocked at [Gama'uun] Mark Johnson's house. And they asked for his gun. "Give me your gun." And he went and handed…his rifle to them.

---

† The road would begin across the Skeena from Hazelton, parallel the river to Kispiox, bridge the Kispiox, and pass through the village and reserve.

‡ The Mounted Police were to deal with Indians, and the BC Police with all others. This separation of duties continued until the BC Police were disbanded in 1950.

One of the white men hit Mark Johnson on his head with a rifle and the rifle broke. And as soon as William Johnson, his brother, saw that he run, one white man shot at him but missed out. White people willing to start war there, but Indians did not like it.

[The] Late Ned Charleson was the chief of the white men.[§] He looked like a general by that time. Also the chief police here [Hazelton] was there and all the police and a big lot of white people were armed. And they took man's name [Gutgwinuxs] Billy Williams and brother's man's name [Wii Bowax] Philip Wilson and they took [Wiidangwax] Richard Morrison himself…and his brother [Gilbil'hlanyuus] Robert Morrison and [Hadaxs'amee] William Stevens and George Robinson…and some others that I forgot.

See how these white people were looking for trouble. And see how these Indians are kindly.

What would have [happened if] the Indian[s] had taken their guns at that time and killed? They would have been slaughtered on both sides on account of the white people. But Indians are very patient. They…brought them [all] to prison in Hazelton. And the report to the government of the white people was awful lies. They said that the Kispayaks Indians had stole all the outfit. And they were tried in Hazelton. Some of the Indians are cleared, and some are not cleared. They stayed in prison for several months. They stayed here. And this is the cause of trouble too. Indian agent should have gone to Kispayaks and made some arrangement about this first.

The Indian Agent had not informed them of what was just and wrong. And the white fired at Mark Johnson's brother (Nagim Wilyee[¶]) and missed him. And Bill Sweeney[**] was the one that had broken the rifle on Johnson's head.

If it had not been for the wise advice of some of the older people in Kispayaks every white would have been killed, the whole town of Hazelton would have been massacred. And all those that went up as a posse, their lives would have been in danger also.

Indians are very good shots…They never miss what they shoot at. They can shoot sparrows on the wing.

[§] Edward Ebbs "Ned" Charleson (1877-1916) enlisted in World War I in October and was killed in action a month later. Barbara and I met and visited Charleson's daughter, Helen, and her husband in Ottawa ca. 1990. Helen (1906-1996) and her brother John (1908-1964) were born in Hazelton.

[¶] Nagim Wilyee was married to my grandfather Charlie Sterritt's sister, Charlotte (1887-1927).

[**] Bill Sweeney was a special constable. *The Omineca Herald* wrote about the incident ("Kispiox Indians Visited by the Special Constabulary." *The Omineca Herald* 6 November 1909: 1.) Charles Martin's 1920 recollection, albeit from a Gitxsan point of view, is accurate.

Every day, right up to this day, the white men are always after the Indian. They are always looking for trouble. And we overlook it all, and lay the blame on the government. These last are my own words.[64]

Martin was at Lorne Creek on business when the big fight at Kispiox occurred. He intended to overnight at Gitsegukla on his way home, but on arriving there, he was told that he would be arrested on his return because of his role in the affair.[†] Martin became very angry and continued on to Hazelton and Kispiox, arriving late at night. There he asked his father's uncle, Haaxxw, for the *laax wan* his father (Kispiox Jim) had once used on the Nass River. Haaxxw refused to give him the knife.

Martin said, "You are making me a coward. I won't shoot the person that will come out [to] arrest me but I will use this knife. The knife will be used on them."[65] Martin was angry, and continued pleading. Finally, Haaxxw relented. Martin returned to Hazelton and sent word that he was there. But, he said, "Nobody came near me. I only heard rumours that the police had gathered and came together to my house at night."[66]

The irony is that Martin's letter on behalf of the chiefs offered a compromise that was ignored, leading to the jailing of Kispiox chiefs. However, sometime very shortly after the raid, a compromise must have been reached. Rather than bridging the river right at the village, which in 1909 was much closer to the junction of the Kispiox and Skeena, the road was extended to the north and the Kispiox bridge constructed very close to where it crosses the river today. My grandfather, who worked on the bridge, said it was completed on January 10, 1910.

There is little doubt that the settlers' road to the Kispiox Valley was the catalyst for increased political activities by the chiefs. Two months later, Charles Martin was present when forty-three Gitxsan chiefs calling themselves "The Committee of Skeena River", met at Andimaul, near Gitsegukla, to organize against reserves and the Indian Act pending resolution of the land question. Martin prepared the minutes of that meeting and, it seems, wrote and typed the following petition that was signed by Kispiox and Glen Vowell chiefs. Stephen Morgan[‡] also signed the petition as president on behalf of the Gyeets (downriver) and Gigeenix (upriver) chiefs.

Meanwhile the Gitanyow, equally concerned about the incursion of settlers into the Kitwanga Valley, continued their decades of resistance in the fall of 1910 by obstructing them and posting notices, leading to the arrest of three Gitanyow leaders:

> The report of these "notices" came shortly after a meeting in Victoria between Premier McBride and ninety-six Indian chiefs and delegates [including Charles Martin] from throughout the province. From the Indian perspective this meeting

---

† Martin had reason to be concerned. Wiigyet/Stephen Morgan (1869-1946) wasn't present either, but was arrested and charged with inciting the Kispiox "rumpus" and drew ninety days "on the wood pile." ("Morgan in Jail." *The Omineca Herald* 4 December 1909: 1.)

‡ Another history could be written about Morgan and his fellow leaders from the downriver villages of Gitsegukla, Gitwangak and Gitanyow. Morgan advocated land rights provincially, nationally and internationally until illness overtook him in 1945.

proved to be unsatisfactory. Their memorial of claims was turned down "curtly and peremptorily," leaving a "bitter feeling."

The Gitxsan took part in one of the responses to this rejection. Charles Martin, of Gitanmaax, was selected as "the man…to speak [about the land issue] for the Skeena River Indians" [with other aboriginal leaders] on a projected trip to England. Owing to the [1911] coronation of King George V, Martin proceeded no further than Prince Rupert.[67]

Martin continued to be involved in the land question into the 1920s and was most likely present in 1924 when a Nisga'a/Gitxsan delegation met with Prime Minister Mackenzie King in Prince Rupert to discuss the land question. The delegations supported each other, and the Gitxsan

```
              The Committee of Skeena River


        We the Committee here assembled at Andimaul, Skeena
  River on the 9th day of March 1910:

        1st.  We decided that we do not want our land
  reserved, we want the reserves to be taken away.

        2nd.  That our land to be given us back again, as
  it belonged to our forefathers.

        3rd.  Also we are pleased to know that King George's
  Act, which ordained on October 7th 1763, has not been changed.

        4th.  Also that each family or tribe should still hold
  possession of the land which is theirs by inheritance


           Do hereby undersigned, under the hand of the Chiefs
           Committee and people of nine villages of Skeena River.

  Chiefs of Kispiox BC.
  on Skeena                        "Stephen Morgan " President

                 Chief"Walter Kaal"   x Kidimkildo
                 "Charles Smith"      x
                 " Paul Clarlahah"    x
                 " Alexander Daimy"   x

  Chiefs of Glen Vowell
  on Skeena B.B.

              (Signed) "Paul Delagumook

                       Sam Barlow     x

                       Paul Green     x

                       Mark Green     x

                       Peter Brown    x
```

"delivered two written statements on their own account…The first of these, signed by Walter Gale and thirteen other chiefs from Kispiox and Glen Vowell, and endorsed by chiefs from Kitwanga, Kitsegukla and Gitanmax, is important and merits quotation:"[68]

Re: Indian Land Question:

[Our] forefathers were the occupants and possessors of the land of this country in the days before the coming of the white people, and in view of the fact that for that reason we are now the proper inheritors of this land; and furthermore in view of the fact that in 1908 the Indian people petitioned the Dominion Government for a settlement of our Land Question, We the Chiefs of the Kispiox Band of Indians now resident on the Kispiox and Glen Vowell Reserves, comprising in all a population of four hundred people, being dissatisfied with the present arrangement of the Indian Land Question as it concerns our people respectfully ask,

First: That the present Indian Reserve System be abolished.

Secondly: That in place of the present reserve system the peoples of the Kispiox Band now living in Kispiox and Glen Vowell villages be granted *A Clear Title* to a strip of land watered by the Kispiox and Skeena rivers; said strip of land to extend from the Kispiox sawmill, midway between Hazelton and Kispiox village to the Brown Bear Lake approximately eighty miles north; said lake bordering on the headwaters of Kispiox river and draining into the Nass river. And furthermore, we desire that this strip of land shall embrace the territories fifteen miles to the east and fifteen miles to the west of the Kispiox river, thus including the mountain ranges on both sides of the Kispiox Valley.

In short it is desired that a strip of land eighty miles long and thirty miles wide as defined above be granted with full title to the same to the Kispiox peoples of the Kispiox and Glen Vowell villages in place of the present Reserve System.[69]

It is said that during this meeting government officials tapped brief Morse code messages to each other with spoons. Martin, an experienced telegrapher, knew what was happening but sat tight. As the meeting came to a close, Martin tapped his own message and startled the officials.[†]

Martin and his family moved from his property near Anlaw to Paul Ts'iiwus's house at Gitanmaax in the 1930s. By then Martin was working for the Canadian National Railway (CNR), which took over the bankrupt Grand Trunk Pacific Railway in 1923. He had been lame for many years and could barely walk.

Nevertheless he was frequently seen struggling with a wheelbarrow near China Grade Hill on his way to his fishing site above Gitanmaax. He parked the wheelbarrow beside the road and

---

† Peter Martin (1930-ca. 1997) to the author, Dec. 1987.

walked down a narrow trail to the river. He emptied his net and packed a few fish at a time to the wheelbarrow, making several trips. Then he pushed the wheelbarrow home.

Martin became ill after walking home in the rain from Bulkley Canyon where he was working for the CNR. He died of pneumonia shortly afterwards in April 1938.

Charles Martin was a remarkable Gitxsan man, but by no means was he the exception. Like so many of his people, he met his rapidly evolving environment head on and adapted to change even though the odds favoured the settlers' business networks and partnerships.

Martin and his fellow students were in the first generation of residential school participants at Metlakatla. Although he and his father sometimes disagreed, they were of one mind about education. Liluxws/Kispiox Jim recognized the need for his son to be able to read and write and compete in this new world order, and Martin did so without sacrificing his Gitxsan ways, values and identity.

ENDNOTES

1 "Barbeau and Beynon Fieldnotes", Charles Martin 1920 B-F-79.11.
2 1881 Canada Census, Dist. 187, BC (Indians) Upper Skeena, p. 15, Lines 22-25.
3 "Barbeau and Beynon Fieldnotes", Charles Martin B-F-235.14.
4 Usher, 6.
5 Begg as quoted in Usher, 3.
6 Usher, 7.
7 Murray, 139.
8 Murray, 139.
9 Murray, 140.
10 Murray, 142.
11 St. Peter's Anglican Church, Hazelton: Hazelton Mission, 2.
12 "Barbeau and Beynon Fieldnotes", Charles Martin, B-F-235.14.
13 "Barbeau and Beynon Fieldnotes", Charles Martin, B-F-235.14.
14 "Barbeau and Beynon Fieldnotes", Charles Martin, B-F-235.14.
15 "Barbeau and Beynon Fieldnotes", Charles Martin B-F-658.4.
16 "Barbeau and Beynon Fieldnotes", Charles Martin, B-F-658.4.
17 "Barbeau and Beynon Fieldnotes", Charles Martin, B-F-658.4.
18 "Barbeau and Beynon Fieldnotes", Charles Martin, B-F-658.4.
19 "Barbeau and Beynon Fieldnotes", Charles Martin, B-F-658.4.
20 "Barbeau and Beynon Fieldnotes", Charles Martin, B-F-658.4.
21 Moeran, 16-18.
22 "Barbeau and Beynon Fieldnotes", Charles Martin, B-F-658.4.
23 "Barbeau and Beynon Fieldnotes", Charles Martin, B-F-658.4.
24 Canada: 1891 Census of BC, Indians, D. 2 New Westminster, S.D. Naas, p. 18, lines 5 – 6.
25 "Barbeau and Beynon Fieldnotes", Charles Martin, B-F-658.4.
26 "Barbeau and Beynon Fieldnotes", Charles Martin, B-F-658.4.
27 "Barbeau and Beynon Fieldnotes", Charles Martin, B-F-658.4.
28 "Barbeau and Beynon Fieldnotes", Charles Martin, B-F-658.4.
29 "Barbeau and Beynon Fieldnotes", Charles Martin, B-F-658.4.
30 "Barbeau and Beynon Fieldnotes", Charles Martin, B-F-658.4.
31 "Barbeau and Beynon Fieldnotes", Charles Martin, B-F-658.4.
32 "Barbeau and Beynon Fieldnotes", Charles Martin, B-F-658.4.
33 Berton, 313.
34 Large, 49.
35 Lawrence, 37.

36 Miller, 44.
37 Miller, 142.
38 "Barbeau and Beynon Fieldnotes", Charles Martin, B-F-658.4.
39 "Barbeau and Beynon Fieldnotes", Charles Martin, B-F-658.4.
40 "Barbeau and Beynon Fieldnotes", Charles Martin, B-F-658.4.
41 "Barbeau and Beynon Fieldnotes", Charles Martin, B-F-658.4.
42 "Barbeau and Beynon Fieldnotes", Charles Martin, B-F-658.4.
43 Canada Sessional Papers, Patrol Report, 1906: 47.
44 "Barbeau and Beynon Fieldnotes", Charles Martin, B-F-658.4.
45 Pierce, 26 March 2014 Wikipedia. Also see Pierce, *From Potlatch to Pulpit*.
46 "Barbeau and Beynon Fieldnotes", Charles Martin and Mrs. Cox, 1920 B-F-68.38.
47 Healing Words, 37.
48 "Barbeau and Beynon Fieldnotes", Charles Martin and Mrs. Cox, 1920 B-F-68.38.
49 "Barbeau and Beynon Fieldnotes", Charles Martin and Mrs. Cox, 1920 B-F-68.38.
50 "Barbeau and Beynon Fieldnotes", Charles Martin and Mrs. Cox, 1920 B-F-68.38.
51 "Barbeau and Beynon Fieldnotes", Charles Martin and Mrs. Cox, 1920 B-F-68.38.
52 Sargent notes.
53 "Barbeau and Beynon Fieldnotes", Charles Martin and Mrs. Cox, 1920 B-F-68.38.
54 "Barbeau and Beynon Fieldnotes", Charles Martin and Mrs. Cox, 1920 B-F-68.38.
55 "Indian Reserves of British Columbia." The Omineca Herald 26 June 1909: 1.
56 "Indians Meet With Commissioners." The Omineca Herald 17 July 1909: 1.
57 "Indians Meet With Commissioners." The Omineca Herald 17 July 1909: 1.
58 "Indians Meet With Commissioners." The Omineca Herald 17 July 1909: 1.
59 Galois, "The History of the Upper Skeena Region", 143.
60 "Barbeau and Beynon Fieldnotes", Charles Martin, B-F-235.13:1.
61 Galois, "The History of the Upper Skeena Region", 148.
62 "Barbeau and Beynon Fieldnotes", Charles Martin, B-F-235.13:1.
63 "Barbeau and Beynon Fieldnotes", Charles Martin, B-F-235.13:1.
64 "Barbeau and Beynon Fieldnotes", Charles Martin, B-F-235.13:2-4.
65 "Barbeau and Beynon Fieldnotes", Charles Martin, B-F-235.13:5.
66 "Barbeau and Beynon Fieldnotes", Charles Martin, B-F-235.13:6.
67 Galois, "The History of the Upper Skeena Region", 152.
68 Galois, "The History of the Upper Skeena Region", 160-161.
69 Galois, "The History of the Upper Skeena Region", 160-161.

CHAPTER SIXTEEN

Starrett and Cummins: Tracing Family, Father's Side

[In 1904] I acquired [my] grandfather in curious circumstances, and Dad for the first time met his father. Even quiet lives have their moments of high drama and surely this was one of them. Grandfather Starrett had long been a legend in the family and might have remained a legend if it had not been for Mother. He had left home to make his fortune in the Canadian West, leaving his family behind him in Toronto. Later his eldest son followed him and neither had returned. Dad had been then a babe in arms and had reached the age of forty-odd without ever knowing his own father. Learning that the old man was alone, Mother offered him a home with us in Chicago; and one memorable day he arrived.

—Vincent Starrett 1965[1]

Charles Vincent Starrett, a Chicago writer, was my grandfather Charlie's first cousin—their fathers were brothers.[†] My search for that side of my family really started in the mid-1960s. Amax Exploration hired me in 1966 as project operations manager for a geophysical survey and drilling operation in the Thompson, Manitoba nickel belt area. I spent the next seven years with Amax, working in Manitoba, Ireland and Arizona.

---

† See Starrett and Cummins Family Tree.

The author pictured in an industry magazine in Manitoba before his transfer to Northern Ireland.

My wife Barbara and I, with our infant son Gordon (b. 1967), spent the winter of 1967-68 in Wabowden, located on the rail line running north from Winnipeg to Churchill. Later in 1968 we moved to Winnipeg where our second boy, Jamie, was born in 1970.

In addition to its Manitoba nickel belt holdings, Amax also held about 180,000 hectares of exploration leases in Northern Ireland, with its base of operations in Omagh, the county town of County Tyrone, Province of Ulster. As the leases were due to expire, a multinational body of Amax professionals was marshalled to complete the required work on time. I was the operations manager, moving to Omagh in October 1971 and bringing my family over in mid-December.

When the Irish Republican Army (IRA) unrest began in August 1971 most incidents, including the deaths of civilians, policemen and soldiers, occurred in and around the cities of Londonderry and Belfast. Omagh was relatively peaceful when we arrived in December, but this changed with Bloody Sunday:

> …on January 30, 1972 in the Bogside area of Londonderry, Northern Ireland…26 civil rights protesters and bystanders were shot by soldiers of the British Army. Thirteen males, seven of whom were teenagers, died immediately or soon after, while the death of another man four-and-a-half months later was attributed to the injuries he received on that day. Two protesters were also injured when… army vehicles…ran them down. The incident occurred during a Northern Ireland

Civil Rights Association march; the soldiers involved were members of the First Battalion of the Parachute Regiment.[2]

Leon Gouin from New York was Amax's geologist in charge of the Omagh project. He invited Barbara and me to join him for dinner one evening. Before leaving our house we saw a plume of smoke rise several kilometres away and heard the sharp crack of a bomb. Half an hour later, the road to the restaurant took us near the site. The bomb had detonated at a Royal Ulster Constabulary station. I don't recall anyone being injured that time.

With violence increasing, Amax decided to transfer me to another project in 1972. Gouin asked if I would be interested in working in Miami. Puzzled, I asked what we were looking for and what kind of a project it would be. Leon said it would be a drill project to define a possible deep copper ore deposit and that Amax had retained a consultant to negotiate real estate options on private properties nearby. This sounded exciting. After I explained the project to Barbara, she was surprised and delighted too. Having worked primarily in wilderness Canada and urban Ulster we thought Florida would be a unique experience…until Leon explained the project was in Miami, Arizona.

The town of Miami is located in Gila County 130 kilometres east of Phoenix and twelve kilometres west of Globe. Prospectors found high-grade silver and low-grade copper in the area in the 1870s. Businessmen, miners and their families settled there and incorporated the town in 1876.[†]

When we arrived in 1972, arid, desert-like Miami presented a stark contrast to the lush green hills of County Tyrone. Although the mines were no longer operating, half a century of production had left piles of tailings several hundred metres high and perhaps a kilometre long near town. The wind often blew tailings dust clouds through the streets of Miami.

Amax geologists reasoned that copper mineralization about 800 metres below the original mines might be extracted by a process known as *in situ* leaching, which involves piping an acidic liquid down into an ore deposit and recovering the dissolved minerals. About ten of us worked in the Miami office and lived in Globe.

In Omagh Gordon had completed the equivalent of Grade One. Nevertheless, the principal in Globe had five-year old Gordon enter kindergarten, setting him up for frustration and boredom. Our moves from place to place were beginning to be an issue for our children's education.

It was at this time we got word of a possible job for me back in Hazelton. Long considered a depressed economic area, the community had undergone a minor resurgence during BC's centennial year in 1958 with the opening of the Skeena Treasure House Museum in downtown Hazelton. It proved extremely popular with tourists and acted as a catalyst for a much more ambitious project starting in 1969. Polly Sargent, Dick Sargent's daughter-in-law, along with community leaders in Hazelton and Gitanmaax, began lobbying for funds to build an entire Gitxsan village as it would have looked a century before. The proponents argued the upper Skeena River economy could be boosted through the development of a replica village, museum and RV

---

† 'Globe' is derived from Western Apache, *Besh Baa Gowah*, which means 'place of metal'.

'Ksan, on the right bank of the Bulkley River, was opened in August 1970 and remains a showcase of Gitxsan culture. (Sheila Peters photo)

park, along with tour guides, craftspeople and the production of Gitxsan arts and crafts such as silkscreens, totem poles, bentwood boxes, and silver and gold jewelry.

The Gitanmaax Band Council designated land for the project at the confluence of the Skeena and Bulkley rivers with the village and museum operation located next to the Bulkley Slough and a state of the art RV Park beside the Skeena River. 'Ksan was officially opened August 12, 1970 and by 1973 the volunteer board had a going concern on its hands.

That is when the board obtained funds to hire a project director. Family members told me about the position and we decided to consider it, partly because of our children. Not only would this be an opportunity for them to gain some continuity in their formal education, they would also get to know their Gitxsan family and learn how to fish, hunt and trap.

I flew to Hazelton for an interview, was offered the position of project director and returned to Arizona to submit my resignation, albeit with regret, as our friends at Amax had become like family. We sold our house, hired movers to pack our belongings and drove to Hazelton in July 1973.

Gordon entered Grade One in Hazelton that fall and soon afterwards his teacher invited Barbara in to discuss Gordon's 'learning disabilities'. The teacher was skeptical when Barbara said Gordon was just bored, that he had already covered the current material in Omagh. Halfway through the year the class began to cover material new to Gordon and his interest in school was rekindled. The teacher acknowledged he had indeed been bored and the next year he was fine.

The author's son Jamie with his first grouse at Temlaham. (NJS photo)

At 'Ksan my job was to manage the entire operation. This involved buying arts and crafts from local artists and carvers for resale, managing finances and staff, organizing special projects such as the carving and erection of totem poles and promotion. I did that for two years and then resigned, enrolling in the Kitanmaax School of Northwest Coast Indian Art.

Not long after I started the 'Ksan job I was invited by Gitksan-Carrier Tribal Council leaders to be an advisor, along with two other men—Don Ryan and Freddy Wale—on a volunteer basis. I accepted and continued to work under that arrangement until June 1977 when the tribal council hired me as their land claims director to start work on the Gitxsan and Wet'suwet'en land claim. In 1981 I was elected leader of the tribal council and in 1983 we instructed our lawyers to commence an aboriginal title and rights case against the federal and provincial governments. In developing an outline of evidence needed to prove our case, our lawyers determined we needed family histories showing that we owned and managed Gitxsan territory before the middle of the 19th century.

That is when I became really curious about my ancestors, especially after our lawyers discovered my paternal grandfather's marriage registration. It stated that his parents were Lucy Simpson of Hazelton and Charles Sterritt from England.

This was interesting because, while we were living in Omagh, we had to take Jamie to hospital when he accidentally burned himself. Barbara called me and I raced home in my vehicle and took them to the hospital. The nurse who admitted Jamie was named Jean Sterritt, as was my mother. Jamie recovered fully from his burns and our interest in the Sterritts of Omagh had been piqued.

In 1986, Barbara and I combined a European holiday with family research in Ulster and London. We stayed in Omagh with a former neighbour and asked her about Jean Sterritt. She was related to her and directed us to other Sterritts she knew in Tyrone and Donegal. We met many of them, but none were related to us.

A stop in London to see if we could find "Charles Sterritt from England" was also unsuccessful, but on our return home from Europe we stopped in Toronto where we discovered the Perkins Bull papers in the Provincial Archives of Ontario.

William Perkins Bull was a wealthy Toronto lawyer. In 1931 he had a serious car accident and while convalescing "…decided to write a brief family history to help pass the time." It was then that the Perkins Bull Historical Series was born. The modest project grew into a massive undertaking comprising over a dozen volumes.[3] The Perkins Bull papers included notes on the pioneer families of Peel and Halton counties near Toronto, including Robert Starrett:

> …[he] lived for some years in Bolton [Ontario]. At the time of the gold strike in Cariboo, B.C. he went west and joined this gold rush. He was not heard of for some years but his son Charles went out and found him and they lived together for some years. Robert Sr. died in Chicago at the home of his son [Robert Polk Starrett and grandson Charles Vincent Starrett].[4]

Could Robert Sr.'s son Charles have been my great grandfather?

Robert Sr. spent his winters at Lac La Hache and worked his Barkerville diggings during the summer. There is nothing to indicate that he was successful in his gold mining ventures and by 1875 he was working at Blackwater Depot west of Quesnel on the Canadian Pacific Railway Survey.

In 1875, Robert Sr. bought the 122 Mile House Ranch at the north end of Lac La Hache, which is where his twenty-two year old son Charles found him in 1877.[†]

Charles bought the ranch from his father in 1878, but sold it a year later. Afterwards, Charles moved to Manson Creek and took work there as a driver and butcher while boarding with the pioneer gold miner, Ezra Evans.[5] Evans spent his winters in Hazelton, and Charles Starrett went there with him in 1884 rather than making the longer trip to Lac La Hache.[‡] It was then that Charles met Lucy Simpson and, while they were never to live together, Lucy delivered Charles's son the next year. That boy, born in Gidumgaldo's longhouse on the bank of the Skeena, was my grandfather Charlie Sterritt. This discovery added three generations to my genealogical map.

Charles returned to Manson Creek the following spring and spent the next three years there. He may have spent 1888 with his father at Lac La Hache but was in business with Robert Leatherdale as Starratt & Leatherdale Fashion Stables, at the corner of Abbott St. and Trounce Alley in Vancouver in 1889. He disappeared from BC in 1890. Four years later, his name appeared

---

† "The 122 Mile House…was constructed of enormous logs felled on site in 1867…the last of several roadhouses built by the Walters brothers. Having passed through several hands, by 1893 the ranch and roadhouse were purchased by George Forbes, originally of Scotland, who, with his wife and six children, operated it until the mid-1930s…" (Patenaude, 55).

‡ The trail distance from Manson Creek to Hazelton was 270 kilometres versus 650 kilometres from Manson Creek to Lac La Hache.

122 Mile House near Lac La Hache on the Cariboo Wagon Road ca. 1900. The author's great grandfather and great-great grandfather owned the ranch in the 1870s. (Forbes coll.)

in a BC voters' registration list as one of the "Names of those who are supposed to have left the country."[6]

After a ten-year search, I found information about Charles Starrett during the time he was living in what was then known as the Northwest Territories. Charles had been living in Fort Saskatchewan, east of Edmonton, since 1890.

Charles continued working in the livery business there. He and his partner, Joseph LaRose, sold their business in 1903 and purchased the Dennis Avenue Stables in March.[7] In December Charles became seriously ill. He died in the Edmonton hospital January 1, 1904 and was buried at the Fort Saskatchewan Cemetery.[8]

Surveyors often named creeks (re-named, for they already had Gitxsan names), lakes and landforms throughout the province. In 1952, the creek known to the Gitxsan as Xsa'is was given the name Sterritt Creek after Charles Starrett, my great-grandfather, rather than my father or grandfather as I once thought.[9]

Just recently, my father said when he was young their surname was spelled 'Starrat'. The 1921 federal census bears this out.[10] But in that same year his father worked as a clerk at a store in Hazelton. The store manager said the proper spelling of Charlie's surname was 'Sterritt' and it has been spelled that way since.

Andrew Starrett and Nancy Cummins emigrated from County Tyrone to Upper Canada in 1819. They had ten children, eight of whom were born in Tyrone and two in Canada.[11] Robert Starrett was their tenth child.

Robert Starrett married Harriet Johnston in 1854 in Albion, Ontario. She was born in the USA. Her parents, James and Catherine Johnston, were born in Ireland. Robert and Harriet had five children; Charles, Catherine, Ella, Bella and Robert Jr.[†]

Robert Jr. was the father of Vincent Starrett (1886-1974).

Unfortunately, government and church records showing when and where the parents of Robert Starrett Sr.—Andrew Starrett and Nancy Cummins—were born and married may not exist. When the Irish declared independence from Britain during their 1919 rebellion, the Irish Public Records Office (PRO) in Dublin housed the vital records and censuses for the entire island. On June 30, 1922 forces loyal to the British bombed insurgents in the PRO, which led to a fire that destroyed "one thousand years of archives."[12]

The loss of the Dublin archives left huge gaps in the historical record, making it difficult for anyone seeking information about their ancestors in Ulster and the Republic. Despite the gaps, clues about the possible birthplace of Robert Starrett's parents are beginning to emerge.

A Toronto lawyer, Richard Houston, developed an interest in genealogy after he retired. He wrote a book about the Standish family of Ireland, *Numbering the Survivors*, which mentions other families, including the descendants of Andrew and Nancy Starrett. Houston said, "The ancestors of the Leslie, Lyons, Starrett and Gamble families were certainly all natives of Tyrone; it is interesting to speculate whether they may not all have come from a single parish in that county."[13]

Houston may have been right. Andrew and Nancy's fourth child, John, enlisted in the 90th Foot Soldiers, 2nd Battalion, Canada at age 18 in 1828, and gave "Leak [Leat][‡], Co. Tyrone" as his birthplace.[§] Leat is in the parish of Donagheady. Barbara and I, with Gordon and Jamie, lived in Ulster for ten months. Assuming that Leat is also Andrew and Nancy's birthplace, we lived just forty kilometres from the Starrett ancestral home while in County Tyrone.

As this situation evolved, I thought back to a discussion precipitated by my Grade Twelve English teacher in Vancouver thirty years earlier.

TEACHER:		Are you related to Vincent Starrett?
ME:		Who is he and where is he from?
TEACHER:		He is an author from Chicago.
ME:		How do you spell his name?

---

† Catherine Anne Starrett was also known as Lilian Madeline Starrett. Her nephew, Vincent Starrett, always referred to her as Lilian, or Aunt Lil.

‡ There is a 'Townland of Leat' in County Tyrone, but not 'Leak'.

§ In his service register, Starret was described as being 5' 7 3/4" tall; 18 years; dark complexion, grey eyes, fair hair, oval face; bo. Co. Tyrone, [Townland of] Leak; labourer; attestation at Glasgow (Scotland), 8th October 1828, enlisted by Lt. J. Pollard (90th Foot Soldiers, 2nd Battalion, 1821-1831 (Ancestry.ca). He was promoted to Corporal/Sergeant May 1831 to Jan 1831; Jan 1833 to Dec. 1837.

Teacher:	S-T-A-R-R-E-T-T.
Me:	No! I don't think so. Our name is spelt S-T-E-R-R-I-T-T.

Vincent (born Charles Vincent Emerson Starrett) and my grandfather were first cousins. Vincent was an author and book columnist at the *Chicago Tribune.* He was born in Toronto in 1886 and moved with his parents to Chicago four years later.

He was part of Chicago's early 20th century literary renaissance with contemporaries Ben Hecht, Christopher Morley and Arthur Machen, to name a few. He was also a Sherlockian and one of the Baker Street Irregulars, which he helped found. He wrote mysteries and was known for discovering young, aspiring authors and promoting them and their literary efforts: in other words, he was a 'bookman'. Vincent's "most popular book, which has been called a classic, is *The Private Life of Sherlock Holmes*, the standard life of a man who never lived."[14]

My grandfather Charlie Sterritt never met his grandfather, but Vincent did when Robert Sr. moved to Chicago in 1904.

Vincent Starrett, as drawn by Frank D. McSherry Jr. for The Last Bookman *(The Candlelight Press) a book to honour Starrett's contribution to the American literary community.*

> I witnessed his arrival from the front window. He came down Adams Street in a city hack drawn by a single horse, his long black sea chest, like a coffin, upright on the box beside the driver. The cab window was open; his lean old face was half out of it. I saw a dominating nose and a fringe of white hair. When he disembarked I saw that he was more than six feet in height. He looked like what he was, a frontiersman. I rushed out of the house to greet him. "Grandfather!" I shouted; and the old man—he was nearly eighty—answered timidly, "Is it Bobby" and put his arm around my shoulders. He had mistaken me for my father.

Then Mother came bustling out of the house and we hustled him inside and established him in the living room. But he would not be left alone. He followed Mother to the kitchen where he sat and talked while preparations for tea went on around him. Suddenly, he whipped out a little black bottle. "Will you have a nip, Maggie?" he asked, and chuckled at her shocked refusal.

He was not much of a drinker, however, in spite of his frightening introduction. He was a simple and delightful old man and, although he sometimes scandalized Mother, he settled down with us like a friendly puppy and gave no trouble to anybody until he began to die.[15]

Vincent himself died in 1974 and was buried with his wife at Graceland Cemetery in Chicago. Vincent's grandfather—my great, great grandfather—was buried at Forest Homes Cemetery in 1907, also in Chicago.†

† The rest of the family ended their days as follows: both Ella (1859-1953) and Harriet (1827-1906) in Fort Saskatchewan, with Harriet next to Charles; Catherine, aka Lilian (1857-1947), and Bella (1862-1946) in Toronto.

ENDNOTES

1. Starrett, 65-66.
2. "Bloody Sunday (1972)": Wikipedia, Aug. 18, 2014 (en.wikipedia.org/wiki/Bloody_Sunday_(1972).
3. Bull. "Who Was William Perkins Bull?"
4. Bull Collection 1930s: 64463.
5. Canada: 1881 Census of BC, Omineca and New Caledonia, p.1, family no. 9: Charles Sturret, Henry Froats, Chas. Montgomery and Ezra Evans.
6. PABC: Registration of Voters, Starrett, 1894: xxvii.
7. Ream, 255.
8. "Starrett".
9. Canada: "W. H. Hutchinson letter to Lt. Col. C. H. Smith, June 7, 1952, Victoria, BC, Surveys and Mapping Service, Dept. of Lands and Forests: Sterritt Creek – after Charles Sterritt [sic], old resident who lived in the area around 1885." Canadian Permanent Committee on Geographical Names, Ottawa, Ontario (author meeting with Charles Maclean, Secretariat employee, Oct. 23, 1990).
10. Canada: 1921 Census of BC, Hazelton, Skeena, RG 31; Folder No.: 17; p.5, lines 45-50.
11. Bull Collection 1930s: 64453-64455.
12. "Battle of Dublin" Aug. 22, 2011. (en.wikipedia.org/wiki/Battle_of_Dublin).
13. Houston, 104-05.
14. Starrett, flyleaf.
15. Starrett, 65-66.

CHAPTER SEVENTEEN

Russell and Weir: Tracing Family, Mother's Side

While still working for Amax in northern Manitoba I had occasion to visit Povungnituk, an Inuit village located on the eastern shore of Hudson's Bay. Many years later I learned my mother and her family also once lived on the eastern shore of Hudson's Bay, albeit several hundred miles south, in the Cree/Inuit community of Fort George.

My mother's childhood years were largely unknown to me until twenty years after she died in 1967. I knew where she was born—Newfoundland—and thought I knew the place—St. John's—but in the latter I was mistaken. It was Mom's sisters, Essie and Shirley Ann, who filled in the gaps and said her birthplace was in the outport community of Little Bay Islands.†

Little Bay Islands is in Notre Dame Bay, 560 kilometres northwest of St. John's. It is a small island of about 1000 hectares. Most of the residents live along the harbour on the east side of the island, with two smaller communities at Sulian's (aka Suley Ann) Cove and Northern Harbour. Students at the United Church school described the island:

> ...an undulating tableland of approximately 100 feet [elevation], with a narrow coastal strip around the main harbour and the coves at the back of the Island. The highest hills are about 300 feet. There are five small ponds but no large brooks. Because of the hilly nature of the Island, there is very little arable land except a narrow strip surrounding the coves at the back of the Island. There is also very little pasture land....The first people to live on our Island were doubtlessly the Beothuks.[1]

The first people of European descent to settle Little Bay Islands were John Campbell and his family who arrived in the early 1830s from St. John's.[2] Others followed, but it seems the first of my

---

† See Map 11: Eastern Canada and New England

ancestors to arrive were Isaac Weir (ca. 1795-1876) and George Bragg Oxford (1805-1892). The Weirs arrived in the 1860s and the Oxfords two decades later.[†]

My grandmother Ann's parents were Francis (Frank) Weir (1864-1940) and Hannah Oxford (1867-1963). Both were born in Little Bay Islands.[‡]

Frank Weir was a ship's captain and ship-builder. Frank's cousin, Reg Weir, said, "Frank could cut the 'knees (ribs) of a ship' and only the devil could fit them" (the result being so fine no mortal could match it). Frank captained a schooner for William Strong—the *W.S. Monroe*—at Little Bay Islands.

Ann Weir was a stubborn teenager and had the nickname 'Chinnie'. My aunt, Shirley Ann, said her mother came by the name because she tended to thrust out her chin in defiance when her mind was made up. My grandmother once said to her mother, "I'm not staying in this place all my life. I want to see the world."

Ann's first job away was in St. John's, working as a maid for a minister and his wife. However, Ann chose not to join them when they moved. Instead, she got a job with the Hudson's Bay Company (HBC) district manager at Weymontachingue[§], Quebec. His wife was ill and needed help with her children and housework. This, it seems, was the first leg of my grandmother's world travels. She travelled by boat, likely to Halifax and rode the train alone to Montreal with just apples to eat. "A lovely lady befriended me," she said. "She had a special picnic basket all made up with food and saved my day. It was wonderful to have chicken legs."

Weymontachingue lies within the homelands of the Atikamekw Nation on the north shore of the Saint-Maurice River in the Mauricie region of Quebec. In 1912, Weymontachingue was an HBC post serving the area's aboriginal trappers. Ann Weir arrived by train in December 1911, on the same train, it turns out, as William Selden Russell, the man she would marry.

His parents were Herbert Elmer Smith (1867-1953) and Fannie Parker Goff (1868-1955), both born and raised within a mile of the Canadian border at Richford, Vermont. Herbert's mother, Orpha Olmstead (1846-1877), was born nearby in Sutton, Quebec. My grandfather, Russell Smith (aka William Selden Russell), was born in Easton, Pennsylvania on April 1, 1892. His siblings were Harvey, Orpha and Ethel.[¶]

Herbert worked as a salesman in Richford when he and Fanny Goff married in 1887. By 1892, the family had relocated to Easton, Pennsylvania where Russell and Ethel were born. The family returned to Vermont after Ethel's birth but Herbert and Fanny separated in 1900.

Herbert returned to Easton, where he married Mamie Markley, their former housekeeper, while Fanny remained in Richford with the children. Fanny found it difficult to make ends meet. When Harvey was old enough, he went to work for his father as a salesman; Russell ran away when

---

† See Russell and Weir Family Tree.

‡ Ann Weir's siblings were Julia (1886-1888), Gordon (1888-1963), Kathleen (1889-1891), Alban (1892- nk), Thyrza (1896-1959), Jo-Anna (1899- nk), Elfreda (1900- nk) and Pearl (1902- nk).

§ Weymontachingue ('Wemotaci' now) is located next to La Tuque, which has grown from a small forest industry community in 1912 to a city of about 11,000 today.

¶ Two other children died soon after they were born.

he was eighteen. He said, "Dressed in a dark gray suit two sizes too large for me, I boarded a train for Montreal. I had tried to grow a mustache with the result that my appearance resembled that of a newly arrived Swede."[3] It would be fifteen years before his mother saw him again.

He assumed the name William (Bill) Selden Russell and spent the next year working at odd jobs around Montreal until the HBC hired him as a clerk on a three-year contract and sent him by train to Weymontachingue. During this trip he noticed an attractive young woman. When he started work in December 1911, he met her—Emma Ann Weir. In May 1912, Bill was transferred south 130 kilometres to Manawan as post manager but made frequent trips to see Ann at Weymontachingue.

After he was re-posted to Weymontachingue as post manager, the young couple took the train to Montreal where they married on June 21, 1913. During the next twelve years, in addition to Manawan and Weymontachingue, Bill and his family lived at Mingan on the lower St. Lawrence River, Cochrane in northern Ontario, Fort George on James Bay, and Senneterre.[**] During that time, except for my mother, each child was born at a different HBC post.[††]

For my mother's birth Ann wanted to visit her family and be near a doctor. She and her first daughter, Essie, traveled by train to Halifax and boat to St. John's and north from there around the northeast coast of Newfoundland to Notre Dame Bay. It was a frightening trip, Essie said, as in 1915 German boats were known to be patrolling the waters off Newfoundland. My mother, Alma Jean Russell, who was called Jean, was born in Little Bay Islands April 18, 1915. She was baptized there on May 29 along with her two-year-old sister, Essie. She was four months old when they left and Mom never went back.

The family's most remote posting, two years later, was to Fort George in northern Quebec on the eastern shore of James Bay. The HBC founded Fort George in 1803 but relocated to a large island at the mouth of the Grande River in 1837. Fort George eventually became a permanent settlement of the James Bay Cree. However, they relocated to a new village site, Chisasibi, after Hydro Quebec began to dam the river in the 1970s. Chisasibi, with a population of about 2000, is the James Bay Cree's most northerly village.

The family of five—Bill, Ann and their three children Essie, Alma Jean (my mother), baby Louise and their dog 'Brown Prince'—moved there in June 1917. According to Aunt Essie they traveled from Cochrane to Moose Factory mainly by canoe but sometimes they walked and sometimes Cree men carried them on their backs.[‡‡] Their route was north down the Abitibi River to Moose River, then down the Moose River to James Bay at Moose Factory, Ontario—a distance of

---

[**] Bill Russell resigned the HBC and worked for Eby-Blain in New Liskeard, Ontario from June 1921 until September 1922. From October 1922 until July 1925, he was HBC post manager at Senneterre, Que.

[††] Essie was born at Weymontachingue in 1913, Louise at Mingan (1916), and Herbert (Bertie) at Fort George (1918). Shirley Ann was born in Auburndale, Massachusetts in 1928.

[‡‡] Moose Factory is in the Cochrane District of Ontario at the southern end of James Bay.

240 kilometres. They had a "temporary stay at Moose Factory pending the opening of navigation,"[4] then sailed 300 kilometres aboard a schooner[†] north up the east coast of James Bay to Fort George.

Although it seemed hardly believable to us as children, my mother sometimes talked about living among the Inuit and of their igloos. In 1989 Aunt Essie showed me photos from that time confirming my mother's stories. Most igloos were built as one would expect, but one photograph showed an igloo with a wall tent attached, likely added with the onset of warmer weather in the early spring.

Fort George had many large frame buildings and a church with cranberries growing in front that Essie recalled picking. There were barns, a hayfield and a large haystack to feed the workhorses and cattle. Another photograph showed a very large fenced garden with acres of potatoes. And there was the obligatory HBC stockade for storing incoming freight and outgoing fur. Kayaks and canoes lined the beach in front of the village.

The HBC provided the family with a two-story frame house with a porch. The house had a dining room, living room, kitchen and bedrooms. The living room included a player piano. Bill and his family once travelled south to Toronto to visit Ann's family and when they returned it was obvious someone had been in the house. Aunt Shirley Ann said there was nothing missing but Grandpa could tell the piano had been used because the canister was still in the piano and it and the piano keys bore fingerprints in whale oil. It seems that music-loving Inuit might have been the intruders. The canister they repeatedly played was *It's A Long Way to Tipperary*.

My mother was two years old when she arrived in Fort George. All three children were dressed in clothes made by their mother. My mother continued this practice for us as we grew up in Hazelton and made her own outfits for weddings and other special occasions. In winter the children wore mukluks and moccasins made by the James Bay Cree and Inuit. The parka hoods were adorned with beautiful crescents of wolf fur. In warmer weather, but with snow still on the ground, they wore toques and wool coats. Summers must have been warm enough for sun bathing and sports, as the girls—Essie, Louise and my mother—appear seated on a sandy beach in one photo and in another, the Inuit were celebrating with a kayak race.

Ann was pregnant in 1918 and the HBC brought a doctor to Fort George for the birth of Herbert Frank Russell, nicknamed 'Bertie'. After three girls, my grandfather was delighted. Everyone loved the cheerful boy and spoiled him terribly. In 1920, the family moved again, retracing their journey to Moose Factory, then south up the Moose and Abitibi rivers to Cochrane, and from there to Weymontachingue by train.

By this time Essie and my mother were of school age. Frank Weir, Ann's father, had moved to Toronto to join his son Gordon after the Little Bay Islands fishing season ended in 1913. His wife and three daughters followed Frank and Gordon to Toronto in 1916. Ann and her children spent

---

[†] Historian Arthur (Skip) Ray is an authority on the fur trade around Moose Factory and Fort George. He said schooners were built by the HBC at Moose Factory into the early 20th century. Motorized vessels were used later. My grandfather took a photograph of his daughters on a vessel with sails. Skip Ray also said James Bay often remains frozen into June and sometimes freezes again in early September (personal communication, July 17-18, 2014).

(L – R) The author's mother Jean, aunts Essie and Louise and his maternal grandmother, Ann, at Fort George, Quebec, ca. 1919. (Bill Russell photo)

the 1920-21 school year at her parents' home before re-joining Bill at Weymontachingue. In the fall of 1922 they moved to Senneterre, Quebec.

A few settlers founded Senneterre as a trading post in 1904. The township was created when the National Transcontinental Railway was built through the area in 1913. From then on Senneterre began to grow as a centre for forestry, commerce and tourism and became a township municipality in 1919.

At first, life for the Russell family in Senneterre was routine, apart from visits to Bill's family in nearby Vermont and Massachusetts. Richford was the eastern terminus of the Missisquoi Valley Rail-Trail and connected with Canada's train system at Sutton, Quebec. Stateside visits were an adventure because Bill was a 'Russell' in Canada and 'Smith' in the USA. Essie said, "Dad used to feed us apples when crossing the border so we wouldn't have to give our names to the customs officer."

On their return from one trip to Vermont everyone in the family became seriously ill with typhoid except for Bill and Essie as they had been inoculated. As the medical authorities nailed a quarantine sign on the front door of the house, Bill and Essie were going out the back door.

Ann and the other children lost their hair and Bertie's fever led to spinal meningitis. He died on May 29, 1924. Not being Catholic, my grandfather had to lay Bertie to rest on June 5 in "the unblessed part of the cemetery."[5] In his grief, Bill wrote the following poem ca. 1925:

The Memory of a Lad

It ain't the lack of money; it ain't the cruel word;
It ain't my wicked deeds that make me sad.
It's the memory of a baby, a blue-eyed baby boy;
A golden headed tiny little lad.
The pudgy little fingers, the stubby little toes,
The chalk marks on the wall we can't efface.
The slivers in his fingers, the toys around the floor;
The little things that no one can replace.
The little boy a-sittin' in the evening with his dad,
So sleepy—with the earphones on his head.
He'd close his tired eyelids and murmur a little prayer
As mother came to tuck him up in bed.
No, it ain't for wantin riches, and it ain't the cruel word;
It ain't for need of friends that I'm bereft.
It's the memory of a baby, just a tiny little lad;
God took him—and the memory's all that's left.

The William Russell family. (L –R) Bertie, William, Louise, Jean (standing in front), Essie and Ann. Shirley Ann was born after this picture was taken. (Sterritt Family coll.)

Life was never the same for the family after Bertie's death. As all three girls were of school age, Bill resigned "in order to secure more advanced education for his children."[6] They moved to Auburndale, Massachusetts in July 1925. Bill resumed his birth name, Russell William Smith, and the girls attended school as 'Smiths'. Bill worked as a salesman for his father and uncles at the Burnham Soluble Iodine Company in Auburndale for six years. In fact, their youngest daughter, Shirley Ann, was born a 'Smith' in Auburndale and has dual citizenship.

Ann and her daughters relocated to Toronto in 1931 while Bill remained in Auburndale but sought work in Canada. This was the time of the Great Depression. Finding work was not easy but Bill eventually landed a job with the HBC in Hazelton.

Hazelton would be a new experience for the entire family as the farthest west any of them had been was Moose Factory. Bill was curious about his new posting and wrote the provincial game department in Smithers inquiring "about sporting possibilities and interesting features" between Vancouver and Hazelton.

Telkwa Game Warden Cecil Muirhead responded with a remarkable letter in which he described points of interest, illustrated with photographs, along the 1100-kilometre route.

> Armed with…a full tank of gas, spare tires and motor in good running condition we leave for and pass through New Westminster, cross the Fraser River and then along the Pacific Highway for about ten miles, where we turn east onto the 'Cariboo Highway' which leads to Chilliwack and points north. Pass through Chilliwack then on to Hope and then Yale, the latter being famous for its establishment during the Gold Rush of 1850. The valley here begins to narrow and ahead it would seem as if the mountains were closing in and such indeed is the case. It is not long now before we are threading our way along the sides of mountains hundreds of feet above the famous 'Hells Gate Canyon' of the Fraser River, where there are many magnificent views. This canyon if not the worst, is one of the deepest, longest and most treacherous in British Columbia, through which riding on the water, no human being has been known to pass alive. Probably Simon Fraser in 1808, when he explored and named the river, came nearer navigating it than any one and although he was traveling light with light canoes and had the assistance of a number of the best Indian canoe men in British Columbia, he was forced to make long portages.[7]

Muirhead continued his essay in this vein for six legal-size pages.

My grandfather drove from Massachusetts to Vancouver where he met Ann and the girls who had travelled by train from Toronto. With Muirhead's essay as a guide, they drove to Hazelton. This was an adventure because the Fraser Canyon highway was dirt and gravel with bridge-like cribbing around steep cliffs. Because Louise was prone to carsickness, she and Shirley Ann rode in the rumble seat at the back of the car. Louise also feared heights and Shirley Ann had to ride on the river side of the vehicle through the canyon.

Shirley Ann recalls arriving in Hazelton and parking at their new home next to the Skeena. If Hazelton was anything like the village I knew, the arrival of three pretty teenage girls—Essie, Jean and Louise—wouldn't have gone unnoticed.

Bill started work as post manager on March 15, 1932 with a salary of $1600 a year, free living quarters, light and fuel and—beginning June 1, 1933—a one percent commission on all sales.

Ward Marshall (1908-2008) and my father-to-be, Neil B. Sterritt, were good friends. Ward and his siblings were born in Langley, Washington. His family moved to Hazelton in 1921. Ward, who described Hazelton as he found it in 1921, said the HBC "stone house was originally for rum storage, but later was used to store fruit during the winter…and was located slightly down river from the post residence." Ward added that it was built partly above ground, "but most of it was below ground level, much like a root cellar."

The HBC also had a warehouse near the post residence. Ward and his brother Tom (1910-1989) began their freighting business in 1929. One of their first contracts was to move the HBC warehouse closer to the store. Ward said, "Tom and I didn't have a clue how to do this. We hired an old Nova Scotia man who knew how to handle horses and work a stump-puller. It took us a full day to set the anchor. We had to do this twice before we got the warehouse to its future location. Bay Street didn't exist then." Bay Street was built afterwards and the warehouse sat at the corner of Bay and Field streets until about 1960.

Shirley Ann said the 1936 flood destroyed the stone house and, shortly after, their house was moved to higher ground above Government Street where it still sits today, opposite the house I grew up in on Bay Street.

Shirley had a sweet tooth for jawbreakers. She took fifty cents from her father's wallet, went to the drug store and, at ten jawbreakers for a penny, bought 500 jawbreakers. Shirley and her friends ate the jawbreakers in a nearby car. A few days later, she saw an elderly man, Henry Bratzine, sitting on a public bench eating a jawbreaker. When she asked Henry for one, he said "You won't like it," but Shirley insisted. Henry obliged her and she popped it into her mouth. It was a plug of tobacco and she became sick. Henry exclaimed, "Your momma will never speak to me again."

Bratzine and Shirley became fast friends. When the family moved from Hazelton, Bratzine continued to write to Shirley and put a stick or two of spearmint gum or ten cents in his letters. "Say hello to your mother," he said, and signed, "Your dear friend, Henry."

Shirley loved Hazelton. It had an outdoor skating rink lit at night by one electric light bulb, sleigh riding, masquerades, May Day at the hospital, baseball, softball and other sports activities.

My aunts Shirley Ann and Louise visited Hazelton in 1999. While driving along the Kitwanga Backroad from Hazelton to our farm at Temlaham, Shirley asked, "Where did the Coxes live?" "Right there!" I said, for at that moment we were at the entrance to the Coxes' former farm.[†] Shirley said, "Oh! I once went there with Emily Carr. Mom and I picked her up at the railway station [in

---

[†] Ed Beauvillier owned the Cox farm in 1999.

Shirley Ann Russell (L), the author's aunt, with painter and writer Emily Carr on a reaction ferry at Hazelton in the 1930s. (Ann Russell photo)

South Hazelton]. We walked from the station across the bridge [from Mission Flats to today's 'Ksan] and took the ferry across [to the right bank of] the Skeena. I have a photo of me and her on the ferry. She spent a week with Mrs. Cox."

At about the same time, Sir Patrick Ashley Cooper became the first HBC governor in 264 years to visit the company's territories in Canada. He was the thirtieth governor and "finally managed a fast-paced ceremonial tour in 1934" with Hazelton on his itinerary.[8] Sir Cooper and a friend arrived by train in September, with my grandmother Ann concerned that her lovely garden with flowers would wilt with the cold before he arrived. The weather held and Sir Cooper's visit went well.

It was about that time when my mother, Jean, watching Neil B. Sterritt play baseball, said to her sisters, "I'm going to marry that man." She pursued him, but he wasn't about to be caught. Dad said he was shy and "when Jean came down the street, I crossed to the other side." There aren't many streets in Hazelton, and eventually Dad ran out of streets to cross. By 1936, when Mom was twenty-one, they began dating.

But life took a left turn for the Russell family that year. Aunt Essie said that after Bertie died, her parents' marriage was never the same. Shirley Ann said her schoolmates were talking one day about her father getting fired. She didn't know what this meant and the children wouldn't explain it. To her young mind—she was just eight—her father was going to be shot by a gun and she ran home to defend him. There she learned what being fired meant and why. As it turned out, my grandfather had begun a liaison with his secretary at the post and, as Shirley Ann said, "to the Hudson's Bay English that was a terrible thing and he was going to be fired for it." He was dismissed April 30, 1936.

The entire family left Hazelton in May with my grandmother and her daughters moving to East Vancouver where they boarded with a family. My mother worked in an ice cream parlor nearby but kept up a correspondence with my dad.

In June 1936, the Skeena experienced one of its worst floods, with houses, barns, chicken sheds and totem poles from Kispiox washing down the river. In Hazelton water rose up to the

Several Hazelton buildings on the left bank of the Skeena, including the Hazelton Hotel, top, were damaged or destroyed during the 1936 flood. (NBS photos)

houses along the south side of Government Street and over the veranda of my grandparent's house. My father was twenty-three years old then and had taken a keen interest in photography. He photographed Hazelton as the Skeena and Bulkley rivers crested and flooded the town. His photos and comments, which he mailed to my mother in Vancouver, capture the event.

Mom and Dad kept up their correspondence and Dad may have made an occasional trip to visit Mom in Vancouver. She returned to Hazelton and married Dad in a civil ceremony in November 1938. As happy as the two of them may have been, there were likely some raised eyebrows in the community. Mixed marriages were uncommon, especially when a 'white' woman married an Indian man. But it was my grandfather Russell who was most upset. Aunt Shirley Ann said he disowned his daughter when she married my dad.

Neil B. and wife Jean with the author and his sister Shirley in the 1940s. (Sterritt Family coll.)

Mom and Dad lived with my grandparents, Kate and Charlie Sterritt, for the next three years. Kate was extremely involved in her Gitxsan responsibilities with respect to funerals, burials, and feasts and caring for her extended family. This aspect of Gitxsan life would have been an eye-opener for Mom despite spending the first ten years of her life in aboriginal communities.

My sister Shirley was born in 1939, and in 1941 Mom and Dad bought their own house at the corner of Bay and Government streets. I was born in that year, Jamey in 1943, and Arthur in 1948.

My mother had a busy life. She took a Red Cross lifesaving course in Vancouver, taught swimming and oversaw us children while we swam at the slough. She began work as a telephone operator at Hazelton and became BC Tel's chief operator there during the mid-1950s. She held this position until she passed away in 1967. Seven years earlier she'd had an emotional reunion with her father. With all four of his daughters in Vancouver in 1960, Bill Russell apologized to my mother for disowning her.

Mom put in many hours of volunteer work for the Red Cross, teaching dancing and helping others put on school concerts and plays. After her death, the cooking area in the old Gitanmaax Hall near Gidumgaldo's totem pole was named the 'Jean Sterritt' room.

My Russell grandparents, Bill and Ann, divorced in 1939. In 1940, Grampa Russell married Mazel Cox, the daughter of Ruxton and Connie Cox. Grampa and Mazel had one child, Bruce (1940- 2013). My grandfather died in 1964; my grandmother Ann died in Duncan at the home of her daughter, Shirley Ann, in 1985.

ENDNOTES

1. "Little Bay Islands", 3.
2. "Little Bay Islands", 4.
3. Russell to Fanny Goff Smith.
4. HBCA. Russell, March 15, 1932, RG3/40C/2.
5. Ancestry.com, Albert [Herbert Frank] Russell.
6. HBCA. Russell Staff Records 1911-1925.
7. Muirhead to Russell.
8. Newman, 160.

CHAPTER EIGHTEEN

Haaxxw/Charlie Sterritt

At my grandfather's place, Gwin Wijix, stood the house where many people were staying. After they had got ready to go to the mountain to pick berries, they had gone up and had come upon the invaders. Immediately, they returned in flight. The women…jumped in their canoes [and] loaded them to capacity…[and] remained hidden among the high rocks…so that the Nass raiders were unable to go up or down the river to catch them. They were in the shelter of a huge precipice, and the men on the opposite shore sat down and were advising the women what to do.

—Woosimlaxha/Jimmy Williams (1859-1924)[1]

With the decline of the sea otter trade along the north Pacific coast, fur traders, in particular American free traders known to the Gitxsan as 'Boston men', looked to inland aboriginal peoples for new sources of fur. Some Boston men, as well as the HBC traders at Fort Simpson, sought to trade inland with the Gitxsan and Wet'suwet'en. But Legaic of Metlakatla "…had the supreme power [over trade] on the Skeena River starting from the mouth…up to where the Gitxsan lived in Kispiox."[2] To sustain his monopoly, Legaic sometimes attacked those Gitxsan who had dealt directly with free traders on the coast. The Nisga'a, travelling overland to the Skeena in search of fur and caribou hides, also attacked the Gitxsan. During one Nisga'a attack, the women and children of Kispiox had taken refuge in a *ta'oots'ip* (fort) built on a rocky island in the Skeena four kilometres above Kispiox.[3]

Continuing his narrative, Woosimlaxha said:

> My grandfather, Dini,† directed them, "Stay where you are! Don't move out! I will tell you when to move," he said. He then used his powers as a *halayt*, and when he thought they were safe, he called out to them to come across [the Skeena]. They came over at once, and then the Nass invaders shot [arrows] at them and into the canoes, but were unable to wound or hurt anyone in these canoes, however close they were. So, in a taunting rebuke, my grandfather called over to the Nass raiders, saying, "Go ahead and shoot at me again—you people from the Nass—you can't hurt me. I have already brought the canoes over," meaning that he had exercised his high powers to make it impossible for the invaders to…do any damage to anyone in the canoes. As soon as the canoes landed, the women rushed out and went into the hills.
>
> Then the Nass River raiders turned their attention to the fort, where they knew that all the people had gone. Although they shot their arrows at the *ta'oots'ip*, no damage was done…[The Kispiox warriors] were all preparing themselves for a big *Halaiyt* in the hills when they looked down and saw the Nass raiders shooting arrows into the *ta'oots'ip*. Then they [Gitxsan] returned and got their guns‡…and spread out in the rear of the Nass invaders, ready to massacre them. The Nass had now shot away all their ammunition and were returning home…[Two Nisga'a men] were recognized as relatives…so they did not shoot them, but shot over them. And when the Nass raiders heard the shots, they immediately took to flight and scattered in all directions…The Nass survivors reached their home in a very scattered condition; first one would arrive, and then…two or three more. This was the last time that the Nisga'a invaded Kispayaks.⁴

During this attack in about 1835, a woman from the House of Haaxxw gave birth to a daughter in the *ta'oots'ip*.⁵ This baby grew up and as an adult held the name Sabasuuxw, 'Bas for short. 'Bas was the sister or cousin of Liluxws/Kispiox Jim and married a man from the House of Ts'iibaasaa. 'Bas and her husband were baptized Selena and Joshua Simpson at Port Essington in 1886.⁶ They had four daughters: Matilda, Selena, Nellie and Lucy.

'Bas's daughters grew up when Gitxsan families still traveled widely throughout their territories and far beyond. Joshua and Selena had promised Lucy to Gidumgaldo's son, Ladaix, when she was fifteen or sixteen. However, Lucy met Charles Starrett from Ontario in 1884 either at Manson Creek or Hazelton when he spent the winter there.

They fell in love and when Charles set out for Manson Creek in the spring, sixteen year-old Lucy was with him. But they got no farther than the banks of the Skeena before her parents caught

---

† Dinii, House of Gitluudaahlxw, Kispiox Fireweed. Gwin Wijix is a fishing site belonging to the House of Gitluudaahlxw.

‡ Kliiyeemlaxha/Martha Brown (1900-1987) described how the guns were loaded. She said, "They stuff it down [the barrel] with a stick before they can fire it" (*Delgamuukw v. BC*, SCBC No. 0843, 1985).

up to them and brought the resisting, wailing Lucy back. This happened several times, and there was quite a commotion, but finally, although pregnant with Starrett's child, Lucy agreed not to go with him. Starrett left Hazelton and never returned.

Gidumgaldo had one of the larger houses in Gitanmaax, accommodating twenty-two people in six families in 1881, including Ladaix (later, Kitanmaax Jimmy). Charles Sterritt, my grandfather, was born there in May 1885. In the 1891 census, the family included Kitanmaax Jimmy, his wife Kinyax/Lucy and her children, Chimilikh/Charlie (my grandfather) and Edohush/Charlotte.§

Jimmy and Lucy separated in 1893, and in the 1901 census we learn that the family consisted of Nos Madam/Lucy, Kitksun/Charles Stirrit and two young sons, Kitksun Duk and Kitksun Olie.¶ Lucy, Duk and Olie died between 1901 and 1911, as they do not appear on the 1911 census.**

My grandfather,†† however, survived and entered joyfully into one of the busiest and most exciting periods of the Gitanmaax/Hazelton history.

The HBC and Omineca miners needed tons of freight and supplies. In 1888, for example, the HBC hired Veith & Borland from 150 Mile House to pack their freight between Hazelton and Babine Post.[7] Between July 8 and September 14, 1894, packer John Harris made eight return trips to Babine on their behalf.[8] Since his mule train consisted of about fifty animals, each capable of a 110- to 140-kilogram load, Harris transported about fifty tons of freight to Babine that year, and each year for many years.

Gitxsan families also backpacked supplies to the Omineca. On February 6, 1895, Joseph Lyon, on behalf of the HBC, "gave out packs to the Indians for Tom's [aka Tom] Creek and Vitale."[9] On June 2, "Kispiox Jim arrived from Babine with letters from McDonald."[10] On June 24, "Big Louis left for Tom's Creek with a load of freight for Old Sam the Chinaman….On July 3, Vieth & Borland's Pack Train arrived [from 150 Mile House] at 4 o'clock p.m., John Harris in charge."[11]

By 1901 Hazelton/Gitanmaax was truly the hub of the north with sternwheelers bringing men, equipment and supplies to Hazelton and pack trains conveying tons of cargo east to the HBC posts and the Omineca mines, and north and south to linesmen in their cabins along the Telegraph Trail.

It was the heyday of packing. In 1900 Charles Barrett won the packing contract between Hazelton and Ninth Cabin on the Telegraph Trail. Barrett, in partnership with Ned Charleson and Jack Sealy, owned the Diamond D Ranch near Houston. In 1902 the HBC replaced Veith & Borland with Jean Caux, better known as Cataline, perhaps the most famous packer of his day. In 1907 Cataline bought Barrett's pack train and took over the Hazelton to Ninth Cabin contract.[12] In 1910 the government awarded Cataline the contract to service the cabins from Quesnel to Ninth Cabin, making it the "largest single contract in the district and an important factor in making Hazelton the centre of the largest packing business on the continent."[13] After nearly sixty years in the business, Cataline retired in 1913 and sold his outfit to George Beirnes.[14]

---

§ Several knowledgeable elders said Charlotte was the daughter of Yal/Donald Mowatt (ca. 1867-1960).
¶ No ages are given for persons enumerated in the 1901 Canada Census for the Babine Agency.
** Lucy is buried in Gitanmaax Cemetery, but the locations of Duk and Olie's gravesites are unknown.
†† See Haaxxw Family Tree.

A pack train leaving Hazelton with supplies for linemen and operators on the Telegraph Trail. St. Peter's Anglican Church is in the left background with Gitanmaax longhouses to the right. (Image B-05848 courtesy of the RBCM & A)

It is little wonder that my grandfather and his friends became packers. They travelled widely as teenagers, wintering in the Cariboo after trailing the horses and mules south. Some of them were notorious—the two Charlies (Clifford and Sterritt) in particular. Bessie, the daughter of Manson Creek gold miner William Keynton, traveled to and from Manson Creek with her father each year until he retired in 1900.† "Those two terrified me," Bessie said, "They were wild and came riding into town [at Manson Creek], hooting and hollering." The two Charlies (born 1881 and 1885) were teenagers in the late 1890s and likely 'put on the dog' for Bessie's benefit. They may have wrangled for Big Louis or Veith & Borland as they freighted to and from the Omineca during the 1890s. Big Louis continued packing as late as 1913 when surveyor Frank Swannell noted that "Kispiox Louis with wife Margaret arrives with 10 pack-horses for Manson Creek."[15]

Once, while I was still attending Gladstone high school, I hitched a ride with my grandfather down to Vancouver. While going through Williams Lake, he pointed westward and said that years before he caught wild horses in the Chilcotin. I asked him how he did that.

> We had wing fences many miles long. They narrowed to a large corral with two gates. With both gates open, we chased small herds of horses between the fences, and through the open corral. We didn't push them hard, and they grew used to

---

† Keynton and his daughter had property near McIntosh Landing at Temlaham, and wintered there.

it. When we were ready to catch and break a large number of horses, we closed the exit gate, rounded up the horses and herded them between the fences into the corral where they milled about as we closed the entrance gate behind them. Afterwards, we broke some to saddle and others to pack.

(L-R) Alfred Shanoss, Charlie Clifford, and Peter Barney with Cataline (standing) before he retired in 1913. (Image I-51525 courtesy of the BBCM & A)

Thomas Hankin's son, Arthur (1882-1971), was working in the Cariboo in the fall of 1897. He was just fifteen years old but this wasn't considered unusual at the time. There was endless work for keen youths on a pack train: wrangling, saddling, shoeing and grooming, cutting wood, packing water and bull-cooking. My grandfather and other teenagers from Hazelton were likely with Hankin that winter for Charlie spoke of wintering in the Chilcotin and being on a cattle drive to the Yukon. The Klondike gold rush was on and Cariboo "ranchers were struggling for a living on the Chilcotin plateau of British Columbia."[16]

Chilcotin rancher Norman Lee kept a diary of his experience driving cattle to the Klondike. He left Hanceville, about ninety kilometres west of Williams Lake, in mid-May "with about two hundred head of beef cattle…[a] pack train of nine horses" a cook, boss packer and seven men.[17] Three other Chilcotin ranchers were also bound for the Klondike: "Jim Cornell…with about seventy-five head, Jerry Gravelle…with one hundred…and Johnny Harris[‡] with his two hundred was trying hard to catch us up."[18]

Arthur Hankin (and perhaps my grandfather) was with Harris:

---

‡ The same John Harris who packed for Veith & Borland.

Geel/Big Louis, Kispiox Margaret (not to be confused with Margaret Kispiox) and baby at Takla Lake. Big Louis was one of several Gitxsan packers supplying goods to HBC posts and Omineca miners in the early 1900s. (Image I-33189 courtesy of RBCM & A)

> There were two [men]…Harris and Knight, owners of the cattle. They possessed 200 head of cattle to drive to Dawson from Chilcotin country. And [we] started over the trail of '98 with the cattle from the Chilcotin.
>
> The cattle started out and he had trouble losing them, [they were] hard to drive. He had trouble as he was in bushy country and the cattle used to get lost at night, and he used to herd them, that is, camp watching them at night to prevent them from getting away. The cattle wanted to go back to the ranches he had bought them from. They were mixed bunches of cattle. This sort of thing continued until the cattle got used to one another and nearly two months of drive till he got to Hazelton, about six hundred miles from the starting point.[19]

Johnny Harris and his crew caught up to Norman Lee at Stoney Creek:

> Harris passed us with his band of 200 cattle. As he had purchased his stock in Chilcotin, I took the opportunity of looking through his band, and found one of my own steers. This, I tried to induce Harris to hand over at once, but he declined, saying that he had bought and paid for it. My men were all in readiness to take the animal forcibly, but on consideration, I thought the best course would be to go for

the man who had sold the steer as Harris's men were quite ready for the fray and they appeared to be a stouter lot of men than mine, though my outfit were better mounted. Harris camped that night three or four miles further on.[20]

Harris and Lee again joined up at Fort Fraser, where Lee observed:

> One reason for the haste with Harris, having been packing for years on this trail as far as Hazelton, [he] knew the good camping places; so that he sent his pack train ahead of our cattle to secure good camping ground for the night. For two or three days I was annoyed by Harris and his pack train, and at last determined to let him pass again in order to be rid of him.[21]

Lee arrived in Hazelton and spent three or four days there. He left on July 14 and, well north of Hazelton on Sunday July 31, wrote:

> We now concluded to drive the cattle in future on foot in order to give the horses every chance. We also now perceived the mistake of having allowed Harris and the other cattle men to get ahead of us, as the trail almost all the way was a sea of mud—such as I have never seen before. Whenever animals moved down a hill the mud rolled down too after the manner of a river, thick pasty mud about the consistency of porridge. It was now borne in upon us that horses were getting weak. This would have been a nice point to have turned back from, but we did not turn back. We threw away now everything that was not necessary.[22]

This is consistent with my grandfather's account. He said their horses were so weak they had to put packs on the cattle. Hankin said it took the Harris party two months to get from the Chilcotin to Hazelton.

> North of Hazelton, trouble began. Our horses all gave out on him. But he had only a very few of the strong ones that followed us and he started losing cattle in the timber country north of [Hazelton]. The cattle then began to get sore feet and short of feed. When he came to grassy mountains where he let them rest and get some feed awhile. Then he continued on till he got to Stikine country, losing many on the way. He ran short of provisions and he used to kill cattle and eat beef and it was about all he had until he got to the Stikine. Then from Stikine he continued to Teslin Lake. There he arrived with the remnants of the outfit of cattle: 125 head of cattle and seven head of horses....[23]

My grandfather told me that when he got to Telegraph Creek, he had had enough. He quit the drive, took a boat down the Stikine to Wrangell, then on to Port Essington and up the Skeena to Hazelton. It was a good decision as all of the cattle were lost when the ranchers tried to float the animals down the Yukon River in wooden scows to Dawson City.

In 1900, after his cattle drive adventure, Charlie Sterritt signed on with Charlie Barrett and Ned Charleson to work at the Diamond D Ranch near Houston. He spent the next six years packing for Barrett and Company on the Telegraph Trail north of Hazelton.

One of the more famous events of the day occurred near Hazelton in June 1906 involving a local man, Alexander 'Alex' McIntosh. McIntosh not only worked as a miner but also for Charles Barrett as a packer. He was one of twelve siblings born to Angus McIntosh and Mary Axgoot.[†]

Mary Axgoot was Gitxsan and belonged to the House of Guuxsan from Gitsegukla. Alex and his siblings, therefore, were also Gitxsan. Their father, born in Scotland, came to Canada in 1862.[24] He worked for the HBC at Fort Babine where he lived with Mary for about fourteen years. They married in September 1886. Alex, their third child, was born in 1882.

David Ricardo Williams, a retired lawyer from Duncan, described Alex McIntosh in *Trapline Outlaw*.

> Alexander…was of stocky build, about five feet eight inches in height, weighing 180 pounds. A powerful and hardworking man who could always find employment, he worked as a packer when the riverboats were laid up for the winter.…Nothing in the background of the McIntosh family foretold violence or tragedy. Alexander's only surviving sister…remembers him as an affectionate brother, 'a good man' and a member of a 'good family'. Yet this same Alexander had a darker side to his character which led to his violent death on June 19, 1906; he persistently got into trouble with the law. It was probably the result of a gregarious nature, or more particularly, a gregarious nature which led him to drinking with Indians, an activity which was declared to be illegal.[25]

Alexander and his fellow packers were camped at Two Mile, between Gitanmaax and Hagwilget, near a roadhouse owned by two brothers and managed by the 'Geezer', James Cameron. The packers were drinking there when Simon Gunanoot stopped by on June 18. There was bad blood between Alex and Simon and they fought, with Simon on the losing end. After the fight, Gunanoot left the roadhouse warning McIntosh that he was going to get him.

My grandfather would agree with Williams that Alexander was a powerful man. He said that he carried 100-pound bags of flour, one under each arm, while unloading boats all day. Alex won most of his fights, but not all. Once, while drinking in Hazelton near the Skeena, Alex took on a man who thrashed him. Alex said, "I'm going to clean up" and walked down to the Skeena to wash the blood from his face. On his return Alex said, "Let's shake on it." His adversary extended his hand and Alex hit him in the face with a rock he had hidden in the other hand.

As they travelled the northern wilderness, the packers often wrestled after setting up camp. Once Alex and a Nisga'a man were wrestling when Alex lost his temper and the fun suddenly turned serious. The Nisga'a man walked away and said prophetically, "Someday you're going to find yourself with a knife in your back."

---

† Mary Axgoot was the sister of Alfred Sampare's wife, Bonita.

McIntosh's pack train was to leave on June 19. The men rose at 4:00 a.m. to round up the horses and mules. Knowing Gunanoot's threat was serious, Grandfather told McIntosh to join him, but McIntosh's hands were so badly damaged from the fight that he rode off to the hospital. His body was found at the bend in the road near today's Hazelton ice arena. He had been shot in the back and died instantly.

Shortly after, about three kilometres away, a second man met his fate. Max LeClair, a newcomer to Hazelton, was about to depart for Kamloops on a packhorse trip. He was riding to town and encountered Gunanoot, whom he likely did not know, near the Salmon River turnoff. Gunanoot told my Uncle Percy what happened:

> I ran into LeClair. He saw the blood on my face and laughed at me. I told him to be careful and he said, "You couldn't hit anything with that old gun." I said, "Take off before I shoot you." LeClair laughed and whipped his horse into a run and I shot him.

Thus began one of the longest manhunts in Canadian history. Simon Gunanoot was pursued for the next thirteen years through thousands of square kilometres of northern BC wilderness. He was never captured; when he finally gave himself up in 1919, he was acquitted for lack of evidence. Simon travelled with his family the entire time, a fact that caused the authorities much aggravation and frustration and, on occasion, considerable embarrassment.

As an aside, Simon Gunanoot owned hay land along the left bank of the Skeena at Anlaw, two kilometres below Hankin's ranch. After Simon took flight, Richard Loring, the Indian agent, leased Simon's land and deposited the money in a local bank. Simon was concerned about this and talked to Charles Martin, possibly when Simon's family spent the winter of 1913-14 with my grandparents at Xsuwii Aks (Sustut River).

Martin did write to Ottawa on Simon's behalf, and Ottawa promptly wrote Loring, who, as David Ricardo Williams said, "…fired off a highly indignant reply…[and] had some choice words for him." Of Martin, Loring wrote:

> His invidious activities are stimulated by an hatred of me since punishing him for supplying liquor to fellow Indians, which he at the time had carried on to a far greater extent than then suspected, and his animus proved in keeping with his bloated scrofulous body from which aught else can emanate but poison when disturbed.[26]

Martin was known to be an advocate for his people on aboriginal rights and the land question. He likely sold liquor while in the retail business, as did other merchants and hoteliers in Hazelton. If his body was bloated and scrofulous, it wasn't from drinking. He was a teetotaler. And if Loring was suggesting he was morally corrupt, Martin's life story reveals that he was an honest, forthright man, but perhaps too trusting of others.

Martin's letter, nevertheless, had the desired effect. Loring immediately sent Gunanoot's Anlaw earnings to Ottawa as he should have done years earlier. Gunanoot later used this and other money to pay his lawyer's fees during his trial.

It is easily forgotten that the Gunanoot-McIntosh matter was an issue between two Gitxsan men and two Gitxsan Houses: Gunanoot from the House of Geel in Kispiox and McIntosh from the House of Guuxsan in Gitsegukla. Had Gunanoot shot McIntosh fifty years earlier House leaders might have dealt with it right away with a different result.

Charlie Sterritt continued in the packing business and in 1907 was working for a provincial land surveyor, John Hamilton Gray. Gray established a sub-office in Hazelton as his base of operations for surveys to be conducted in the Bulkley Valley. He hired my grandfather as his head packer. The party of nine left Hazelton in the spring of 1907 with eighteen horses.

Ned Charleson (centre right) and Charlie Sterritt (far right) with other members of a government pack train en route from Quesnel to the upper Nass River, ca. 1906. (Image B-05434 courtesy of the RBCM & A)

They spent the summer laying out section lines and pre-emption claims mainly in the Bulkley Valley. Gray started surveying on May 9 in the Smithers area at Seymour and Chicken (Lake Kathlyn) lakes and finished in October at the headwaters of the Bulkley River and Tsinkut Lake.[27] Rather than return to Hazelton in November, the survey party left for the Lower Mainland and Victoria. Charlie herded the horses south to a farm in the Fraser Valley near New Westminster. He spent the winter in Victoria with monthly trips to New Westminster to check on the horses.

He may have hoped to find his father, Charles Starrett, on his way south. Years later he told at least one person—Delbert Turner—that his *wil'suwitx* (father) lived at Lac La Hache. He talked to old timers at Lac La Hache who said that the Starretts had left the area years before.

Charlie spent the winter in Victoria where, on January 20, 1908, he witnessed the opening of the Royal Empress Hotel. When the survey party prepared to return north in the spring, Charlie asked Gray to hire his Hazelton friend, Charlie Clifford. During the coming season, "J.H. Gray [was] to survey the Crown lands in the Nechaco and to report on the necessary roads and trails, which will greatly facilitate the newcomers to establish homes."[28]

As they travelled north the two Charlies often stopped at roadhouses. Sometimes locals harassed them, perhaps because they were aboriginal. My uncle Percy laughingly said, "That damn Charlie Clifford was always getting into fights, and when that happened my dad had to help him out." In the 1990s, after a funeral service at St. Peter's Church in Hazelton, I offered Charlie Clifford's daughter, Violet Smith, a ride to the Gitanmaax Cemetery. I asked Violet whether her father talked about his travels with my grandfather. "Oh yes, he did." Violet said. "When they went into bars, Charlie Sterritt would get into a fight, and then my dad ended up in the thick of it too."

The two Charlies returned to Hazelton in December 1908. My grandfather had won a mail contract between Hazelton and Kitimat that was to begin November 1 but he was a month late arriving from Ootsa Lake. In the meantime, an article in *The Omineca Herald* read, "Until he can reach here and assume charge, arrangements are being made for others to handle the mail at his expense."[29] On December 12 Charlie was on the job and on his way to Kitimat with his dog team.[30] In January, "The incoming mail arrived Sunday evening after the quickest trip from Kitselas that has been made in the history of the river. The carriers left the canyon Saturday morning and covered the distance to Hazelton, 80 miles, in 36 hours, including all stops."[31]

Charlie had a one-year contract and did not renew it because he found the snow between Kitimat and Terrace was too wet.

In 1911 he drove stage from Hazelton to Aldermere. Martin Starrett, a fur trader who worked between Fort Babine and Hazelton, travelled to Round Lake near Aldermere on an errand for his fur trader uncle C.V. Smith of Hazelton. He asked a worker at the telegraph cabin for messages, and got the following reply: "No, there was a message here for Charlie Sterritt who drives the stage. No, there's none here for M. S. Starrett. Sorry, boy."[32] Neither Martin nor my grandfather knew they were second cousins.[†]

Martin Starrett told his life story to CBC radio producer Imbert Orchard during the early 1970s. Of some 900 interviews, Starrett's was considered amongst Orchard's best. However, nowhere in Starrett's stories does he say that he and my grandfather were related.

The two Charlies (Clifford and Sterritt) worked as packers with K'aatim Hayatsxw/Andrew Mowatt and Woosimlaxha/Peter Barney. Andrew Mowatt did double duty as cook and as Sterritt's helper. All were hard workers. Many years later my Uncle Percy said when these old-timers were lashing on packs "the ropes whistled and snapped in a blur." When he was packing horses to take

---

† Andrew Starrett and Nancy Cummins were the grandparents of Charles (Charlie Sterritt's father) and William Andrew (Martin Starrett's father). See Starrett and Cummins Family Tree.

supplies out to the trapline for the winter, Charlie Sterritt's sons often helped. While 'throwing the diamond', he entangled one or the other in the diamond rope—probably deliberately—while they struggled to keep up with their father.

In the early 1900s homesteaders throughout northern BC relied upon Hazelton for government services, medical needs and provisions. In 1911, an immigrant from Scotland—John Glen—settled at Francois Lake and made frequent trips to Hazelton for supplies:

> The arrival of a boat and the departure of a pack train brought out most of the population. Charlie Sterrat was considered the fastest and most reliable packer in that district and being a quiet, conscientious man, he believed everything that was said to him. Knowing this, some of the onlookers would tease him. Mules mostly were used in the packing business. Not only were they stronger than horses, they were less troublesome. Packs were weighed and piled in front of the animal that was to carry it. Two men worked as a team, or rather as a head packer and his helper. Charlie would be stripped to his overalls with the sweat pouring off him. He would grab a side pack and place it on with a light rope. In the meantime, his helper would put the pack on, on his side, and Charlie would throw on the top pack, put the canvas cover over the entire pack, and reach for the lash rope. This is when the fun generally started. Charlie would be throwing the diamond hitch and

The author's paternal grandfather, Charlie Sterritt (R) and Andrew Mowatt. Charlie, born in Gidumgaldo's longhouse in 1885, worked as a trapper, packer, stage driver, road builder and logger throughout Gitxsan territory and beyond. He died in 1968. (Sterritt Family coll.)

one of the onlookers would have his watch in his hand. "What's the matter Charlie? You're getting slower every day."

Charlie would give him a black look over his shoulder and then that rope would just seem to sizzle. I have watched many packing contests and have travelled with packers and guides, but I have yet to see a man who could pack a horse faster than Charlie. It certainly was wonderful the way those boys could handle freight. Nothing seemed to stump them: heavy mining equipment, circular saws, sawmill shafts and pulleys, crosscut saws and delicate survey equipment, together with crates of eggs. All seemed to reach their destination safely. Suitcases were something that the packers frowned upon. If the owner insisted, after being advised to put the contents in something else, the suitcase would be on top of a pack and the rope tightened until it seemed to groan. From that time on, the insides generally accompanied their owner in a gunnysack.[33]

Years later Charlie's son Percy witnessed a packing contest in Hazelton. Percy said Charlie was once the *cargidor* (pack boss) for George Beirnes on the Telegraph Trail, managing eighty-six horses and mules with Andrew Mowatt, Gidumgaldo/Charlie Clifford and Peter Barney, to name a few.

The way they do it is they grab the pack box, flip it to their knee and in the same motion, onto the side of the horse; the pack settles as they tie the lash ropes; the mantle flies on the load and just as quickly the diamond rope is flying, with Charlie shouting to Andrew, "Breaker, breaker, cut him in two!" as they took up slack and tied off the diamond.

Packing contests weren't the only sport enjoyed by the Gitxsan. Some communities, like Glen Vowell, had baseball and hockey teams. The Glen Vowell baseball team included Alfred and Eddy Russell, Billy Bird (Aunt Edith's husband), Phillip Brown and my grandfather, among others. The team uniforms had large red initials, GV, on the front. They traveled to Hazelton and New Hazelton to play, and on May 24, 1917 beat an experienced non-native New Hazelton team. Alfred Russell was their pitcher.

The Gitxsan people loved all sports—hockey, soccer, baseball and basketball. During the early 1930s, visionary Gitxsan community leaders established the Young People's Educational Association (YPEA).[†] The YPEA sponsored sports activities and supported young people who wished to participate. At the same time, the leaders created an outdoor sports area on reserve land near Hazelton where they later built concession stands, a kitchen, and a covered grandstand[‡] along with a soccer pitch and a baseball diamond. A grateful Hazelton community provided food to the workers during the building project, as the field would be available to everyone.

[†] In about 1942, the elders changed the name of the YPEA to the YPAA: Young People's Athletic Association.

[‡] At the time, it may have been the only covered grandstand in all of northern BC.

Portion of Haaxxw's pole carved and erected in Kispiox in about 1885. It was considered one of the finest in the village. In the 1940s, Charlie moved the pole to Totem Park in Gitanmaax where it still stands. (Image 49248 courtesy of NAC).

The sports field became known as Totem Park when some Gitanmaax chiefs, concerned there could be a repeat of the 1936 flood, decided to move their riverside poles there. The first pole, that of Shanoss, was moved from Gitanmaax to Totem Park in 1942.

Also, by 1940, some of the Kispiox village poles had fallen and were lying in the grass rotting, including my grandfather's[†] Gans' Niigyamks pole. This may have been why he too decided to relocate the pole to Totem Park, despite the protests of his House members. He ignored their protests, or convinced them otherwise, and hired Marshall Brothers to haul the pole from Kispiox to Gitanmaax in 1947.[‡]

[†] Charlie Sterritt accepted the name Haaxxw, and with it responsibility for the pole, when his uncle died in 1933.

[‡] In about 1947, another aged pole from Gitanmaax was moved there. In the same year, Guuhadak/Tommy Muldoe raised a new pole at the park; as did the House of Luutkuts'iiwus in honour of Tom Campbell. My grandmother, Kate Sterritt,

The controversy didn't end there. Another pole being carved for the opening of Totem Park had a crest that my grandfather said belonged to him. He instructed two of his House members to chop the figure from the pole. Finally, on opening day, the celebration began. I recall wandering around the field, watching the poles being raised, but I had no idea what the pole raisings signified. Today, the only pole from the mid-1940s still standing at Totem Park is Haaxxw's Niigyamks pole.

The totem poles (L-R) are those of Sanoos, Haaxxw, Spookxw, Guuhadak, and Luutkuts'iiwus. The first three poles were carved ca. 1885, and were moved from Gitanmaax Village (1 & 3) and Kispiox (2) to Totem Park; the two on the right were carved after 1945. (C.L. Botham photo from Bill Heath coll.)

My grandfather stopped packing and trapping in the mid-1930s and began logging cedar poles during the winter and commercial fishing and farming during the summer. He continued in these occupations until the mid-1950s when he retired. He died in 1968.

I now realize that my grandparents and parents lived in two very different worlds: the first, of course, being their Gitxsan world; the second, both socially and economically, as entrepreneurs in the rapidly evolving economy: hunting, trapping, packing, commercial fishing and logging.

---

intended to have a pole carved and moved a cedar tree to Totem Park in the early fifties. She died before it was carved, and the log eventually decayed.

There was undoubtedly tension due to differing cultures but my grandparents and parents were determined that their children be part of both worlds.

After my grandmother Kate died in 1955, I asked my grandfather if I could come and stay with him for a few days. He agreed and I took a couple of library books with me. One of the books had stories about American folk heroes like Paul Bunyan, Pecos Bill, Davy Crockett and Daniel Boone. When I got up for breakfast the next morning my grandfather was reading the book. It might have been a struggle for him but he could read and write a bit and was fascinated by the stories and told me so. This was a side of him I hadn't seen. But as Freddy Jackson told me, my grandfather often told Wiigyet stories after everyone bedded down for the night. Paul Bunyan and Pecos Bill don't seem to have much in common with Wiigyet, yet my grandfather found the American folk stories appealing. Like all skilled storytellers, he recognized a good yarn when he found one.

ENDNOTES

1. Barbeau and Beynon, "Raven Clan Outlaws", 409-411.
2. Beynon, *The Last Raid of Legaick*, 26-30.
3. Canada: Dept. Of Indian Affairs, Green fieldnotes 1911. Green described the site as, "A large rock in the centre of the [Skeena] river used as a fort in olden times."
4. Barbeau and Beynon, "Raven Clan Outlaws", 409-411.
5. *Delgamuukw v. BC*, Martha Brown, Vol. III 1985: 40.
6. PABC. "Baptism record of Joshua and Selena Simpson," Jan. 10, 1886, Methodist Church, Port Essington Register 1883-1946.
7. Morrow, 106.
8. "HBC Diary", 1, 3.
9. "HBC Diary", 5.
10. "HBC Diary", 8.
11. "HBC Diary", 9.
12. Morrow, 117.
13. "Packing Contract Let: Supplies for Yukon Telegraph Line to be carried by 'Cataline'", 1.
14. Morrow, 117.
15. Sherwood, 111.
16. Lee, 10.
17. Lee, 18.
18. Lee, 24-5.
19. "Barbeau and Beynon Fieldnotes", Arthur Hankin B-F-199.8, 1923: 1.
20. Lee, 25-26.
21. Lee, 27.
22. Lee, 37.
23. "Barbeau and Beynon Fieldnotes", Arthur Hankin, B-F-199.8, 1923: 1-2.
24. Canada: 1901 Census of BC, Cassiar (Skeena), Burrard, p. 1, line 23, Family No: 11. McIntosh emigrated to Canada in 1873.
25. Williams, 25.
26. Williams, 87.
27. PABC: Surveyor General's Office, J.H. Gray Fieldbooks (P.H. No. 18, 1907).
28. "Ashcroft: The Gateway to the Nechaco Valley and Northern British Columbia", 1.
29. "Local and District News", 7 Nov. 1908: 1.
30. "Local and District News", 12 Dec. 1908, 1.
31. "Local and District News", 16 Jan. 1908, 1.
32. Orchard, 66.
33. Glen, 23-24.

CHAPTER NINETEEN

Wii Bowax/Percy Sterritt

[The]interweaving of people from various Houses into seasonal round activities brings the whole community into play when work is being performed, and it articulates the extended family relationships that make up daily life.

—Anthropologist Richard Daly 2005[1]

My grandfather Charlie Sterritt married sixteen year-old Margaret Johnson of Kispiox in 1905. Margaret's parents were Axgigii/Solomon Johnson (1854-1931) and Naagahl Banda/Sophia Wilson (1861-1956). Soon after their marriage Charlie applied to pre-empt 160 acres along the left bank of the Skeena River opposite Glen Vowell at Skanii'mahl'hoohl'gan, where the cedar tree for Gidumgaldo's totem pole became stuck ca.1880.[†] Margaret's older brother, Jonathan Johnson, held the name Wii Bowax, which my uncle, Percy Sterritt, inherited when Jonathan died.

The family lived there most of the time, but also in Kispiox if Charlie had work there. Charlie and Margaret had three children: Simon (c.1905-1915), Gertie (1907-1990) and Percy (1910-1998). Sadly, Simon died at about age ten after suffering for several years from a leg injury that Percy thought led to cancer.

Charlie helped build the first modern bridge to span the Kispiox River at Kispiox. The men completed the bridge on January 10, 1910. When Charlie came home from work that day he discovered Margaret had delivered their third child, Percy.

---

† My grandfather's property was located at District Lot 2160.

Charlie was always taking jobs that took him away from home for long stretches of time, and he and Margaret separated in the spring. While their parent's separation was hard for Gertie and Percy, they nevertheless lived long, healthy, useful lives, lives that were a testament to the resilience and support to be gained from an intact extended family.

After Charlie and Margaret separated, Solomon Johnson and Sophia raised Simon, Gertie and Percy in Kispiox. Everyone's diet then consisted mainly of fish, wild animal meat, berries and what they grew in their gardens. Sophia, with Gertie and Percy, had rabbit and grouse snares set in the bush north of Kispiox which they checked daily. Gertie and Percy often checked the snares alone. By the time they were teenagers, they had bush-knowledge, survival skills and a work ethic that would stand them in good stead to the end of their busy lives.

For example, while trapping with their grandmother on their Kispiox Valley territory near Xsi'an Seegit (Murder Creek), they found a live lynx in their trap. Sophia gave Gertie a red polka dot handkerchief and said, "Wave this in front of the lynx's eyes." Gertie did and the lynx became drowsy, nodding its head. Sophia made a snare of fine rope, looped it over the lynx's head and neck and strangled it. Percy said the old people didn't believe in clubbing an animal to death.

Sophia's brother, Wo'os Sa'lo'op/Philip Wilson (1867-1940) had a hunting ground far to the north near the headwaters of the Nass River at Miin Lax Mihl. Philip's great-nephews George Brown and Percy accompanied him to this hunting ground when they were perhaps twelve or younger.

One of the Gitxsan men Percy trapped with was 'Niist/Charles Sampson (1886-1963). Sampson belonged to the Kuldo Wolf Clan and was the son of Haaxxw/Mark Sampson. Mark Sampson and Charlie Sterritt were cousins, which meant that Charles Sampson and Percy were second cousins. Percy admired and respected him:

> Charles Sampson was the best woodsman I ever knew. He was full of fun and very clean on the trap line. Old Indians believed that they should never change their clothes while trapping. It was bad luck. But throughout the winter Charlie bathed himself and washed his clothes in the creek by our camp every two weeks without fail.

> Charlie and George Wilson once carved an eight or ten-foot totem pole when they had nothing to do. Then Charlie cooked a big moose stew. No one knew what he was doing until he jokingly called everyone (eight to ten people) to his 'feast' while he raised the pole.

> He got up every morning at 4:00 a.m. and cooked breakfast for everyone. He patiently sat by the fire waiting for everyone to get up and, when they did, he would say, "Well, you guys were sleeping and I didn't want to wake you up." He was a very kind man.

Trappers made new snowshoes each year before setting out for the trap line. But sometimes a person would be caught unprepared and emergency snowshoes had to be made. Percy described how this was done:

> [Good] snowshoes can be made from grey willow—*giist*—which grows on the mountain. The wood looks like maple, but it's not as soft. In order to bend the wood, you leave the bark on and gently heat it by the fire. If there are lots of moose near the trapping area, you don't need to bring the heavy foot filling—*am nax*[†]—with you [as it can be made from fresh moose hide].
>
> At Sixth Cabin [on the Telegraph Line] there are lots of moose. After shooting a moose, and while the animal is still warm, you can pull the hair off the rump and lower back and pack the hide to your camp. When you have time, you can cut the hide into strips for filling or re-filling your snowshoes.

Percy soaked the *am nax* and *winx* to make it more pliable when filling his snowshoes. It tightened up when dry but was slippery and difficult to manage when wet. Percy overcame this with charcoal or wool, so he could grip and pull the filling. In those days men and women knit and mended their own socks and gloves and they packed wool with them for that purpose.

Percy used a dull knife to cut the foot filling because a sharp knife cut too fine and the filling broke easily. He had a handy gauge when cutting the hide—his notched thumbnail—to ensure the filling was of a consistent width.

In the spring of 1964 Joshua McLean, his brother Thomas, Joe Wilson and I snowshoed to Kuldo to look at timber. Early one morning we heard a keening noise coming from the mountainside nearby. Joshua said it was a grizzly bear. This occurred each morning for a couple of days and then we returned to Hazelton. I told Percy about this and he said:

> When bears come out of the den in the spring, they have a ritual called *sii'sagenxw* [making new tracks]. The bear walks from the den a few steps at a time, then, walking backwards in the same tracks, retraces its steps. He walks a little further each day, until the weather is right. He does it for three or four days. After that, the bear walks away from the den and finds a good place where he will spend the night.

In 1924 Percy and his uncle, Philip Wilson, were hunting bears at Ts'im Aks in the mountains northeast of First Cabin. They checked about half a dozen dens but they were empty. Finally, Philip noticed a hole high in a big dead hemlock and said, "There is a black bear in that tree. You will have to climb up and kill it." They felled a tree with limbs to lean against the hemlock tree providing rungs for Percy to climb.

[†] *Am nax* supports the wearer's feet, and fine filling—*winx* (aka babiche)—is used in the rest of the snowshoe.

The author's son, Gordon, at Temlaham with snowshoes made by Percy Sterritt. (NJS photo)

I could tell there was a bear in there but he wouldn't move so I poked a stick in there and all at once the bear came at me. I backed up…while the bear snapped at me. Its snout was three inches from my face, and it slobbered on my face and down the front of my clothes. I was terrified. Suddenly, the bear backed into the tree. I don't know how he did it—the hole was so small. I climbed down and Philip told me to go back up and shoot the bear. I said, "No." Then Philip climbed to the bear. He took a branch and rattled it around in the den. I could hear the bear climbing up and down inside the tree. Philip waited and shot the bear in the head when it appeared. We tried to get the carcass out, but couldn't. So we chopped the tree down, and chopped the bear out. It was huge. When we were gutting the bear, my uncle told me to look at its *'ts'imko'o* (anus). I did, and there was a dirty object there. It looked like rolled up thimbleberry leaves.†

Percy told me how a grizzly bear attacked and almost killed Philip's brother, Robert. He had shot two mountain goats and was returning to pack out the second animal.

---

† Hibernating bears emerge in the spring with an anal plug, which forms during hibernation. Because the plugs are found just inside or outside the dens of bears that have just emerged, it is thought the plug keeps the bear from defecating inside the den during hibernation.

Robert heard a noise, and found himself between two grizzly cubs. The sow suddenly attacked, grabbing his foot and swiping him on the head. She threw him through the air. He finally got his knife, and while he was going for the sow's throat, she ripped off his little finger. He lay as if dead, but the bear attacked his head and back and leg, then it sat on him. When the bear finally walked away, Robert shouted, "Why didn't you finish me off?" The sow returned and bit his eye and mouth, and part of his head. The bear finally left. Robert, taking four days, dragged himself over the mountain and down to the Kispiox River at Geel/Henry Aluux̱w's camp. Henry took Robert to First Cabin where Doctor Wrinch met them.‡ Robert was wrapped in a blanket, which stuck to him because of all the dry blood. He lived.

Philip Wilson had fifty-four pack animals in 1923 and a contract with the HBC to provision Fort Babine. According to Percy they were up at 3:30 am to gather the horses and were packed and ready to go by breakfast time. In Hazelton the men packed at Philip's place or at Two Mile Creek. They camped three times between Hazelton and Babine Lake: at Seven Mile (if they packed in Hazelton); Nine Mile (if at Two Mile), and then at Eighteen Mile and Stump Camp. After leaving Stump Camp, they climbed east to the summit and could see Babine Lake twenty kilometres below. They camped just once—at Eighteen Mile—on their return trip.

Working with horses and mules on a pack train is challenging, even for adults who cherish such work. The camaraderie and teasing that goes with that life appeals to teenagers and Percy treasured it. But a great deal of responsibility accompanied the trust the pack boss placed in all his men, the animals and their equipment. The trips weren't without their hazards, some self-inflicted, others—like disturbing a hornet nest—are the bane of pack trains. The first few animals stir up the insects, the animals following bear the brunt of the attack and then, with hooves stamping, heads rising sharply, ears pricked forward, the remaining animals stampede in panic.

During one of their trips Philip led the pack train, Percy following on his horse behind the bell mare. As they were approaching the bridge at Babine Lake Percy leaned to pick high bush cranberries and spied a yellow-jacket nest. He jerked a nearby branch to irritate the yellow jackets and rode on. Daisy, Philip's wife, was behind Percy carrying two pails of blueberries. Daisy screamed as her saddle horse, attacked by yellow jackets, bucked its way across the bridge, pursued by the entire pack train. Packs were thrown and scattered as were Daisy's blueberries. Philip was furious. He and Daisy refused to feed Percy that night.

Percy told how during another trip Jonathan Johnson was injured.

> He put his foot in the stirrup and while putting his right leg over the saddle the horse took off, pulling his left leg out of the socket. He couldn't get off his horse at Stump Camp. From there on we had to lift him on and off his horse on our return to Hazelton. He was laid up in Kispiox all winter until April.

---

‡ The mauling occurred in 1922 and was reported in a local newspaper under the caption, "Native Badly Mutilated by Grizzly Bear".

> Mrs. Louis Wesley was a healer. She felt Jonathan's hip. She said, "It's already rotten in his joint." Mrs. Wesley laid Jonathan on his side on a table. She put blankets between his legs and around his legs, and a plank along his side. Samuel Johnson stood on the plank. He jumped twice, but it didn't work. Jonathan passed out from the pain for a long time.
>
> James Angus's mother was helping. Everyone else left. Wiis'dis/James Angus (1902-1988) stayed to hold Jonathan while Arthur and Samuel Johnson stood on the plank. Jonathan said, "Go ahead. You might as well fix it." They barely jumped and his leg went back into the socket with a loud bang. Jonathan passed out again. His eyes rolled back, his face was twisted and his tongue twitched. I watched all this. He was walking in two days and played baseball that summer. When Jonathan died [in 1968] his whole leg [and his side] up to his arm was blue.

This wasn't the only time Jonathan needed help for an injury.

> We were trapping at Kwinageese and he pulled a muscle while snowshoeing. My grandfather made a saw-tooth like scraper with a piece of tin and put it on a stick. Then he told Jonathan to hang onto a roof beam in their cabin. Solomon scraped Jonathan's leg four times on four sides. Blood came pouring out. Then my grandfather wrapped his leg with cloth and some kind of medicine. He was OK in two days. Jonathan was really brave. He was brave because they gave him the heart of a *gibuu* (wolf) when he was young. He was mean [in the warrior sense], and very quiet.

In 1925 George Beirnes still serviced the linesmen between Hazelton and Ninth Cabin each summer and had made his last trip of the season. Afterwards, he guided big game hunters at the headwaters of the Skeena and Stikine rivers where there were mountain sheep and goats, grizzlies, caribou and moose. He intended to rendezvous with his hunting party at Fourth Cabin and had hired Philip Wilson to get the hunters that far.

Philip, Jonathan Johnson (Percy's uncle), and Percy herded the packstring—ten horses and four mules—to Four Mile above Kispiox, where they packed the animals. The hunting party included three adults—all doctors—and a doctor's son.

Philip was busy and had fifteen-year-old Percy bring the hunters and their guide—Simon Gunanoot—from Four Mile above Kispiox to Fourth Cabin. Percy was in good company with Dave Wiggins and 'Ot' Adler as helpers. Percy sensed that "people were afraid of Simon," but Percy found him pleasant to be with. They bunked together during the trip and Simon talked about his life. It was then that he told Percy about the incident with McIntosh and LeClair.

Whenever the lakes or streams had fish, the doctors fished. They camped thirteen miles north of First Cabin at Trout Lake on their second day out. Trout were rising and the doctor and his son went fishing on a decrepit raft. The raft broke apart, and the men fell in the water with the doctor

A pack train at Fourth Cabin on the Yukon Telegraph Line. (Image A-05356 courtesy of the RBCM & A)

trying to save his son and the son trying to save their rods. Simon Gunanoot rolled around on the ground laughing while the cook hollered, "When do you want me to cook the fish?"

Percy and his colleagues took another two and a half days to get to Fourth Cabin. Beirnes's men were there with their packhorses. Feed had been scarce and Beirnes's animals were gaunt and had saddles sores. The doctors asked Percy to continue to Groundhog Mountain with his packstring but he said no, that he had other commitments.

He returned to Hazelton and continued packing for the rest of the summer helping Philip, Ot Adler and Dave Wiggins pack cables for the Red Rose Mine tramline which was being built from the railroad near Carnaby to a ridge on the mountain at the headwaters of Comeau Creek.

Twelve pack animals were needed as each cable weighed at least 1300 kilograms, and the animals, when loaded, would in effect be cabled to each other. Loads comprised eight loops per animal (four loops per side), with slower animals in the lead. The packstring settled into a routine after two trips.

When the cable contract was finished, Philip hired Percy to supply the mining camp on a weekly basis. Percy used three packhorses and a saddle horse. He loaded the horses at Dick Sargent's store in Hazelton, crossed the bridge from what is now 'Ksan to Mission Point and took the Comeau Creek trail to the camp on the ridge where he unloaded and spent the night.†

---

† The government built the bridge across the Bulkley River ca. 1920.

The bridge across the Bulkley River between Mission Flats (aka Anderson Flats) and what is now 'Ksan was used by Percy en route to the Red Rose Mine. It was wrecked in 1942 when attempts to dynamite a log jam took out one of the middle sections (Sterritt Family coll.)

A man by the name of Dick McLaren was in charge at the camp. He ordered two cases of vanilla extract† weekly and expected Percy to take good care of it. The extract was the first item to be unloaded at camp. McLaren opened a bottle and downed it while Percy looked on in amazement.

---

† Vanilla extract has a high alcohol content.

Simon Gunanoot returned to Hazelton with Beirnes and the hunters in the late fall of 1925. They had taken two grizzly bears and some sheep and caribou. Percy said Simon earned $5.50 a day with Beirnes while Phillip paid Percy $3.00 a day, and Dave Wiggins and Ot Adler $4.00 each.

Several years later, Percy, C.W.D's son Charlie Clifford (1881-1953) and other trappers were on their way to their hunting ground near the headwaters of the Nass River. They camped one night on Poison Mountain, which lies between Third and Fourth Cabins. While the men made camp, Clifford (who later held the name Gidumgaldo) went off into the bush and shortly after, called the others to join him. He pointed to the telegraph wire hanging there, according to Percy, and said:

> I worked with a crew of men cutting trail from the Hazelton side, and there was a second crew of men cutting trail from the Ninth Cabin side. We were slower because we had a smaller crew. We started through the timber and had just come out on top here. The crew from Ninth Cabin had come over Poison Mountain. We would have missed each other but not by much. The crew from Ninth Cabin had flatter, easier ground, so they recut their section so the line would meet us head on, instead of at an angle.

"Charlie showed us the splice," Percy said. "It was about eighteen inches of wrapped wire. Charlie Clifford said they built a big camp and partied for three days afterwards."

The 1901 celebration Clifford participated in almost didn't happen. The federal government had been ambivalent about the telegraph project and had avoided making the decision to connect Dawson City with southern Canada until December 1899 when J. B. Charleson was authorized to start the wheels rolling to complete the gap between Quesnel in the south and Atlin in the north, a distance estimated to be about 1500 kilometres.[2]

Trappers routinely coped with cold weather but on rare occasions severe conditions could seriously challenge their abilities. Percy and his cousin George had been trapping near the head of the Nass River at Miin Lax Mihl when, during normal winter weather, they packed up and started for Hazelton with their dogs. By the time they got to the Third Cabin, the weather had turned bitterly cold. Percy became worried and they hurried on to Second Cabin where they would have telegraph contact with Hazelton.

> At Second Cabin, we phoned [telegraphed?] Hazelton and asked Nikateen/John Smith to meet us with horses and a sleigh. We kept on travelling and met John, Charlie Clifford and Philip Wilson near First Cabin. We made camp late and couldn't warm up. We built a big fire with two fallen trees. The flames were twenty feet high, and I was standing close to the fire. George said, 'Look at your buttons.' They were melting and dropping off, but I couldn't feel any heat. I told George, 'Come on! I'm not staying in this damn place. I'm walking.'
>
> John Smith told me not to go, but we left anyway. When the dogs gave up, we carried their packs as well as our own. The dogs followed way behind us. We got

to Kispiox at 4:00 a.m. My grandmother broke into tears when she took my rubber boots off. There was crushed ice on both sides of my feet inside the boots.

An hour and a half later, my grandmother saw a team of horses and sleigh come into her yard. It was John, Charlie and Philip. They couldn't stand the cold either. John Smith had covered Charlie and Philip with hay and then burrowed into the hay for shelter while he drove the team.

Percy didn't say how cold it was, or the year, but said it was the coldest weather he had ever experienced. Other reports from that period suggested it was not unusual for the mercury to drop to minus 55° Celsius.

Percy, like most of his generation, led an exciting, eventful life. Steeped in Gitxsan ways, he easily made the transition to the emerging life style and economy. At fourteen, he spent the summer packing with Philip Wilson. That fall, for the first time, he went commercial fishing with Ts'iin/Joshua Campbell. He continued commercial fishing along the west coast for the next sixty years, and worked at many other jobs.

> I worked at every pole camp around here: with Old Man Cook at Xsi'anhl Guuxs; at Beament for Louie Mero, where I drove a team of horses; at Nash Y; at Bell Lake (aka Keynton Lake) for Elliott; across the Skeena here for my father. I worked at Silver Standard Mine here, and as a miner for Nicholsen Creek mines at Usk.

> At Usk I cut wood for a man named Arnold. He had three cabins, a bunkhouse and a cook shack. I used three saws. Arnold had two people doing what I was doing and they couldn't keep up to me. I was over five cords of wood ahead in April.

Percy married Nancy, the daughter of Wallace and Martha Morgan of Gitwangak, in 1945. She was from the House of Guuxsan. They had seven children.[†] As Percy said, "After I was married and looking after the kids, I stopped travelling."

Percy and his family lived in Two Mile, near Hazelton, during the 1940s. There, Percy's kids learned to play Old Tom Gwats, a ball game the Gitxsan played for many years.

> We played Old Tom Gwats when I was a kid at Kispiox. We used to play all afternoon. The older people played too: Simon Angus (James Angus Sr.'s brother) played. He could run fast and chased us and hit you hard on the back or head with the ball, putting you out.

> My kids learned from Stanley Blackstock and Eddy Olson in Two Mile. They played in my backyard every night. The kids played in Terrace after we moved there. All the white kids joined them. I used to go out and play with them too.

Percy explained how the game was played:

---

† Mamie (Percy's step-daughter), Marvin, Ron, Vincent, Simon, Valient and Valerie.

The field could be any size, with a batter's line and a runner's line across the field from side to side; a catcher's plate or base, and a pitcher's plate. The bat was made from a fence picket or a short carved pole. The ball was a rag hand-sewn into cloth or canvas. There could be any number of runners to a team, but usually between nine and twelve.

The objective was to hit the ball and get from the batter's line to the runner's line. But you could stand at the batter's line until it was safe to race to the runner's line. At times, six or seven or more runners might be standing behind the batter's line, waiting to get to the runner's line.

A batter, and the batter's side, was out if the catcher caught a ticked ball three times in a row. A runner was out when a player on the field side threw the ball and hit the runner. A side scored when a runner successfully made it to the field line and back without being hit.

The author (back right, with snowshoes he made) and his uncle, Percy Sterritt, with sons Gordon (L) and Jamie (ca. 1977). (Valerie Belina photo)

We played Old Tom Gwats in Hazelton too in the schoolyard next to our house. The Robinson twins—Perry and Ronny—were merciless and could throw the ball so hard it stung. I still remember the terror I felt running to or from the field line when one of the twins had the ball.

Soon after we returned to Hazelton in 1973, Percy and Gertie adopted my wife Barbara and our two sons into their House. Percy still trapped then and taught Gordon and Jamie. Gordon ran his own line next to Percy's at Skansna'at Lake (Skunsnat Lake). Percy died in March 1998 at Wrinch Memorial Hospital in Hazelton.

Percy Sterritt (centre), son of Charlie, was a packer, commercial fisherman, logger, miner, storyteller and mentor to the author. He died in 1998. Pictured here with his brother, Neil B. and Neil's B.'s second wife Barbara. (Valerie Belina coll.)

The next year, our genealogist in the *Delgamuukw v. BC* court case, Heather Harris, wrote a wonderful poem about Percy. Heather is of Metis and Cree ancestry and lived in Gitxsan territory for many years. She was married to a Gitxsan man, David Harris. 'Niist/David Blackwater adopted her into his House.

"I would like to thank…Percy Sterritt/Wii Bowax," she said, "for telling me the best story I ever heard."[3]

Percy's Stories

Gee-zus Cur-ist! I never gonna forget
what I seen as long as I live.

Percy's lived his long life.
Gone on to the spirit world now.
Left his stories with me.
His words hang in my mind
in his blue room.

"Gee-zus Cur-ist!
Me and Joe was 'bout sixteen.
We was sneakin' aroun'.
Out by where the *halaits*
had their place at Anlaw.

They had a ol' log cabin.
They was a bunch of them inside.
We was lookin' through the cracks.

They was dressed up.
Bear skins, bear claws,
'roun their necks,
on their heads.

Aprons, *aatai asxw* an' stuff.
They dance, sing, rattle, drum.
Got a fire in the middle
o' that dirt floor.

They got Matilda there.
She been sick a year or so.
She dressed up like them *halaits*.

One ol' *halait* spread out
the hot coals
into a path 'bout eight feet long.
I start to get real scared
'Joe, what they gonna do?'

'She gonna walk on it.'

'Mathilda in her bare feet.
She walk on them burning coals.
She drag her feet real slow
through them coals.'

Percy shuffled his hands in the air.

"Them ol' *halaits* keep singin', drummin',
rattlin', dancin'.

Mathilda, she go slowly,
slowly through them red hot coals.
I get the hell out of there.

Later, me and Joe, we ask her,
'What's it feel like?'

She say, "They tell me it's *siiyun*—glacier.
It feel like ice."

Gee-zus! That's one thing
I couldn't get over.
I never gonna forget that.[4]

ENDNOTES

1   Daly, 163-64.
2   Miller, 91.
3   Harris, H., 7.
4   Harris, H., 109-10.

CHAPTER TWENTY

Wiik̲'aax/Neil B. Sterritt

A big bird came from the sky...it was from the bird's wings...The big bird from the sky told [Ts'ooda] to come up the Skeena River and there will be seven houses and they will be called villages....and then [Ts'ooda] travelled all the way up to the Yukon...and they just scattered all over the place...[then] they went to Kisgegas.

—Guuhadak/Thomas Wright, 1986[1]

One of the early coastal peoples was the People of Ts'ooda who played a very significant role in the history of the Skeena River peoples. They established early settlements at the mouth of the Ecstall River, up the coast at Kadu and in the upper Kispiox, G̲aldo'o and Kisgagas area as well as at the headwaters of the Nass and Skeena Rivers. Some of their numbers also settled at Dehldan [Tahltan Village] on the Stikine River and in the Tagish Lake area. In these northern areas they merged with inland groups and together they became known as the Wolf Clan.

—Susan Marsden 1987[2]

Luu Uuxs[†]/Kathleen (Kate) Morrison

My grandmother Kate considered Kisgegas to be her home, a village which was for centuries the largest of all Gitxsan villages because of the huge Babine Lake salmon runs that converged in the canyon below the village. Based on fur traders' observations the village population may have exceeded 600 during the mid-1800s. Kate's mother, Galuua/Jessie, was born at Kisgegas in 1865 and married Ma'uus/Job of Kispiox by custom in 1881.[‡] A few months after their marriage, Job went to the Nass River to harvest oolichan, leaving Jessie in Kispiox. Job failed to return when the oolichan season ended and Jessie learned that he was living with a woman in a Nisga'a village.

After several months with no sign of him returning, Jessie went to Hazelton where she met a man, lived with him and became pregnant by him.[§] In the fall, as Jessie and the man walked from the church in Hazelton, Job suddenly appeared, grabbed Jessie by the arm and said, "This is my wife and I'm taking her home." My grandmother, Kathleen (Kate), was born at Kispiox in March of 1882.[¶]

The family participated in the commercial fishery at the coast where Job fished while Jessie worked in the cannery and mended nets. According to Aunt Edith, Kate's birth father was in Port Essington. He approached Jessie and Charles Martin's sister Maggie (Margaret Kispioks) and said he wanted to take his six-year-old daughter south so she could go to school. Jessie was in favour of this and Maggie agreed to bring Kate to her birth father at Port Essington while Job was out fishing.

When Job returned and found Kate missing, he was enraged and demanded to know where she was. He immediately went to Port Essington and took Kate from her birth father. Jessie was disappointed that Kate had lost the opportunity for an education. Job and Jessie had other children, including two who survived to adulthood, James (1895-1940) and Eva (1904-1964).

Strange as it seems, Job and Jessie may have taken the surname Morrison from that of Kate's birth father.

Uncle Percy phoned me in the fall of 1956, not long after I had moved to Vancouver for school. Percy and other Skeena River commercial fishermen were docked at Steveston, a salmon-canning centre at the mouth of the south arm of the Fraser River. They were there for a fall opening and Percy asked me to join him on the weekend. After school on Friday I took a bus to Steveston. We fished for a while and that night slept on his gill-netter. The next morning I explored the docks while Percy cleaned his boat. I saw a woman mending nets on the dock and went over to watch her work. I was startled, for sitting there working was my grandmother, or at least a remarkable likeness of her. I said hello and asked her name. She said, "I'm Irene Harris. What is your name?"

I told her, and she said, "Your grandmother and I are sisters. We have the same father."

[†] Luu Uuxs, meaning 'inside the copper'.
[‡] At the 1881 Canada Census, Gitxsan people had only Gitxsan names. Within a few years they began taking baptismal names.
[§] The surname of this man may have been Morrison, as we shall see later.
[¶] See Wiik̲'aak Family Tree.

She said the two of them had spent time together when they were young. Irene, the daughter of Agnes McDames (1855-1943) from Gitsegukla, was six years younger than my grandmother.[3] One of her sons, Wiiyagadeets/Elijah (Eli) Turner, said Irene's father's name was Morrison and that he traveled widely with Agnes while he lived in the north searching for gold. When he finally found it, he told Agnes he was returning to his wife in southern BC. Irene was born after Morrison left.

My grandmother Kate's first husband was Gwiiyeehl/Joseph Brown. They had four children, Edith (1902), Jane (1904), Esther (1907) and Harry (1909).[4] Brown was a member of a Kispiox Fireweed Clan but was closely related to Niistahuukw/Walter Wright of Kitselas. Their cabin sat on the right bank of the Skeena opposite the mouth of Legate Creek. The Grand Trunk Pacific railway built a way station, Pacific, at or very near the cabin and totem pole.

My Aunt Edith/Wiilixsha'os said:

> My father [Joseph Brown] brought two donkeys from Manson Creek—Jennie and Fannie. He shot a caribou at Xsina'gwoot (Legate Creek) and had it in his canoe. I thought it was one of the donkeys. I cried and told my mother. We stayed in a big cabin…by the Skeena River at Pacific…They had a totem pole standing there… They called the trapping ground Xsina'gwoot…the log house was on the [west] side and the totem pole was there too. Every year we went there to trap in March and came back in June by riverboat. The Kitselas people know all about this.

The Kispiox of my grandmother's day was a divided community. Jonathan Johnson and Johnson Williams said the Christians ran a *gokhl* (cedar rope) down the centre of the village with Christians on one side and heathens on the other. Johnson Williams said, "The only problem was that the good-looking girls were on the heathen side, and I was on the Christian side. So I used to sneak under the *gokhl* and have fun with the girls."

The Kispiox 'Christians' were those converted by Robert Tomlinson Sr. in the 1880s. The so-called heathens were those who belonged to the Salvation Army. My father told me that two Gitxsan youths saw the Salvation Army preaching on a street corner and found their music and prayers more exciting than those of the Methodists. Ward Marshall learned, possibly from Charlie Clifford, that the two youths were Clifford himself and Charlie Sterritt. A fierce rivalry ensued between the Methodists and the Salvationists in Kispiox and this led to a physical confrontation in 1898.

Reverend William Henry Pierce was living in Kispiox and had built a water-powered sawmill south of the village. Pierce had difficulty building the flume and asked Robert Tomlinson Jr. for help, as Robert Jr. and his father had already built several water-powered sawmills.

Tomlinson arrived when trouble was brewing:

> Mr. Pierce had some trouble with some disgruntled villagers at Kispiox. A good-looking young Indian had raped a Kispiox girl, and her family and friends hauled him to the District Indian Agent, who found him guilty and sentenced him. He felt absolutely disgraced, so when he returned to the village, he gathered his friends

around him, and together they decided to break from the Methodist mission there and start a mission of their own. These natives of Kispiox called their group the Salvationists.

In time, the two factions had developed so much hostility between them that one night they came to blows. I had been in Kispiox that day, and I heard the two groups were planning a showdown that evening to decide which group would win out in Kispiox. Deciding I wanted no part of the trouble brewing, I left that afternoon and went into Hazelton. That night I stayed at the home of Mr. Loring, the Indian agent.

The next morning the Salvationists arrived at the Loring house, badly bruised and beaten. They begged Mr. Loring to set apart a place for them where they could worship and live as they wanted.

The Kispiox tribe owned a second…reserve…a few miles downriver, where their village sawmill was located. Mr. Loring decided to divide that land in two and give half to the Salvationists. Everyone was happy with this arrangement, and Mr. Glen Vowell† was called in to survey the ground and lay out the lots. Later still, the official Salvation Army heard about this group of lost sheep and sent in officers from headquarters to shepherd them.[5]

The agricultural potential of Glen Vowell, as the village came to be known, was good with its deep, fertile soil. Each lot of several acres or more stretched back from the river in long, narrow, fenced fields. The villagers built their homes and hay sheds beside the wagon road that ran along the top of the riverbank. Winters were much colder then and families crossed the river on the ice on foot, and by horse and sleigh. Sometimes they travelled to and from Hazelton along the frozen river.

The religious dispute in Kispiox led to the creation of Glen Vowell, but it too was divided, with a thirty-foot border of trees between the Salvationists to the north and the Methodists to the south. Families from Kuldo and Kisgegas also moved there. Gwiniiho'osxw/Alfred Shanoss, for example, lived in a little log cabin on the north side of the trees; Duuk and his wife, Noxs Ts'aa, lived on the south side.

My grandmother Kate's life, never an easy one, got more difficult in 1909. Four people—Geel/Big Louis, Robert and Sarah Williams, and an orphan white boy—set out on a hunting expedition to Madii Lii, a campsite fifty kilometres east of Hazelton. Joseph Brown, Kate's husband, joined the hunting party at the last minute. Unbeknownst to the others, he was suffering from a heart condition. His doctor had told him not to ride a horse.

The party arrived at Madii Lii and set up camp. Complaining about his heart, Brown told Big Louis that "…he had not done as the doctor ordered him." On September 13, the Williamses

---

† The surveyor was Arthur Wellesley Vowell. He was appointed Indian Reserve Commissioner in 1898 and laid out Gitxsan reserves.

A religious dispute within the village of Kispiox led to the establishment of Glen Vowell a few kilometres downriver. Pictured here is a Salvation Army parade at Glen Vowell. (Image A-06061 courtesy of RBCM & A)

stayed with him in camp while Big Louis and the young boy went hunting mountain goats. They were away two days. On their return, they heard shots signalling the need for help and learned that Joseph had been dead for a day and a half.

Sarah Williams said Joseph appeared to be in good health but in the morning they found him dead.[6] Big Louis brought the body to Hazelton. At the inquest, Garnet Graham testified that he had examined the body "…and found no marks of violence and nothing to indicate anything other than a death from natural causes."[7]

After Joseph died, Kate and her children moved from Kispiox to Hazelton where she worked with her uncle, Charles Martin. Aunt Edith said Charles was protective of them and made them go to the 'white' school that Jessie Lumm also attended. But living with Charles was a challenge, Edith said, because "Old Man [Dick] Sargent wanted to marry my mother after my father died, and Charles Martin wouldn't let her."

Edith said, "We got a kick out of Charles. He used to dress up and walk around town with his cane in the evening." It was dark when Charles returned one night and thought he saw Dick Sargent lurking in the shadows. Charles punched Dick, but 'Dick' was a post, and he smashed his fist.

Dick finally arranged to meet with Charles, and Edith overheard them talking. Charles said, "There is no way my niece is going to marry a white man. She will marry an Indian." Dick was angry. He stood up and said, "Well, I won't be back."

Dick later went to Prince Rupert where he married Emily Agnes Barbeau in September 1911,‡ and Kate and her children moved to the farm she had inherited in Glen Vowell. Her stepfather, Job

---

‡ Emily Barbeau, her sister and father were living in Prince Rupert in 1911. Emily and Marius Barbeau were second cousins.

Kathleen (Kate) Sterritt (nee Morrison) (R), the author's paternal grandmother, was born in Kispiox in 1882 and died in 1955. She lost her first husband, Joseph Brown, in 1909 and married Charlie Sterritt shortly thereafter. She is pictured here with her daughter Edith (L), from her marriage to Joseph Brown, and granddaughter Katie. (Sterritt Family coll)

Morrison, had built a frame house there at a time when most houses—especially in the original Gitxsan villages like Gitanmaax and Kispiox—were longhouses. For example, while visiting in Kispiox, Dad and his family stayed with Gutgwinuxs/Billy Williams, who lived in a big one-room building.† The stove in the centre of the room was used only for cooking and didn't really heat the building. Dad said, "We were warm. We dressed as we would outside, and had feather mattresses and blankets. We slept comfortably."

Aunt Edith said my grandfather, Charlie Sterritt, began courting Kate in Glen Vowell:

> When Charlie came back from horsepacking, he had lots of money and built a big house across from Glen Vowell. Charlie was all over the world when he was young. He was always with white men. He was even at Prince George when they first

---

† Billy Williams, Jimmy Williams and Peter John were brothers (Johnson Williams to Bruce Rigsby, ca. 1967).

surveyed it. Charlie and his first wife had a big wedding. Then he had twelve mules and horses and went packing on the telegraph line. I used to see him. George Beirnes and his packers camped at Mission Flats. They waited there until they were ready to go out again. They usually made about three trips out there every summer.

Charlie and Kate had their first child, Walter, in April 1911. He was born at Glen Vowell, as were my father, Neil B. (1913), Agnes (1916) and Jack (1920). Arthur (1923) and Margaret (1925) were born in Hazelton.‡ My grandmother's 'farm', as Edith called it, was south of the Salvationist/Methodist dividing line in Glen Vowell.

A wagon road ran south from Kispiox through Glen Vowell, past the Kispiox sawmill at Xsi Muula (aka Mill Creek, Alipakh Creek and Mero Creek) to Four Mile Bridge and Hazelton. Another road ran down the riverbank in front of my grandmother's house. It was used only in winter and shortened the distance to Hazelton by several kilometres.

Glen Vowell had a population of 105 in 1915, with half the population being twenty years or younger. The Department of Indian Affairs gave their religion as 'Other Christian Beliefs.'[8]

Early Years

My father and his siblings spent their early years in Glen Vowell. But within a few months of my father's birth in August 1913, his parents, Charlie and Kate, took him to Xsuwii Aks accompanied by Charles Martin, Edith, and Walter. They travelled the frozen Skeena from Hazelton with five dogs pulling a toboggan with their supplies and two-year-old Walter. They snowshoed up the river and carried heavy packs. My grandmother carried a pack and her infant son.

Edith said, "We stayed out in the open in a three-sided tent. That's how we lived in those days." Fur prices were high and although Charlie Sterritt made a lot of money, Charles Martin didn't do so well. They lived on moose meat, rabbits and grouse all winter. When their supplies ran low, Charlie and Walter went "…to the big Hudson's Bay post [Fort Connolly] at Bear Lake to get supplies we needed." Bear Lake was forty kilometres, a one-day walk from their camp at the junction of the Skeena and Sustut Rivers (Xsuwii Aks).

People living at Bear Lake were in bad shape. Edith said, "Simon Gunanoot and his family were at Bear Lake but they decided to live with us at Xsuwii Aks, as did Wiik̲'aax/Daniel Wiigaak. Simon was still hiding from the government. Simon's wife (Sarah) was from the House of Niik'yap and was related to my mother." David Gunanoot, Simon and Sarah's son, was seven years old and years later recalled Walter running about on his little snowshoes, tumbling here and there.

One day Charles Martin was boiling water in a large pail on the fire while Edith made bannock. A fire-log rolled, spilling scalding water on Edith's leg. It was spring and the water was rising in the river but Edith's leg had to heal before they could leave. Daniel Wiigaak took spruce

---

‡ See Wiik̲'aax Family Tree.

pitch, balled it up and put it on Edith's leg. Her leg finally healed but by then the Skeena was in flood and they needed to cross to the trail on the other side of the river.

The men built a raft with four large spruce logs. Kate covered the raft with a tarp to keep their bedding and the children dry. They loaded the raft with their winter's catch, some food, the children and dogs. As Edith said:

> I was really scared. I thought I would drown. When we all got on the raft it went below the water. There was water over top of the logs…what a sight. We should have got a picture of that. It would have been a funny picture. There were six of us, and the five dogs sitting right there too. We had a paddle but the water was so strong. We went way down the Skeena before we finally landed on the shore.

Edith said the trip along the trail from Xsuwii Aks to Fourth Cabin and south to Hazelton was difficult. Because of their late start they were short on food but telegraphers living in the line cabins offered them food as they traveled home. The trip to Hazelton took seven days. Edith was pleased that Charles, walking with a limp, slowed them, as she had difficulty walking too.

The year before their trip to Xsuwii Aks, my grandfather applied to pre-empt 167 acres of land on the right bank of the Kispiox River at Date Creek.[†] Several years later he hired George Moore, Andrew Mowatt and Billy Bird to clear brush on the property. James Angus was also looking for work. He walked up the left bank of the Kispiox River and waded across near Date Creek. My grandfather was so impressed he hired young James on the spot.

Later, after the land was cleared, someone in Kispiox noticed fires burning near the farm. They went to check and discovered my grandmother throwing lit matches about, burning underbrush so wild berries would grow.

Walter and Dad (Neil B.) frequently played and worked together. But Walter, being two years older, often dared his younger brother to copy him. For example, when he was four, Dad and his family lived briefly with Charles Martin in Kispiox. His two-story house had a hole in the ceiling with a pole from floor to roof. Walter often slid head first down the pole, and told Dad to do the same. He didn't hang on properly and dove straight down, landing head first with a thud.

Walter, Edith and Dad were always snaring rabbits and playing in behind Glen Vowell and across the Skeena near Gisgamaawin. A few years ago, Dad asked Edith if she remembered this.

> Yes. You and Walter were always scheming. My mother had two hats covered with fruit in a round-top trunk. I was babysitting you and Walter. You guys took out the hats, put them on, and ran all over the field chasing our cows. It was hilarious. You put the hats away before mother returned, and we said nothing.

Walter and Dad often fed the cattle at Date Creek. When he was six Walter dared Dad to walk on the ice of a creek near the farm. Dad took the dare, inching his way until he fell through and got

---

† Lot 2540, Cassiar District, was crown granted to Charles Sterritt on January 30, 1922. Two other Gitxsan men, Gidumglado/Charlie Clifford and Johnny Angus also pre-empted crown land near Charlie Sterritt's property.

soaking wet. They fed the cattle and hurried back to relatives at Kispiox for Dad was freezing. This was, of course, child's play in a relatively shallow creek compared to other more serious dramas that unfolded only too often along the Skeena at Glen Vowell.

The Gitxsan were familiar with the Skeena's many moods. It is a dangerous river. In recognition of this, residents hung emergency ropes by their house or gate. Dad explained how they were used:

> One spring when I was small, I heard the rumble of thunder. My father [Charlie] heard it too and knew it was the ice breaking up. Phillip Brown was coming across the Skeena from Anlaw with a team of horses, but he was walking behind his sleigh. He didn't know the river was open on our side. Charlie grabbed his lasso and ran from our house to the edge of the river, shouting, "Beat those horses into a gallop and make them swim." Phillip leapt to his sleigh and whipped the horses. They hit the open river with a huge spray of water, and my Dad and others lassoed the horses and helped pull them to shore. They wouldn't have made it if they hadn't galloped.

On another occasion, Charles Stevens, who lived across the river above Anlaw Reserve, was installing a phone line from Hazelton to the Salvation Army school in Glen Vowell. He drove his team down to cross the Skeena and was almost to the Anlaw side when one of the horses broke through the ice. He beat the horse, which struggled to free itself, but couldn't. Then the other horse fell through. There was nothing Charles could do and both horses drowned.

One day, the only people around were my five-year-old father and eight or nine-year-old Herbert Morrison, who lived just upriver with his grandparents. Dad heard someone shouting

Charlie and Kate Sterritt with sons (L – R) Neil B., Art, Walter and Jack. (Sterritt Family coll.)

frantically from the river. He grabbed a rope and ran to the other side of the road where he could see that an old man—Ts'ogo Wil—had fallen through the ice. Herbert was already down on the ice and threw his rope to Ts'ogo Wil, who wound the rope around his arm several times and put the free end in his mouth. Herbert struggled and got the old man onto the ice, but he broke through again. He finally got him to shore. Dad said Herbert was lucky that he didn't fall in too.

Another tragedy occurred on the river at Glen Vowell but during the summer. My grandfather—with Kate, Edith, Esther and Dad—was building a road for the Silver Standard mine on the mountainside east of Glen Vowell. Jacob and Elizabeth Gelakgen, an elderly couple, were there too. Kate, Edith and Esther left for Glen Vowell to tend their garden at the same time as the Gelakgens, who walked so slowly they were left far behind.

The old couple, with their dog, finally arrived at the river and signaled their grandson, John Gwoimtqu, to come get them. John paddled across the river and retrieved his grandparents and the dog. He tied the dog to the canoe. As they beached at Glen Vowell the dog leapt for shore, spilling John and his grandparents into the river. Elizabeth and Jacob managed to join hands across the overturned canoe as it floated down the Skeena. John disappeared. No one knew what happened until the elderly couple was seen in the eddy above Four Mile Bridge. By then they were exhausted, let go of each other and disappeared before anyone could rescue them.

Someone brought the news to Charlie and Dad that three people had drowned at Glen Vowell. They raced to the village where they learned that Kate, Edith and Esther had crossed the Skeena and were gardening before the elderly couple arrived at the river. They were unaware of what had happened.

Christmas was a special time at Glen Vowell. Dad recalled a concert he attended at age five:

> Everyone was there. The teenage girls performed with hoops, and the boys performed with clubs. They put on a wonderful show, and people in Hazelton invited them to bring their concert to Hazelton. They performed at the Hudson's Bay Hall. My dad took us to town in the cutter, and Esther was in the concert.

On Christmas Eve it was common for families to go house-to-house in Glen Vowell carolling. Those who wanted the carollers to sing and had snacks for them left their lamps on. Those who chose otherwise turned them off. As Dad said, "The carolers came to our house and sang on and on without being invited in. When they finally left, Charlie said to Kate, 'I know what's going on. Walter and Neil have their lamp on upstairs.'"

Children were expected to be self-reliant in the early part of the century. Charlie owned a Model T Ford in 1919 and drove Kate, Edith, Esther and my dad, aged six, to Four Mile on the Babine Trail. They went berry picking on Mohawk Mountain and Charlie returned to town. Dad had his own *gal enk* (cedar berry box). After picking for a few days, Kate said to my dad, "You will be the messenger. Go down to Four Mile and put your *enk* on a beam under the bridge. Then go to town and get your dad."

Dad described another occasion:

Three of us—Esther, my mother and I—went to Date Creek by horse and wagon to dig potatoes. After we loaded the wagon, she sent Esther and me across Date Creek to Ellen May's. From there, we crossed the Kispiox River, and went up a steep hill. Esther unloaded the wagon and we returned to the farm to get my mother and the remaining sacks of potatoes.

Dad's first trip to the coastal canneries was in 1916 when he was three years old. Kate had taken a summer job working in the cannery at Oceanic on Horsey Island. They took the train from South Hazelton to Inverness and the boat from there to Oceanic on Smith Island at the mouth of the Skeena. Many Gitxsan people from all the other villages were on the train too. Kate and the others had made the train trip a number of times by then and knew when they were approaching a tunnel. At the tunnel, Dad was running about when suddenly everything went black. He was startled and, as they emerged from the tunnel, Dad's older siblings said he was spinning around wildly with his hands flailing about in the air. Kate bought some green bananas at Prince Rupert. Dad took one and ate it, peel and all. He has never lived that one down.

Salmon canneries, such as the Dominion Cannery at Inverness, employed hundreds of Gitxsan people in all aspects of the industry from the late 1870s well into the 1900s. (Image A047826-v8 courtesy of NAC)

Dad said that when his mother was young, she and her parents went to Washington State to pick hops after the Skeena canneries closed in mid-August. She said, "Working in the hop fields was an excursion. It was like a picnic." They traveled by boat to Tacoma, gathering people from coastal villages along the way.

In Autumn 1891, for example, over 500 Aboriginal people from the North Coast and the Skeena River converged in Victoria on their way home. Such bottlenecks offered opportunities to link labor travels with visits to extended kin and attendance at Aboriginal gatherings. Workers must have welcomed the days of festive enjoyment that punctuated the arduous cycle of migratory labor.[9]

A Gitxsan man, David Louie, the uncle of Luutkuuts'iiwus/Ben McKenzie, lived at Yakima for so many years while working in the hop fields that he was nicknamed 'Yakima David'.

In 1919 my father attended the funeral of his great-grandmother Selena Simpson who was about ninety years old. The Haaxxw family bought an ornate coffin and a silver bird that was to sit on top. Kate knew that her son wanted the bird and kept him away from the graveside ceremony. The bird sank out of sight as the coffin was lowered and Dad began to cry. Women wailed on cue in sympathy for the child who they assumed was crying for his great-grandmother.

Charlie, who liked to spoil his son, later asked Kate what Neil was crying about. Kate said he wanted the silver bird. Charlie said, "Why didn't you tell me? I would have given it to him." Kate said, "I know. That's why I didn't tell you."

Later that year Simon Gunanoot gave himself up. Edith was married to Gutgwinuxs/Thomas Danes and living at Gwo'goots, near Anlaw Reserve. Simon had a house with acreage about a kilometre away at Anlaw. Dad, who was visiting Thomas and Edith, said, "We could hear the keening from Gwo'goots. It carried clearly to us. They must have thought Simon would be put in jail."

Charlie and Kate moved the family to Hazelton in 1921, perhaps because Charlie was working as a clerk at one of the stores in town, but also for their children's schooling. Dad had completed Grade Three in Glen Vowell, but repeated it in Hazelton. He went home for lunch every day. One day he arrived home to find his mother and Connie Cox together. Kate had a suit for Dad and told him to put it on. The two women looked him over, fed him and said, "Okay. You can go to school now." Dad was incredulous, "Like this?" Kate said, "Yes." He didn't dare defy her and went to school. He was teased mercilessly.

There was no housing available to purchase, so Charlie and Kate rented a two-room log house while Charlie Sampson built a house and a four-horse barn for them on River Road. My grandfather later bought a piece of land from Marianne Brown near the ferry where he built another barn. Eventually, after he bought Jim Hodder's property on Government Street (Lot 19), he dismantled his house near Anlaw, hauled it to town and rebuilt it there. My grandparents lived in the Government Street house until the mid-1950s.

Dad was riding his horse Tiny from Hazelton to Glen Vowell in 1927 or 1928. He stopped to water Tiny at Xsi Muula. Tiny was so tame Dad removed the bridle to allow him to drink in the shallow creek. Suddenly two riders on galloping horses came around the corner.[†] Tiny bolted as Dad tried to grab him around the neck. He fell to the ground, hit his head and was knocked out while the riders raced away. When he came to, he found he had walked from the creek to the south

---

† Gwilanamax/Tom (aka John) Sampson (1868-1941) and his wife Kliiyeemlaxha/Martha (1901-1987).

end of Glen Vowell near Walter Geel's house.‡ When his father saw the bruise on Dad's face, he said, "What have you been doing? Drinking home brew?" Dad went to bed and slept and remembered what happened when he woke up.

They couldn't find Tiny so the next day Kate took Dad to see Maria, Mark Sampson's wife, who was a seer. Kate explained why they were there. Maria said, "You know, I'm not always right, but I'll see what I can do." Then she said, "You don't need to worry, your horse isn't lost." Dad and Kate were seated facing the door. Someone opened the door and there was Walter leading Tiny. He had just returned from Babine Lake and found Tiny between Hazelton and Glen Vowell.

Trapping at Xsuwii Aks

My grandfather, Percy and Walter continued to trap at Xsuwii Aks until the mid-1930s. They often played pranks on each other and on the 1928 trip my grandfather was on the receiving end. He kept his whiskey bottle in a knapsack, and throughout the journey one son or another, including my fifteen-year-old father who rode in with him, hid small rocks in the knapsack without Charlie noticing. They arrived on the right bank of the Skeena at Xsuwii Aks, unpacked the horses and crossed the Skeena in a dugout canoe he had built. He threw his knapsack to the beach where it landed with a crunch, shattering his treasured whiskey bottle. After the others settled in, my father returned to Hazelton with the horses.

Uncle Walter and Kate's brother, Ts'aan/James Morrison (1895-1940), were responsible for the territory at Xsuwii Aks in the 1930s.§ Percy, Charlie's youngest son from his first marriage, often trapped with Walter and Charlie there. One year, packer George Beirnes, who serviced the operators along the Telegraph Trail for two decades, became lost near the headwaters of the Skeena while checking some mining claims. He wandered downriver for many miles. Uncle Walter, who was out checking his traps, saw a strange object lying on the ice. He thought it was a moose but when he got closer, he discovered it was George Beirnes. He was snow blind, had badly infected eyes and was starving to death. He wept when Walter found him.

Walter took the old man back to the cabin. Percy was there at the time, but Charlie was away checking his traps so they put George in Charlie's bed. Over the next two weeks they fed him and nursed him back to health. When George felt he was ready, he offered to pay Percy "really well" to accompany him to his ranch on the Kispiox River. Since it was spring and the season was coming to an end, Percy, encouraged by his father, set out down the Skeena with George in tow. Charlie was happy to finally get his bed back.

It took the two men a week to walk from Xsuwii Aks to Beirnes's ranch. When they arrived, Mrs. Beirnes ran from the house and leapt into George's arms. They tumbled to the ground with Mrs. Beirnes landing on top of and kissing George. Percy and a woman watching both laughed. Percy said, "It was the Russian girl who was trying to walk home."

---

‡ Walter Geel was also known as 'Big Louis'.

§ Walter was being groomed to be a chief in the House of Wiik̲'aax, as we shall see later.

Walter Sterritt at First Cabin on the Telegraph Trail. Even as a teenager, he spent months on the family's traplines. (Sterritt Family coll.)

Percy was mistaken about the identity of the woman at Beirnes's ranch. Lillian Alling, the Russian girl, had walked through Hazelton in the fall of 1927 and again in June or July of 1928.[10] Uncle Walter discovered Beirnes on the Skeena at Xsuwii Aks in mid- to late April of 1932.

But the woman could have been nineteen-year-old, Manitoba-born Anna Mae Ullman. She arrived in Hazelton with the intention of walking the trail to Telegraph Creek in April, 1932. But the creeks would soon be flooding and, as with Lillian Alling in 1927, the provincial police stopped Ullman at First Cabin.

According to Bill Miller, author of *Wires in The Wilderness*, "Ullman [got] a job as a cook at the nearby ranch of George Beirnes where she spent the next three months flipping sourdough hotcakes for his wranglers."[11] When conditions were right, Ullman continued her journey. By all accounts it was a difficult trip but with the help of linesmen and aboriginal people along the way, she arrived in Telegraph Creek where she spent the winter. Ullman later became lost during a snowshoe trip. If a Tahltan man, Joe Coburn, hadn't found her she would have frozen to death. Coburn brought Ullman to Telegraph Creek and she was flown to the hospital at Atlin for treatment. She lost both legs below the knees due to gangrene.[12]

George Beirnes paid Percy fifteen dollars for bringing him home.

Walter often returned from Xsuwii Aks to Hazelton for Christmas. He camped late at night, building a large fire against rock cliffs near the river. As the rocks cooled, he arose early in the morning when it was still dark, ate a light breakfast and continued his trip, covering 160 kilometres in three days.

Given the many steep canyons the Gitxsan had to cross, bridges were essential. And accidents occurred. Xsugwinhliiyuun (Mosque Creek) runs west into the Skeena River about thirty kilometres north of the Sustut River. It is a boundary between the territories of Wiik̲'aax and Wiiminoosikx, with the latter's territory commencing on the north side of Mosque Creek.

Antgulilbixs/Mary Johnson was married to Peter Angus (1893-1950), a member of the House of Wiiminoosikx. Mary explained how Peter Angus's father died when trying to cross a bridge over Xsugwinhliiyuun:

> When we went up on the ice and the snow was deep, there was a creek that Peter showed me. This time, we got to Xsuwii Aks, and we saw Walter Sterritt there. I don't know how far we walked after that and we got to this creek, called Xsugwinhliiyuun. Peter told me what happened to his father on this creek.† Peter and Robert Angus were very small. They were out hunting at Xsuwii Aks. At that time, Peter's father was going to put Peter in as a chief when they returned to Kisgegas because of the death of the other Wiiminoosikx.
>
> It was spring and the creek was really high. They were on their way [home] to Kisgegas. They had to go up the creek to a canyon. They had a bridge there made with logs and cedar bark rope. Peter's father, Gyats'ees, from the House of Wiik̲'aax, a brother of Daniel Wiik̲'aax, wanted to see whether the bridge was strong enough for the family and the dogs. When he got to the middle of the bridge, it fell down and he fell into the canyon. Peter tried to save him. He ran along the canyon edge but couldn't get down to the creek. After that his mother was strong. She fell some trees across the river and they got across.
>
> They continued on toward Kisgegas, and past Xsuwii Aks they came to a camp. It was G̲asx̲ [Peter Brown] and his family. When they saw Peter and his mother, they knew right away something had happened, and they started to cry.‡

---

† Peter Angus's parents were William and Ellen Angus.
‡ Mary Johnson re: Gyats'ees at Xsuwii Aks: October 29, 1996. Peter and Mary were married March 9, 1931.

Am Hat'al—Western Redcedar in the 20ᵗʰ Century

While trapping is a seasonal activity, logging can take place year round. The Grand Trunk Pacific (GTP) railroad was the prime catalyst for early logging along the Skeena and Bulkley rivers as thousands of railroad ties were needed to lay the track. A young Swedish immigrant, Olof Hanson, recognized the opportunity in 1907. Hanson had immigrated to the United States from Tannas, his hometown in Sweden, in 1902 at age twenty. He spent three years in the USA, working and learning English. In 1905 he emigrated to Manville, Alberta, which was near the route of the GTP.[13] There, he homesteaded during the summer and cut ties and bridge timbers for the GTP during the winter. He quickly realized homesteading held little promise for him. Instead, in 1907, he walked west 1200 kilometres to Hazelton, studying the timber potential along a route the GTP had yet to survey. Hanson was in Prince Rupert in 1909 when the GTP "…called for tenders to build one hundred and forty miles of railroad from Kitselas Canyon to Aldermere [later Telkwa]."[14]

> As a 27-year-old entrepreneur in the Prince Rupert of 1909, it would seem Olof Hanson was trying to define either the limits of his own ability or the capacity of this rough, new port town to accommodate his considerable ambition. Whichever, few men confronted with the travel and communication restraints of that era could have kept pace with the one who became known as northwestern B.C.'s Timber King.
>
> It was his involvement with the production of railway ties and cedar poles for which Hanson is mostly remembered today. Between Terrace and Endako his timber interests made him the single largest employer next to the Canadian National Railway, then the Grand Trunk Pacific.[15]

Hanson, who served as the Skeena MP from 1930 to 1945, thus set the stage for the pole and lumber businesses on the upper Skeena River that would be the mainstay of numerous Gitxsan and Wet'suwet'en extended families, including my own, for the next half century.

Archaeological finds along the Pacific's northwest coast reveal that woodworking tools were being used at least 8,000 years ago. And, as the glaciers receded along the upper Nass and Skeena valleys, a variety of tree species began to grow and were likely available when Temlaham was founded. The Gitxsan have been using cedar—*am hat'al*—for up to 5,000 years for building houses, sheds, boxes, masks and totem poles. The inner bark—*hat'al*—was used to make baskets, coats, hats, raincoats, floor mats, cedar rope, water bags and cooking bags.[16] Stripping the bark involved taking a single, vertical, up to nine-metre strip from a young cedar tree. Although a scar was left the tree was not killed.

Provincial forest legislation was in its infancy when Hanson established the Hanson Lumber and Timber Company in Prince Rupert in 1909. Hanson acquired large timber licenses, also known as limits, from the province giving him the harvesting rights to cedar and hemlock forests along the Skeena River. To meet the huge demand for railway ties Hanson sub-contracted local people to log hemlock. The demand for cedar, which was rot resistant and light, was growing as well due to the need for pilings, telephone and telegraph poles throughout North America. In the absence of roads and suitable trucks, the challenge of getting poles and ties to the GTP and the outside world was met through river drives—floating poles down the Skeena and Kispiox rivers to a suitable landing site near the railroad.

Within ten years, Hazelton had become the centre of a huge pole and tie industry. Ward Marshall said he and his father cut cedar poles soon after they arrived in Hazelton in 1921. Within that year Olof Hanson had "…shipped over three hundred carloads of poles and pilings along the line of the GTP…[and almost] all the poles came from west of Beament [21 kilometres east of Hazelton on the Bulkley River] and along the Skeena River." By 1922, Hanson was preparing to take out even more poles and pilings than he had for several years.

The involvement of Gitxsan people in the pole business was not without detractors. In 1926, an editorial in *The Omineca Herald* stated:

> [T]here is another forest enemy at work which few have heard of yet, but which is becoming very serious. We refer to the depredations of the Indians among the cedar trees. They use the bark for some reason unknown to us, and to secure this bark they take a single strip off each tree, with the result that the tree becomes no longer of any value as a pole or piling. It dies and becomes a menace to the rest of the forest.[17]

Maik George, who was incorrect in his assertion the cedar strips killed the trees, was one of the largest cedar pole contractors in the Hazelton area. In 1924 he married Maggie McLean, a Gitxsan woman from Glen Vowell. Maik George had two complaints: that Indians had destroyed more than $50,000 worth of timber in the Silver Standard Mine area and they refused to take strips of bark from trees on reserve.[18] Many of Maggie's Gitxsan relatives and friends worked in the pole industry and George's attitude may have affected their relationship. She divorced him in 1929.

He continued to prosper in the pole and piling business. In 1927, he hired Leo Spooner to haul his poles to the railroad at New Hazelton, from where "…hundreds of thousands of feet of poles and thousands of ties will be shipped…."[19] Even so, poles trucked to New Hazelton from throughout the district were but a small "…portion of the cedar that will go out of this district."[20]

In 1928, despite Gitxsan "depredations", Maik George "[Wound] up His Biggest Season" and proceeded to build a large pole camp north of the Shegunia River during the summer.[21] Hazelton area logging continued at a remarkable pace for many years, even after Maik George died in 1936.

Hanson established two destinations near the GTP along the Skeena where cedar poles would be gathered: Nash Y, below Gitsegukla and Cedarvale, below Gitwangak. *The Omineca Herald* made a note of the annual event:[22]

Gitxsan families working in the cedar pole business for many decades included Nikateen/John Smith, above the Salmon River, and later on the right bank of the Skeena, opposite Hazelton; Ts'iin/Joshua Campbell, right bank of the Skeena, opposite Hazelton; Guuwasan/Roy Wilson, east of the Kispiox River above Seventeen Mile Bridge; Gwingalagantxw/Ben Woods, near Beament on the Bulkley River; Haxbagwootx/Arthur McDames, near Gitsegukla; Jonathan Brown, left bank of the

Skeena fifty kilometres north of Hazelton; Wii Seeks/Pete Muldon, Kispiox, near Tenas Mountain; Woosimlaxha/Peter Barney, left bank of the Skeena twenty-five kilometres north of Hazelton; my grandfather Charlie Sterritt, right bank of the Skeena opposite Hazelton, and later, right bank of the Skeena thirty kilometres north of Hazelton; and my father, Neil B. Sterritt, Nine Mile on the Babine Trail and left bank of the Skeena at Sidina Creek.

> **Boom Swung At Cedarvale During Week**
>
> Plans were complete for swinging the boom across the Skeena river at Cedarvale to catch the cedar poles to be driven from the upper Skeena and the lower Kispiox rivers. The Hanson Timber & Lumber Co. have the greatest lot of cedar poles on the banks of the rivers this year that has ever been cut in this district. They expected to start driving this week. There will be three driving crews this season and at Cedarvale there will be two loading crews. Orders have been placed with the railway for at least thirty flat cars a week for the entire shipping season. In addition to more than a million lineal feet that will be shipped from the Cedarvale yards there are many carloads to go out from other points along the line with New Hazelton as the biggest contributor. At this point several cars a week have been going forward since the winter and there are many more car loads to bbe brought in and loaded.

All of these people were aware of traditional house territories. If someone like my dad wished to cut poles on someone else's territory, he acknowledged the ownership and hired workers who belonged to that house.

For example, when my father planned to cut cedar poles at Sidina Creek, he knew that territory belonged to the House of Gutgwinuxs. In respecting that, he hired men who belonged to that House or who had married into it. He hired Joe and Thomas Brown who belonged to the House and he hired Niist/Charlie Sampson who was married to a woman from the House of Gutgwinuxs. He also hired Charlie's son, Ts'ago Gaak/Perry Sampson, who was a Gutgwinuxs member through the matriline.

My grandfather continued packing, trapping, farming and commercial fishing until the mid-1930s. In 1935, perhaps earlier, he acquired a timber limit across the Skeena opposite Hazelton in a good western redcedar stand and logged there for the next fifteen years.† It was mostly a family operation and included not only his sons, but also members of my grandparents' extended families from the Houses of Haaxxw and Wiik'aax and their spouses. There were also members of the House of Luutkuts'iiwus, which owned the territory, employed there.

The camp consisted of four or five log cabins, a barn and shed. From there his loggers worked in the forest nearby, felling trees by hand with crosscut saws, delimbing them and peeling the bark with double-bitted axes. He used Percheron workhorses to drag poles from the forest to skidways or landings where they were piled.

From the landing, teamsters with horse-drawn, single-bob sleighs hauled up to seven or eight poles to the riverbank at the ferry crossing below Hazelton. By springtime, thousands of poles were piled there. Other contractors had similar piles far above and below Hazelton. Later, after the spring flood, men spent many days putting the poles into the Skeena. River drivers kept the poles floating to the booms at Nash Y and Cedarvale.

Although wages were low during the 1930s, men were happy to be working. The Hanson Lumber and Timber Company bought poles and paid a sliding scale for peeled, green, and sound cedar poles and pilings F.O.B. Nash Y and Cedarvale. Poles were cut in lengths between thirty feet and ninety feet (in five-foot increments). Depending on the grade, Hanson paid contractors up to three dollars for a thirty-foot pole and $10.80 for an eighty- or ninety-foot pole. But contractors paid pole cutters by the foot as follows: three cents a foot for a thirty-foot pole (i.e. ninety cents), and six cents a foot for eighty- to ninety-foot poles ($4.80 to $5.40).[23] A hard-working, experienced logger might peel 500 lineal feet per day in the springtime when the sap was running but somewhat less during the rest of the year.

Men from nearly every Gitxsan family worked on the river drive at one time or another and an *esprit de corps* developed that produced exciting tales around campfires and in warm kitchens.

Albert Elliott, who was born in Ontario in 1883 and came to Hazelton in the early 1930s, hired my father in 1934. Elliott had a large pole contract with Olof Hanson along the right bank of the Skeena below Temlaham and built a pole camp west of there that consisted of two bunkhouses, a cookhouse, and a cabin for the foreman. He owned one team of horses but since his contract was so big, Olof Hanson provided more teams.

My twenty-one-year-old father was new to the business. He learned quickly and then worked in every phase of the operation with experienced pole cutters, teamsters, road builders and river drivers. In 1993, Dad described each aspect of cedar pole logging: camp layout; the building of skid roads and skidways; hauling poles on horse-drawn sleighs; care of horses; and river driving. In most cases, poles were cut and peeled along terraces high above and well away from the Skeena.

---

† The provincial government provided a license to log on crown lands, i.e. to cut cedar for poles and spruce or hemlock for lumber. These licenses were called timber limits and allowed a person to log, but did not confer ownership or title to the land where logging took place.

Because hillsides above the Skeena were often very steep, contractors built landings at the top of the hills and slid the poles down log chutes to the river.

> At Elliott's landing up river, we used two teams of horses and a single horse, and we worked ten hours a day. We started at seven in the morning, worked 'til noon to give the horses a rest, had lunch, then worked from one 'til six, no coffee breaks. All day long there was a steady stream of poles fed down the chute into the river.
>
> My job was to feed the poles into the chute. They were brought in on the side hill by a team of horses. As soon as the team stopped, I grabbed the pole with a peavey so it wouldn't roll. The teamster unhooked the chain and then I let the pole run into the chute. Once it hit the chute it was all downhill and away it went. Near the end of the chute, the ground leveled off a bit, and at the end of the chute there was an apron: a big raft of logs anchored at the end of the chute. The poles left the chute and leveled out on the apron, which prevented the poles from breaking or splitting on the bottom of the river at the end of the chute.
>
> One man worked as a hook tender at the landing above the chute. He had a chain that he hooked the poles with. If the poles were small, he hooked two or three at the same time. If he had three poles at the same time, my job was to catch the pole on the lower side, and hold all three from rolling. As soon as the horses were gone, I let one [pole] go down the chute, and immediately caught the next pole, letting each pole go down one at a time. We put 500 poles a day into the river for six weeks without stopping for a single day. We worked and worked, Saturdays, Sundays, every day of the week. That is, roughly, 20,000 cedar poles that we put into the river in six weeks.[24]
>
> The chute was made of logs with railings on the side to contain the logs, because once a pole went down there, it had to stay inside the chute....We waited until after high water in the spring before putting the poles in the river. Just below Kitseguecla, on the [right] side of the river was a place called Nash Y. Here they had a big boom of logs tied together. It was about a mile long. The boom extended from one side of the Skeena to the other, at an angle down the river. The upper end of the boom was anchored on the east [left] side of the Skeena, and the lower end was anchored on the west [right] bank at Nash Y.
>
> There was a chute on the Nash Y side of the river too, [which] went from the river bank to the top of quite a high, steep hill. There was a 'donkey' [engine] on top of the hill, and a long cable [which] pulled the poles up the chute to the landing at the railroad.
>
> I didn't work on the river drive [in 1934], but I did later on…and I'll tell you about that to give you an idea of what the river drive was like. People experienced on the

river drive really knew the river. I was inexperienced as it was my first time on a river drive. Willy Smart and Johnny Moore were very experienced. Our boss, Vic Gerow, was from Smithers. They knew all the back eddies where poles got held up. Some of the poles grounded on the beach and others just went round and round with the flow of water. At this time, the river drive crew was small. We were driving from Hazelton to Nash Y. We had a cook who had his own boat and he carried our tents, blankets and food. We had a boat as well.

Neil B. Sterritt, the author's father, and his family started in the cedar pole business in the 1930s and he continued until the mid-1960s. (Sterritt Family coll.)

These guys knew their business. They come to a back eddy with poles laying in there. Each back eddy is different. Willy and Johnny knew each eddy. They knew where to push the poles out so they would carry on downstream, instead of getting drawn back in to the eddy. In some eddies they pushed the poles out near the middle and in others they pushed them out at the top end of the eddy.

Steamboat Eddy is a big eddy. We had to use a boat there. There were four of us in the boat, two were rowing on the same side of the boat…on the outer side of the eddy. And the other two guys stood in the boat and hooked their pike poles into a cedar pole. They did this until they gathered about half a dozen poles of different lengths. Then they fastened their pike poles into the sixth or outer pole and they pulled all those poles up against the boat. It was just like a raft, and we were rowing up stream until we got to the head end of the eddy. Here the river caught us and we started to swing out into the Skeena, and as soon as you start to swing out you have to row…we were trying to get the raft of poles as far out as we can into the middle of the river, or even beyond, otherwise we will end up back in the eddy again. As soon as they are far enough out into the river they give their pike poles a turn to get it out of the pole and turn them loose and the poles are gone. Then we go back into the eddy with our boat and do it all over again. So that is river driving. From there the poles go down to the boom and up to the railroad track at Nash Y.[25]

Charlie Sampson, my grandfather's cousin, also worked for my grandfather at his pole camp. Charlie (1888-1963) was a member of the Kuldo Wolf Clan and the son of a former Haaxxw, Mark Sampson. He worked for my grandfather for about fifteen years and then for my father for another eight years when he began harvesting cedar poles along the Skeena in 1950. Charlie's son Perry, born in 1934, grew up helping his father cut poles. Perry cut poles and also worked on the river drive before the road between Hazelton and Kisgegas was built in 1951.

Perry lived with his father and mother during the winter at the pole camp opposite Hazelton. During the early 1940s, he walked to school each day at Glen Vowell. Other children, including my cousin Katie, lived there too. Perry said, "We used to walk to school from … the camp. Katie used to leave … ahead of me and once, [when] I caught up to her, [she] said to me, 'Did you see that big dog back there?' I said, 'No, but that was a wolf.'" They heard wolves howling all the time. It took two hours each way for them to go to and from school, so they left early and returned late. Perry's father made a lantern for them, using a jam can with a candle inside.

Jonathan Brown, a Gitxsan man, contracted to cut poles about fifty kilometres up the Skeena from Hazelton. His timber limit was on a high terrace east of the Skeena. His crew cut poles all winter and skidded the poles to a landing above his camp on the Skeena. A chute much the same as the one Dad worked with at Elliott's had been built down to the river. Brown's crew spent weeks sending thousands of poles down the chute into the Skeena. The river drive began when Brown's last pole was in the water. Meanwhile, other camps below Jonathan Brown's had also been dumping their poles into the Skeena: Arthur Hankin[†] at 'Xsan (a treacherous canyon on the Skeena), Peter Barney near Pinenut Creek and John Smith near Salmon River.

The problem of course was that cedar poles, like sheep and cattle, need to be herded. They got hung up on rocks and caught in the numerous back eddies and canyons between Johnathan Brown's and Nash Y. A huge boulder—named *Gil'dip Nakw* by the Gitxsan—sits in the middle of

---

† Hankin abandoned this camp (cabins and barn) and Dad used them when he logged there after 1950.

the Skeena River at the Utsun (Cariboo) Creek confluence. Water flowing over and around *Gil'dip Nakw* caused huge log jams during the river drive. Perry said two poles once jammed against each bank and the boulder and other poles gathered against the two poles creating a log jam they could walk across from one side of the Skeena to the other. The two poles were finally freed and sent down the river, but a larger log jam had developed farther down the canyon.

> Edward Sampson [from Glen Vowell] had a head for figuring out which pole was the 'key' to breaking the log jam. There's only one log that will break it. There was a cliff there and the older men said, "Perry, you are the lightest, so we will lower you down with a rope, and you chop the pole off. Don't worry about your axe. Let it go and we'll pull you up." They had the rope tied around my waist, and looped around a tree and they watched me. I chopped and chopped and then the pole broke with a loud bang. When the pole snapped, they pulled me up. I weighed about 120 pounds then, and I was in good shape.

The War Years and After

During the years leading up to World War Two, Dad took work as it became available. In the winter of 1939 he and a friend from Hazelton, Earl Simpson, worked at the Big Missouri Mine twenty-five kilometres east of Stewart. The mine was then owned by the Consolidated Mining and Smelting Company and was in production from 1938 to 1942. Dad didn't enjoy the work, so he quit after about six months and returned to Hazelton.

The Geological Survey of Canada (GSC) was conducting fieldwork in the Hazelton area at that time and hired Dad as their guide and packer. Using his father's horses, Dad and the GSC worked east of Kisgegas at the headwaters of Xsimatsi'ho'ot (Tomlinson Creek), at Thoen Basin north of the Babine Trail and east of Hazelton, and east of Moricetown on the Debenture Trail.

Dad skippered a commercial fishing boat during the summer of 1940. That fall almost 100 Hazelton area men and women had enlisted in the army, at least forty percent of them of Gitxsan and Wet'suwet'en ancestry. Dad and his brother, Arthur (Art), enlisted at Prince Rupert on November 20 and, along with Tom Marshall from Hazelton, were assigned to the Second Searchlight Coast Defence Battery.

Dad began as a gunner with pay of $250 per year and was made a sergeant December 1, 1942. He was stationed in Prince Rupert, Nanaimo and Esquimalt, during which time he qualified as a Mechanic Class B and took electrician's training. He continued mechanics training in 1944 at three automotive plants in Ontario at Oshawa and Windsor. He was shipped overseas as a trainer, arriving in London in December 1944.

Not everyone went into action overseas. In Dad's case, not only was he provided further training as a mechanics and electricians coach and instructor, his superior officers recognized his skills in track and field. He participated in the Canadian Army Track and Field Championships in Aldershot, England in July 1945, and also in Nijmegen, Holland in August. There Dad and his running mates came in second to the Dutch 440 relay team. They defeated Canada's number one team, which finished in third place. Dad returned to Hazelton when the war ended in September 1945.

Art Sterritt, Dad's brother, was seventeen years old when he enlisted at Prince Rupert in 1940. He moved through the ranks as gunner, lance bombardier and, upon transfer to Victoria, as a bombardier and anti-aircraft instructor. The army transferred Art from Victoria to Halifax. On April 1, 1943, Art shipped out to Europe on the *Queen Elizabeth I*, 'stacked' into the ship with 15,000 other men. Art thus became the first 'Hazelton Sterritt' to reverse the trend begun by his great-great grandfather, Andrew Starrett, who emigrated to Canada with his family in 1819.[†]

Uncle Art entered active duty with the 4th Light Anti-aircraft Regiment, 100th Battery, landing at Normandy, France on June 12, 1944, six days after D-Day. This regiment was noted for shooting down more enemy aircraft throughout the war than any other British or Canadian Regiment.

In the fall of 1944 Art was transferred to Lille, France, then to Ghent, Belgium after which he was to be transferred to England for infantry training. However, early one morning his regiment was called out with full kit to the parade square to answer as their names were called.

Those whose names were called would go as one group to England for infantry training. Those who remained were to stay on in Europe as artillery reinforcements. Six remained, including Uncle Art, and he ended up in the 3rd Light Antiaircraft Regiment as a gunner. He left Europe and visited his family in Hazelton in May 1946.

Art served in Korea as a sergeant with the 3rd Regiment, Royal Canadian Horse Artillery (RCHA) from March 1954, and returned with the last Canadian artillery regiment in December of the same year. He married Ada Moore on August 20, 1955 at the military church in Picton, Ontario.[‡]

Art eventually retired from the military in 1969 as Warrant Officer, second class, in the 4th Regiment RCHA at Camp Pettawawa. At one point late in his career Art was being congratulated on achieving his rank and commendations by a superior officer who said, "That's pretty good for an Indian." Art told the officer what he could do with the 'compliment' and was assigned to KP duty.

My father and his siblings have been blessed (some might think otherwise) with an unusual independence and strength of character as Uncle Art demonstrated above. Uncle Walter also enlisted in the Canadian Army. He was working near Hope as a logger in 1940 when he decided to enlist and went to Vancouver. However, he couldn't tolerate his superiors ordering him about. He went AWOL and walked the 150 kilometres back to Hope.

Dad returned to Hazelton after the war and obtained work running the diesel generator that provided electricity to Hazelton. At the same time he registered his trap line at Nine Mile Creek on the Babine Trail where he and Ward Marshall trapped occasionally over the next five years. Trapping was an excursion for both families. We all rode out on the back of one of Marshall

---

[†] See Chapter 16: Starrett and Cummins.

[‡] They adopted three children: Wayne, Margaret, and Michael.

Brothers trucks and camped at Nine Mile on weekends. We alternated trapping with fishing for trout at Robinson Lake.

Premier John Hart established the BC Power Commission (BCPC) in 1947. Its mandate "…was to amalgamate existing power and generating facilities across the province…and to extend service to the many smaller communities without power."[26] Hazelton was one such community, and BCPC soon established a large diesel plant near Hazelton. Dad worked there for a couple of years until he, Ward Marshall and Earl Simpson formed a partnership to log cedar poles on a timber limit they obtained at Dad's Nine Mile Creek trap line.

All logging along the upper Skeena, whether for cedar poles or spruce and hemlock trees, from the 1920s to the mid- to late 1950s, was by selective logging. Despite the hundreds of thousands of trees taken, a person walking through the forest would see only a few stumps here and there. A person flying over would see the intact forest canopy. Fur bearing animals and larger game weren't affected. That changed with clear-cut logging. As Kliiyeemlaxha/Martha Brown (1900-1987) said to the Minister of Indian Affairs, Hugh Faulkner, at Kispiox in 1977, "Now all we have left are bald-headed mountains."

Dad, Ward and Earl lived in Dad's trap line cabin at Nine Mile along the Babine Trail.[§] They built a corral and shelter for Earl's workhorse and purchased an old steel-wheeled tractor. The tractor, even though it had lugs on the wheels, was a dangerous machine. It could easily tip backwards while dragging poles or when going up too steep a grade. But the men were careful. They backed up steep hills and limited the number of poles they skidded.

Dad described a typical day at the Nine Mile pole camp:

> We worked eight hours a day. We ate a big breakfast in the morning. Then we made two sandwiches each and took a jar of water or tea. At 10:00 a.m. we ate our two sandwiches and drank our tea. Then we went right at it again until 12 noon. Then we went back to our camp, made and ate a big lunch, and made two more sandwiches and another jar of tea and we ate at three. That's how tough that work is.

> Nobody made any money. But things were cheaper then. Blue jeans only cost a dollar and a half. I remember buying good Pierre Paris low shoes for $1.50. That same shoe today [1993] would cost about $150. In proportion it's still the same.

> Hanson Lumber and Timber Company bought our poles. We didn't auction the poles off because Hanson was the biggest logging contractor in the country. … He owned a lot of timber in the area. He owned the Bell Lake area; he bought that up. And he financed us. I worked for him too when we finished logging at Nine Mile.

---

§ Biiyoon/Sarah Mowatt and others belonging to the House of Guuhadak, which has close connections to the House of Wiik̲'aax, said Dad could register the trapline at Nine Mile, as that is part of Guuhadak's territory. Guuhadak was originally a member of the House of Wiik̲'aax at Kisgegas.

In 1950, Dad obtained a timber limit along the left bank of the Skeena at Xsugwa Mahlit (Sidina Creek), thirty kilometres north of Hazelton. My grandparents moved from their timber limit opposite Hazelton to another cedar pole area on the right bank of the Skeena River also thirty kilometres above Hazelton.

Uncle Walter, who moved to the Prince George area in the late 1930s, met Phyllis Storrings there and they married in 1939.† In 1940 the family moved south where Walter worked on the Fraser River log booms. In 1944, the owner of Jones Lake Logging hired Walter as his boom foreman. In 1947, Walter took on a log booming contract at Ruby Creek on the Fraser River until 1952 when he moved home and applied for a timber limit beside his father's new pole camp north of Hazelton.

He set up a sawmill and ran that business for eleven years. In 1966 the family moved to Terrace where Walter resumed work as a boom foreman on the Skeena River. When he was sixty-nine he hired on as a faller with McGillis and Gibbs, a cedar pole company, and outworked younger men on the steep mountainsides along the Skeena below Terrace. Several of the men Walter worked with told Walter's son that "Walter was always ahead of us and out of sight going up the hillsides near Remo. He sat and waited for us and jokingly asked, 'What's your problem?'"

This reminded me of a story I had heard about Walter when he was much younger, probably in 1927 or 1928. For many years sports days have rotated among the Gitxsan villages each spring. Events include soccer, baseball, softball and various kinds of races. Gitwangak sports days included a men's foot race across the field and up *Gwin Lalt*, the steep hill at the edge of the field. Men raced to the bottom of the hill and up to the finish line. Witnesses said Uncle Walter ran in the race and won it handily, reaching the finish line well ahead of the pack. Not unlike the young men's story about Remo forty years later, Walter was sitting down and smoking a cigarette when the other runners arrived.

Uncle Walter retired, left Terrace and spent his retirement years working his gold claims at Manson Creek. It is likely that Walter got his start there with Luke Fowler (1872-1950) during the 1930s. Luke held the name Luugantxw from Gitwangak, although he was born in Kisgegas and raised in Gitanmaax. After Job Morrison died, Luke married my great-grandmother Jessie in 1919.[27] Although Luke had been travelling to and from Manson Creek for many years, he was working his own property in the Blackjack area in 1933, which is probably when Walter first went to Manson Creek.[28]

Luke Fowler died at Manson Creek in June 1950 and was buried there. Uncle Walter continued to work at Manson after he quit logging and died there in October 1983 from injuries he suffered in a vehicle accident. He was buried in Prince George.

For centuries Xsan, the canyon between my father's and my grandfather's pole camps, supported an incredible Gitxsan fishery where Babine Lake-bound salmon were harvested. In Hazelton one day, my dad went to the river to fetch water and was startled to see hundreds of salmon carcasses floating tail-first down the river. He later learned that a massive slide containing

---

† They had five children: Patrick, Margaret (Jo), Charlie, Gerry (1943-2014) and Reta.

about 100,000 cubic metres of rock had blocked the Babine River above Kisgegas.[29] This resulted in a severe loss of salmon in 1951 and 1952.

The Department of Fisheries and Oceans (DFO) immediately began to build a road to the slide. What had always been known as *Genim Kisgegas* (trail to Kisgegas) would become known as the Babine Slide Road. The road was built quickly without much of a base and during spring breakup or heavy rain it was a sea of mud. The DFO road-builders got by because they had four-wheel drive Power Wagons with winches. We had horses and a two-wheel drive pickup. Several years later, when Dad and Bob Blackstock were hauling poles during the winter from Jonathan Brown's pole camp further up the river, Jack Hanson, Olof Hanson's younger brother, said to Dad, "This is not a road, it's a ski jump!"

Thomas and Joe Brown and Charlie Sampson with his son Perry began working for my dad in 1950. They cut poles in a first growth cedar grove beside T'am Similoo'o, a lake a couple of kilometres east of Dad's pole camp at the base of Sidina Mountain. The cedar trees around T'am Similoo'o were huge and because little light could get through the forest canopy, the entire area at ground level was a park-like blanket of moss. This was in 1951 or 1952, and Perry was old enough to work with

The author's Uncle Walter working a gold claim in the Omineca gold fields at Manson Creek. (Sterritt Family coll.)

his dad then and, using a crosscut saw and a double-bitted axe, he and his father cut, limbed and peeled some very long poles, including some near the lake that were thirty metres long. It was a challenge for Dad's workhorses, Beauty and Lil, to drag each of those poles down the hill to the skidway beside the road. Dad once said he made good money even if all he hauled to the railroad at New Hazelton was a single thirty-metre pole.

By this time Dad had a forty-pound Pioneer power saw. He babied this marvel of engineering, and packed it to and from his cabin every day. In 1952, he bought a D-4 Caterpillar and built a road to T'am Similoo'o though he still needed horses to bunch poles in the bush.

Eventually Dad bought a five-ton single axle truck and a trailer. He used the truck to haul his own poles and those of others to the railroad. Peter Barney, James Morrison, Solomon Jack and Jonathan Brown also hired Dad to build logging roads and skidways for them.

In those days, the men loaded poles onto their trucks by hand. A skidway was a deck of logs built at the bottom of a hill at right angles to a road. The deck had to be at least the height of the truck beds. The truck and trailer were parked parallel to the road, but at right angles to the skidway

Hauling cedar poles the old way and the new. Neil B. is atop the sled and his first wife Jean is standing beside the 'modern' truck. (Sterritt Family coll)

and light, sturdy poles were laid between the skidway and the truck. Men with peavies rolled the poles down the hill onto the skidway and then lengthwise along the bed of the truck. As the load got higher, rolling the poles upwards became more difficult. During my early teens I helped Dad on many occasions. Sometimes the poles were so heavy my only purpose was to hold the pole while Dad took another grip with his peavey and rolled the pole another foot or so.

Pole cutters were experts with a peavey. They could flip the cant hook and grab a pole, stopping it from rolling, or increasing its roll, or sliding it forwards or backwards so that it sat in the right position on a truck. They could reach under a pole and use the peavey as a lever to raise it into a more suitable position. And men standing opposite each other at the same end of a pole could grab a small or moderately sized pole with their peavies and lift it off the ground.

We worked up and down the Babine Slide Road for years. In 1956 or 1957, Peter Barney had a skidway deep in the bush near Xsa'is (Sterritt Creek). Bill Maitland for Marshall Brothers and three other truckers—Bob Blackstock, George Hagen and Dad—hauled poles for Peter. I drove the Cat from the road through the bush to the landing, towing four empty pole trucks at once (connected by chains). Coming out of the bush, I towed one loaded truck at a time.

Dad continued in the cedar pole business until the mid-1960s. Barbara and I spent the winter of 1964 in Hazelton. Dad had a small crew then consisting of myself and brothers Tommy Green and Joshua McLean. Tommy and Joshua cut and peeled poles, while Dad and I used his D-4 Cat to skid the poles to his landing. In 1954 Dad had bought 360 acres of forested private land from Jack Frost. The property was located just north of Cariboo Creek on the Babine Slide Road. We worked on his property all that winter. In the spring I hauled poles from his landing to Bell Pole's yard by the railroad in New Hazelton.

While Terrace was long considered the pole capital of the world, Hazelton ran a close second.[30] My father, who got into the cedar pole business in 1948, was one of the few remaining pole suppliers in the Hazelton area by the mid-1960s.

After Dad left the pole business he continued to work his private property above Cariboo Creek on a seasonal basis. With his D-4 Cat and a power saw, he cut enough cedar or spruce to earn a bit of money each summer. He hired a local person with a self-loader to haul his timber to market.

Wiik̲'aax

My father never sought the name Wiik̲'aax: that is not his way. In fact Dad's brother, Walter, was groomed as a potential heir, which is why he and his uncle, James Morrison were once responsible for the Xsuwii Aks territory. Dad said after feasts were held in Bear Lake during the 1920s and 1930s, messengers brought small gifts for Walter to my grandparents in Hazelton in recognition of this. However, during the mid-1930s, Uncle Walter began working at Manson Creek and logging out of the Hazelton area, and dedicated himself to his family and his work.

After a recent successor,[†] Wiik̲'aax/Kenneth Campbell, died in 1973, the Wright brothers from Kisgegas asked Dad to accept the name. He declined and the seat remained empty for nine years. However, on March 8, 1982, Ax Moogasxw/Jack Wright died and Haspaiyets/Henry Wright approached Dad again, asking him to accept the name. This time Dad agreed. As Dad recently said, "Henry Wright must have known what he was doing" because Henry died a week after the feast on March 22, 1982.

Wiik̲'aax is the *miin wilp* (head) of the House of Wiik̲'aax. The House has many members and extensive territories. Jack Wright's funeral was held on March 13, 1982. The ceremony officially began with a chief's farewell at Jack Wright's house, followed by the funeral at Kispiox Community Hall and his burial in the cemetery nearby. The feast began shortly afterwards.

The House of Wiik̲'aax hosted the feast with Wolf Clan members from other houses helping. The Wolves seated 290 witnesses from the Frog, Fireweed and Eagle clans. The feast began with a prayer and short speech, the calling in of my father and Murphy Green (Jack Wright's successor), and a lament from the House of Wiik̲'aax sung by Antgulilbixs/Mary Johnson.

The Wolf Clan fed the guests, making sure that the *simgiiget* (chiefs) were served first, and in greater quantities. Afterwards, the Wolves contributed financially to the feast, beginning with my father and Murphy Green who deposited their money in a large basin at the front of the hall. Others followed, contributing according to their rank.

These funds were used to pay various individuals, chosen according to Gitxsan custom, to buy a coffin and clothes to dress the body; watch over the body while it lay in state; and pay pall bearers, grave diggers, and others who carried out related tasks.

After the workers had been paid, the balance of funds, which were considerable, was paid to the witnesses, again according to rank. Children present would receive a token amount. At the same time, gifts by way of clothes, tools, perhaps rifles or snowshoes were given to those who had been kind to the deceased at one time or another.

Finally, the host chiefs began their closing comments, at which time they announced when another feast would be held to place the deceased's headstone, and closed with a general reference to their House territories, If the need arose, a more detailed description might be given at the headstone feast. They then thanked the witnesses for attending. This was the signal for the leading chief at each of about twenty tables to rise and thank the hosts for the food, gifts of money and goods, after which the feast closed with a prayer.

As demanding as the feast was, my father's work had just begun. He and his fellow chiefs were responsible for territory near Kisgegas, Bear Lake, and the upper Skeena. Given the existence of the Groundhog coal deposits along with logging and, in time, pipelines and other industrial activity, he had much to oversee. And having such a large house, perhaps 400 members, many of whom were aged, annual funerals and feasts were a certainty. Although the work and costs are shared, the *sim'oogit* (chief) bears the brunt of the burden.

[†] Simon Wright (1895-1966) inherited the name when Daniel Wiik̲'aax (1867-1925) died. Simon had four brothers: Jack, Thomas, Edward and Henry.

My father has always seen his role as Wiik̲'aax as one of service to his House, to the members, and to the protection of their lands and resources, not as a badge of honour. And that is what it should be. A capable person who shied away from the task was often chosen by elders because that person understood what the job entailed.

There are many stories that can be told about my father, but my favourite is his experience with a grizzly.

In the early 1990s, Dad and his lifelong friend, the late Charlie Smith (1917-2005), were picking huckleberries at a large berry patch in the Burrage Burn near the Stikine River. When picking berries, it is common to wander about from patch to patch and become separated from other berry pickers. Soon my dad and Charlie were about half a mile apart. Dad was concentrating on finding berries when he heard a noise. He turned to see a female grizzly bear charging him. Her shoulder hair was standing on end, her ears were laid back and she was snarling and growling.

Dad didn't have time to think. He told me, "I threw my berry picker at her and then I tried to pull out a small dead tree to use as a weapon. She was coming at me and by now she was roaring and I was roaring back at her. Well, to tell you the truth, I was screaming."

She charged right up to him.

Neil B. Sterritt on his 102nd birthday, August, 2015. (Jamie Sterritt photo)

> I stood my ground, raising my arms, trying to make myself appear bigger and I was screaming at her. When she got to me, she stopped and stood up. At that moment I was staring right into her eyes. She was so close I could not see her snout. It was under my chin. We were face to face, eye to eye, inches apart. She was still roaring, and I was still screaming. That's the last thing I remember, her eyes, and then I blacked out.

I asked my dad, "Did you fall down?"

"No," he said.

I asked him, "How long were you out? What happened?"

> I blacked out for ten or fifteen seconds, maybe longer. I don't know. When I came to, I was still standing there, unharmed, and she had walked a little ways off. I grabbed a club to use as a weapon. She came back towards me, threatening me, and then I heard a cub call to her and she answered it. Still growling, she slowly moved away and then she gathered the two cubs and left.

Charlie Smith later told Dad, "I could hear the roaring and screaming, and it went on for a long time. Suddenly, everything was quiet. I thought you were dead."

When we discussed what had happened, I asked Dad why he reacted to the grizzly the way he did.

> I was with Yal/Charles Mowatt, his wife Biiyoon/Sarah, and my grandmother, Jessie, picking berries along the Kispiox River near Seventeen Mile Bridge. I was five or six years old. The women left me in camp with Charles who was crippled.[†] Because it was salmon and berry season, there were bears around, grizzlies and black bears.
>
> Charles said, "If a grizzly bear attacks you, grab a club and defend yourself. Stand up to the bear. Don't run. You have to defend yourself." I remembered what Charles said and so that is what I did. I stood my ground and defended myself.

My dad was raised in the bush. He is a brave man but naturally was frightened when the grizzly sow charged. He respected the bear but stood his ground and, by his response, invited the grizzly to respect him as well.

I am fond of this story because it deals with the value of cultural continuity. Charles Mowatt was the son of a former Gidumgaldo, Alexander Mowatt (1855-1915). Charles took the time to tell a five-year-old boy what to do in the face of imminent danger and eight decades later my father heeded Charles's words, which may have saved his life. One never knows when and where the teachings of an elder will be useful.

---

† Charles Mowatt (1874-1927), as did many other Gitxsan men, enlisted in World War I. He may have been injured during his time overseas, as this was about 1920, and he used two crutches to walk.

ENDNOTES

1. *Delgamuukw v. BC,* Thomas Wright, 1986, Vol. 1: 3 - 18.
2. *Delgamuukw v. BC,* Atlas, Map 1: Ancient Times – the arrival about 10,000 years ago.
3. Harris, K., 1974.
4. Canada: 1911 Census, BC, Comox-Atlin, p. 20, lines 33-37, family 815.
5. Tomlinson 1991: 341-42.
6. PABC Inquisitions 1909, B2384, File 176.
7. PABC Inquisitions 1909, B2384, File 176.
8. Canada, Indian Affairs Annual Report, year ended March 31, 1915.
9. Raibmon, 103.
10. Miller, 223-24.
11. Miller, 226.
12. Miller, 229.
13. Shervill, 16-21.
14. "Tenders Called for 140 Miles", 1.
15. Shervill, 17.
16. GWES Gitxsenimx – Gitxsanimax Dictionary, Tab 12, 6-7.
17. "Destroying the Cedar Trees", 2.
18. "Destroying the Cedar Trees", 2.
19. "Cedar Poles are Being Hauled Several Camps", 1.
20. "Cedar Poles are Being Hauled Several Camps", 1.
21. "Maik George Winds up his Biggest Season", 1
22. "Boom Swung at Cedarvale During Week", 1.
23. Sterritt, N.B.
24. Sterritt, N.B., 10-12.
25. Sterritt, N.B., 12-13.
26. BC Hydro, History (Wikipedia, Jan. 2, 2015, <en.wikipedia.org>.
31. "Marriage of Luke Fowler to Jessie Morrison," Aug. 21, 1919, Hazelton Methodist Church, Hazelton, BC. Copy in possession of author. PABC 1919.
32. Hall, 70.
33. Moore.
34. Terrace, British Columbia, Economy (Wikipedia, Jan. 1, 2015, <en.wikipedia.org>.

CHAPTER TWENTY-ONE

The *Ansgiyast* (Cemetery)

Gamlaxyeltxw/Edgar Good: What do you think of the Hungry Thirties?

Alvin Weget: Our people lived off the land. They had fish. They trapped. They had berries and vegetable gardens. They were wealthy. If you don't believe me, go look through the graveyards. Look at the headstone Shanoss had at Gitanmaax and Alexander Gitluudaahlxw at Kispiox. They had six- or seven-foot monuments. Moses Shanoss ordered his from England.

—Gitluudaahlxw/Alvin Weget

The Gitanmaax *ansgiyast* sits on the high terrace overlooking the villages of Gitanmaax and Hazelton.† It is a peaceful place, a refuge where squirrels, rabbits and grouse, crows, and sometimes a bear, live nearby among the poplar trees and hazelnut bushes. It is where family members go to honour loved ones, leave flowers, mementos and a few tears at gravesites. For many years free-ranging horses and cattle grazed there. It wasn't always this way. Before settlers arrived well over a century ago, people followed the ancient Gitxsan practice of cremation.

Most tribal groups in northwest BC, including the Gitxsan, cremated their dead. This was practical because death could occur when family members travelled far from their village. While burial is time-consuming, a body can be cremated at or near the place of death and the deceased's

---

† *An toosim gyat* is the formal Gitxsan name for a cemetery.

ashes brought home.‡ Each village had a cremation site—an *ant'gelaa*—located near plentiful wood, preferably pine.

The Gitanmaax *ant'gelaa* was located about three kilometres from Hazelton near today's Salmon River Road turnoff. My grandfather once showed Uncle Walter and my dad the site. Dad said it was obvious from the ashes and soil that it was an *ant'gelaa*. When cholera, probably carried by the Omineca miners, came to the new village of Hazelton in 1872, deaths occurred in such great numbers that the villagers had to forego cremations at their usual site and build large fires in the centre of Gitanmaax.

While the cremation process may have varied from village to village, Constance Cox, Thomas Hankin's daughter, described what happened in Gitanmaax:

> There was cholera here. Hundreds of Indians died. My father saved dozens and dozens of them by giving them quicksilver…it saved them in some way. In those days they always cremated their dead. They would pull dry gummy [pine] sticks lengthwise and lots of kindling wood under, checker like, and they lay the body on it and built more gumwood on it. And the pallbearers with long poles stood there and lit the fire after the bodies were put on. And then they would poke the bodies with sticks. They were burning these dead with cholera, they were afraid.

> There was a boy, Johnny Lulaxs, who was working for my father, about fourteen years of age. And he told my father that his uncle was very sick, that he would go for a while. My father said all right, and he went home and my father went to see through the village who was sick, and who was not.

> He heard a lot of crying when he got to Johnny Lulaxs's house.§ He met a man and asked who is dead. And he said, "Johnny is dead and his uncle is dead. They are getting ready to burn them now."

> …he was keen on watching the funeral. He said he would go to Johnny's funeral and the Indians said all right. They burnt them right in the village. They had a burning place. They lit a big fire. And [lit] John's uncle first. And then they…took Johnny [to his pyre, and put him] right on top and lit the fire.

> The heat of the fire brought Johnny to and they rolled him off in a great hurry and the Indians ran for their lives. They thought it was a Skot [ghost]. And Johnny rubbed his eyes and staggered over to his mother. And she said, "Don't, don't touch me, I don't want to die."

---

‡ Early French fur traders named the Nedut'en, Wet'suwet'en, Sekani and other Athapaskan speaking peoples, 'Carriers', as they also practiced cremation and carried some ashes of the dead for months afterwards.

§ At the original village near the slough.

> And he went to where his brother was but his brother ran away. And it was awful cold and Johnny had no pants on, and my father put his overcoat around him and took him down to the store and put him to bed. He was very sick.
>
> The next thing was to get Johnny a pair of pants but there were no pants in the store…the only thing was bright green beige (table cloth). And he made Johnny a pair of pants. And Johnny did not care for them much. But he wore them and strictly in dress. My father said that it was his green pants that saved his life. So he did not like to go out without them.
>
> My father explained to the Indians that Johnny had only fainted and he advised them to be very careful before burning. That is, holding the hand up in front of a light and look through it, and if it shows no red, then they are dead, or open their eyes and pick the eyelids and if the eye does not flinch, they are dead, otherwise they will move. So after that they were more careful. Poor Johnny told me often the narrow escape he had, and [of] the green pants. [Johnny went home and gave] the green pants…to his parents…and went naked…He was not an Irishman.¹

Gwininitxw/Solomon Jack described a cremation that his grandfather managed in the early 1900s:

> My grandfather cremated two women at the *ant'gelaa* between Kisgegas and Bear Trap Creek.† He [alone bundled] and packed each woman to the site, as most considered it *hawahl* (unlucky). No one looked towards the smoke during the cremation because that was unlucky too. The heart didn't burn (because it was in the rib cage) and was buried with the ashes.

Solomon's grandfather, being from the deceased women's father's side, was the *'t'iluulak'at*, the person who cared for the body by tying it up and packing it to the cremation site, lighting the fire, and burying the ashes.

Reincarnation

My father said no one would visit the cremation site later because the deceased was coming back anyways, by reincarnation.

'Niist/Bill Blackwater Sr. confirmed this and added that the person who comes back is the *hots'imo witxw*, while the mother of the child is the *widintxw*. Bill also said that the person who has been cremated continues to exist within the ashes. Therefore when the child arrives or is recognized, a bit of food is put into the campfire or, in recent times, into the stove.

Heather Harris, our *Delgamuukw v. BC* genealogist, wrote about Gitxsan reincarnation in her 1994 MA thesis:

---

† Xsigenusmax.

The Gitxsan believe very strongly in reincarnation. Nearly every Gitxsan knows who he was in his last life, sometimes for two or more generations. Reincarnation is usually within the house. When it is outside the house it is always another kind of relative. There are many ways in which the returning person is recognized including dreams by a pregnant woman or her relatives telling who the new baby will be, birthmarks which match the scars or marks of the former person, memories of younger children, and affinities in young children for relatives or friends of the former personality (Mills 1994)…Because of the firm belief in reincarnation, the Gitxsan see life as cyclical in nature; past, present, and future are not entirely distinct. A new baby born in the house is seen very much to be a continuation of the past and continuity into the future.[2]

Moses Shanoss (1847-1928) was a chief in the House of Nikateen. Moses had a brother, Arthur Nelson, who drowned in 1907. When Arthur Sampson, a great-nephew of Arthur Nelson, was born ten years later, he was said to be *witxw* Arthur Nelson or 'Arthur Nelson arrived'.

Examples of reincarnation occurred in my grandparents' day. One of Charlie Sterritt's great uncles was hit in the eye by an arrow during a battle. Some years later, when Charlie's cousin Tom Sampson was born, he had a black eye and was said to be the reincarnation of their great uncle. And my grandmother Kate had a relative named Yimist. Kate's youngest son, Arthur (1923-2001), came to her and asked for something that belonged to Yimist. Afterwards, he was nicknamed, 'Art Yimist'.

Despite the need for immediate cremation during the 1872 cholera outbreak, it seems there were also a few burials at the old village near 'Ksan. My dad was once hired to do some bulldozing there and inadvertently exposed several graves. He stopped work and reported his findings. Evidently the villagers began burials soon after Thomas Hankin and other settlers brought Christianity to the area and by 1900 burials had replaced cremation.

A 1906 sketch map of the cemetery and Hazelton reveals that by then there had been at least 136 burials at the cemetery—mostly Gitxsan—in eighty-one grave houses and fifty-five fences.[3] Early photographs depict a village of expertly built miniature houses. While grave houses were built for both adults and children and held their cherished worldly possessions, chiefs continued to erect totem poles carved in tribute to a deceased chief and his or her House history in Gitanmaax itself. Many grave houses remained during the 1940s but grass fires wrought havoc and none exist today. The sketch also shows that the southwest corner of the graveyard was for use of the white people.

For many years, the three Hazeltons—New, Old and South—buried their dead at Gitanmaax.‡ Today, at least sixty non-native people are buried there, including the remains of three people of Chinese ancestry. Many other Chinese residents were temporarily buried there until friends and relatives later held a ceremony, recovered the remains and returned them to China.

After half a century the cemetery at Gitanmaax was beginning to fill up, and "the natives [wanted] the whites to get a cemetery of their own."[4] A number of potential sites were considered

---

‡ Most Wet'suwet'en people, and some Gitxsan, buried their dead at Hagwilget and Moricetown.

At one time there were more than eighty grave houses at the Gitanmaax cemetery on the hill above Hazelton. Most were lost to grass fires in the 1940s and after. (Wrathall photo VPL Photo No. 39320)

and rejected until the 1950s when a site was chosen at Two Mile, a community between Gitanmaax and the Hagwilget Canyon Bridge. Most white folks, including my mother, and some aboriginals have since been buried at Two Mile.

While there once appeared to be unlimited space for graveyards when settlers arrived on the Upper Skeena, it is no longer the case. Thus, an interesting trend is emerging, whereby some Gitxsan people are choosing cremation rather than burial, albeit in crematoriums rather than at an *ant'gelaa*.

As Constance Cox explained, gravesites became elaborate memorials to the deceased:

> [The Gitxsan] don't do the graveyard as they use to. They use to take as much care and pain to build a [grave house] as they would a bungalow. It had painted windows [and] they would prepare it inside and they put all the worldly belongings of the departed [into it]. And if it was a woman they always cut her hair off and put it in the grave house; [they] hung it, and all her clothes [and] her trunks. And the same way [for men].

> And the things were never touched. They stayed there quite safe until they rotted; no one thought of robbing them. It was quite a job when the [railway] construction came through here. Many graves were robbed by the whites. They would pick whatever they had a sense to. Sometimes there was carelessness on the grave. And a [*halayt*] had all his instruments and some of that was taken.

> Once I was with three tourist ladies…[who] were taking photographs and examining the graves, when their eyes took sight of all the dishes with a pattern that they said was very valuable, and I said it was because it had belonged to that Indian for at least 60 years. They used to trade…[with] the Nass Indians for dishes. And most likely other dishes had come from there. The ladies did not hear where they came from [and] she took it and what is [strange] enough, she climbed over the grave and I kept [watching] and she took a dish: it looked like a pot but it had a fine spout on it. It may have been a belly pot.[5]

One may speculate that the belongings placed in Gitxsan grave houses provided items of value to the 'incarnation' of the deceased: a woman's sewing machine, a child's boots, a *halayt*'s regalia and charms, hair hanging in the grave house. These would be important items in the afterlife and available to the person who was going to return.

Although most graves in the cemetery have headstones, not all graves contain the deceased's remains. For example, Arthur Nelson, the younger brother of Moses Shanoss, was a river man. While taking gold to the coast by canoe, he drowned when his boat overturned near Gitsegukla, and his body was never recovered. Moses Shanoss, John Smith and other members of Nelson's extended family bought a monument and installed it in the Gitanmaax cemetery.

> Died
> Sept. 18, 1907
> Aged 37 Years
> Lead Kindly Light, Lead
> Thou To Me
> NELSON

Another Gitxsan chief, Daniel Skawill (1871-1945), whose territory lay 270 kilometres northwest of Hazelton near Stewart, was a maternal uncle to Wiigoobil/Jessie (Lumm) Sterritt (my grandfather's third wife). Gitxsan chiefs were wealthy, as Alvin Weget noted. They lived off the land and, because revenue from trapping was surplus to their needs, they were able to afford fine headstones.

Daniel wanted to be buried at Gitanmaax. Albert Allan, Daniel Skawill's nephew from the Nass River, brought Daniel's monument to Gitanmaax by train. Daniel was pleased when he saw the tombstone beside his house. He put up a feast and placed the stone at his intended gravesite.

Unfortunately when Skawill died in 1945, he was buried in the Barney's Gulch Creek cemetery near Stewart. An early snowfall in the fall of 1958 was followed "…by days upon days of warm rain. Flooding was everywhere and the steep banks of Barney's Gulch…sloughed into the little river and dammed it up…The cemetery was buried under 30 or more feet of gravel …."[6] Daniel Skawill's grave was also buried. Nevertheless, thanks to his foresight, his undated memorial stands in Gitanmaax Cemetery and reads, "IN LOVING MEMORY OF DANIEL SKAWIL".

Many Gitxsan gravestones replicate crest images—a frog, bear, grouse or raven, for example. These monuments were made elsewhere, but by whom? Several stonemasons set up businesses in

Victoria during the 1870s, including George Rudge (1854-1934) from New Brunswick. Rudge, who apprenticed under his father, traveled west and worked as a 'marble maker' in San Francisco and Seattle. He worked in Victoria until 1891 and then moved to Port Simpson. He became "…noted for his totemic images in stone to be found in native Indian cemeteries on the Queen Charlotte Islands, Port Simpson, Port Essington, Kitimaat, and Hazelton."[7]

Many of the gravestones at Gitanmaax bear the names of pioneers such as miners James May, J. H. Lyons, Ezra Evans and William Keynton. The location of the grave of one of BC's most famous pioneers, Cataline, had been lost to memory until recently. He is buried next to James May and Ezra Evans. The stone cairn put up in his honour reads JEAN CAUX/THE PACKER / 1832–1922 and is about fourteen metres east of his gravesite.

Gitxsan chief Daniel Skawill so wanted to be buried at the Gitanmaax cemetery he had his undated head stone erected there before his death. Unfortunately, he died in Stewart. His remains were interred there and then buried under a further thirty feet of gravel when the graveyard was flooded in 1958. (Harry Kruisselbrink photo)

To a certain extent, the cemetery reflects aboriginal and non-aboriginal preferences. For example, the house fronts and totem poles of northwest coast peoples always fronted on a river or beach so visitors could locate the houses of clan relatives from the water. Similarly, nearly all Gitxsan gravestones in the Gitanmaax cemetery face one of the roads running through it. Hazelton's pioneers, on the other hand, seem to have preferred a 'room with a view' as many of their graves face the valley and mountains along the brow of the hill in the southwest quadrant.

A few gravestones in the cemetery were made locally. James and Isabella McLeod immigrated to Canada from Scotland in 1906. They bought land on the north side of Salmon River above

Hazelton where they established the Silver Spur Ranch. James was a mason's laborer in Scotland and he and his sons fabricated monuments from Silver Standard Mine tailings. The monuments have since weathered badly and the inscriptions are gone. James (1861-1932) and Isabella (1864-1927) are buried in the Gitanmaax cemetery.

In 1958, I was walking through the graveyard when I saw a headstone that took me back to a warm day in May 1954. Some of us were playing in my grandparents' yard on Government Street when my grandmother called me to her kitchen. I was wearing my favourite t-shirt, which bore a handsome horsehead framed in a horseshoe. She asked, "Can you draw that horse?" I did what she asked and resumed playing with my friends. My grandmother died the following year and I completely forgot about the matter until that day in 1958. There was my sketch, carved into the weathered headstone of my grandmother's fellow house member, Guuhadak/Beal Muldoe.

Hazelton's undertakers and gravedigger were local men. Ward and Tom Marshall were the undertakers, and Long Frank Wilson, a Gitxsan man, worked for many years as Hazelton's gravedigger. Although he disliked "picking nuggets" in the rocky part of the cemetery, Long Frank took pride in his work. He had a keen sense of humour and regularly dropped by Marshall Brothers' office to visit. One day, the conversation went like this:

LONG FRANK:	Hello Tom, how are you?
TOM:	Just fine. How are you?
LONG FRANK:	Good. Did anyone die today?
TOM:	Nope.
LONG FRANK:	Too bad.

The image of a horse's head, carved into the headstone of Beal Muldoe, was based on a 1954 drawing by the author. (NJS photo)

Charlie Yeomans

Eulogies provide a brief but important record of a person's life. In exceptional situations—a heroic accomplishment, accidental death, or murder—the deeds or misdeeds of an individual survive in oral histories, court records and other historical documents. Any number of the people buried in the Gitanmaax cemetery—native and non-native alike—met their end at a time when Gitxsan culture was in flux. Two gravestones bear silent witness to the clash of cultures on the upper Skeena: those of trader Charlie Yeomans and Gitxsan chief Spookxw/James Spaagh. They are but two of the many stories that can be told.

> In Memory of
> Amos Charles Yeomans
> Died June 16, 1884
> Aged 45 Yrs

Little is known about Charlie Yeomans[†] before he arrived in Hazelton except that he may have been lured there by the Omineca gold rush in 1871 or 1872. Like so many others, he wintered in Victoria and travelled to the interior during the summer and fall. Yeomans established a trading business in Hazelton and lived with a Gitxsan woman, Emma Holland from Gitwangak. Their daughter Martha, the first of five children, was born in 1874.

Yeomans bought supplies for his business at Port Essington and hired Gitxsan men to bring his provisions upriver by canoe. The death of Billy Owen, a Gitxsan man hired by Yeomans, had tragic consequences, as described by two Gitxsan men, Gamayam/Charles Mark and Ts'igwii/Isaac Tens. Charles Mark said:

Trader Amos Charles (Charlie) Yeomans was killed at Hazelton in 1884 because he failed to observe Gitxsan law "regarding accidents and death". (Sheila Peters photo)

---

† Also spelled Youmans and Homans.

Tom Hankins always had his freight canoe and Indians freight for him. And Charles Yeoman had his canoe and Indians freighting for him. By this time, I was quite a big boy. And was quite able to understand what was going on. Ch. Yeoman was here at his store, and it was very high water, and he sent two canoes to get his freight down the river. The freight canoes were on their way up. They had reached the Gitsalas Canyon when one of the men in the freight canoe fell out and was drowned. His name was His'duuhl'gana'aw. His father's name was Ha'atu [Haa'atxw]…

When the first canoes arrived the news soon spread that Ha'atu went down to Yeomans and asked him to pay a ransom for the death of his son. Ha'atu was very sad. His heart was very heavy when they talked and when he talked to Yeoman. Yeoman did not pay attention to Ha'atu's request. He did not even reply to him. Ha'atu went back to his house. I have seen the knife which Ha'atu went to get at his house. It was a knife belonging to a white man, a soldier's knife. He carried the knife up his arm, concealed inside. There was a white man sitting off a piece, just talking near Yeoman's store, there was a large veranda.[8]

Isaac Tens explained what happened next:

There were many Gitxsan people in the store and many outside. They were all talking of the death of the man [Billy Owen]…saying Charlie Homans was in the wrong for not informing them before, and he saw Ha'atu coming along to the place where was the store, and he had a coat on, a large coat like an overcoat. [He] had his hands crossed over his body and one hand concealed within one arm of his coat. Charlie Homans was leaning over the counter on his left elbow…talking to Dr. D.

So in comes Ha'atu…into the store. No one knew of his purpose, he still had his hand concealed and he walked right up [to] Charlie Homans and stabs him in the neck. Everybody ran away…including Dr. D. It was with a butcher knife. Charlie Homans fell to the ground. He had a house on the hill, and he started up towards the house holding his hand over the wound.[‡]

I was the only one that stopped by and Charlie Homans saw me and he spoke to [me] "hello". And he went into his house. When he came into his house he fell [under] the table, and the blood flowed over repeatedly. This is what William Holland told [me]. And an hour after, he was dead. He never spoke again before dying.

---

‡ Joseph Augustus (Gus) Sampare (1878-1947), Bonita and Alfred Sampare's son, said he was at the scene of the murder, and that "…the Indian came down the road and walked up behind Yeomans and killed him" ("Barbeau and Beynon Fieldnotes", B-F-90.3).

The following August the police came up. And with them was a man from the Nass named Bathle (Charlie Barton). He acted as interpreter for them. Ha'atu at the time was at Kispayaks and the police never went after him. The police then got a brother of Ha'atu and sent him to Kispayaks…and when Ha'atu saw his brother he got up and followed him…and he walked in to the police himself. And they had the trial right where the school is now, a great big log house.⁹

The Gitxsan people were concerned about how Ha'atu would be treated under provincial laws. On their behalf Gidumgaldo sought clemency for Ha'atu and, explaining Gitxsan law, appealed to the provincial secretary in a letter:

> Geddum-cal-doe, Head Chief, to the Provincial Secretary
> Kit-au-max (Forks of the Skeena)
> September 7th, 1884
>
> SIR—We, the Chiefs and people of Kit-au-max, the place where the late A.C. Yeomans was murdered, desire to lay before you, and your colleagues in office, our feelings in regard to that unfortunate affair. We are anxious that this matter shall be so settled that the utmost good feeling shall exist between the whites and the Indians, which, unhappily does not now obtain.
>
> We wish to lay before you our law in regard to accidents and death that occur in company with others. It is expected that survivors shall immediately, or as soon as possible, make it known to the friends of the injured or deceased, what has taken place. If this is not done, it is taken as evidence that there has been foul play.
>
> In the case of the death of Billy Owen, Mr. A.C. Yeomans arrived at this place, and remained in the midst of Billy's friends of the deceased, though we asked Mr. Yeomans if those with him were all well. His answer was: "yes, except one had sore feet". At the expiration of two days and three nights a canoe came up, and the news was conveyed to the friends of the drowned man, and they thought there had been foul play on Mr. Yeomans part, as he had not made the matter known.
>
> The general custom among the Indians is that if anyone calls another to hunt with him, to go canoeing, etc., and death occurs the survivor always makes a present corresponding with his ability, to show his sympathy and good will to the friends of the deceased, and to show that there was no ill-feeling in the matter.
>
> Mr. Yeomans failed in this. He gave no present, thus showing no sympathy or good will. We did not know that the father of Billy Owen was going to kill Yeomans. When the officers of the Government came to arrest the murderer, we gave no opposition to their work. We believed that Billy's father would be justly dealt with, and that all the circumstances of the case would be taken into consideration. While we do not justify the murder, we believe that it was the

strange way in which Mr. Yeomans acted that exasperated the man to do the deed. For this reason we ask that clemency be shown the murderer, particularly as he was a quiet, inoffensive man.

We hope, sir, you will take all things into consideration, and that peace be firmly established between the whites and the Indians. I am, Sir, on behalf of the other Chiefs, and the people,

Signed GEDDUM-CAL-DOE

Head Chief

His   X   Mark

D. J(ennings)[10]

This is a remarkable letter. Gidumgaldo, on behalf of Owen's father, made a clear case for clemency, explaining how under Gitxsan law Yeomans could have dealt with Owen's accidental death in a reasonable way. But colonial law trumped Gitxsan law and "Haatq was found guilty of murder and sentenced to be hanged on 25 February 1885."[11] Although Ha'atu's sentence was later commuted to imprisonment he died two years later in jail.[†] His death contributed to already heightened tensions on the upper Skeena and was a factor in the Skeena Uprising a few years later, when, once again, Gitxsan and settler laws clashed.

Spookxw/James Spaagh[‡]

A dispute over the succession of a chief's name—Hanamuxw—arose between Kamalmuk of Gitanyow and Neatsqua of Gitsegukla. Kamalmuk believed that Neatsqua had used his shaman's powers to kill his son. Kamalmuk shot Neatsqua in February 1888 and retreated to Gitanyow territory at Meziadin Lake. This triggered a series of events that may have contributed not only to Kamalmuk's death in 1888 but to the death of James Spaagh and his family five or six years afterwards.

The provincial government sent five special constables to apprehend Kamalmuk. In May, the constables learned that Kamalmuk had returned to Gitwangak. Several were dispatched to make an arrest but it was botched. A constable shot Kamalmuk in the back and killed him, creating turmoil and anger not only in Gitwangak but upriver at Gitanmaax and Kispiox. The white residents of Hazelton reinforced the HBC stockade and prepared to defend themselves, even though some among the settlers thought this response was unwarranted.

One of the five special constables dispatched to arrest Kamalmuk was Constance Cox's soon-to-be stepfather, Richard Loring. Loring (1849-1934) was born in Dresden, Germany and had a military education. After visiting New York relatives in 1874, Loring mined in Colorado and California for about six years and then relocated to BC. He spent several months on the upper

---

† Ha'atu was also the father of Abel Oakes.

‡ Spaagh is the spelling used in the records of this story.

Skeena as a constable in 1888, then returned to Victoria and worked in the provincial jail as a guard. He was appointed Indian Agent for the Upper Skeena and Babine District in August 1889 and married Thomas Hankin's widow, Margaret, the same month.[12] As Indian Agent, Loring was required to oversee and investigate the death of James Spaagh and his family.

> IN MEMORY
> OF
> JAMES SPAAGH
> TWO CHILDREN
> PERISHED IN THE OMINECA
> DECEMBER 20, 1893
> May they rest in peace

James Spaagh was likely only a teenager during the 1888 Skeena Uprising. Constance Cox said, "Spox was the man whom the government recognized as the only Chief on the Skeena River on account of his loyalty to the whites during the time of the uprising, the year before Mr. Loring became [the Indian] Agent."[13]

A winter journey to the Omineca in 1893 resulted in the tragic death of James Spaagh and his immediate family. His wife and two children are buried in the cemetery. Spaagh himself was cremated in the Omineca and his ashes brought to Gitanmaax. (Sheila Peters photo)

If Cox was right, some among the Gitxsan may have resented Spaagh's intervention. Being favoured by the 'whites' could have been as much a curse as a blessing and, as a result, Spaagh may have believed a *haldawgit* (a practitioner of witchcraft) was conspiring against him. Whatever the reason, Spookxw/Steve Robinson said James Spaagh chose to go to the Omineca at an unusual time as the mining camps were empty and he and his young family would be alone until the miners began to return in the spring.

The family set out for Tom's Creek on February 27, 1893 with sufficient provisions to carry them through the winter. Spaagh probably worked at Tom's Creek during the summer of 1893 but, rather than return to Gitanmaax in the fall, he went east to the Germansen Lake area where, as Loring said, he would be trespassing on "Sicanee territory".[14] In December, perhaps because he was short of food and unable to hunt due to heavy winter storms, Spaagh and his family set off for Tom's Creek mining camp seeking food.

About fifteen kilometres west of Germansen River and fifty kilometres short of the mining camp, Spaagh sought refuge for his wife and children in a cabin near the Omineca River. With his family safe in the cabin, Spaagh continued his desperate journey westward. It seems he made it to Tom's Creek but on his return "broke through the ice…and shortly after must have frozen to death as the distance from the hole in the ice to where he was found frozen was only about 100 yards. In consequence of this perishing, his wife and children died from hunger and exposure."[15]

Exactly when their deaths occurred is unknown, but "…according to all signs and indications, [they] must have died some time after Xmas last [1893], the time of the heavy snow storm. Their bodies were brought in…on toboggan, that of husband and father is still missing."[16]

Loring's reports to BC's Superintendent of Indians, A.W. Vowell, provide clues as to what occurred next, although Loring acknowledged that his April and May report was, "…somewhat conflicting as to the death of Spaagh, etc."[17]

The valley bottoms in the Omineca rise from 732 metres elevation at Germansen Landing to 1588 metres at Old Hogem, and very heavy (three metres and more) snowfalls are common. Spaagh's body—no doubt covered by deep snow shortly after he died—was found in May 1894 "…on the Omineca River, nearly opposite to the old trading post [of] Hogem."[18] Spaagh likely made it to Tom's Creek and on his return broke through the ice of the Omineca River.[†]

Two aboriginal men, Daniel Teegee and Bear Lake George, each then twenty years of age, lived at Takla Landing and knew the Omineca region intimately.[‡] They became brothers-in-law when Daniel married Lucy Alexis.[§] As Carrier-Sekani Grand Chief Edward John explained in 1986, the men were hunting caribou when they found an upright stick with four charcoal marks on it pointing towards a nearby cabin. At the cabin, the men found three bodies lying on the bed. On closer inspection they found that the infant child had a sugar-bag rag in her mouth. They believed she was the last to die. The fourth person was nowhere to be seen. Teegee and George recognized the deceased as Spaagh's wife and children. They searched for Spaagh but could not find him. Bear Lake George immediately began a remarkable 280-kilometre snowshoe trip to Hazelton. He took two very long days to get to the HBC post at Babine Lake, arriving there exhausted. He slept and

---

† See Map 9: Routes to the Omineca Gold Fields.

‡ Daniel Teegee (1873-1938) was Sekani, and Bear Lake George (1874-1954) was of Gitxsan and Sekani heritage.

§ Bear Lake George was orphaned when his mother (Lucy Alexis's aunt or great-aunt) died.

resumed his journey the next morning, climbing the 1,372 metre summit twenty kilometres west of Babine Lake, and snowshoed on to Hazelton to report the tragedy.†

After Bear Lake George set out for Hazelton, Daniel Teegee barricaded the cabin to prevent animals from entering and returned to Takla Landing. The police and Spaagh's relatives accompanied Bear Lake George back to the Omineca. The police examined the bodies and could see that there had been no foul play. It appeared they starved to death as there was nothing in their stomachs.

Teegee and George also worked as packers and miners in the Omineca and may have been present when Spaagh's body was found:

> [Spaagh] was burnt by the Indian who brought his bones and ashes. The [family] placed the box on a platform in front of his house in Hazelton, where it was nailed to the totem pole. His was a thin trunk. The mother and children were brought to Hazelton and buried in the cemetery on the brow of the hill. The name is on the tombstone, 'Perished in the Omineca'...I saw the bodies...they were not decayed, but [were] like mummys.[19]

Daniel Teegee and Bear Lake George found Spaagh's wife and children in midwinter when the trail to Gitanmaax was covered with snow. Spaagh's relatives brought their bodies by toboggan to Gitanmaax where they were buried. James Spaagh's body was discovered in the spring. It was too early for packhorses and carrying his body 240 kilometres was impractical. As had been done for millennia, James Spaagh's body was cremated and his ashes brought home to Gitanmaax.

During the mid-1980s, the tribal council hired Heather Harris to research and write the genealogies of Gitxsan and Wet'suwet'en families for the court in *Delgamuukw v. BC*. After the Supreme Court of Canada decision in December 1997, I continued recording family information written on headstones at Gitanmaax and other village cemeteries. One Sunday in 1998, while researching and photographing each headstone at Gitanmaax, my father arrived and told me what he knew about many of the names on the gravestones. On another occasion, Ward Marshall, the local undertaker, and his nephew Toby accompanied me to the cemetery where Ward also explained what he knew about the various families there, along with the structure of the cemetery.

Afterwards, I approached chief councillor Victor Robinson for funds to hire a surveyor to produce a map of the cemetery. The council agreed, and the result is a map and spreadsheet of all marked and unmarked gravesites.‡ Two roads run through the graveyard at right angles to each other, creating four quadrants (northeast, northwest, southeast and southwest) for general location purposes. The surveyor located 504 gravesites, of which 340 have headstones, with the remainder being grave depressions. At least ninety-six graves from 1906 are included in the total. However, trees and underbrush in the northwest quadrant hid another forty sites known to be in that area. The total number of known burials in the cemetery from the mid-1880s to June 2000 was at least 544.

---

† The parallels between the Dakelh oral history of 1986, told here by Edward John, and that of the Gitxsan by Constance Cox in the 1920s, is striking.

‡ McIlhenney Engineering of Smithers conducted the survey. The Band Council and Village of Hazelton each have a copy of the map.

ENDNOTES

1. "Barbeau and Beynon Fieldnotes", Constance Cox n.d., B-F-203.2.
2. Harris, H., "Only Their Skins", 25-26.
3. Canada, DIA, Gitanmaax cemetery sketch 1906.
4. "Looking for a Cemetery Site for Hazelton." *The Omineca Herald* 11 Jan. 1939.
5. "Barbeau and Beynon Fieldnotes", Constance Cox, 1920, B-F-111.2.
6. McLeod, 172.
7. Adams, 19.
8. *"Barbeau and Beynon Fieldnotes", Charles Mark* and Mrs. Cox, 1923, B-F-658.1.
9. "Barbeau and Beynon Fieldnotes", Isaac Tens nd. B-F-90.3: 3-4.
10. Galois, "The History of the Upper Skeena", 134-135.
11. Galois, "The History of the Upper Skeena", 135.
12. Loring to Gosnell, Sept. 5, 1896.
13. "Barbeau and Beynon Fieldnotes", Constance Cox, nd, B-F-203.2: 1-3.
14. Canada, Babine Agency Letterbook (BAL): Loring to Vowell, Oct. 16, 1894.
15. Canada, Babine Agency Letterbook (BAL): Loring to Vowell, Oct. 16, 1894.
16. Canada, Babine Agency Letterbook (BAL): Loring to Vowell, July 23, 1894.
17. Canada, Babine Agency Letterbook (BAL): Loring to Vowell, Oct. 16, 1894.
18. Canada, Babine Agency Letterbook (BAL): Loring to Vowell, May 31, 1894. Two miners (one named Wm. Williamson) found Spaagh's body.
19. "Barbeau and Beynon Fieldnotes", Constance Cox, nd, B-F-203.2: 1-3.

CHAPTER TWENTY-TWO

The Land Question

The white man staked the land over there at Temlaham and got preemption or bought it I don't know. The government sold that land. Sold it to George Swan, an operator in Hazelton about 1901 before the early telegraph party. There were over one hundred cords of wood cut there and piled up there. It belonged to the Indian boys from their own lands there.

I had some wood and had about five cords. Billy Green had lots of cord wood about 40 cords. And Fred Hart 10 or 20 cords, and Luke Sampson probably had 5 to 10. And Peter Brown with his brother I don't know how many cords, and William Brown too. Swan knew that they cut wood there and after he cut the wood he took it all. Got the policeman and hauled it.

Some wanted to take Swan and hang him and start war after that. Me and Gidumgaldo make peace, did not want war. We go in jail one month each about that trouble. I did not want so many people killed after that. We wanted to settle the 'Land Question' before that, and we started, but not quite yet. The Indians did not want all of BC but only want from Kcigonget Creek† (fifteen miles below Kitwanga) to Bear Lake and Blackwater. That is all we want.

---

† Xsigwink̲'aat (Fiddler Creek).

I heard that he had lost that property since. I heard it. George Swan got that wood and sold it. George Beirnes worked for George Swan. He was poor man he pulled the wood for Swan with Swan. And Dutch Clyne worked for Swan and he helped Swan to sell the wood out. And Indians got nothing.

At that time the Indians wanted to start a fight. Me and Gidumgaldo go in jail to stop that war. Whiteman he did not know. The Indians had a great meeting here when we were arrested and wood hauled. Some Indians said, "What is the matter that is our place here for generation and generation? That wood belongs to us not George Swan."

Me and Chief James White (Gidumgaldo) were arrested and put in jail one month because I cut some wood on my own land after that. That was at the same time. He kept my wood too. That is the reason why the Indians in BC are in trouble. The government took the land away from the Indians and never tell before. And we go to the priest Mr. John Field and ask for his help and he said that he had nothing to do with it. And we go to Indian Agent—Billy Green [go] too and tried to get help. He [Loring] says he cannot do it.

So we quit all the Indian Agent and the church too. Never listened to them after that, the Indian Agent and the church. Suppose we Indian get in trouble we go to lawyer Anderson and Williams and Thompson at Prince Rupert to fix up right about troubles. Never go for Indian Agent or anybody else. Suppose there is trouble between Indians or white men we get lawyer go court to fix it right like anybody else.‡

—Naalaxha/Abel Oakes 1920[1]

Naalaxha/Abel Oakes (1879-1956) was a member of the House of xGwoimtxw from Anlagasimdeex near Kisgegas on the Babine River. He was perhaps five foot eight and solidly built. He seemed always to be wearing leather top boots. As children, some of us wore such boots too, but didn't call them 'leather tops' or 'shoe pacs' as adults did. We spoke proudly of them among ourselves as our 'Abel Oakes'.

---

‡ Abel Oakes's strategy ultimately proved effective; however, it took many years to be tested. A 1927 amendment to the Indian Act prohibited fundraising to advance a land claim in BC. Until an early 1950s revision removed both fundraising and potlatch prohibitions, it was illegal for aboriginal groups to pursue their land claims in the courts.

Abel Oakes had a clear sense of who he was and how life around him and his people was changing. He was right about money, policemen, the government and their laws. And he, along with other Gitxsan leaders, was concerned about the 'land question'. Abel Oakes knew that the members of the House of xGwoimtxw owned their territories collectively. This wasn't wishful thinking. In 1812 Daniel Harmon, a North West Company employee based at Stuart Lake Post (later Fort St. James) recognized it:

> Every tribe [west of the Rocky Mountains] has its particular tract of country; and this is divided again, among the several families, which compose the tribe. Rivers, lakes and mountains serve them as boundaries; and the limits of the territory which belongs to each family are as well known by the tribe, as the lines which separate farms are, by the farmers, in the civilized world.²

This became a contentious issue in BC when Sir John A. MacDonald appointed Joseph Trutch as BC's first lieutenant governor in 1871. Trutch reviled aboriginal people, considering them a hindrance to development. Rather than negotiate treaties, as was done elsewhere in Canada, Trutch took land from natives and gave it to developers and settlers. Aboriginal and government leaders alike referred to the dispute over native land rights as the 'land question'.

Captain Cook

The land question has its roots in Captain James Cook's voyage to the South Pacific a century before Trutch's appointment. As an accomplished navigator, Cook was at the vanguard of British imperialism from Canada to New Zealand and Australia. During his relatively short lifetime, he not only circumnavigated the world but was also present on the east coast of Canada (acquiring his considerable mapping and navigational skills) when King George III issued his 1763 proclamation which established the constitutional basis for negotiating treaties with aboriginal nations.†

Cook recorded a solar eclipse in British North America in 1766. The quality of his report on the event led the Royal Society and the British government to commission Cook to observe the transit of Venus in the South Pacific in 1769 during the first of his three historic voyages.‡ He recorded the eclipse and subsequently sailed around New Zealand, determining it to be two islands, then sailed to the east coast of New Holland (Australia) and northwards along that coast, finally returning to England to report his findings in 1771. In the summer of 1778, on his third epic voyage, he sailed along the west coast of North America and north to the Aleutian Islands and Bering Strait before turning back. He returned to Hawaii where he was killed in a confrontation with local indigenous people in 1779. Others of his party continued the search for the Northwest

---

† Almost two and a half centuries later, the proclamation would finally apply to BC in the *Delgamuukw v. BC* court case.

‡ A transit of Venus occurs when the planet Venus passes between the sun and the earth. Venus appears as a small black dot moving across the face of the sun. It is a rare event, occurring in patterns of about 243 years, with pairs of transits eight years apart (as in 2004 and 2012). They are of scientific importance because they helped determine the size of the solar system, which is why Captain James Cook went to the South Pacific. Others made observations throughout the known world at the same time as Cook. By chance, Barbara and I witnessed the transit of Venus while in Townsville, Queensland in June 2012.

Passage after Cook was killed, including Captain William Bligh of *Mutiny on the Bounty* fame. Also serving as a midshipman during Cook's second and third voyages was a talented young man, George Vancouver. He became a captain in his own right and surveyed the Pacific coast in the vicinity of the Skeena and Nass estuaries in 1792.

Cook had an enormous impact on the peoples inhabiting the continents he visited because he paved the way for Great Britain to colonize Australia, New Zealand and Canada. However, the new colonial land policy established in 1763 was applied differently in each place.

Cook was well aware of the new policy. The Royal Society sponsored his 1769 voyage and provided him with instructions reflecting the Royal Proclamation of 1763. As society president James Douglas (1702-1768)§ pronounced, "No European Nation has a right to occupy any part of their country, or settle among them without their voluntary consent. Conquest over such people can give no just title."[3]

The Royal Navy was paying the cost of the expedition and expected Cook to determine the existence of a fabled southern continent, *Terra Australis Incognito*.[4] After observing the transit of Venus, Cook sailed from Tahiti to New Zealand and then continued west towards Van Diemen's Land (Tasmania) and New Holland (Australia). With regard to Australia, the navy told Cook that he was "…with the consent of the natives to take possession of convenient situations in the country in the name of the king of Great Britain".[5] Cook anchored in Botany Bay from April 29 to June 5, 1770 and then sailed north up the east coast of New Holland.

On August 22, 1770 Cook sailed around the north end of Cape York, anchored and went ashore on what came to be known as Possession Island.

> [He] hoisted the English colours in the name of His Majesty King George the Third [and] took possession of the whole eastern coast from the above latitude [38 degrees south] down to this place by the name of New South Wales, together with the Bays, Harbours, Rivers and Islands situate upon the said coast, after which we fired three Volleys of small arms which were answered by a like number from the Ship.[6]

After Cook returned to England in 1771, the ensuing debate and British policy in Australia became rooted in the belief, based on Cook's report, that the Australian Aborigines were few in number, less technologically advanced, had no clothing and only rudimentary shelter. As the British colonized Australia, a consensus emerged that the Aborigines were "… the least civilized human beings they had ever seen."[7]

As Stuart Banner wrote, "…Australia, from Cook and [naturalist Joseph] Banks's reports, seemed to present sparseness of an entirely different magnitude. North America had some empty places, but Australia sounded like an empty continent."[8]

---

§ Douglas, no relation to HBC's factor and Vancouver Island's first governor James Douglas, was the 14th Earl of Morton, a Scottish astronomer and Royal Society president from 1764 until his death October 12, 1768. Cook named Moreton (sic) Bay, Queensland after Lord Morton.

Diane Smith, a colleague who has worked with aboriginal people throughout Australia, said British colonizers went further in terms of their self-justifying philosophy and regarded indigenous Australians as having "no government, no kings, no rule of law" and downgraded them to what might be termed *governance nullius* along with *terra nullius* (nobody's land). In their eyes, the British settlers brought law and government to a lawless land and a lawless people and they essentially ignored the Royal Proclamation of 1763.

A similar pattern emerged in Canada where the British and French had been established on the east coast since the 1600s. After much warfare, and in particular after the Anglo-French Seven Years War ended with an English victory and the Treaty of Paris in 1763, King George's 1763 proclamation recognized the rights of North American natives. In eastern Canada, from 1701 to the early 1800s, the British negotiated peace and friendship treaties for the purpose of ending hostilities and encouraging cooperation between the British and aboriginal peoples.[†] Peace and friendship treaties did not require that aboriginal nations surrender rights to their lands and resources, nor did treaties negotiated post-confederation. After 1867, Canada went on to create treaty policy, appoint treaty commissioners and ratify treaty agreements. Eleven such treaties, known as the 'Numbered Treaties', were agreements with the Government of Canada, administered by Canadian law and are overseen today by a federal cabinet minister assigned that specific responsibility.

The colony of Vancouver Island was created in 1849 with James Douglas (1803-1877) as governor.[‡] Douglas applied practices consistent with those east of the Rocky Mountains and was aware of the Treaty of Waitangi that the British had negotiated in 1840 with the Maori in New Zealand recognizing their rights. The text he used in the treaties he negotiated with Vancouver Island tribes between 1850 and 1854 was taken from "New Zealand precedents for purchasing Maori land".[9]

In the case of the Douglas treaties, the aboriginal signatories and their descendants understood that they retained existing village sites and fields for their continued use, the "liberty to hunt over unoccupied lands" and the right to "carry on their fisheries as formerly." Contrary to current belief, the original text of the Douglas treaties did not contain extinguishment language, or the notion that an area of land was surrendered "entirely and forever" in exchange for cash, clothing, or blankets.[§] That was added later.[10]

[†] Tension existed as early as 1701 between the east coast aboriginal peoples and the British Crown. By 1722, as New England colonies expanded northward, hostilities led to war. Three years later, the 1726 treaty between the British Crown and the Abenaki—an alliance of the Mi'kmaq, Maliseet and Passamaquoddy nations—became the first 'peace and friendship treaty' in what came to be known as Canada (see Wicken).

[‡] Chief Factor James Douglas became governor of the colony of Vancouver Island in 1849 after the British transferred Vancouver Island to the HBC. Therefore, the fourteen treaties Douglas negotiated were on behalf of the HBC, not Britain (see Banner, 204-205).

[§] The notion of extinguishment is an interpretation advanced by Crown governments based on the written text. Those who concluded the numbered treaties did not understand "surrender" and don't accept that the treaty accomplished this (Louise Mandell, personal communication, August 2012).

Joseph Trutch

Until Alexander Mackenzie's journey to the Pacific in 1792, the Rocky Mountains represented a physical barrier to the westward march of explorers, fur traders and settlers. Soon after Mackenzie arrived by land and Captain Vancouver by sea, the region began to open up. The crown colonies of Vancouver Island and (mainland) BC became a single colony in 1866. When the colony of British Columbia joined Canada in 1871, successive provincial and federal governments argued that the royal proclamation did not extend west of the Rocky Mountains. And the policy adopted in 1871 by BC's first lieutenant governor, Joseph Trutch (1826-1904), had the hallmarks of Australia's *terra nullius* policy.

Born in England and a surveyor by profession, at twenty-two Trutch made his way to the California gold fields. He worked in the western USA for about ten years and arrived in BC in 1859. Trutch was hostile to and contemptuous of aboriginal people. In an 1850 letter to his wife regarding the Indians of Oregon,¶ Trutch wrote, "I think they are the ugliest and laziest creatures I ever saw and we should as soon think of being afraid of our dogs as of them."[11]

Trutch refused to recognize the legitimacy of reserves established by James Douglas and had them re-surveyed in 1867, reducing their size by ninety-one per cent. Trutch's animosity towards Indians didn't abate with continued exposure to other BC aboriginal tribes. In 1870, referring to the Tsimshian at Metlakatla near the mouth of the Skeena, Trutch wrote, "I have not yet met with a single Indian of pure blood whom I consider to have attained even the most glimmering perception of the Christian creed."[12]

Historian Robin Fisher summed up the Trutch legacy:

> In reality Trutch's views and actions left British Columbia not only with growing Indian discontent, but with a legacy of litigation that in the long run was to cost the province more than extinguishing Indian title and laying out reasonable reserves would have done. In most areas of Canada the Indian land question has been tied up in a neat European legal package called a treaty. In British Columbia by 1876, largely thanks to the influence of Trutch, it was still in the category of unfinished business.[13]

The land issue came to a head on the northwest coast at Metlakatla by way of the Duncan – Ridley dispute. As the official Church Missionary Society (CMS) representative, Ridley finally took control of the buildings (church, house and store) in the middle of the village. With Duncan's support, "…the Metlakatlans protested the land was theirs…and had never been given to the Church Missionary Society",[14] although a reserve, as Charles Martin said, had already been established. The bishop, with friends in the provincial government, obtained a deed to two acres of land for the CMS within the village. Duncan and a Metlakatla delegation went to Ottawa to plead their case but got only empty promises. Back home, Duncan's Metlakatlan supporters prevented

---

¶ The HBC had operated throughout Oregon Territory until Britain and the United States signed the Treaty of Washington in 1846, when the 49th parallel became the boundary between the two countries.

a provincial land surveyor from surveying the CMS property for months. When the provincial government arrested and jailed the protestors, Duncan and his followers made plans to move to Alaska.[15]

The McKenna-McBride Royal Commission

To understand the obstacles Abel Oakes and the Gitxsan people faced thirty years later, the transcripts of royal commission hearings in 1915 are revealing. The hearings were held due to aboriginal discontent with Indian reserves and because government and industry wanted clear title to land in BC to advance development. The BC government was concerned that reserves established at the turn of the century were too large, and that those near cities or along railroads were better suited to industrial development and agriculture. At the same time, aboriginal people wanted the federal parliament to deal with the land question and eliminate Indian reserves altogether.

The commission was headed by BC Premier Richard McBride,[†] who was born and raised in BC, and J. A. J. McKenna, a federal Department of Indian Affairs official. They held hearings between 1913 and 1916. Even today it's clear that the "McKenna-McBride Royal Commission had a significant impact on Indian people's reserve land base by adding to, reducing and eliminating reserves throughout the province."[16]

The commission travelled to the upper Skeena and held meetings with Gitxsan and Wet'suwet'en leaders from the Babine Agency. Almost without exception, the leaders asked the commissioners to eliminate Indian reserves and deal instead with the land question. The meeting with Gitanmaax village leaders was typical. The following exchange took place at Hazelton on April 21, 1915. It is quoted below in its entirety.[‡]

> EDWARD SPOUK [Spookxw][§] addresses the Commission as follows:
>
> I am very glad to see you all here today right in our Getanmax Reserve. We were born right here and God gave us this little place and I feel happy because I see you gentlemen here. Seven years ago we sent a petition right down to Ottawa—our petition meant that we were asking for the Government to give us our land back and also all our hunting grounds and all our fishing camps, and we want to hold these for our own use—we want to hold it just the same as a white man holds his land and we want to hold our land in the same way, and we have been asking the Government to get rid of the Indian Act for us—this is what we have been asking the Government for the last seven years.
>
> COMMISSIONER CARMICHAEL:

[†] McBride (1870-1917) held office as premier from 1903 to 1915. He resigned on December 15, 1915 due to illness.

[‡] With Moore (probably George Moore, House of Miluulak) interpreting.

[§] Edward Clark (1860-1925), House of Spookxw, Gitanmaax Wolf Clan.

> Thee committee of Skeena River
>
> We the committee here assembled, at Andimaul Skeena River on the 9th, day of March 1910.
>
> 1.st. We decided that we do not want our land reserved, we want the reserves to be taken away.
>
> 2.nd That our land to be given us back again, as it belonged to our forefathers.
>
> 3rd Also we are pleased to know that King George's act. which ordained on October 7th. 1763, has not been changed.
>
> 4th Also that each family or tribe should still held possesion of the land which is theirs by inheritance.
>
> Do hereby undersigned, under the hand of the chiefs committee and people of nine villages of Skeena River.
>
> Chiefs of Kispiox B.C.   Stephen Morgan President
> on Skeena
> (Sign) chief   Walter Kaal x   Robim Kaldo
> "   Charles Smith   x
> "   Paul Clarkahak   x
> "   Alexander Dairy   x
>
> Chiefs of Glen vowell on Skeena B.C.
> sig Paul Dalagymoak
> " Sam Barlow +
> Paul Green x
> Mark Green x
> Peter Brown x

The petition Edward Spouk told the Royal Commission about in 1915 may have read much like the 1910 petition Gitxsan chiefs wrote—calling themselves the Committee of the Skeena River—when they met at Andimaul to express their concerns about the loss of traditional lands. Signatures are on the next page. (Image courtesy of SFU's Native Land Claims Letters: Nass and Skeena Rivers coll.)

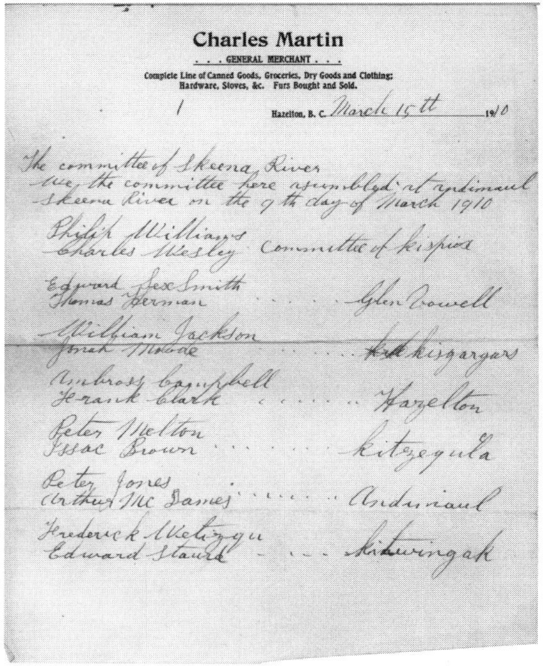

Charles Martin
GENERAL MERCHANT
Complete Line of Canned Goods, Groceries, Dry Goods and Clothing; Hardware, Stoves, &c. Furs Bought and Sold.

Hazelton, B.C. March 15tt 19/0

1

The committee of Skeena River
say the committee have assembled at Gitxsimdeax
Skeena River on the 9 th day of March 1910

Ralph Williams — Committee of Kispiox
Charles Nesley — Committee of Kispiox
Edgrard Jos Smith
James Forman .... John Crwell
William Jackson .... Kithigayor
Fred Moore
Anthony Campbell .... Hazelton
Frank Clark
Peter Milton .... Kitzeguela
Isaac Brown
Peter Jones .... Andimaul
Anthony McJames
Frederick Westry .... Kitwangah
Edward Sewill

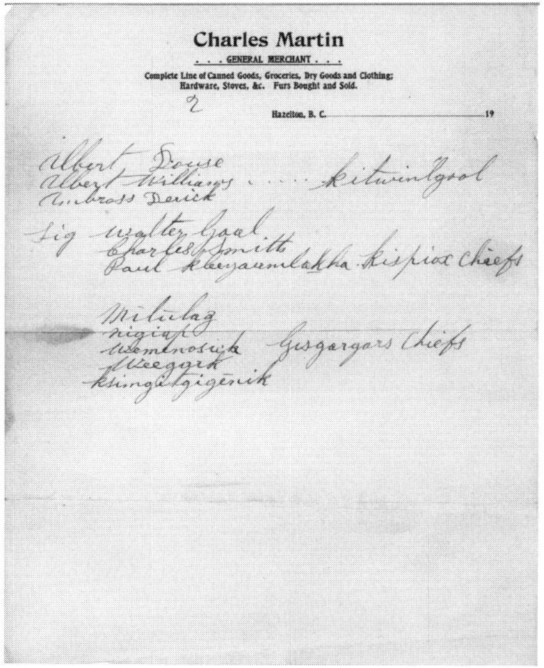

Charles Martin
GENERAL MERCHANT
Complete Line of Canned Goods, Groceries, Dry Goods and Clothing; Hardware, Stoves, &c. Furs Bought and Sold.

Hazelton, B.C. _____ 19___

2

Albert Doggie
Albert Williams .... Kitwangal
Andrew David

Sig Walter Eggel
Charles Forrest
Paul Haryamledha Kispiox Chiefs

Mitalay
Niget
Wamnock Gyagars Chiefs
Liwegett
Kningelgegenck

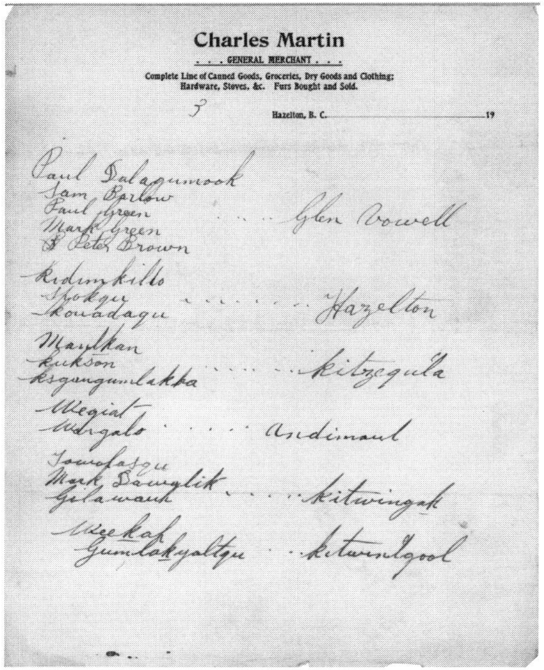

Charles Martin
GENERAL MERCHANT
Complete Line of Canned Goods, Groceries, Dry Goods and Clothing; Hardware, Stoves, &c. Furs Bought and Sold.

Hazelton, B.C. _____ 19___

3

Paul Delaguinock
Sam Barbue
Mark Logan .... John Crwell
& Chris Brown

Kedurykillo
Spotzin .... Hazelton
Nowadayu
Mayathen
Judom
Logungamketha .... Kitzeguela
Wegiat
Natzyale .... Andimaul
Jamdaizu
Week Daryleh .... Kitwangah
Litamand
Nigelockayatzu .... Kitwangah
Gwudebzyalzu

Q. You are the Chief of the Hazelton No. 1 Reserve?

A. Yes.

Q. Have you a map, like this one which I hold here in my hand and which belongs to your Indian Agent?

A. No.

Q. Well, there are 2704 acres in that reserve—do you know that?

A. Yes.

Q. Do you know how many people live on that reserve?

A. What is the reason you are asking me all these questions—what I want to get is my own land back again.

Q. We are asking you these questions in order to help you—In addition both Mr. McKenna and myself, who represent the Dominion Government, want to find out the condition of your reserve and also what additional land you want.

THE CHIEF: We want to get our own land back; that is all.

COMMISSIONER CARMICHAEL: There is no use in this Commission, which is a very important Commission and travelling all over British Columbia, wasting its time here if you don't want to talk to us and won't answer the questions that are being put to you. This Commission has been through hundreds of Reserves in British Columbia, and the only way we have been able to help the Indians on those Reserves is where they have given us the information we want to get and in many cases reserves will be added to, but it is quite impossible for us, outside the help of the Indian Agent, to get information unless the Indians want to give it to us. As we have a great deal of British Columbia yet to cover it is your chance to talk to us. It is no use for you to say that you want all the land back because we have nothing to do with that matter at all. As far as we are concerned, we are here to listen to you and if you don't want to speak to us, well, we have done our duty in coming to see you. If you have made up your mind that you are not going to answer any of our questions, then we have nothing more to do but say good-bye and go away, and we won't come back. This morning we spent with the Rocher de Boule [Hagwilget], and they gave us information of a very valuable nature which may enable us to help them; but if you have made up your mind not to answer the question, that is your funeral and not ours.

THE CHIEF: My representative will answer your questions—his name is Mr. Holland (an Indian).

HOLLAND IS CALLED AND SWORN.

MR. HOLLAND: The Indians say they would like to put it to a vote as to whether or not they will answer your questions.

MR. COMMISSIONER CARMICHAEL: (To the Commission)

I think we should adjourn for ten minutes in order to give an opportunity to the Indians present to take a vote as to whether they are willing to answer the questions put by the Commission, so that the responsibility for refusing to answer would remain entirely with the members of Reserve No. 1 of the Hazelton Band. [adjourns and resumes after ten minutes].

MR COMMISSIONER CARMICHAEL addresses the Chief and Indians as follows:

We left you so that you could talk among yourselves and decide if you wish to give us the information we desire or not. We have returned and we ask you what decision the members of this Reserve have come to?

MR. HOLLAND: You heard what the Chief said a while ago—We don't want no reserve at all, we want to get our own land back. You want to ask us questions, which are not in our petition† at all. We did not give our petition for a reserve at all—we signed it for our own land. The reservation is not so good for us at all—it is of no use to us. They are all fenced all around so we can't do any business outside the reserves. We are just tied up in the Reservation, and that is the reason we signed our petition that we don't want any more reserves for the whole of the Skeena Nation. We sent a couple of gentlemen down to Ottawa and we sent the petition with those gentlemen. Our petition is right in Ottawa and the other one has gone to the King. We want to get our own land back and we want to hold it for our own use. We would like to [live] just the same as a free man so that no one is going to watch us all the time just like we are watched when we are in a reserve—we cannot be helped in our reserves at all. It is the wish here that we get the petition settled. I guess all you gentlemen misunderstand the petition—you think we sent our petition in for a reserve, but that is not right, we did not send in our petition for a reserve, larger or smaller—we did not sign our petition for that at all. Where we are now is just the same as if we were being tightened all the time with the fences all around us; that is the reason we sent the petition.

MR. COMMISSIONER CARMICHAEL: We have heard your explanation regarding the petition—we have told all the Indians who have sent in [a] petition of that kind that this Commission has no power to deal with that petition, and we would be deceiving the Indians if we let them think that we had that power; but I understand that the Indians, after consultation, refuse to answer the questions which we require in order that we may carry out the powers which we have—they don't wish to answer the questions, is that correct?

---

† This may refer to the document Charles Martin drew up for the Committee of the Skeena—see Chapter Fifteen.

Mr. Holland: We could give you all kinds of answers if we made our petition that way, but we did not make our petition for reservations at all. The reservation is no good for us—it is no good for white men, it is no good for anyone. We cannot sell it or do anything and that is the reason we won't give you an answer.

Mr. Commissioner Carmichael: We are sorry that the Indians have refused to give answers to the questions we have asked them; but it is done on their own responsibility.

The Chairman addresses the Assembled Indians as follows:

We quite understand the view that you take—We think, though, that you have made a great mistake, because if we were in a position to give the Indians here more reserves that would not hurt them in the claim that the Indians are making— If we gave them an additional 1,000 acres for their reserve it would not hurt them in still holding to the claim that they have. We also notice that the Chief said "That he wanted the Indian Act to be done away with"—This statement surprises us, because the Indian Act protects the Indians in all their rights and privileges, and the Dominion Government, who are the trustees for the Indians, passed that Act for the very purpose of protecting them and benefitting them; however we are glad to have met you here today, and while you have refused to give us the information for which we came here to get, we may not be able to benefit you as much as we would have liked, yet we wish you well and wish you all prosperity in the future.

Mr. Holland: We are not mistaken when we ask for our own—we are born citizens in this country—we were born in this place—we were born here and we own this land and we want to get it back.

The Chairman:

We are not discussing the fact that you own this land; only they are two different matters altogether. If we were to give you an additional 1,000 acres of land, your right to this question is still open and you could still go ahead and make your claim without fear of hindrance.

This concluded the meeting.[17]

Aboriginal leaders like Edward Spookxw and William Holland faithfully carried the land question torch throughout their lives. They, as did each of their fellow chiefs in other Gitxsan villages, addressed McBride and McKenna with dignity and confidence about their rights as citizens of the Gitxsan nation and of their title to Gitxsan land.

The challenge was that aboriginal people throughout BC lacked a provincial organization capable of sustaining a united, informed front against the federal and provincial governments, even though some tribal groups had presented petitions to the government beginning in the 1880s.

For example, in 1887 the Nisga'a and the Port Simpson Tsimshian presented a petition "for the return of their lands…and a treaty guaranteeing their rights to those lands forever."[18] During the 1890s Arthur Calder was instrumental in creating the Nishga Land Committee and in 1912, in the same year that the federal and provincial governments initiated the McKenna-McBride Royal Commission, the Nisga'a retained a lawyer—Arthur O'Meara—to draft the 'Nishga Petition'. Before then other tribal groups throughout BC had been organizing and in 1915 Interior Salish groups met at Spences Bridge to form an organization—the Allied Tribes of British Columbia—in support of the Nishga Petition.[19]

A year later, two young men, Andrew Paull from Squamish and Peter R. Kelly from Skidegate, came into prominence. Well-educated and highly respected, they took up the cause of the Allied Tribes. They travelled throughout BC visiting nearly every village, including Kispiox. On behalf of the Allied Tribes, they made valiant efforts to be heard by drafting petitions to BC, Canada and London. Finally, in 1926 the Canadian parliament established a "Joint Committee, consisting of a committee from the Senate and one from the House of Commons, authorized to hold hearings and to make recommendations to Parliament which would bring the problem to an end."[20]

The Joint Committee held hearings in March and April 1927. Kelly and Paull understood the issues and made important contributions during the hearings. Unfortunately, some Interior groups with their own lawyers arrived uninvited and contradicted Kelly and Paull. This combined with the fact that the Allied Tribes' lawyer "…unfortunately antagonized the committee…[made it difficult for the Committee] to arrive at a just decision."[21]

The Joint Committee reported:

> …there was no real basis in fact to the claims of aboriginal right in British Columbia; and that, while no compensation was required to extinguish title, it was true that they received no annuities as other Canadian Indians did. Hence, it was recommended that $100,000.00 per annum, over and above normal appropriations for education, medical care, etc. in British Columbia be provided the Indian Department…in lieu of 'treaty monies.'[22]

The $100,000 annuity came to be known as the 'BC Special' and the federal government continued paying it until the mid-1980s.

Native Brotherhood of British Columbia

After the Joint Committee report, the Allied Tribes organization fell apart but the need for a provincial aboriginal body still existed. A Haida leader, Alfred Adams of Massett, had relatives in Alaska, often visited them, and sat in on at least two Alaska Native Brotherhood (ANB) meetings. Adams saw the ANB as a model for BC. Others from the northwest coast, especially fishermen with whom Adams discussed the idea—Ambrose Reid, Rufus Dudoward and William Beynon—were favourably disposed to pursuing the idea further. A meeting was held in Port Simpson in December 1931 with delegations from Massett, Hartley Bay, Kitkatla, Port Essington and Metlakatla, BC.[23]

During this meeting, the participants agreed "that they would organize permanently as the Native Brotherhood of British Columbia [NBBC]."[24]

Between 1931 and 1936 other prominent leaders joined the NBBC and took up the cause: Chief Heber L. Clifton of Hartley Bay and Chief Edward Gamble of Kitkatla, with other members from Klemtu, Bella Bella, Bella Coola, Kitimaat, Kispiox, Skeena Crossing, and Gitanmaax, for a total of fourteen active branches and 474 members. In 1942, Andrew Paull became the business agent of the Brotherhood and organized throughout BC.

Several Gitxsan men were active members of the Brotherhood during the 1950s. In the fall of 1956, Geel/Walter Harris, and Dee/Howard Wale (Abel Oakes's great nephew) attended meetings in Vancouver. Walter invited me to join him in his room at the Niagara Hotel. When I arrived, Walter and Howard were with seven others, all of whom had been pursuing the land question for years: Johnny Clifton†, Robert Clifton, Guy Williams, Andrew Paull, Peter Kelly, Ed Nahanee and Heber Maitland. They understood success would come in part through the courts and encouraged me to take law at university. I never seriously considered going to law school but never forgot the honour they bestowed upon me by suggesting it nor their understanding of and commitment to the land question.

The NBBC leadership believed in the Royal Proclamation of 1763 and trusted that the Queen of England could and would settle the land question. They had no reason to trust Canadian governments to do so. Peter Kelly testified before a joint hearing of a Senate and House of Commons committee on Indian Affairs in 1959: "But, gentlemen," Peter Kelly said, "so long as that title question is not dealt with, every Indian in British Columbia feels that he has been tricked, and he will never be satisfied...Let us say that it [will] be dealt with by the Supreme Court of Canada."[25]

Cowichan chief, Dennis Alphonse,‡ led the creation of another aboriginal political organization, the Union of BC Indian Chiefs (UBCIC), in 1969 when Prime Minister Trudeau and Indian Affairs Minister Jean Chrétien issued a White Paper intended to "...abolish the Indian Act and dismantle the established legal relationship between Aboriginal peoples and the State of Canada in favour of equality. The federal government proposed that, by eliminating 'Indian' as a distinct legal status, equality among all Canadians would result."[26]

Recognizing the need for a united front in order to survive, aboriginal leaders rallied throughout BC. Gitxsan leader Niis Noohl/Ray Jones and others like him who had formed alliances while attending residential schools in Alberta and BC were among those who advanced the cause. Jones and Wet'suwet'en leader, Misilos/Victor Jim, led the Gitksan-Carrier Tribal Council for many years and established a foundation for future political and legal action.

---

† My brother Art married Patricia Clifton (Johnny Clifton's daughter) in 1969. She was working on the *Calder* case with Frank Calder at the time.

‡ Chief Alphonse was joined in this initiative by Rose Charlie of the Indian Homemakers Association, Philip Paul of the Island Tribe Federation and Don Moses of the North American Indian Brotherhood.

Calder v. BC

During the same period, in 1969, the Nisga'a sued BC in *Calder v. British Columbia*, seeking a declaration that they had aboriginal title to their land which had not been extinguished. In 1973 the case went to the Supreme Court of Canada (SCC). The decision, which was divided, determined that aboriginal title does exist in BC but did not clarify the nature and scope of that title. David W. Elliott wrote, "The real significance of *Calder* is in its strong suggestion that Aboriginal title is not necessarily limited to the confines of the Royal Proclamation of 1763, but may be based on the concept of prior occupation of lands."[27]

Frank Calder, who served in the BC provincial legislature for 30 years, launched an aboriginal rights case that went to the Supreme Court of Canada. (Image 01657 courtesy of the RBCM & A)

The decision in *Calder* forced the federal government to abandon its White Paper in 1975 and implement a land claims policy to resolve outstanding land claims in non-treaty areas of Canada.[†] While any number of aboriginal groups could get funding to conduct research in preparation for negotiations, Canada would actively negotiate with just six groups at a time, only one of which would be in BC—the Nisga'a.

The Calder decision and regional boundary issues prompted a 1975 meeting of Gitxsan elders that ended with a decision to prepare for a Gitxsan land claim. Provincial government attitudes also played a role. In that same year I had a meeting with then BC Minister of Aboriginal Affairs, Alan Williams. Out of the blue Williams said, "Just because a bunch of Indians wandered up and down the Rocky Mountain Trench for a few hundred years, doesn't mean they own it." Obviously he didn't realize I was aboriginal and felt free to express his personal opinion.

The tribal council worked with Gitxsan and Wet'suwet'en elders to prepare for negotiations. By 1981, however, it was obvious that it would take years for the Nisga'a process to reach an

---

† In the Yukon and Northwest Territories, northern Quebec and nearly all of BC.

agreement.‡ Negotiations were painfully slow because, following Joseph Trutch's 110-year-old *terra nullius* policy, BC refused to participate.

In 1981, another process presented itself. Canada had been governed by a constitution that was a British law and could be changed only by an act of the British parliament with the consent of the Canadian government. Prime Minister Trudeau decided to patriate the Canadian constitution.§

The aboriginal peoples of Canada were incensed that the prime minister intended to patriate the constitution without their participation. Thousands of individuals and leaders from local, provincial and national aboriginal organizations descended on Ottawa demanding that aboriginal people be involved in the process. Under tremendous pressure, Trudeau relented and scheduled four first ministers' conferences (FMCs) with Canada's national aboriginal leaders to be held between 1983 and 1987.

The idea of including Canada's aboriginal peoples in the FMCs was unprecedented. However, it was clear by the close of the first conference in 1983 that aboriginal expectations would not be met in the constitutional forum alone. Those of us involved in the process realized that we needed to educate not only the first ministers and their advisors but all Canadians. We felt that another process was needed because the government lawyers and bureaucrats taking our people to the courts on fisheries, forestry and hunting-related issues were the same people who were advising politicians in the FMC process. In 1983, we again crossed paths with Alan Williams just before a national conference called by Prime Minister Trudeau with aboriginal leaders and provincial premiers. The purpose of the conference was to determine how aboriginal rights and title would be incorporated into the constitution. Williams, as attorney general of BC, was there.

Before Trudeau's meeting, another aboriginal leader, Tl'azten Grand Chief Edward John, and I requested time with Williams to discuss aboriginal rights. We felt we had to try to tell him what we thought was at stake in this conference. He gave us fifteen minutes.

We began the meeting thinking we had to talk fast to someone who wasn't really interested in what we had to say. We told him about the nature of aboriginal nations. We talked about our connection to our territories, our histories and our laws. We explained the purpose and role of the feast system. We tried to convey to him who we were as peoples and as nations. To our surprise, he listened. He listened carefully and asked thoughtful questions. The meeting lasted more than an hour.

Later, at the conference, the aboriginal leadership was trying to convey to the prime minister and premiers the meaning of aboriginal title and rights. At one point we saw Williams raise his hand and Trudeau asked him to speak. When he spoke, he relayed what we had said to him privately. He put our views forward with force and conviction, speaking on behalf of the recognition of aboriginal title and rights. His intervention was important. It was one of many things that contributed to the long effort to provide constitutional protection to the aboriginal and

---

‡ Almost two decades later, on May 11, 2000, the Nisga'a Final Agreement came into effect. It was BC's first modern-day land claims agreement under the 1970s comprehensive claims process. The Nisga'a agreement has the status of a treaty under Canada's constitution.

§ Patriation was the process of transferring autonomous authority from Great Britain to Canada.

treaty rights of aboriginal peoples in Canada under Section 35 of the constitution—an historical development in Canada and for our people.

Later on, after Alan Williams retired from politics, he served on the commission that established the treaty process in BC. You never know what people will do when you take the time to talk with them respectfully, intelligently and patiently.

In 1920, Abel Oakes recognized that he and Gidumgaldo might need lawyers to help them deal with white people who were taking over their land and resources. Sixty years later, we were in the same position. On October 23, 1984, elders Delgamuukw/Albert Tait and Gisday Wa/Alfred Joseph, accompanied by a small delegation, filed the writ and statement of claim in the Smithers court registry. A total of forty-eight plaintiffs stood up for the case: thirty-five Gitxsan and thirteen Wet'suwet'en.

It took over fifty years—from 1920 to 1973—before the first aboriginal rights and title challenge in BC by way of *Calder* made its way to the Supreme Court of Canada. It would be another decade before the Gitxsan and Wet'suwet'en became so frustrated with Canada and BC's unwillingness to deal with aboriginal title and rights that our chiefs filed their own case October 23, 1984.

A Smithers court clerk receives the writ and statement of claim from the Gitxsan-Wet'suwet'en Tribal Council in 1984. Filing the writ are (L-R) Misilos/Victor Jim (Moricetown), Delgamuukw/Albert Tait (Kispiox), the author, and Gisday Wa/Alfred Joseph (Hagwilget). (Ian Lindsay, Vancouver Sun)

ENDNOTES

1. "Barbeau and Beynon Fieldnotes", Abel Oakes, 1920, B.F. 94.1.
2. Lamb, 237.
3. Banner, 14.
4. Hough, 134.
5. Banner, 14.
6. Parkin, 441.
7. Banner, 24.
8. Banner, 17.
9. Foster, 51.
10. Lambert (also see J. Lambert in Regina v. Bartleman, BC Court of Appeal 1984).
11. Lambert (also see J. Lambert in Regina v. Bartleman, BC Court of Appeal 1984). 5.
12. Lambert (also see J. Lambert in Regina v. Bartleman, BC Court of Appeal 1984). 7.
13. Lambert (also see J. Lambert in Regina v. Bartleman, BC Court of Appeal 1984). 33.
14. Drucker, 88, fn 38.
15. Drucker, 88, fn 38.
16. Canada: McKenna-McBride, Minutes.
17. Canada: McKenna-McBride Report for the Babine Agency, 1915: 39-53.
18. Drucker, 89.
19. Drucker, 95.
20. Drucker, 100.
21. Drucker, 100-101.
22. Drucker, 101.
23. Drucker, 105.
24. Drucker, 106.
25. Berger, 235.
26. "1969 White Paper".
27. Elliott, 75.

CHAPTER TWENTY-THREE

Delgamuukw v. BC

Our people did not understand that our hunting territories were going to be taken away. In the first place, we did not refer to the territories as "a trapline". This is the way government referred to it. I do not know why some people call it a trapline. It is our hunting territory.

My uncle George Williams registered our territory. He always understood that he was registering his territory. He never considered that he was only registering a trapline. George formerly held the name Antgulilbixs and then he took the name Ts'iibaasaa. My uncle George was told that if he did not register the territory then the white people would take it away from him. The Indian Agent used to come out and they would meet about the land and the hunting ground. The Indian Agent came out and told my uncle George that it would protect his territory if he registered it.[†]

—Antgulilbixs/Mary Johnson

Frank Calder and his Nisga'a colleagues made history by taking their title case against BC to the Supreme Court of Canada. When the federal comprehensive claims process began in 1975, the Nisga'a were the only BC tribal group allowed at the negotiation table, but the government did agree to provide resources to other BC aboriginal groups to research

---

[†] Antgulilbixs/Mary Johnson, 1986 Preparation of Evidence,

and prepare for future comprehensive claims negotiations. To qualify for research funds, tribal groups had to provide a map showing the external boundary of their territory and a statement as to who sought to participate in the negotiations. In other words, we had to explain who we, the Gitxsan, were and what lands belonged to us.

Antgulilbixs/Mary Johnson sang at Jack Wright's funeral feast in Kispiox in 1982 when Neil B. Sterritt accepted the name Wiik̲aax. Mary Johnson was a plaintiff in the Delgamuukw v. BC case, as was Neil B. (Steven Bosch photo)

Gitxsan elders, wary that the Nisga'a might encroach on Gitxsan territory when settling their title with Canada, recognized how important it was to define the external boundary of Gitxsan territory and present it to our neighbours and the federal and provincial governments on a comprehensive map. To this end nearly 100 Gitxsan elders and chiefs held a series of feasts in 1975 and instructed the Gitksan-Carrier Tribal Council, as it was known then, to file a map and to engage Canada in the comprehensive claims process. Delgamuukw/Albert Tait from Kispiox was one of those chiefs. Three of us—Gary Patsey, Alan Mason and I—volunteered to develop a draft external boundary map of Gitxsan territory. Gary and Alan were called to other duties but that mapping dominated my life for the next fourteen years.

Documenting Gitxsan place names was critical to our mapping as those names reflect and embody the rich oral histories, laws, and traditions of the Gitxsan. The place names are the geographic markers of spiritual and historic events showing the breadth and depth of our Gitxsan ancestors' long-standing presence on, and occupation of, the land. The chiefs who provided this information to me were the contemporary voices of our ancestors, the repositories of the knowledge of their own House territories. Their knowledge had to be carefully documented and recorded.

At the outset of my initial mapping research in 1975, I interviewed Luus/Chris Harris, a leading chief from Kispiox. He had been gathering place names, hunting and fishing sites and House boundaries from other chiefs since the late 1960s and showing them on a map of Gitxsan territory. He had the assistance of anthropologist Wilson Duff, linguist Bruce Rigsby, the National Museum's anthropologist, Marie Françoise Guedon, and my brother Art Sterritt. He showed me his map and, assuming I spoke Gitxsan, liberally sprinkled his part of our conversation with Gitxsan words. I told Chris that speaking Gitxsan was a challenge for me, and he optimistically said, "You can learn to speak our language by mapping Gitxsan territory." Chris was right. By the time the *Delgamuukw* case got to court in 1987, I could, after working with fluent speakers for years, name hundreds of geographic features in Gitxsan, although I remained far from fluent in conversation.

I was still a student in the carving course at 'Ksan and two years into mapping in my spare time when in June of 1977, Bill Blackwater Sr., then chief councillor of Kispiox and a member of the tribal council, came to me and said, "There is an office for you in Kispiox, and a salary. We want you to work as the Tribal Council Land Claims Director."

I accepted the offer and went to work immediately, continuing to gather place names and territorial ownership information from both Gitxsan and Wet'suwet'en[†] sources to be included in the map. I also began preparing the background documents needed to meet the federal comprehensive claims policy requirements.

It was important to record the chiefs' knowledge and to write down the oral histories as they pertained to our land and our laws. We began hiring a research team that would work with the elders and other knowledgeable people over the coming years. We held meetings in different Gitxsan communities where the elders identified and named Gitxsan mountains, rivers, villages, camps, trails and land features, and described the external boundaries of their House territories. Twelve advisors,[‡] all chiefs, met with us bi-weekly to review our progress and verify our work as we delineated external and internal boundaries. I recorded what I was told in field books, diaries, and on hand-sketched maps.

On November 7, 1977 the chiefs presented a map delineating those external Gitxsan (and Wet'suwet'en) boundaries along with an accompanying declaration to then Minister of Indian Affairs, Hugh Faulkner. This was the first such map by our chiefs, and it laid the groundwork for the more detailed territorial maps we later presented in *Delgamuukw* in 1987-90.

In early 1978 the Office of Native Claims in Ottawa approved our research budget setting off eight years of preparation for our land negotiations. About this time some members of the initial planning team met to lay out a longer term strategy for recognition of Gitxsan and Wet'suwet'en

---

[†] The Wet'suwet'en (known as 'Carrier' at that time) were part of our initiative. Administratively, the Wet'suwet'en and Gitxsan were part of the Department of Indian Affairs' Babine Agency, and the Wet'suwet'en have been closely allied with the Gitxsan since Hagwilget was established in the mid-1820s.

[‡] Charles Austen, Richard Benson, Andrew George Sr., Alfred Joseph, Dan Michell, David Milton, Roy Morris, Steve Robinson, Alvin Weget, Peter Williams, Stanley Williams, Walter Wilson Sr.

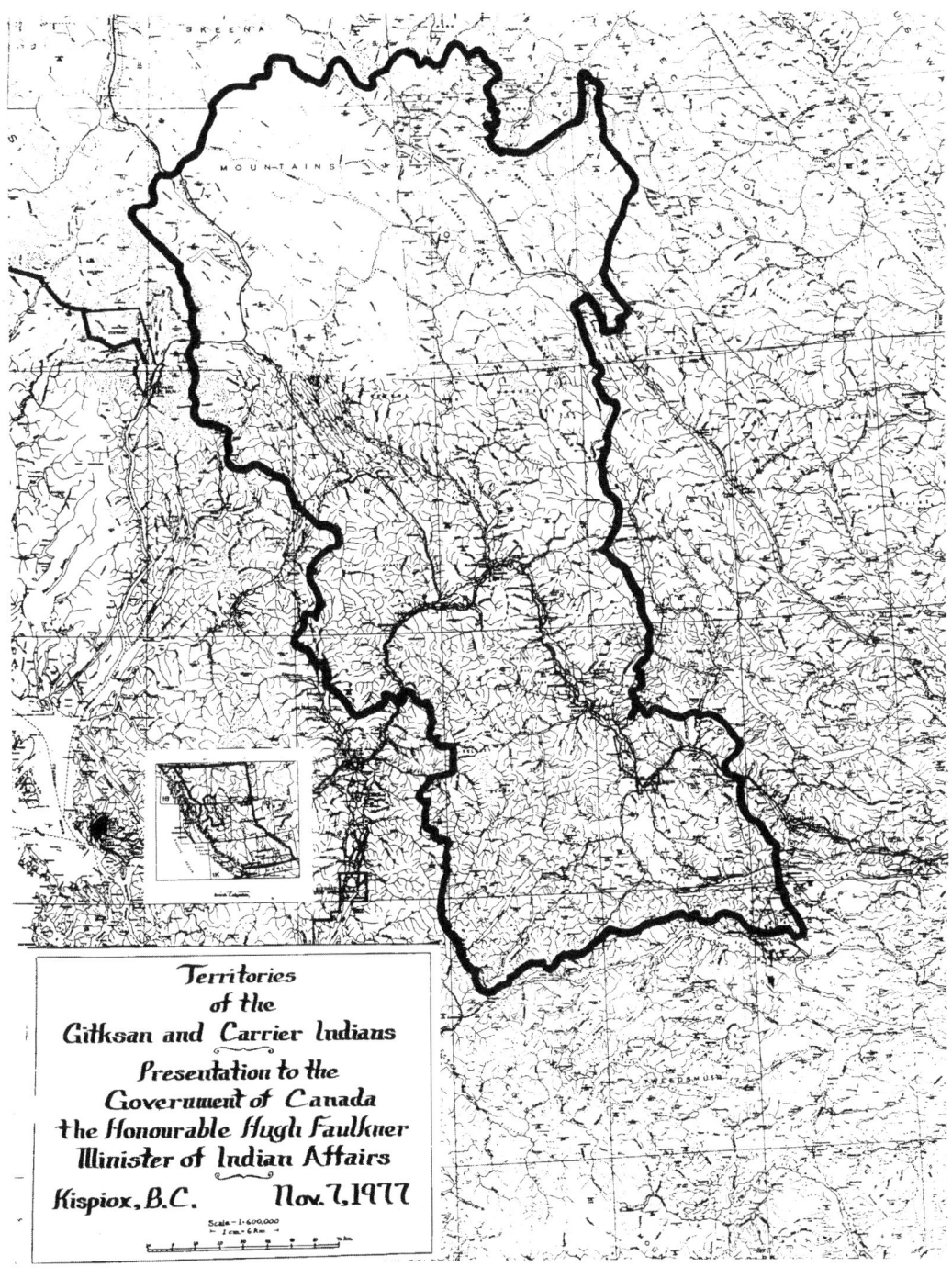

The 1977 Gitxsan and Wet'suwet'en external territorial boundary map.

lands. The team consisted of Gary Patsey, Ardythe Wilson, Don Ryan, Herb George and myself. One of the first things we did was to create a research-training program in association with Carleton University in Ottawa. If we were going to negotiate, we needed more specific information, so we sent eight Gitxsan and Wet'suwet'en students east to verse themselves in the academically acceptable methodology necessary to research all aspects of our culture—history, language, laws, economy, demographics, governance, fisheries and territories.

Our research also involved interviewing elders about Gitxsan and Wet'suwet'en history and culture, their lives on the land—hunting, trapping, berry picking, fishing, selective logging—and the House territories. We continued to document Gitxsan and Wet'suwet'en place names and boundaries with those elders and chiefs who were most knowledgeable about their territories.

One of those chiefs was my grandfather's third wife, Wiigoobil/Jessie (Lumm) Sterritt, who rolled out name after name in 1985 when describing the route to her uncle's House territory at Xsuwii Aks:

> NEIL: Jessie, your aunt was married to Daniel Wiik'aax. Did you ever go to Xsuwii Aks, near Bear Lake, with them?
>
> JESSIE: Yes.
>
> NEIL: Do you remember the trail you took, and can you describe it to me?
>
> JESSIE: Yes. We walked from Hazelton to Kisgegas. From there we went up over a pass beside Ts'im an Makhl (Kisgegas Peak), and then down the mountain. We came to Angil Galaanas, one of the Wright family's berry patches, and then to Tam Xsigintaayin (Sicintine Lake). There was a cabin there, and lots of whitefish in the lake. I don't know who owned the cabin. After that, we climbed Ts'im Maltwit (Motase Peak), a steep mountain. We crossed a glacier, and had to cut steps down the other side. That is when we came to Gwiis Xsigwingyilaa. This creek flows into Xsigwingyilaa (Squingula River). Wiik'aax had a cabin there, and he got coho there in the fall. Thomas Lumm, my brother, drowned near there, where Xsuwii Aks (Sustut River) and the Skeena join.[†] He was young and the river was deep. He slipped in. I was fourteen years old then.

While our objective was to use this mapping work in negotiations, we knew there was a possibility it would end up in court because the Nisga'a negotiations were moving so slowly.

Initially Prime Minister Pierre Trudeau's plan to repatriate the constitution seemed to present a better opportunity to entrench our rights within the Canadian legal system. I also thought it could bring about something the chiefs have always said they wanted—a meeting with the Queen. However by the close of the initial First Ministers' Conference on Aboriginal Rights in 1983, we realized that the legal and political advisors to the prime minister and the premiers were the same

---

† The distance from Kisgegas to the Skeena/Sustut confluence is eighty kilometres as the crow flies. Given the terrain, it would have taken the family about a week to make the journey.

DANIEL WECAHK OF HAZELTON WITH 162 BEAVER, 309 ERMINE, 72 MARTEN, 55 MINK, 14 FISHER, 3 WOLVERINE, 4 OTTER

Daniel Wiik̲'aax, an uncle to Jessie (Lumm) Sterritt, was chief of the House of Wiik̲'aax from Kisgegas. (Image A-06042 courtesy of the RBCM & A)

people who were responsible for bringing fisheries and wildlife prosecutions against aboriginal peoples across Canada, including our own people. We understood we would never achieve recognition of our title and rights in the constitutional forum alone. This was a bitter realization, as we had placed a lot of hope in the federal constitutional process. After many weeks and months of deliberations at feasts and in meetings, the chiefs decided to go to court, a decision that was the culmination of many factors:

- The option of treaty negotiations did not, in fact, exist because it was federal policy to negotiate with only one First Nation at a time and the Nisga'a were first up. Although we had spent six years preparing, we were not going to get to the negotiation table in the foreseeable future and certainly not while many of our elders were still alive.

- There was no political will on the part of the provincial government to negotiate land issues. BC refused to participate in treaty negotiations with the Nisga'a and, during the 1983 First Ministers Constitutional Conference, took a narrow approach claiming that aboriginal title in BC had been extinguished; in short, a denial of our aboriginal title.

- We needed to educate Canadians about Gitxsan and Wet'suwet'en issues. People born and raised on the land testifying in court would be speaking openly and directly to the 'Queen' and to Canadians. There was urgency to this as some potential witnesses were in their eighties and frail. Thirty-four of the plaintiffs were born between 1890 and 1920. They had grown up on the land and knew their histories, territories and laws. Their memories reached back to and beyond the time the first Europeans started to settle on our lands. We recognized that within a few short years the legacy of those witnesses could be lost.†

Today, more than thirty years later, of those plaintiffs who started the case only a handful are still living.

Between 1981 and 1984, there had been lively debates about going to court during a series of meetings among the elders, with the Gitxsan and Wet'suwet'en sometimes meeting separately due to language differences. Finally, at the end of a lengthy Gitxsan meeting, Albert Tait summarized what he had heard and what he believed, and said he approved going to court. The Gitxsan elders decided then that Albert would be the lead plaintiff for the Gitxsan. The Wet'suwet'en chose Gisday Wa/Alfred Joseph as their lead plaintiff.

When we filed the writ and statement of claim with the BC Supreme Court registry on October 23, 1984, a key part of our strategy was to build on the mapping work already underway, transferring the chiefs' extensive knowledge of the land onto maps that would form a permanent Gitxsan aboriginal title record. Introducing the territorial maps and their underlying data in court would be a forceful means of showing House ownership. We also knew that the province's lawyers, in upholding the position that all aboriginal title had been extinguished, would go to great lengths to undermine the validity of all that evidence and would try to attack the credibility of the chiefs.

Our research during the comprehensive claims process took us part way there. But we were now face-to-face with the challenge of seeking a court remedy so we needed to prove our ownership House territory by House territory in a formal court process. That was a formidable job given our limited resources and the pressure that would come with a trial under strict time lines.

We worked intensively with the chiefs and elders to set forth the territories and boundaries of each House confirming specific names and descriptions of landmarks and places and we showed the full extent of Gitxsan land on a composite map that was exhibited in court.

The decision to go to trial had not been an easy one as much was at stake. The Gitxsan and Wet'suwet'en have always had a clear sense of their territory and their rights. For the chiefs to face cross-examination by government lawyers to prove to the colonial governments that they existed as peoples and held title to territory on which they and their ancestors had lived for millennia was humiliating and exhausting. And the chiefs knew from experience that not only was the court environment unfriendly and foreign to them, but their resources were far outmatched by the governments' resources.

By 1984 we had amassed an extensive body of historical and scientific information which would later form the evidentiary base for our case at trial. Unlike all earlier aboriginal title cases, our case would be built on the direct testimony of Gitxsan and Wet'suwet'en men and women, especially our elders, the real experts of our title. Contrary to the strategy used in the *Calder* case where one expert witness was called to prove title, our strategy was to defeat the extinguishment argument and to prove Gitxsan and Wet'suwet'en title by placing a substantial body of evidence

---

† Gitluudaahlxw/Moses Morrison (1897-1985) died a year after the writ was filed. Maxlaxleek/Johnny David (ca.1890-1994) died before the Supreme Court decision in 1997.

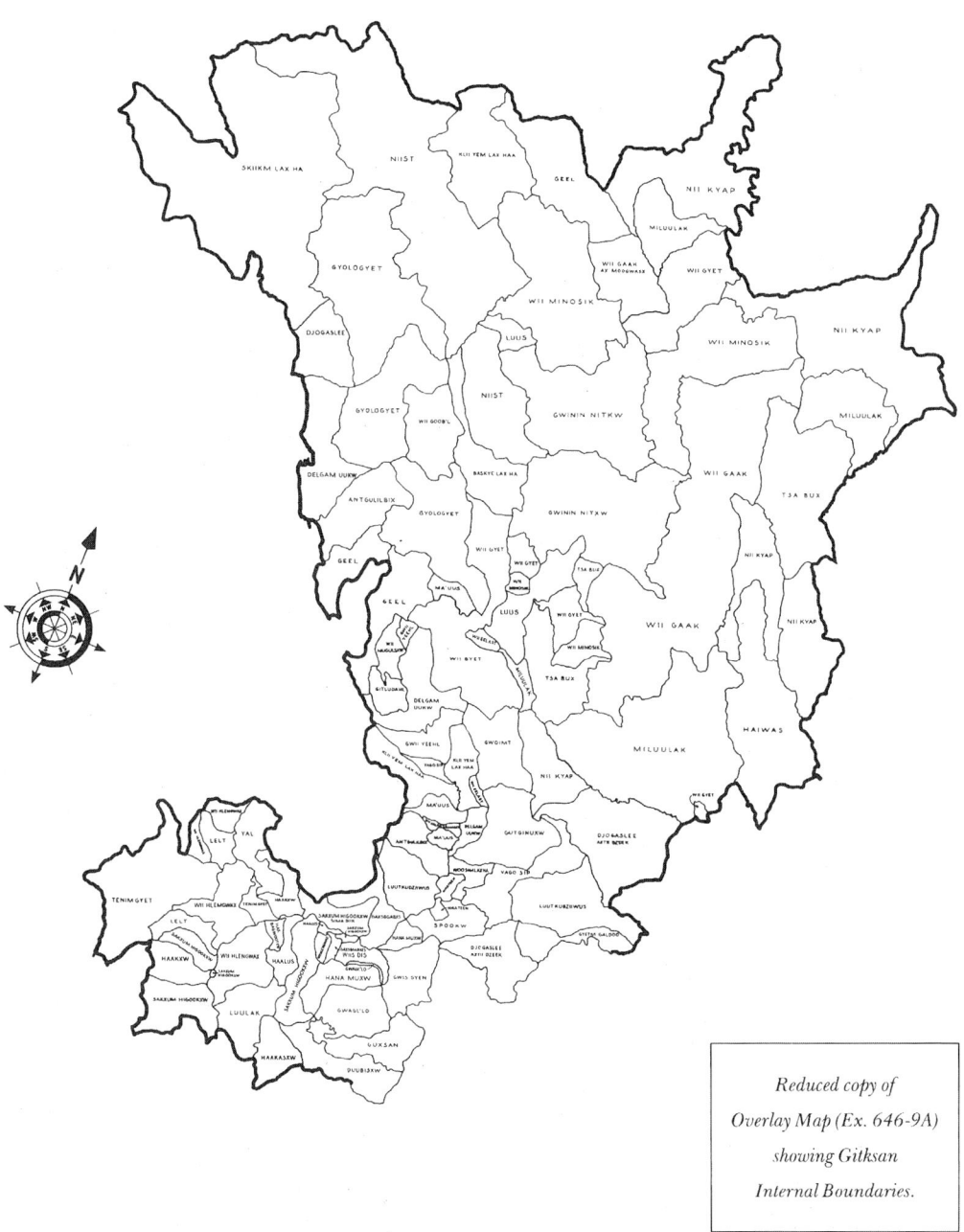

1987 Map of Gitxsan House territories and the external boundary. (Exhibit 646-9A, *Delgamuukw v. BC*)

Reduced copy of Overlay Map (Ex. 646-9A) showing Gitksan Internal Boundaries.

Gisday Wa/Alfred Joseph (1927-2014), the Wet'suwet'en chief who played a major role in the gathering and presentation of evidence for the Delgamuukw v. BC court case. (Steve Bosch photo)

from the elders about our land, laws and oral histories against the meagre evidence of the crown and its sovereignty assertions.

One of the precedent-setting elements of *Delgamuukw* was the central importance of showing the crown and the courts the scope and extent of Gitxsan and Wet'suwet'en knowledge and territory.[†] Given the primacy we placed on mapping to demonstrate our title, it was necessary to complete the mapping process. The chiefs decided to show the external boundaries of the Gitxsan and Wet'suwet'en nations by proving the internal boundaries of each House territory. From 1984 to 1987, Alfred Joseph, Marvin George and I spent most of our time gathering the underlying information and developing maps for use in the case. In addition to conducting one-on-one interviews with elders and chiefs, attending House meetings and participating in feasts,[‡] we also traveled to distant parts of the land with elders to name features and confirm boundary locations.

[†] This was in sharp contrast to the Nisga'a case. Professor Wilson Duff, an expert witness in the *Calder* case wrote Frank Calder and said, "As I recall, it was not the intention to settle the question of tribal boundaries for all time, nor to jeopardize any future settlement of that question, but to establish an agreed-upon area for which to establish the unextinguished existence of aboriginal title. . . .The Nishga case was therefore a test of the concept of native title, and not of specific boundaries between tribes" (Duff to Calder, Aug. 8, 1974 in Wilson Duff Files, UBCMAA, 1974).

[‡] I found that elders wanted to share their knowledge of the land with me, and occasionally at a feast an elder would talk to me about his or her land. To be sure of what I was told, I often drew a sketch of the area the elder was talking about and wrote each Gitxsan place name (creek, lake, mountain, etc.) on my sketch. I put together this information with the other information we were told by the elders and it demonstrated the power and depth of our chiefs' and elders' knowledge of our territory and resources.

Sometimes we traveled by vehicle and other times we needed helicopters to get to the more remote parts of Gitxsan territory.

Malii/Glen Williams from Gitanyow often accompanied me to meetings and on field trips, as he is a fluent Gitxsan speaker, having been raised by his grandparents, Nits'iits Hahlma/Maggie and Lalt/Fred Johnson. Though young at the time, Glen was already respected by the elders and could converse freely with them.

Gitxsan elders took an active part in preparing for Delgamuukw. Here Txawok/James Morrison and Niik'yap/David Gunanoot (L-R) in the foreground work with Glen Williams mapping in the Foster Peak area along the upper Skeena River. The pilot, Doug Whelan, is standing by the helicopter. (NJS photo)

A typical day in the field involved flying out with elders to strategic locations, usually on a mountaintop or ridge with a good view of the surrounding terrain. There we asked the elders to describe what they knew about the vista before us—the geography, the names of landmarks, resources, the stories. I wrote down what I was told in my field books, took photographs of the landscape and often sketched specific mountains and creeks. We also traveled to the territories by horseback, snowmobile and fixed wing aircraft. Being out on the land was the only way to know the land. Alfred Joseph and his team followed much the same process in Wet'suwet'en territory. After these trips I met with our advisors, clarified issues, and provided my information to cartographer Marvin George who transferred the information on to his maps.

During the 1960s, while working north of Hazelton with Amax, a minerals exploration company, I was curious about the origin of some place names that appeared on government maps.

Who, for example, was 'Slowmaldo', and where did the name 'Sally's out' come from? How did Motase Lake and Shegunia River get their names? Where did the name 'Damsumlo' come from? In my map fact-finding, I learned from Gitxsan elders the answers to such questions:

- Xsiluu'am'maldit (creek cottonwood trees): Slowmaldo Creek and Mountain;
- Xsitk'aliix'awit (creek that flows opposite the Nass R): Sallysout Creek;
- Dam Mootixswit (lake milky): Motase Lake (and therefore, nearby 'Motase' Mountain);
- Xsigwinya'a (river of spring salmon): Shegunia River;
- Dam Similoo'o (lake bad spirit): Damsumlo Lake.

Mapping at Kisgegas are (L-R) James Morrison, David Green, the author, Henry Wright, unknown child, and Joshua McLean. (NJS coll.)

As we prepared our evidence for trial, the lawyers explained that the elders and chiefs with first-hand knowledge of their territories and boundaries would be the best witnesses to testify as second-hand evidence would be deemed hearsay.† Traditionally when western courts dealt with aboriginal rights cases, experts, or as Ardythe Wilson called them, the 'ologists', would be considered the primary witnesses. In our case, we decided that the chiefs would take on the primary role of giving evidence in court—a fundamentally different approach in advancing

---

† Generally speaking statements witnesses make based not on their personal knowledge but on something they've been told is hearsay. If this rule applied to oral histories, they could never be used in evidence. The SCC made clear this restriction on evidence could not apply to oral histories.

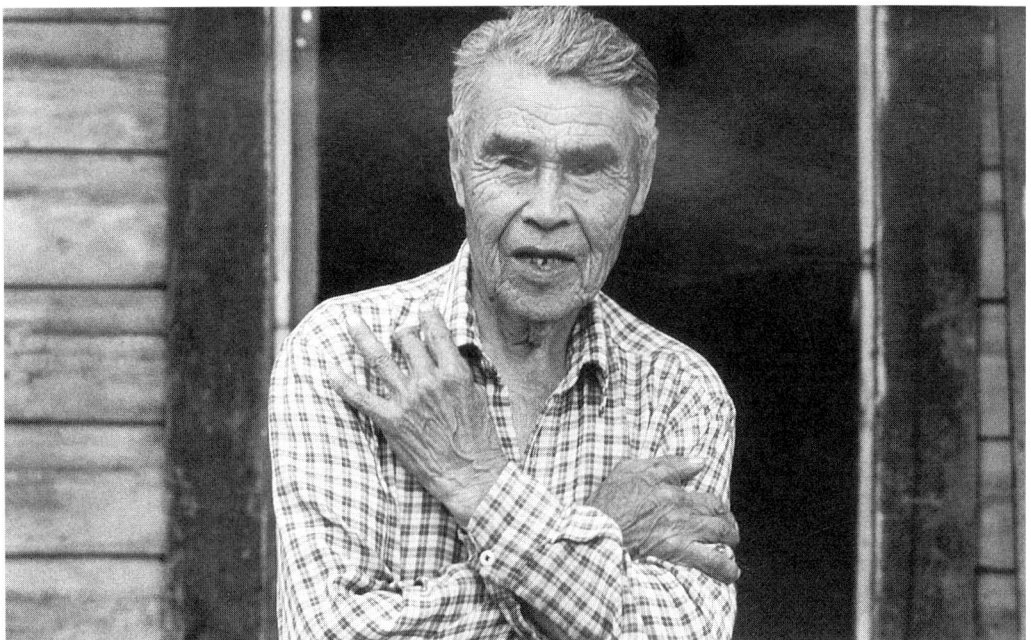

Albert Tait (Steve Bosch photo)

evidence in First Nations litigation, a strategy which was later endorsed by the Supreme Court of Canada. As Ardythe Wilson said, "Oral history based on intimate knowledge and experience, and scientific history based on rational knowledge and accreditation—two solitudes coming together and applying different shades to the same picture."[1]

Because we wanted to both demonstrate and emphasize the elders' intimate and detailed knowledge of the land and our laws, we decided to present all-inclusive evidence about place names and boundaries through written affidavits and individual maps of the chiefs' House territories. In this way every chief gave evidence of their House territory and every House territory was before the court.

The task of preparing territorial affidavits and maps fell largely to Alfred Joseph, Marvin George, research coordinator Richard Overstall and myself. Our role was to record as accurately as possible the chiefs' descriptions of their territories and boundaries as well as principal landmarks.

We took pre-trial deposition evidence, under oath by commission, of elders who were aged and frail and might not make it to trial. We wanted to be sure to preserve their knowledge of their territories and the histories and laws of the Gitxsan and Wet'suwet'en for the record.

Given that Albert Tait was healthy and very active throughout the trial preparation phase, we did not take commission evidence from him. One Sunday evening four months before the trial was to commence, I phoned Albert about some territories and place names. Fifteen minutes after our conversation ended, the phone rang. It was my sister Shirley, who said, "Neil, Albert is dead." I said, "He can't be. I just finished talking to him and he was fine." She said, "Yes. He got up from his chair, went to the refrigerator and fell to the floor." Albert Tait died January 18, 1987. This was a great loss for the Gitxsan and for me personally. I had worked with him for years recording information about our people and our land gathered over many decades.

Within a week the new Delgamuukw, Ken Muldoe,[†] was named and assumed his responsibilities in the court case. Albert Tait's contribution to the case was integral to its success, but Ken Muldoe shouldered his new and unexpected responsibilities well.

The remedy we sought at trial in the Supreme Court of BC was for a declaration of ownership of and jurisdiction over the territory. Gitxsan and Wet'suwet'en ownership includes the right to use, harvest, manage, conserve and transfer the lands and material resources and to make decisions about those rights. Our jurisdiction involves the right to govern the territory and the members of the Houses represented by the plaintiffs in accordance with Gitxsan and Wet'suwet'en laws and administered through Gitxsan and Wet'suwet'en political, legal and social institutions as they were then, and as they would develop. The chiefs also put forward a case of aboriginal title and aboriginal rights.[‡] These rights had not been abandoned or lawfully extinguished.

One of the lawyers for the plaintiffs, Peter Grant, said when the case finally got to the Supreme Court of Canada, the court gave a lot of weight to aboriginal title, treating it much like ownership, except for two points. Aboriginal title (to land) can only be alienated to the crown and cannot be otherwise sold or alienated, and the aboriginal title holders cannot destroy the title lands in a way that future generations will not be able to benefit from aboriginal title.

The *Delgamuukw* trial began on May 11, 1987, in the BC Supreme Court in Smithers. The Gitxsan and Wet'suwet'en chiefs stood before Chief Justice Allan McEachern and started what became the longest aboriginal title trial in history up to that day by explaining in the opening statement:

> For us, the ownership of territory is a marriage of the Chief and the land. Each Chief has an ancestor who encountered and acknowledged the life of the land. From such encounters come power. The land, the plants, the animals and the people all have spirit—they all must be shown respect. That is the basis of our law.
>
> The Chief is responsible for ensuring that all the people in his House respect the spirit in the land and all living things. When a Chief directs his House properly and the laws are followed, then that original power can be recreated. That is the source of the Chief's authority…
>
> My power is carried in my House's histories, songs, dances and crests. It is recreated at the Feast when the histories are told, the songs and dances performed, and the crests displayed. With the wealth that comes from respectful use of the territory, the House feeds the name of the Chief in the Feast Hall. In this way, the law, the Chief, the territory, and the Feast become one. The unity of the Chief's authority

---

[†] Upon Ken's death in 1990, his brother, Earl Muldon, was named to succeed him. Muldoe and Muldon are anglicizations of Gitumgaldo.

[‡] Collective right to the use of and jurisdiction over a group's ancestral territories.

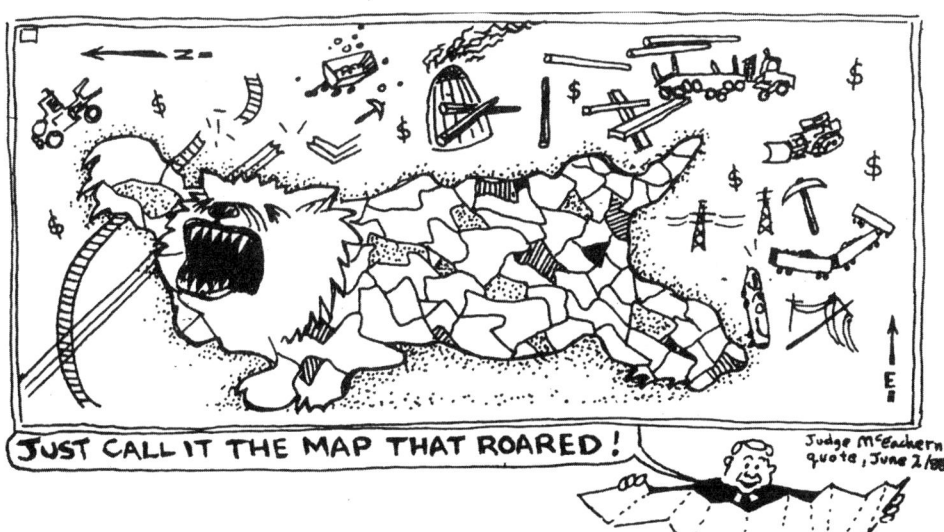

A Don Monet version of the land claims map prepared for the court case. In Colonialism On Trial, Monet produced a visual record of the three and a half year court case, including the portrait of the author on the stand (above).

and his House's ownership of its territory are witnessed and thus affirmed by the other Chiefs at the Feast.[2]

This was the first time in Canadian legal history that aboriginal chiefs directly addressed the court in the opening statement. Thus commenced the celebrated *Delgamuukw*[3] trial, which continued for 387 days in court including over 150 days of cross-examination on territorial affidavits and commission evidence of elders. The trial ended on June 30, 1990.

The chiefs were relying heavily on the 1982 constitutional promise of Canada and the provinces to recognize and affirm the aboriginal rights of indigenous peoples in Canada as stated in Section 35 of the constitution. However BC denied that there was any aboriginal title in BC and therefore interpreted Section 35 as meaningless as it applied to land.

A voluminous body of evidence was given by the chiefs on oral history, laws, ways of life, description of territories, boundaries, genealogies, and use and management of land and riverine resources. We called expert historians, genealogists, archeologists and anthropologists who supported that evidence and told the court about indigenous relations with the crown and first settlers. Pivotal to the chiefs' case were the maps of the territories showing place names, trails, villages, resources and boundaries. As Gisday Wa and Delgamuukw explained in the opening, our Gitxsan and Wet'suwet'en oral histories were rooted on the territories.

It was an exhilarating but trying and frustrating experience for me as a witness. I was on the stand for thirty-four days, the longest of any witness, and I was cross-examined aggressively by provincial lawyers. They pulled out all stops to undermine the territorial maps and the chiefs' evidence that underpinned the maps. Each chief had given evidence of his or her territories supported by a hand-drawn map showing the boundaries.

The focus of the province's attack on me was fundamentally misplaced. Government lawyers did not understand or accept that the location, extent, character and borders of the territories were derived from House histories and the chiefs' knowledge of the land and the resources on it. The province summarily dismissed as 'myth' our laws and oral histories and tried to counter our mapping case with a suite of maps that showed provincial administrative boundaries throughout the territory. This was their demonstration of assumed crown jurisdiction. They also said pre-confederation colonial land laws extinguished the chiefs' title.

Chief Justice McEachern rendered his decision on March 8, 1991, dismissing our case and concluding that aboriginal title of the Gitxsan and Wet'suwet'en had been extinguished by pre-confederation colonial land legislation. He dismissed our laws, including ancient oral histories, as mere beliefs. He said that if any rights existed they were use rights and were present only in a reduced land area.

The chiefs were incredulous. Their ancient laws and oral histories had been completely rejected by the chief justice and he had concluded that our title and rights to the land had been extinguished not only by a process of which we had no knowledge, but which occurred before any white man had any real knowledge of who we were.

At first we mourned McEachern's decision and then we realized that his dismissal of who we are and of our rights to our territory could not be allowed to stand. The Gitxsan and Wet'suwet'en decided to appeal the decision to the BC Court of Appeal.[†]

A five-member bench heard our appeal over thirty-nine court days.[‡] The central issues which we raised in challenging the BC Supreme Court included:

- The finding that Gitxsan and Wet'suwet'en title had been extinguished by colonial laws (a decision that, if upheld, would affect most of BC and those indigenous nations that had never concluded a treaty);
- Whether reliance on the detailed knowledge of oral histories, place names and territorial boundaries was a valid means to prove title; and finally,
- Whether aboriginal title was 'non-exclusive' (meaning governments had equal access to aboriginal title lands and resources).

The June 25, 1993 Court of Appeal judgment unanimously overturned McEachern's finding that our aboriginal *title* had been extinguished. This was a huge victory and engendered a renewed sense of optimism on our part.

While agreeing title had not been extinguished, the court was split on whether or not we had proved title: three judges upheld McEachern's dismissal of our case while two dissenting judges found that the chiefs had indeed proved aboriginal title to our land and they would have granted a remedy.

The Court of Appeal also found that aboriginal *rights* (for example, to hunt and fish) did exist, but only over the reduced part of our territory which McEachern arbitrarily defined as the distance of one day's travel from the present and ancient villages. And the court found that such rights were non-exclusive, which meant governments retained access to our land and its resources.

The chiefs decided to seek leave to appeal to the Supreme Court of Canada, but initially decided to put the appeal in abeyance. Believing our hand would be strengthened in negotiations by the legal process we had pursued, the Gitxsan and Wet'suwet'en decided to see what we could achieve in the newly established BC Treaty Commission process.[§] We entered negotiations in 1994 but talks were suspended two years later over fundamental differences.

In spite of the court's rejection of government demands for extinguishment of title, governments continued to make it a condition of any treaty settlement. In other words, the BC government refused to negotiate unless the aboriginal group agreed in advance that any final agreement or treaty would include the extinguishment of aboriginal rights and title not covered by the treaty. The government negotiation mandate also reflected an impoverished view of aboriginal title and rights maintaining there was no title and rights were restricted to hunting, fishing and trapping.

---

† [1993] 5 W.W.R. 97.

‡ The longest appeal ever heard by the BC Court of Appeal.

§ In 1991, BC reversed its longstanding denial of aboriginal rights and recognized them as official policy.

BC's aboriginal affairs minister recommended clarification by the Supreme Court of Canada. We agreed. By this time the Wet'suwet'en had decided to present their arguments as a separate nation, but we jointly brought our appeal to the SCC on June 16-17, 1997.

On December 11, 1997, the SCC handed down the seminal decision on aboriginal title in Canada. *Delgamuukw* achieved significant legal victories. The court found that it was appropriate for the chiefs to base their case on their traditional knowledge, laws and oral histories and directed lower courts to give equal weight to aboriginal oral histories and perspectives as they gave to western written history.

The mapping work the Gitxsan chiefs undertook twenty years earlier as a method of proving title to their land was endorsed by the court as one of the proper ways to prove title.

The court unanimously ruled that aboriginal title had not been extinguished in BC and that the province had no jurisdiction to do so without the consent of the aboriginal nation.

Neither BC nor Canada—with the help of many corporate and government interveners—could raise a single legal theory to justify the denial of aboriginal title since confederation, nor could they justify the dispossession of the Gitxsan and Wet'suwet'en from our territories. Aboriginal title—our laws—exist, and the court held that title had not been extinguished.

The court rejected the government's claim that aboriginal title was confined to specific practices and limited to small areas, the position embedded in the government negotiation mandates brought to the BC Treaty Commission. The court held that aboriginal title arising from our original occupation of the land is a communal right to land, held by the nation, embracing the exclusive right to use the land, and the right to choose the uses to which the land can be put, including an 'inescapable economic component', meaning that finally the courts have confirmed that aboriginal peoples of Canada have a legal right to share in the economic wealth of their aboriginal territories. Aboriginal title also has an inherent limit in that one generation cannot destroy the land in a manner that prejudices the rights of future generations.

The court concluded with these words:

> As was said in *Sparrow [v. the Queen]*, Section 35(1) 'provides a solid constitutional base upon which negotiations can take place.' Moreover, the Crown is under a moral if not a legal duty to enter into and conduct these negotiations in good faith. Ultimately, it is through negotiated settlements, with good faith and give and take on all sides, reinforced by the judgments of this Court, that we will achieve…a basic purpose of s. 35(1)—'the reconciliation of the pre-existence of Aboriginal societies with the sovereignty of the Crown.' Let us face it, we are all here to stay.[4]

The chiefs sought a declaration of title to specific territories, but we did not achieve that remedy. The SCC stated that the claim should have been based on the Gitxsan Nation as opposed to individual House territories. This was a technicality and allowed the court to avoid finding aboriginal title. Instead the court sent the case back for a new trial based on a technical defence as to the pleadings. However the court urged the parties to negotiate a settlement which implied negotiating a treaty relating to our territories and resources.

We, the Gitxsan, together with the Wet'suwet'en, led the SCC to recognize our laws and their exercise as proof of our aboriginal title, and the court declared that such title existed in Canada.

The Legacy of *Delgamuukw*

The SCC decision was a significant victory not only for the Gitxsan and Wet'suwet'en but for indigenous peoples throughout BC, Canada and the Commonwealth. But the governments continued business as usual—no changes were made to the government negotiation mandate brought to the BC Treaty Commission. For example, the province granted a multi-year, long-term logging tenure to a company on Haida Gwaii without consulting the Haida, who brought a judicial review of that decision. The province argued before the SCC that "until the Haida people formally prove their claim, they have no legal right to be consulted".[5]

The SCC rejected the province's position and relying on the principles set down in *Delgamuukw*, stated:

> In all its dealings with Aboriginal peoples, from the assertion of sovereignty to the resolution of claims and the implementation of treaties, the Crown must act honourably. Nothing less is required if we are to achieve 'the reconciliation of the pre-existence of aboriginal societies with the sovereignty of the Crown'.[6]

The court imposed a duty on the crown to consult and accommodate when the crown contemplates decisions that could impact aboriginal title and rights.

More recently, in *Tsilhqot'in*, the province argued the same impoverished view of aboriginal title that the governments brought to our treaty negotiations prior to our appeal to the SCC.

The SCC rejected this impoverished view and ruled in 2014 that the Tsilhqot'in met the legal test for a declaration of aboriginal title[†] as established in *Delgamuukw*. The court declared the Tsilhqot'in hold aboriginal title to 1900 square kilometres. The court recognized that the Tsilhqot'in had and still have the right to decide how to proactively use and manage their land for enjoyment, occupancy, possession and economic benefits. It was the first time in Canadian history that a court had declared aboriginal title to lands outside of a reserve.

The court also made it clear that governments and individuals proposing to use and exploit land—whether before or after a declaration of title—can avoid infringements by obtaining consent. Here the Supreme Court of Canada has aligned with the United Nations Declaration on the Rights of Indigenous Peoples, which defines indigenous rights as inherent human rights and establishes a human rights framework resting on notions of justice, equality, good faith, and principles of engagement based on free, prior, and informed consent. If consent cannot be achieved, the court created a high standard for the crown to justify infringements.

The courts have been a vehicle for setting things straight. Our case in *Delgamuukw* gave the SCC the opportunity to lay the foundation for a new relationship between the crown and

---

† The legal test for aboriginal title requires an aboriginal nation to demonstrate that it regularly, sufficiently and exclusively used the claimed land at the time the crown asserted sovereignty in 1846.

indigenous peoples. The vision of those chiefs with whom I worked for over thirty years has been brought closer by their clear and powerful voices in and out of the courtroom and the record that they have now passed onto the future generations of Gitxsan and Wet'suwet'en. They educated the courts and governments about the depth of our history on Gitxsan land and were leaders in achieving the now internationally recognized legal rights based on that foundation.

Delgamuukw has paved the way for a treaty relationship based on recognition of aboriginal title, including giving expression to our laws, and prohibiting its denial, diminishment or extinguishment. Both crown and indigenous laws and titles are at play on the same landscape. Although they are not the same, these titles and spheres of jurisdictions can interact in a functional and honourable way, sharing decision making, revenue and benefits.

Because our land embodies who we are, concerned Gitxsan *simgiiget* (chiefs) met together to deal with the land question more than 100 years ago and continued doing so through to the mid-1970s. During the contemporary era[†] there was a resurgence of aboriginal political activity. This led in January 1975 to the Gitxsan holding a series of special feasts with the *simgiiget* that continued throughout the year. These special feasts followed Gitxsan tradition of chiefs coming together during times of war and crisis.

The chiefs decided in January 1975 that the Gitksan-Carrier Tribal Council (GCTC) make the resolution of the land question our priority and that their "hereditary lands" be set out on a map.[‡] Several of us undertook to do that work, but when some of us were needed for other important priorities, I continued on my own, working with chiefs and elders like Chris Harris who had started the work. This work culminated, firstly, in the map and declaration the *simgiiget* presented to the Minister of Indian Affairs at Kispiox on November 7, 1977 and finally with the evidence presented during the *Delgamuukw* trial.

Shortly after Bill Blackwater hired me in June 1977 with the support of Ray Jones, Victor Jim and other tribal council leaders, I realized that we were filling an important contemporary need. We were documenting, in writing, the histories, laws and territorial knowledge from an oral culture and we needed a place to store and protect the information we were gathering. This was the beginning of our Gitxsan library and archives, and its contents grew exponentially over the next decade. In addition to the precedents set out in the Supreme Court decision, the enduring legacy of the *simgiiget* includes our territory maps and genealogies; archival material gathered during the land claims and legal processes;[§] and films and photographs.

This invaluable record is also evidence that can be used should the Gitxsan ever choose to return to court seeking a declaration of title. The evidence of the elders now deceased can continue to speak to the courts, to the governments in negotiations and to our future generations.

[†] Beginning in 1969 with Trudeau's White Paper and the Nisga'a suing BC in the *Calder* case.

[‡] Other feasts were held during the year culminating in a large feast hosted by the GCTC at Gitwangak on Jan. 6, 1976 with a large delegation of *simgiiget* from all Gitxsan villages.

[§] For example, the Barbeau and Beynon files contain what our *simgiiget* said between 1915 and 1955 about their histories, territories and laws.

But we should not have to go back to court—the SCC urged us to negotiate aided by decisions of the court, and in *Delgamuukw* the court established an enduring set of landmark legal principles on aboriginal title, including the recognition and validation of our laws, customs and oral histories, along with the determination that aboriginal title has not been extinguished in BC. This jurisprudence continues to provide the Gitxsan (and other indigenous peoples) with a legal platform to move forward to protect our territories and enhance our rights and economic well-being. And we can't forget that this legacy was achieved by having the *simgiiget* take their rightful place as plaintiffs and the leading witnesses in this case.

Less obvious than the wealth of information gathered through to the end of the *Delgamuukw* trial in 1990 were the equally important processes we followed that created a shared vision, strategic goals, flexibility, transparency and accountability, and the inclusion of the multitude of lawyers, expert witnesses, organizers, volunteers and fundraisers who dedicated themselves to our case professionally and ethically. Without this team of people, and the *simgiiget*'s common purpose, we would not have achieved what we did and to them we will always be indebted.

One of our expert witnesses said, "The full impact of the *Delgamuukw* decision on the Gitxsan is still unknown. You never know who will benefit from your work in the area of aboriginal rights—and how they will benefit—until twenty years later at least."¶ These words proved prophetic.

The vision, unity, solidarity and accountability of the entire Gitxsan nation—with the tribal council and band councils working together leading up to and during the *Delgamuukw* case—was critical to the outcome of *Delgamuukw*. Unfortunately, that unity has not lasted. We have since struggled with internal problems that continue today. The hard reality is that the internal struggles among the Gitxsan have frustrated the advancement of the whole nation toward the goals the case was set out to achieve.

Now, in the aftermath, we need to rekindle a new vision and revive broadly shared values that will allow future generations to achieve the outcomes our elders fought for. Important steps in fulfilling the legacy of *Delgamuukw* are to re-establish our library and archives so that all Gitxsan people—including high school students and young Gitxsan professionals—can learn about their rich and remarkable history and laws; to appoint an apolitical board to oversee the library and archives;** and to welcome the next generation of talented Gitxsan youth and encourage them to stay home or come home and work with the Gitxsan nation.

Gitxsan principles and legal traditions are deeply embedded in our culture. These are the constitutional principles by which the Gitxsan long ago were taught to live. We can rebuild our society from these basic values so that the political and economic institutions we create to address contemporary issues rest on that solid foundation.

Back in 1956, nine Native Brotherhood of BC leaders suggested that I attend law school in order to advance the land question. I chose another path that I feel was equally beneficial. That path allowed me to work directly with the *simgiiget* and identify and map the historical territories of the

---

¶ Hugh Brody to Peter Grant, personal communication.

** UBC now holds the documents we developed during the *Delgamuukw* case. With a library and librarian, our records at UBC could be returned to our territory where they belong.

Gitxsan Houses so they would be preserved for all time. There is still much to be done—socially, economically and politically—and the continuation of this work will fall, as it should, to our children and grandchildren. With our support, they will have the means by which to find their way home.

ENDNOTES

1 Wilson in Monet, 105.
2 Gisday Wa and Delgamuukw, 7-8.
3 *Delgamuukw v. BC* [1991] 3 W.W.R. 97.
4 *Delgamuukw v. BC* 1997 3 S.C.R. 1010 at para 186.
5 *Haida Nation v. BC* (Ministry of Forests) 2004 3 S.C.R. 511 2t para. 8.
6 *Haida Nation v. BC* (Ministry of Forests) 2004 3 S.C.R. 511 2t para. 17.

Gitxsan Spelling and Pronunciation Guide[†]

The writing of the Gitxsan language is based on the alphabetic principle, which requires, as linguist Bruce Rigsby said, "…that each sound of a language must have its own letter (or combination of letters) and each letter (or combination of letters) must have its own sound."[1] Rigsby and his Gitxsan advisors chose to use English letters, commas, the apostrophe ', and the underline, allowing Gitxsan words to be written on a standard keyboard.

Although the Gitxsan language lacks several English letters (c, f, q, v, r and z), its alphabet has forty-six letters: ten "short vowels" and "long vowels", thirty-five "hard consonants" and "soft consonants", and a glottal stop. Therefore, for example, the long aa vowel below is considered a single Gitxsan letter, as is the consonant kw', and so on.[1]

VOWELS

Letter	English equivalent	Gitxsan words & meaning
Short **a**:	at, bat, sat	*aks* – water; *am* – good
Long **aa**:	dad	*aat* – ashes; *daala* – money
Short **e**:	wet, bet	*ye'e* – grandfather; *helt* – many
Long **ee**:	make, bake, lake	*nee* – no; *yeen* – cloud or mist
Short **i**:	hit, orbit, lit	*is* – soapberries; *sip* – bone
Long **ii**:	ease, heat	*iis* – necklace; *wii* – big
Short **o**:	go, goal, home	*lo'op* – rock; *wo'os* – plate
Long **oo**:	low, snow	*moos* – thumb; *daboon* – padlock
Short **u**:	ulcer, up, us	*ubin* – pregnant; *'malu* – crazy
Long **uu**:	food, rude	*uut* – baked; *duus* – cat

CONSONANTS and GLOTTAL STOP

Letter	English equivalent	Gitxsan words & meaning
b:	same	*ban* – belly; *bil'ust* – star
d:	same	*daw* – ice; *daala* – money
Front **g**:	same	*gyat* – man; *guxw* – to shoot
Back **g**:	none	*gaak* – index finger or raven
gw:	Guelph	*gwila* – blanket; *gwalga* – all

---

† This guide is based on the Gigeenix (upriver) dialect as in the Hindle and Rigsby dictionary and the GWES (SD 88) dictionary.

CONSONANTS and GLOTTAL STOP

Letter	English equivalent	Gitxsan words & meaning
h:	same	*hap* – to collapse; *ha* – air
hl:	none	*hlap* – deep; *mihl* – to burn
j:	has a *gz* sound	*jin* – hummingbird; *jak* – to kill
Plain **k:**	similar	*naks* – spouse; *ak* – water
Hard **k':**	none	*k'elt* – summit; *k'ets* – chin
Plain back **k̲:**	cut	*eek̲* – coho salmon; *lok̲* – eel
Hard back **k̲':**	kut	*Tk̲'a* – skin; *bok̲'* – to be lame
Plain **kw:**	queen	*ayukws* – crest; *'nakw*– far
Hard **kw':**	quiet	*kw'ast* – broken; *sankw'ax̲* – hiccup
Soft **l:**	let, look, lake	*laaxw* – trout; *lalt* – snake
Hard **'l:**	none	*a'lax* – angry; *'lax* – needle
Soft **m:**	same	*meek* – cone; *mukw* – ripe
Hard **'m:**	none	*'mal* – canoe; *loo'm* – we, us
Soft **n:**	same	*naa* – who; *nda* – where
Hard **'n:**	none	*'niin* – you; *'nax̲* – bait
Soft **p:**	same	*pdal* – rib; *wilp* – house
Hard **p':**	none	*goyp'ax̲* – bright; *goop'* – waves
s:	same	*sdin* – heavy; *haast* – fireweed
Soft **t:**	same	*hlit* – ball; *helt* – lots, many
Hard **t':**	none	*t'aap* – hammer; *t'aa* – to sit
Hard **tl':**	similar to "cl" in clan	*tl'ook* – mud; *tl'ak* – lower lip
Soft **ts:**	none	*yats* – to hit; *hets* – to send
Hard **ts':**	none	*aats'ip* – door; *ts'uuts* – birds
Soft **w:**	same	*wilp* – house; *wis* – rain
Hard **'w:**	none	*'Win* – teeth; *'wiit'is* – big one
Front **x:**	none	*hix* – fat; *wijix* – caribou
Back **x̲:**	none	*bax̲* – to run; *meex̲* – sour
xw:	none	*saxw* – mouth of stream
Soft **y:**	same	*Ya'a* – spring salmon; *yeen* – fog
Hard **'y:**	none	*'Yimk* – whiskers; *'yans* – leaves
Glottal stop **':**	none	*'niin* – you; *ya'a* – spring salmon

ENDNOTES

1 Hindle and Rigsby, 2.

Glossary

A

Aakts'ilaasxwit (mouth of the canyon): Fish camp on the Skeena River at Four Mile Bridge near Hazelton.

Ackwellget Station: Mission Flats near Hazelton. Also Achwylget.

Adaawgam Ts'iisus: Stories of Jesus.

adaawk: Gitxsan histories from time immemorial to the present.

Aiyansh (place of leaves): A Nisga'a village. Also New Aiyansh.

Aluugigat: The indigenous peoples of North and South America.

Aluuxw: Gitxsan chief in the House of Geel.

am giikw (good hemlock bark): Western hemlock tree.

am hat'al (good cedar bark): Western red-cedar.

am nax (good for snowshoes): Heavy foot lacing in snowshoes. Also see 'nax' and 'winx'.

amnigwoot (good father): Limited privilege for using the resources of one's father's territory.

Ana'bisxw: A fishing camp on the right bank of the Skeena River above Kispiox village.

Anda Ap: Gitxsan chief in the House of Gutgwinuxs.

Andamixw (where there is moonlight): Hazelton Peak and Mountain area.

Andisa'm: An ancient house at Gitxandakhl on the Nass River.

anguuxw'uutx: Gitxsan word for a sweat lodge.

Anhla'guu'a: Fish camp on the Skeena River above the mouth of Pinenut Creek.

Ankitlas: Former missionary village on the Kispiox River.

Anlagasimdeex (where store fishing gear and ropes): Former Gitxsan village on the Babine River.

Anlaw (where to cross): The river crossing near Glen Vowell. Also a Gitanmaax Reserve.

Ansa Bilaa (where there are abalone shells): A hill at the fifteen km post on the Kitwanga Backroad.

ansgiyast: Gitxsan word for cemetery. Also see 'an toosim gyat'.

Ansin Gam (where there are saskatoon berries): A rocky ridge along the west side of Sealy Lake.

ansin maa'y: Gitxsan word for berry patches.

Ansi'suuxs (where there is driftwood): The area at 'Ksan village and museum near Hazelton.

An'spa'yaxw (hiding place): Kispiox village.

ant'gelaa: Gitxsan cremation site.

An Togasxw: Red ochre site at the head of Xsi'an Togasxw (Driftwood River).

Antgulilbixs (whirlpool): Gitxsan chief in the House of Ts'iibaasaa.

ant'imahlasxw (to tell): Gitxsan word for stories and fables, like the Wiigyet stories.

an toosim gyat: The formal Gitxsan name for a cemetery. Also see 'ansgiyast'.

Anwok'esxw (where to dig): An area near the village of Temlaham.

Anxhon (where there are salmon): Fish camp on the lower Cranberry River.

Anx Milit (where there are steelhead): Steelhead fish camp on the Suskwa River.

Anxya'gen (chew dry salmon): Fishing area on the Kispiox River near the rodeo grounds.

Anyuusxw: Fish storage pit; also a dip net site at Hagwilget Canyon.

Atnah and Atenas: Gitxsan people, to the Nedut'en (Babine), Dakelh and Tsetsaut peoples.

Axgigii: Gitxsan chief in the House of Delgamuukw.

Axgoodim Tsetsaut: Gitxsan chief belong to the House of Nikateen.

Axgoot (without heart): A name in the House of Guuxsan.

Axmoogasxw (sufferer): Gitxsan chief in the House of Wiik̲'aax.

Axtiits'eek: Gitxsan chief in the House of Ts'ogaslee.

A'yawasxw (not hiding information): Gitxsan chief in the House of Gidumgaldo.

ayook: Gitxsan law, custom or precedent.

B

Bagayt 'Neexhl (middle of fin-back whale): Nisga'a chief of the Gitlax̲t'aamiks Eagle Clan.

banna: A dip-net like fishing device used in a canyon for spring salmon.

Bas: See Sabasuuxw.

Biinix: Gitxsan chief in the House of Gidumgaldo.

bilaa: Gitxsan word for abalone.

bil'ust: Gitxsan word for star.

C

Caskai: A boy's name in the House of Wiik̲'aax.

Chimhoatch: See Xsim Hayetsxw.

D

da'ak: Gitxsan house built partly below ground, often called a 'graded house'.

daganasxw: Gitxsan word for dried berry cake rolls, similar to fruit leather.

Dagmwilgyet: An ancient house at Gitx̲andakhl on the Nass River.

Dakelh: A central BC aboriginal nation of the Takla Lake area, also known as 'Carrier'.

dam: Gitxsan word for lake. Also see 'tam'.

Dam Similoo'o (lake creature): A lake below the west slope of Sidina Mountain. Also Damsumlo Lake east of Kuldo.

Dawamuxw (cold ears): Gitxsan chief in the House of Dawamuxw.

Dee: Gitxsan chief in the House of xGwoimtxw.

Dehldan: Tahltan village at the confluence of the Tahltan and Stikine rivers.

Delgamuukw (talking to copper): Gitxsan chief in the House of Delgamuukw; lead plaintiff in *Delgamuukw v. BC*.

Dii'atix: A boy's name in the House of xGwoimtxw. Also Deadix.

din: Gitxsan word for a fish trap.

Dinii: Gitxsan chief in the House of Gitluudaahlxw.

Duuk (quarrel): Gitxsan chief in the House of Kliiyeemlaxha.

E

Edohush: A girl's name in the House of Haax̲xw.

eek: Coho salmon.

enk: See 'galenx̲'.

G

Gaidaxgyet (very strong): Gitxsan chief in the House of Alaist.

Galaanhl Giist: Slamgeesh Lake area.

galdim aks: Gitxsan word for a water pail.

Galdo'o: See Kuldo.

galenx̲: Cedar bentwood boxes of various sizes, for berries, storage, moving dirt, etc.

Galuua (to call a second person): Gitxsan name in the House of Wiik̲'aax.

gam: Saskatoon berries.

Gama'uun (broken wing of a small grouse): Gitxsan chief in the House of Delgamuukw.

Gamayam: Gitxsan chief in the House of Guuxsan.

Gamlaxyeltxw: Gitxsan chief in the House of Gamlaxyeltxw.

Gamgisti'ltxw: Gitxsan chief in the House of Ma'uus.

Ganada: The Frog or Raven Clan. Also Lax See'l and Lax Ganada.

gan'il: Gitxsan word for guardrails on a bridge.

Gans' Niigyamks ('the sun shines on' pole): Totem pole in the House of Haaxxw.

gapk'ooyp: Gitxsan word for bunchberry.

gawagaanii (deer ceremony): A northwest coast feast held when war, bloodshed or conflict between tribes or nations has been resolved.

Gasx (bitter): Gitxsan chief in the House of 'Niist.

gaytim Boston (hat Boston): Gitxsan name for American fur traders' hats.

Geel: Gitxsan chief in the House of Geel.

gelpgasw: Wooden rings (small hoops) used to allow a fishing platform to float up and down.

gibuu (wolf): Gitxsan word for wolf.

Gidix'uus (taking away the dog): Gitxsan name in the House of Gitluudaahlxw.

Gidumgaldo (man just over there): Gitxsan name in the House of Gidumgaldo.

Gigeenix: The eastern or upriver Gitxsan dialect beginning at Gitanmaax; Gitsxan people from Gitanmaax north. Also see Gyeets.

giist (alder): Grey willow, also known as mountain alder.

Gilbil'hlanyuus (two caches, of large grizzly): Gitxsan chief in the House of Ma'uus.

Gil'dip Nakw (water flows around): A large boulder in the middle of the Skeena River at Utsun Creek. Locally known as Cariboo Creek. See Xsints'ihl.

Giletuhl'hamook (home of wild celery): A Gitxsan territory.

gimdiiyee'asxw: Gitxsan word for relaying backpack loads from place to place.

Gingolx (place of skulls): Nisga'a village at the mouth of the Nass River. Also Kincolith.

Gisday Wa: Wet'suwet'en chief and the second plaintiff in *Delgamuukw v. BC*.

Gisgamaawin (people of 'rasp-like' fern): Gitxsan name for the area surrounding Thomas Hankin's ranch north of Hazelton.

Gisk'aast (fireweed): Gitxsan Fireweed Clan.

Gitangasx (people of wild rice): Former Gitxsan village on the Skeena River east of Fourth Cabin.

Gitangwalkw (people of dry area): Former Gitxsan village near the Sweetin River confluence.

Gitank'aat (people of the cane): Former Gitxsan village on the Skeena River below Gitwangak.

Gitanmaax (people who fish by torch light): Gitxsan village at Hazelton. Also 'Get-an-max'.

Gitanyow (people of the narrow place): Gitxsan village northwest of Gitwangak. Also Kitwancool.

Gitgalaxan (people of fish fence or weir): Gitxsan name for a village near Fort Fraser.

Gitgwinyookhl: Ancient village on the Nass River opposite the mouth of Kwinamuck Creek.

Gitgwooyim (people of springtime): Gitxsan word for the Nedut'en (Babine Lake) people.

Gitlaxt'aamiks (people of the lakes): Nisga'a village on the Nass River near Aiyansh.

Gitluudaahlxw: Gitxsan chief in the House of Gitluudaahlxw.

Gits'abixw (man who made something): Gitxsan chief in the House of Wiik'aax.

Gitsegukla: A Gitxsan village below Hazelton. Also see Xsigyuukla.

Gitwangak (people of rabbits): A Gitxsan village on the Skeena River. Also Kitwanga.

gitwinkxw: To whistle.

Gitw'inkxws Wiigyet (ghost whistled in Wiigyet's ear): A feature on the Kispiox River near Kispiox.

Gitxandakhl: Ancient village on the Nass River near the mouth of Kwinamuck Creek.

Gitxat'in (people of fish traps): Nisga'a people who lived on the lower Nass River.

Gitxsan: People of the Skeena.

Gitzaxhlaahl: One of the nine Tsimshian tribes of the lower Skeena River.

Gotsgim Gipaiyk: Gitxsan name in the House of Gitluudaahlxw.

Gowal Mihl (burned over place): Village of Old Kuldo near Third Cabin.

Gunanoot (from Gam'anhuut, to flee): Gitxsan chief in the House of Geel.

Gutgwinuxs (owl): Gitxsan chief in the House of Gutgwinuxs. Also Nuuxs.

Guuhadak (selfish): Gitxsan chief in the House of Wiik̲'aax; a relative at Gitanmaax with the same name and crests.

Guuwasan: Gitxsan chief in the House of Ma'uus.

Guuxsan (gambler): Gitxsan chief in the House of Guuxsan.

Guuxwo'ot (continually feasting): Gitxsan chief in the House of Gutgwinuxs.

Gwaas Hlaa'm (borrow a shin bone): Gitxsan chief in the House of Gwaas Hlaa'm.

Gwa'gayee: Gitxsan chief in the House of Haalus.

gwalgwa hon: Dried salmon.

gwalgwa maa'y: Gitxsan word for dried berries. Also see 'daganasxw'.

Gwanks Ts'ak: Nisga'a fish camp on the Nass River.

gwats: Gitxsan word for faeces.

gwiikw: Hoary marmot, often referred to as whistler and groundhog.

Gwiiyeehl (small raven): Gitxsan chief in the House of Gwiiyeehl.

Gwilagantxw: Gitxsan chief in the House of Ts'abax/Ts'iiwus.

Gwilanamax: Gitxsan chief in the House of Haax̲xw.

Gwinax'hlo'otw (where there is an avalanche): Inverness Cannery near mouth of Skeena River. Also Woodcock's Landing.

Gwingadak̲ (where there are sandhill cranes): Part of the village of Temlaham.

Gwingalagantxw: Gitxsan chief in the House of Guuxsan.

Gwiniiho'osxw: Gitxsan chief in the House of 'Niist.

Gwininitxw: Gitxsan chief in the House of Gwininitxw.

Gwin Lalt (where there are snakes): High hill north of Gitwangak.

Gwin Ts'ihl: Mission Flats (aka The Forks, Fort Finlayson, Ackwellget Station, Anderson Flats).

Gwin Wijix (where there are caribou): Sidina Mountain; also a fishing site near Kispiox.

Gwis Sgan (small pine pitch): Gitxsan chief in the House of Haxbagwootx.

Gwits'enksim Sim'oogit: Gitxsan chief in the House of Haxbagwootx.

Gwo'goots (fish guts): A camp near Anlaw.

Gyagan: Gitxsan youth who mocked the sun at Temlaham.

Gyahl 'Tin (spearing fish trap): Kiteen River; a Gitanyow fish camp. Also see Xsi'gyahl't'in.

gyamk: Gitxsan word for sun. Also 'hlox̲s'.

Gyats'ees: Gitxsan chief in the House of Wiik̲'aax.

Gyeets: Western or downriver Gitxsan dialect; Gitxsan people from Gitsegukla to Gitanyow. See also Gigeenix.

gyuwadan: Gitxsan word for horse.

H

Haa'atxw (redheaded woodpecker): A Gitxsan man in the House of Ts'iin.

Haatq and Ha'atu: See Haa'atxw.

Haax̲xw (poor, in dire straits): Gitxsan chief in the House of Haax̲xw.

Hadaxs'amee: Gitxsan chief in the House of Dawamuxw.

hagehlast: A pole with a chisel-like end for scraping hemlock bark.

hagemgansxw: A stick or pole sharpened at one end used to loosen earth when digging a garden, digging up potatoes, etc.

Hagwilget (gentle people): Gitxsan word for the village and the people who lived there.

Halal: Nisga'a name in the Gitlax̲t'aamiks Eagle Clan.

halayt (one who hears or listens): A Gitxsan shaman who may be male or female.

haldawgit: Gitxsan word for witchcraft; a person who practices witchcraft.

hamook: Gitxsan word for rhubarb and wild rhubarb.

Hanamuxw: Gitxsan chief in the House of Hanamuxw.

Haspaiyets: Gitxsan chief in the House of Wiik'aax.

hawahl: Gitxsan word meaning unlucky.

Haxbagwootx: Gitxsan chief in the House of Haxbagwootx.

haxgwi'laax: Gitxsan war club.

hayuux: Gitxsan word for spirits.

His'duuhl'gana'aw (pretend humpback frog): Gitxsan man's name in the House of xGwoimtxw.

hlam'gan: A large floating rectangular platform with sides, used when fishing salmon on the Skeena River.

hl'hunhl gitgwooyim: Gitxsan word for Babine-bound salmon run.

Hl'sise'e Hlooxs (sunbeams feet of the sun): A Kisgegas Wolf Clan crest, House uncertain.

hots'imo witxw (again returns): A reincarnated person.

Hul'qumi'num: A large Coast Salish tribal group on southeast Vancouver Island and the lower Fraser River.

I

is: Gitxsan word for soapberry.

J

Jayn: Gitxsan word for 'Chinese' or 'Chinaman'

K

Kadu: An early Tsimshian village between Prince Rupert and Port Simpson.

Kaldixgyet (two-headed person): Gitxsan chief in the House of Luutkuuts'iiwus.

K'aatim Hayetsxw (cane of copper shield): Gitxsan chief in the House of Yal.

k'aliidakhl: Gitxsan word for Steller's jay.

Kamalmuk (Gamgaxmilmuxw): Gitxsan chief in the House of Gwaas Hlaa'm.

k'amksi'waa (driftwood): Gitxsan word for driftwood. Also Gitxsan name for light-skinned Caucasian peoples.

Kincolith: See Gingolx.

Kinyax: A woman's name in the House of Haaxxw.

Kisgagas: See Kisgegas.

Kisgegas (people of gaga'a, sea gulls): Gitxsan village on the Babine River.

Kispiox: Gitxsan village near Hazelton. Also see An'spa'yaxw.

Kitanmaax: See Gitanmaax.

Kitseguecla: See Gitsegukla.

Kitselas (people of the canyon): Tsimshian village near Usk.

Kitsumkalum: Tsimshian village near Terrace.

Kitwancool: See Gitanyow.

Kitwanga: See Gitwangak.

Kliiyeemlaxha (walking across the sky): Gitxsan chief in the House of Kliiyeemlaxha.

k'okhl: Gitxsan word for cedar bark rope. Also 'maa k'okhl'.

'Ksan: Model Gitxsan village on the Bulkley River at Hazelton.

Kuldo (not far over there): Former Gitxsan village on the Skeena River near Second Cabin. Also see Gowal Mihl and Ts'ilasxwm Gansxwit.

Kwinageese: Kwinageese Lake area.

Kyeekw: Nisga'a chief on the Nass River at Gitlaxt'aamiks.

Kyolugyet (only man): Gitxsan chief in the House of Kyolugyet.

L

Laa Good (of no use the heart): Gitxsan name in the House of Gitluudaahlxw.

Laan (salmon roe): Gitxsan chief in the House of Dawamuxw.

Laats: Gitxsan chief in the House of Wiik'aax.

laax wan: Gitxsan name for a twin-bladed knife with a handle in the middle.

Ladaix (useless skin): A Gitxsan chief in the House of Wiik'aax.

lahaal: The Chinook word for gambling. Also see 'xsan'.

lan: Gitxsan word for fish eggs. Also see 'logo lan'.

lasa 'wiihun (time of the big sockeye run): Gitxsan word for month of July.

lasa 'yanja (time of leaves): The month of May.

Lax Ansi Matsa (where hit blue grouse): A berry patch on Sidina Mountain.

Lax Antaahl (berry area): Nine Mile Mountain.

Lax An'xsan Tsetsaut (where gambled the Tsetsaut): A gambling site near Hazelton.

Lax Galts'ap: The Nisga'a village of Greenville.

Lax Gibuu (on wolf): Gitxsan Wolf Clan.

Laxgitangasx: See Gitangasx.

lax ha (on sky): Gitxsan word for sky. Also 'lax'om'.

Lax Kw'alaams (on rose hips): Port Simpson.

Laxnok: See 'naxnok'.

Lax See'l (on frog): Frog-Raven Clan. Also Lax Ganada.

Laxt'ihl: A boy's name in the House of Wiik'aax.

Laxwiiyip (on big land): Where the Luuts'abim Tsimyip people lived.

Laxwillamuut: A Nisga'a chief.

Lax Xsgiik (on eagle): Gitxsan Eagle Clan.

Lee An: See Xsi'yeen.

Legaic: A Tsimshian chief from Lax Kw'alaams. Also Legeex.

Ligi Gimstuutxw (the end of the river, it's gone): Gitxsan chief in the House of Dawanmuxw.

l'iligidum bitxw: A divorce feast.

li'ligit (feast): A Gitxsan feast where house business is conducted. Also see 'yuukw'.

Liluxws (thief, to steal): Gitxsan chief in the House of Haaxxw.

limx bitx: Gitxsan term for a divorce song.

Lip Ha Un: Gitxsan chief in the House of Luutkuts'iiwus.

lixs ta'at: Gitxsan name for an island.

logo lan: Fermented fish eggs.

Lulaxs (in bear wallow): Gitxsan name in the House of Gidumgaldo/Skiigamlaxha.†

Luugantxw: Gitxsan chief in the House of Lalt.

luulak: Gitxsan word for ghost.

Luus: Gitxsan chief in the House of Luus.

Luutkuts'iiwus (bright all around): Gitxsan chief in the House of Luutkuts'iiwus.

Luuts'abim Tsimyip (people who live in the earth): Tsetsaut people who lived in underground houses.‡

Luu Uuk (in copper): Gitxsan name in the House of Wiik'aax.

---

† Gidumgaldo and Skiigamlaxha have the same origin at Kuldo, and earlier.

‡ Probably similar to the 'Kekuli', pit houses built in the central interior of BC.

M

maadim: Gitxsan word for winter.

maa hixs: Gitxsan word for a birch bark torch.

maa k'okhl: See k'okhl.

Madiigam Gyamk (supernatural grizzly of the sun): Gitxsan name in the House of Gitluudaahlxw. Also the 'sun bear' crest on Gitluudaahlxw's totem pole.

Madiigam Gyat (grizzly man): Gitxsan chief in the House of Wiik'aax.

Madiigam Ts'uwii Aks (supernatural grizzly of the water): Grizzly that devastated Temlaham in ancient times.

Madiik: A supernatural grizzly.

Madii Lii: A camp and high hill east of Hazelton on the Suskwa River.

mahlasxwm duutsw (talking metal): Gitxsan phrase for telegraph, telephone and electrical wire.

Maikt: A boy's name in the House of Wiik'aax.

Malii: A Gitanyow chief in the House of Malii; also, Malii (Mary). Also Kisgegas Wolf Clan crest, House uncertain.

matx: Gitxsan word for mountain goat.

Ma'uus (crazy dog): Gitxsan chief in the House of Ma'uus.

maxmaagay: Gitxsan word for rainbow.

Metlakatla: Tsimshian village on an island near Prince Rupert.

miiyahl: Gitxsan word for low bush blueberry.

Miin Lax Mihl (foot of the burn): Gitxsan name for a territory north of Seventh Cabin.

Miluulak (corpse or ghost): Gitxsan chief in the House of Miluulak.

Minhl Ts'uusx (the little frog gets up with difficulty): Gitxsan name in the House of Wiik'aax.

Misa'loos (Mr. Ross): A name in the House of Waiget.

Misilos (Mr. Ross): A Wet'suwet'en chief.

miso'o: Sockeye salmon.

moogan nisgoo: Gitxsan phrase describing children licking berry juice from thimbleberry leaves (nisgoo).

moohl: A small barrel-like trout trap. Also a dip net used at Hagwilget Canyon.

N

Na'a: A Tlingit village at or near present-day Loring, Alaska.

Naagahl Banda: Gitxsan chief in the House of Kliiyeemlaxha.

Naalaxha: Gitxsan chief in the House of xGwoimtxw.

Nagim Wilyee (long distance away, the moon): Gitxsan chief in the House of Delgamuukw.

Nagwa'uun (long arm): Gitxsan chief in the House of xGwoimtxw. A Nisga'a chief has the same name.

nax: Gitxsan word for snowshoes. Also see 'am nax' and 'winx'.

naxnok (spiritual or supernatural power): A chief's power as enacted in a feast or ceremony.

Naxwan (walk by riverside): Nisga'a chief in the Eagle Clan at Gitlaxt'aamiks.

Neatsqua: See Niitsxw.

Nedut'en: The aboriginal people who live at Babine Lake. Also 'Nate-ote-tains'.

Nigitxw (on a difficult place): Gitxsan chief in the House of Haaxxw.

niguis: Gitxsan word meaning 'father of (name of child)'.

nii'a gatsa (to pour berries): Berry mash poured onto berry racks.

Niik'yap (on ten): Gitxsan chief in the House of Niik'yap.

Niis Nawii: Tsimshian chief in the Fireweed Clan.

Niis Noohl: Gitxsan chief in the House of Simoogihl Gyamk.

Niist (man of the mountain): Gitxsan chief in the House of 'Niist.

Niistahuukw: A Tsimshian chief from Kitselas.

Niitsxw: Gitxsan chief in the House of Hanamuxw.

Nikateen (bow): Gitxsan chief in the House of Nikateen.

Nisga'a: The aboriginal nation on the lower Nass River.

nisgo'o: Thimbleberry leaves.

Nola: Gitxsan chief in the House of Luutkuuts'iiwus.

noxs: Gitxsan word meaning 'mother of (name of child)'.

Noxs Doo (mother of Doo, Gidumgaldo): Gitxsan woman in the House of Gidumgaldo.

Noxs Ladaix (mother of Ladaix): Gitxsan woman in the House of Wiik'aax.

Noxs Maak (mother of Mark): Gitxsan woman in the House of Delgamuukw.

Noxs Oop (mother of Oop, Wii Goobil): Gitxsan woman in the House of Gidumgaldo.

Noxs Ts'aa (mother of Ts'aa): A Gitxsan woman, the wife of Duuk.

O

Osii Midoo (white man's dog): A name in the House of Waiget.

P

pdek: Gitxsan word for clan.

Pilse'yax: A boy's name in the House of Wiik̲'aax.

otsi: Otsi Creek. May be the anglicization of the word 'wijix' or caribou.

ploo'ah: A type of fish trap used in Hagwilget canyon.

S

Sabasuuxw: A Gitxsan woman in the House of Haax̲xw (nicknamed 'Bas').

Sanoos (pretending to die): Gitxsan chief in the House of Nikateen.

Satsan: Wet'suwet'en chief in the Gilseyhu Clan.

Sekani: Aboriginal group who lived along the Peace River and its tributaries. Also see Tsetsaut.

Sicanee: See Sekani.

s'id'axt: A topknot tied at the top a man's head.

Sigit'ox: A mountain at Kispiox, known locally as Elephant Mountain.

sii'sagenxw (making new tracks): Gitxsan word describing how grizzly bears emerge from their dens in spring.

siiyun: Gitxsan word for glacier. Also 's'yun'.

sim'algyax̲ (true language): Gitxsan, Tsimshian and Nisga'a word for their respective languages.

simgiget: Gitxsan chiefs; the plural of sim'oogit.

similoo'o: Gitxsan word for an unusual creature in a lake or water. A *halayt* in training may perform a vision quest at such a site.

simmaa'y: Gitxsan word for black huckleberry.

sim'oogit: Gitxsan word for chief.

Simoogihl Gyamk: Gitxsan chief in the House of Simoogihl Gyamk.

Skanii'mahl'hoohl'gan (where the pole got stuck): A place near Gisgamaawin.

Skanu'u: Gitxsan chief in the House of Gutgwinuxs.

Skansna'at (hawthorn bush): Gitxsan name for the area surrounding Skunsnat Lake.

Skawats'eekx̲: Gitxsan chief in the House of Gidumgaldo.

Skawill (in the way): Gitxsan chief in the House of Gidumgaldo/Skiigamlaxha.

Ska'woo: The mythic grandmother (sometimes said to be the mother) whose granddaughter flew to the sky people and gave birth to four sons.

Smax (meat, or black bear): Gitxsan chief in the House of Ts'abak/Ts'iiwus.

Spaksuut (autumn camp): Tsimshian word for Spokeshute near Port Essington.

Spookxw: Gitxsan chief in the House of Spookxw.

Spox: See Spookxw.

Sta'gapsit (high on one side): Porphyry Creek.

Stekyawden (stands alone, or brother): Gitxsan name for Rocher Deboule Mountain.

Suuwiiguus (new great jumping (frog)): Gitxsan chief in the House of Kyoluget.

T

tam: Gitxsan word for lake. Also ''dam'.

Tam Gwinha'moo<u>k</u> (lake near wild rhubarb): Kwinamuck Lake on the Nass River.

Tam Lax̲'antaahl (lake near a berry patch): Robinson Lake.

Tam Stekyawden (lake of Stekyawden): Sealy Lake.

Tamtuuts'whl'aks (lake of black water): Damdochax Lake. Also Blackwater Lake.

ta'oots'ip: Gitxsan word for fort or fortress.

Tawee-welp: A Gitxsan man at Temlaham.

T'axxw'm Waax (paddles): Nisga'a chief at Gitlaxt'aamiks.

Temlaham (prairie place): Ancient Gitxsan village on the Skeena River below Hazelton.

t'imi'yt: Gitxsan word for kinnikinnik, a shrub with dry red berries.

t'iluulak'at: The person from the father's side who prepares and cremates the deceased.

Tl'azten (people by the edge of the bay): A Dakelh village on Stuart Lake.

Toq: Nisga'a chief on the lower Nass River, Wolf Clan.

Ts'abax: Gitxsan chief in the House of Ts'iiwus/Ts'abax.

Ts'akim Eek (nose like a coho): Name of Gidumgaldo's totem pole at Hazelton.

Ts'ago Gaak: Gitxsan chief in the House of Gutgwinuxs.

ts'idipxs: Gitxsan word for highbush cranberry.

Ts'igwii (a small bird): Gitxsan name in the Gitsegukla House of Wiigyet.

Ts'iin: Gitxsan chief in the House of Ts'iin. Also Xsimots'iin.

Ts'ilaasxwit: Four Mile Canyon near Gitanmaax.

Ts'ilasxwm Gansxwit (canyon where there is heather): New Kuldo near Second Cabin.

Tsilhqot'in: The Chilcotin people and nation. Also *Tsilhqot'in v. BC* (2014).

Ts'im Aks (inside the waters): A Gitxsan territory at the source of Corral Creek and Deep Canoe Creek.

ts'imko'o: Gitxsan word for anus.

Tsë Cakh: Wet'suwet'en name for the village at Hagwilget Canyon.

Tsetsaut: Any of several aboriginal peoples who frequented the Gitxsan's north and northeast border.

Ts'iibaasaa (like blinking of lights): Gitxsan chief in the House of Ts'iibaasaa. Also a Tsimshian chief.

Ts'iiwus: Gitxsan chief in the House of Ts'iiwus/Ts'abax.

Ts'iiyee: Gitxsan chief in the House of Kliiyeemlaxha.

Ts'imanluuskeexs: Former Gitxsan village in upper Nass watershed.

Ts'im'ansi'mal (where there are cottonwood trees): A place near Kispiox. Also the site of a Gitxsan and Nisga'a gawaganii.

Ts'im Gaak (inside the raven) and Sk'alaa'nt (behind): Buildings in Wiik'aax at Kisgegas.

Ts'imilix Maadimtxw (inside a snow cave): A child's name in the House of Haaxxw. Also 'Chimilikh'.

ts'imil guut (adoption): Gitxsan term for bringing a person into one's house.

Tsimshian (inside the Skeena): The name of the aboriginal people inhabiting the mid- to lower Skeena River and adjacent coast islands.

ts'in duuhl: Gitxsan snow shovel.

Ts'ixs Gibuu (like the colour of a wolf): Gitxsan name in the House of Gitluudaahlxw.

Ts'ogaslee: Gitxsan chief in the House of Ts'ogaslee.

ts'ogom beehl: A fine cedar net used for winter fishing under ice.

ts'ogo guuxdit gan lax aks (floating a wood staff on the river): A Gitxsan game.

Ts'ogo Wil: Gitxsan man from Glen Vowell.

Ts'ooda: An early coastal people, ancestors of many Wolf clans.

Ts'ugyet: Gitxsan name in the House of Kyolugyet.

Tu Etisht: Gitxsan name in the House of Gutgwinuxs.

U

Utseni: Wet'suwet'en name for the Nisga'a people.

Uuxs Bahlit: Mountain area at headwaters of the Suskwa River near French Peak.

W

Wa'a: Gitxsan chief in the House of Xsim'gwneekxw. See Xsim'gwneekxw.

Waiget (dead fall trap): Gitxsan chief in the House of Wiigyet.

Watsonqua (Watsonkwa): See Widzin Kwah.

weex: Gitxsan word for lynx.

Wet'suwet'en: Neighbours of the Gitxsan who live mainly in the Bulkley River watershed.

Whull-e-mooch: Ancient people who migrated to Haida Gwaii from Whull, Puget Sound, Washington. Also known as Tillamook, a chinook word for a tribal group at Puget Sound.

widintxw: The mother of a reincarnated person.

Widzin Bin: Wet'suwet'en name for Morice Lake.

Widzin Kwah: Wet'suwet'en name for the Bulkley River.

Wii Bowax (sloppy eater): Gitxsan chief in the House of Kliiyeemlaxha.

Wiidangwax (big food): Gitxsan chief in the House of Ma'uus.

Wiigoobil (heart of a salmon): Gitxsan chief in the House of Gidumgaldo.

Wiigyet (big man): Gitxsan chief in the House of Wiigyet.

Wiik'aax (big wings): Gitxsan chief in the House of Wiik'aax

Wiilaxhaa (great sky): A boy's name in the House of Wiik'aax.

Wiilixsha'os (big strange dog): Gitxsan chief in the House of Wiik'aax.

Wiiminoosikx (big wolverine): Gitxsan chief in the House of Wiiminoosikx.

Wii Muugilsxw (big stirring water): Gitxsan chief in the House of Kliiyeemlaxha.

Wii Seeks (big spruce tree): Gitxsan chief in the House of Wiiget. Also a Tsimshian chief's name.

Wiis'dis: Gitxsan chief in the House of Miluulak.

Wiiyagadeets (big wolverine): Gitxsan chief in the House of Haxbagwootx.

Wilgawsuuk (where-keep-silent): Gitxsan territory north of the Sustut River.

Wilgyehlhetxw See's Wiigyet (where Wiigyet's foot touched down): The impression of a foot in a rock near Seventeen Mile Bridge (destroyed when a BC Hydro crew installed a powerline).

wilp haniits'ok: Gitxsan word for a lean-to at a berry patch.

wil'suwitx (coming out): Gitxsan word for one's father, or father's side.

Wiluux t'aas Wiigyet (where sat Wiigyet): A site near Four Mile Bridge where Wiigyet fell from the sky leaving an imprint in the rock. The imprint was lost during bridge re-construction.

winx: Gitxsan word for fine filling (babiche) in snowshoes. Also see 'am nax' and 'nax'.

Wisanskit: A mountain in Gitxsan territory north of the Sustut River.

Witset: A former Wet'suwet'en village near Moricetown. Also Hotset.

witxsw: To mash or squeeze berries.

wo'o: A large barrel-like fish trap for salmon.

Woosimlaxha (sea creature from the sky): Gitxsan chief in the House of Woosimlaxha.

Wo'os Sa'lo'op (stone bowl): Gitxsan chief in the House of Kliiyeemlaxha.

X

Xantxw (killed by a tree): Gitxsan chief in the House of Gwiiyeehl.

xGwoimtxw (springtime): Gitxsan chief in the House of xGwoimtxw.

Xhlex: Gitxsan chief in the House of Yal.

Xsa'alis'awit (runs backward): Sallysout Creek.

Xsa'is (creek where soapberries): Sterritt Creek.

Xsan: The canyon on the Skeena River above Kispiox.

xsan: Gitxsan word for gambling. Also see 'lahaal'.

xsgoogam sim'oogit: The leading chief of each Gitxsan village.

Xsi'an Bin'aast: Shewililba Creek.

Xsi'anhl Guuxs: Gitxsan name for a creek near Beament on the Bulkley River.

Xsi'an Seegit (creek where murder happened): Murder Creek.

Xsi'ansix Moohl (creek small fish trap: Sansixmor Creek.

Xsi'ansix Moohl Ando'o (creek small fish trap): Cutfoot Creek.

Xsi'anskeexs (creek that is shallow): Lorne Creek.

Xsi'anspayaxw: Kispiox River.

xsigis ba'anasxw (creek running water): Gitxsan word for a canal.

Xsigwin Gyila'a: Squingula River.

Xsi'gwin Hu'ums (creek where there is devil's club): Hazelton Creek.

Xsigwink'aat (creek of cane): Fiddler Creek. Original home of the Gitk'aata (Hartley Bay people).

Xsigwinya'a (river of spring salmon): Shegunia River.

Xsigwitselasgwit (creek canyon): Shenismike Creek. Niik'yap's fish camp on the Babine River above Kisgegas.

Xsigwits'iik: Boulder Creek, between Hazelton and Moricetown.

Xsi'gyahl't'in (creek where they spear a fish trap): Kiteen River. Also see Gyahl 'Tin.

xsiisxw: Gitxsan compensation or payment feast for an accidental death or a crime committed. See 'gawagaanii'.

Xsimatsi'ho'ot (first out in spring)[†]**:** Sediesh Creek or Thomlinson Creek

Xsim Hayetsxw (river copper): Copper River, near Terrace.

Xsina'gwoot: Legate Creek.

[†] Wiik'aax/Simon Wright to Bruce Rigsby ca. 1966

Y

ya'a: Gitxsan word for spring salmon.

Yaga'yansit (along slope of leaves): China Grade Hill near Hazelton.

Yee'l: Gitxsan chief in the House of Gitluudaahlxw.

yeen: Gitxsan word for cloud or mist.

yees: Gitxsan word for fence or palisade.

Yimist: Gitxsan name in the House of Wiik'aax.

Xsints'ihl (creek where there are ground squirrels)[‡]**:** Utsun Creek, commonly known as Caribou Creek.

Xsiphetxw (water stands still): Gitxsan name for a river feature between Kitselas and Terrace.

Xsi'yeen (water of mist): Skeena River.

Xsi'yeen Ando'o (Skeena over there): Gitxsan name for the Bulkley River.

Xsigyuukla (river of Gyuukla Mountain): Gitsegukla River. Also Kitseguecla.

Xsim'gwneekxw (woman of cold): Gitxsan chief in the House of Xsim'gwneekxw.[§]

Xsi Muula (creek sawmill): Alipakh Creek (from Xsigalibax).

Xsimxsan (woman of maggots): A Gitxsan chief at Kisgegas. Also a Nisga'a chief at Gitlaxt'aamiks.

Xsi Tsihl'nii'din (so many salmon, like fat bubbling in a pot): McCully Creek.

Xsitxemsem (river of Txemsem): Nass River.

Xsugwa'mahlit (creek running flat): Sidina Creek.

Xsugwinhliiyuun (creek moose skins): Mosque Creek

Xsugwin Lik'insxw (river where there are grizzlies): Babine River.

xsuu'w: Gitxsan word for dried hemlock cambium cakes.

Xsuwii Aks (river with big water): Sustut River.

xwsit: Gitxsan word for the fall season.

[‡] Ground squirrel, or 'ts'ilix' in Tahltan language, or perhaps a pika.

[§] This house has the same myths and crests as Gidumgaldo (Barbeau files).

yuukw (feast): A major feast for raising a totem pole or high chief's gravestone. See Li'ligit.

Acknowledgements

There are so many people to thank that it is difficult to know where to begin, so perhaps the mid-1970s will do. From then to now, I have had the privilege of working with dozens of Gitxsan and Wet'suwet'en elders and chiefs. More recently, during the writing of this book, I have also turned to several people whose knowledge of the Gitxsan language and events has assisted me greatly: 'Niist/William Blackwater, Axgoodim Tsetsaut/Victor Robinson, Ts'ago Gaak/Perry Sampson, Lip Ha Un/Fanny Smith, Dinii/Fern Weget, Gitluudaahlxw/Alvin Weget, Skanu'u/Ardythe Wilson and my father, Wiik̲aax/Neil B. Sterritt. I am grateful for their time and patience. Of course, errors that may have crept in are solely my responsibility.

The following individuals provided encouragement, inspiration and advice: Hugh Brody, Ted Chamberlin, Stephen Cornell, Allen Gottesfeld, Susan Marsden, Mélanie Morin, Richard Overstall, Diane Smith, Peter Grant, Louise Mandell and Stuart Rush.

Thanks to Karen Aird of the Saulteau First Nation who said, "You have to write a book and its title should be 'Mapping My Way Home.'" I had been struggling for a title and Karen provided it.

Thanks also to my family, in particular: sons Gordon and Jamie; Aunt Shirley Ann Dowd, the last of my mother's siblings; cousin Sandra (Colcord) Hunt; my sister Shirley and brother Art; Dad's wife, Barbara J. Dunn; Uncle Bill Heath; and cousin Charlie Sterritt.

Thanks especially to Lynn Shervill and Sheila Peters of Creekstone Press who asked me to write a Hazelton area history almost a decade ago. The time they have spent on this project and their editing skills are truly appreciated. Thanks also to Morgan Hite for his mapping expertise and Harry Kruisselbrink for help with the proofreading.

Finally, my sincere appreciation to the managers and staff of the BC Archives at the Royal BC Museum, the Bulkley Valley Research Centre, the Hazelton Pioneer Museum and Archives, the Manitoba Archives and the National Archives of Canada.

About the Author

Neil Sterritt was born and raised in Hazelton, British Columbia and later lived with his wife and sons for many years at Temlaham, the site of a Gitxsan ancestral village. He is a member of the House of Gitluudaahlxw and was president of the Gitxsan-Wet'suwet'en Tribal Council from 1981 to 1987, key years in the lead up to the precedent-setting aboriginal rights case known as *Delgamuukw v. BC*. He writes extensively on aboriginal rights and governance and serves as a consultant to many aboriginal organizations around the world. He co-authored the book, *Tribal Boundaries in the Nass Watershed* (UBC Press 1999). In 2008 he received an honorary doctorate from the University of Toronto in recognition of his "lifetime contributions to the understanding and expression of aboriginal citizenship in Canada". Neil also served as Director of Self-government, Assembly of First Nations in Ottawa from 1988 to 1991. He currently lives with his wife, Barbara, near Williams Lake, BC.

The author upon the occasion of receiving his honourary doctorate with (L – R) his son, Jamie, wife, Barbara, and his son, Gordon. (Jamie Sterritt photo)

References

Adams, J. *Historic Guide to Ross Bay Cemetery: Victoria, BC Canada*. Victoria: Sono Nis Press, 1998.

Ames, K. "Report of Excavations at GhSv 2, Hagwilget Canyon". Inglis, R. and G. MacDonald, eds. *Skeena River Prehistory*. Ottawa: National Museum of Man, 1997.

Ancestry.ca
- CWD Clifford and family, 2013.

Ancestry.com
- John Starret. *Canada, British Regimental Registers of Service, 1756-1900* [database on-line]. Provo, UT, USA: Ancestry.com 2012.
- Albert [Herbert Frank] Russell. Quebec, Vital and Church Records (Drouin Collection), 1621-1976 [database on-line]. Provo, UT, USA, Ancestry.com 2008.

"Ashcroft—The Gateway to the Nechaco Valley and Northern British Columbia." *Ashcroft Journal* 9 May 1908:1.

Austin, K. F. "The Changing Vista of the Northern Northwest Coast Indian Deer Ritual." MA University of Alaska 1999.

Banner, S. *Possessing the Pacific: Land, Settlers, and Indigenous People from Australia to Alaska*. London: Harvard Press, 2007.

Barbeau, M. *Totem Poles of the Gitksan, Upper Skeena River, British Columbia*. Ottawa: King's Printer, 1929.

Barbeau, M. and W. Beynon. *Tsimshian Narratives Vol.1: Tricksters, Shamans and Heroes*. Ed. John J. Cove and George F. MacDonald. Mercury Series. Directorate Paper 3 CMM Ottawa 1987.

— (n.d.). "Temlarham: The Land of Plenty on the North Pacific Coast." Unpublished manuscript: Canadian Centre for Folk Cultural Studies, Canadian Museum of Civilization, Hull.

— (n.d.). "Wolf-Clan Invaders from the Northern Plateaux among the Tsimsyans." Unpublished manuscript: Canadian Centre for Folk Cultural Studies, Canadian Museum of Civilization, Hull.

— (n.d.). "Raven Clan Outlaws of the North Pacific Coast." Unpublished manuscript: Canadian Centre for Folk Cultural Studies, Canadian Museum of Civilization, Hull.

— (n.d.). "The Marius Barbeau and William Beynon Fieldnotes" (1915-1956). Canadian Centre for Folk Culture Studies, Canadian Museum of Civilization, Hull.

Berens, H. H. (Deputy Governor of HBC, London) letter to Governor James Douglas May 5, 1858 PABC GR 1372, Colonial Correspondence, file 704.

Berger, T. *Fragile Freedoms: Human Rights and Dissent in Canada*. Vancouver: Clarke, Irwin, 1981.

Bergreen, L. *Columbus: The Four Voyages, 1492-1504*. New York: Viking Penguin, 2011.

Beynon, W. "When Tckaimson and Laggabula Gambled." *Tsimshian Stories (VI)*. Metlakatla Indian Community, Metlakatla Alaska, 1985.

— *Tsimshian Stories: The Last Raid of Legaick on the Skeena Gitksan*. Metlakatla, AK, Metlakatla Indian Community (Columbia University Library of Rare Books and Transcripts): 1980.

Boas, F. *Tsimshian Mythology*. New York: Johnson Reprint Corporation, 1970.

Book Builders of 'Ksan. *We-Gyet*. Hazelton: Kitanmax School of Northwest Coast Indian Art, 1977.

"Boom Swung at Cedarvale During Week." *The Omineca Herald* 22 July 1927: 1.

Brock, P. *The Many Voyages of Arthur Wellington Clah: A Tsimshian Man on the Pacific Northwest Coast*. Vancouver: UBC Press, 2011.

Brown, W. "Report of the Establishment of Fort Kilmaurs, Babine Country, New Caledonia 1822-1823." HBCA (B 11 / e / 1).

—. "Report of the Babine Country and Countries to the Westward April 1826." HBCA (b 11 / e / 2, fol. 12).

Bull, W. P. "Who Was William Perkins Bull?" Peel Information Network, Local History Databases, Historical Series. (www.pinet.on.ca Aug. 18, 2014.)

Bull W. P. Collection, STARRAT, 1930s; MS 515, reel 69, pp. 64447-64516, Brampton Public Library, Brampton, Ontario.
Canada.
—. Census of Canada, 1881-1921.
—. Gazetteer of Canada. *British Columbia*. Ottawa: Dept. of Energy, Mines and Resources, 1985.
—. Report of the Select Committee of the Senate, Appointed to Enquire into the Resources of the Great Mackenzie Basin. Session 1888. Ottawa: Queen's Printer, 1888.
—. Permanent Committee on Geographical Names, Ottawa, Ont.
—. Canada Sessional Papers, Vol. 11, Third Session of Tenth Parliament 1906-07, Appendix C, Patrol Report of Inspector A.E.C. McDonnell, Whitehorse to Hazelton, BC Oct. 5, 1906: 47.
—. Canada British Regimental Registers of Service (1756-1900).
Canada. Department of Indian Affairs.
—. Ashdown Green fieldnotes and sketch, survey records, Kispaiax Indian Fisheries on the Kispaiax and Skeena Rivers, FB BC/22A, 12, Aug. 18, 1911.
—. Babine Agency Letterbook (BAL); Loring and Vowell, 1894 re: James Spaagh.
—. Gitanmaax cemetery sketch, 1906, DIA, Black Series, RG 10, Vol. 4086.
—. Indian Affairs Annual Reports, 1864-1990. Babine and Upper Skeena Agency, Hazelton, July 15, 1901.
—. Annual Reports of the Department of Indian Affairs; Glen Vowell and Andimaul Day Schools, The Salvation Army and Indian Education. (www.nlc-bnc/indianaffairs/index-e.html.)
—. J. Lestock Reid, DLS, British Columbia, Babine and Upper Skeena River Agency, Hazelton, July 14, 1905.
—. Laird, David. Indian Commissioner, BC, Babine and Upper Skeena Agency, Hazelton, July 25th, 1899 (Indian Affairs Annual Reports, 1864-1990, Library and Archives Canada).
—. McKenna-McBride Royal Commission, Minutes of Decision 1913-1960. (www.ubcic.bc.ca Jan. 18, 2015).
—. McKenna-McBride Report, Babine Agency, BC, 1915 (UBCIC typescript, author's possession).
"1969 White Paper." No author. (www.en.wikipedia.org May 24, 2015). Also see Canada, "Statement of the Government of Canada on Indian Policy 1969" (www.aadnc-aandc.gc.ca May 25, 2015).
Cannings, R. et al. *Birds of the Interior of BC and the Rockies*. Vancouver: Heritage House, 2009.
Cannings, S., J.A. Nelson, and R. Cannings. *Geology of British Columbia: A Journey through Time*. Vancouver: Greystone Books, 2011.
"Cedar Poles are Being Hauled Several Camps." *The Omineca Herald* 14 Jan. 1927: 1.
Cove, J.J. *A Detailed Inventory of the Barbeau Northwest Coast Files*. Canadian Centre for Folk Studies, Paper 54. Ottawa: National Museums of Canada. 1985.
Chow, L. *Chasing Their Dreams*. Prince George: Caitlin Press, 2000.
Cove, J. and G. F. MacDonald. "Combat between Txamsem and his brother Lagabula." *Tsimshian Narratives 1: Tricksters, Shamans and Heroes*. Ottawa: CMC Paper No. 3, 1987: 25-26.
Cox, C. "The Founding of Hazelton." ca.1956 (unpublished essay, author's possession).
—. "Indian Uprising on the Skeena." *Native Voice. Special Edition*. 1958:16. Also see "Simon Gunanoot: the Authentic Story".
Daly, R. *Our Box Was Full: an Ethnography for the Delgamuukw Plaintiffs*. Vancouver: UBC Press, 2005.
Dawson, G. M. *Report on an Exploration from Port Simpson to Northern British Columbia and the Peace River Country*. Montreal: Dawson Brothers, 1879.
Deans, J. "Tales of the Totems of the Hidery." ed. O. L. Triggs, *Archives of the International Folk-Lore Association* (2), Chicago, 1899: 57.
Deaville, A.S. *The Colonial Postal Systems and Postage Stamps of Vancouver Island and British Columbia: 1849-1871*. Lawrence, Mass: Quarterman Publications, (nd).
Delgamuukw v. BC, "Commission Evidence." Smithers Registry No. 0843, 1985-1986.
—. *Reasons for Judgement*. Smithers Registry No. 0843, 1991.
"Destroying the Cedar Trees." *The Omineca Herald* 18 June 1926: 2.
Dorsey, G.A. "The Geography of the Tsimhian Indians." *American and Antiquarian Journal* XIX (1897).
Downie, W. *Hunting for Gold: Reminiscences of Personal Experience and Research in the Early Days of the Pacific Coast from Alaska to Panama* (1893). San Francisco: California Publishing, 1893.

—. Journal, "A Prospecting Expedition from Victoria and the Queen Charlotte Islands to The Forks and Fort St. James 1859." PABC, Colonial Correspondence (B01326, File 487, 4a).

Drucker, P. *The Native Brotherhoods: Modern Intertribal Organizations on the Northwest Coast.* Brighton, Michigan: US Government Printing Office, Washington, 1958.

Duff, W. ed. *Histories, Territories and Laws of the Kitwancool.* Victoria: Dept. of Education, 1959.

Dunn, J. A., ed. *Sm'algyax: A Reference Dictionary and Grammar for the Coast Tsimshian Language.* Seattle: U. of Washington Press, 1995.

Elliott, D. W. "Chapter 3: Aboriginal Title." Bradford W. Morse, ed., *Aboriginal Peoples and the Law: Indian, Metis and Inuit Rights in Canada.* Ottawa: Carleton University Press, 1989.

Evans, H.R. "The Family History of Jonathan Johnson." 1953 (unpublished manuscript).

Finlayson, R. to William Manson, Victoria 1866, HBCA, (B.226/b/35).

— to W.F Tolmie, Victoria May 1868, HBCA, (A.11/83, fo.418).

Fisher, R. "Joseph Trutch and Indian Land Policy." *BC Studies* 12 (1971-72): 3-33.

Fitzgerald, K. "Collin's Overland Telegraph." *The History of the Canadian West* 1 (l982): 23-63.

Foster, H. and A. Grove. "United States v. Tom and a New Perspective on the Short History of Treaty Making in Nineteenth-Century British Columbia." *BC Studies* 138/139 (2003): 51-86.

Galois, R. M., ed. *A Voyage to the North West Side of America: the Journals of James Colnett, 1786-89.* Vancouver: UBC Press, 2004.

—. "Colonial Encounters: The Worlds of Arthur Wellington Clah, 1855-1881." *BC Studies* (1997-98): 105-147.

—. "The History of the Upper Skeena Region, 1850 to 1927." *Native Studies Review* 9: 2 (1993-1994).

Gisday Wa and Delgamuukw. *The Spirit in the Land: The Opening Statement of the Gitksan and Wet'suwet'en Hereditary Chiefs in the Supreme Court of British Columbia, May 11, 1987.* Gabriola, BC: Reflections, 1987.

Glen Sr., J. *Where the Rivers Meet: The Story of the Settlement of the Bulkley Valley.* Duncan: New Rapier Press, 1977.

Gottesfeld, A., R.W. Matthewes and L.M. Johnson Gottesfeld. "Holocene debris flows and environmental history, Hazelton area, British Columbia." *Canadian Journal of Earth Sciences* 28 (1991): 1583-93.

GWES. *Gitxsenimx – Gitxsanimax to English Dictionary: Learners Edition* Volume 1. Terrace: BC Ministry of Education, 1996.

Hall, R. *Pioneer Goldseekers of the Omineca.* Vancouver: Morriss Publishing, 1994.

Hanna, C. J. P. "Bailliff Macaulay." *BC Historical News* (1992-93): 16-19.

Harris, C. *Making Native Space: Colonialism, Resistance, and Reserves in British Columbia.* Vancouver: UBC Press, 2002.

Harris, H. *Rainbow Dancer.* Prince George: Caitlin Press, 1999.

— "Only Their Skins Change: Gitksan Social Structure, Kinship, and Genealogy." MA Thesis, University of Alberta, 1994.

Harris, K. B. *Visitors Who Never Left: The Origin of the People of Damelahamid.* Vancouver: UBC Press, 1974.

Hudson's Bay Company Archives (HBCA)
- Brown, Wm. Biography, Hudson's Bay Record Society, V. 1, appendix 431.
- Manson, Wm. Fort Simpson Journal, B.201/a/9.
- Ross, C. to Connolly, Bear Lake, Oct. 27, 1829, #38.
- Russell, W.S. Staff Record of Service 1911 to 1932.
- Russell, W.S. Staff Records, author's possession (1911-1925, one page).
- Russell, W.S. Hiring Contract, March 2, 1932.
- Tolmie, W.F. to Captain H.G. Lewis, Aug. 31, 1868, B.226/b/44, fo. 37.d.

"HBC Diary," Hazelton, 1894-97, NW Community College Library, typescript.

Healing Words. "Glen Vowell and Andimaul Day Schools: The Salvation Army and Indian Education." *Aboriginal Healing Foundation*, 4:1 (Winter 2003): 37. (www.ahf.ca Jun. 1, 2015.)

Hindle, L. and B. Rigsby. *A Short Practical Dictionary of the Gitksan Language. Northwest Anthropological Research Notes* 7 (1) 1 – 60. Moscow, Idaho: 1973.

Horetzky, C. *Canada on the Pacific: Being an Account of a Journey From Edmonton to the Pacific by the Peace River Valley.* Montreal: Dawson Brothers, 1874.

Hough, R. *Captain James Cook: A Biography.* London: Coronet Books, 1994

Houston, J. R. *Numbering the Survivors: A History of the Standish Family of Ireland Ontario and Alberta.* Agincourt, ON: Generation Press, 1979.

Hunter, D. *The Race to the New World: Christopher Columbus, John Cabot and a Lost History of Discovery.* New York: Palgrave MacMillan, 2011 (e-version).

Hurley, M. C. *Aboriginal Title: The Supreme Court of Canada Decision in Delgamuukw v. British Columbia.* Parliament of Canada, Law and Government Division, January 1998, rev. 2000. (www.parl.gc.ca May 25, 2015.)

"Interview with Johnny Moore," by A'yawasxw/Martha Brown (1917-2011), March 1, 1972, Hazelton, BC, handwritten copy.

"Interview with Smax/Arthur P. Sampson (1911-1981)," by A'yawasxw/Martha Brown, March 8, 1972, Hazelton, BC, handwritten copy.

Jenness, D. *The Carrier Indians of the Bulkley River: Their Social and Religious Life.* Smithsonian Institution, Bureau of American Ethnology, Bulletin 133, Paper No. 25, 1943.

Jorgensen, M. *Rebuilding Native Nations: Strategies for Governance and Development.* Tucson: University of Arizona Press, 2007.

Kari, James., ed. *Ahtna Athabaskan Dictionary.* Fairbanks, AK: Alaska Native Language Center, 1990.

Kitanmaax School of Northwest Coast Indian Art. *We-Gyet: Legends of the Northwest.* Toronto: James-Christen Associates and Eric Rosen Enterprise Limited, 1977.

'Ksan. *Gathering What the Great Nature Provided: Food Traditions of the Gitksan.* Vancouver: Douglas & McIntyre, 1980.

Lamb, W.K., ed. *The Journals and Letters of Sir Alexander Mackenzie.* London: Cambridge Press, 1970.

— . *Sixteen Years in the Indian Country: the Journal of Daniel Williams Harmon 1800-1816.* Toronto: MacMillan, 1957.

Lambert, D. "Three Points About Aboriginal Title." *The Advocate*: 70: 3, May 2012: 340-359.

Large, R.G. *Skeena: River of Destiny.* Vancouver: Mitchell Press, 1957 (5th Ed. 1981).

Lawrence, G. *40 Years on the Yukon Telegraph.* Winnipeg: Hignell Printing Ltd., 1990.

Lee, N. *Klondike Cattle Drive.* Vancouver: Mitchell Press, 1960.

Letters:
- "Loring, R.E. Indian Agent, Babine Agency to R.E. Gosnell, Librarian to Legislative Assembly," Hazelton, BC Sept. 5, 1896, copy in possession of author.
- "Muirhead, C.D., Game Warden to W.S. Russell," Jan. 17, 1933 [s.b. 1932]. Copy in possession of author.
- "Russell, W.S., to Fanny Goff Smith," July 21, 1929. Copy in possession of author.

Lewis-Williams, D. *The Mind in the Cave.* London: Thames & Hudson, 2002.

"Little Bay Islands, Past, Present, and Future: An Historical Review." United Church School Magazine 1942, N. pub. Author's possession, TS [typescript].

"Local and District News." *The Omineca Herald.* 7 Nov. 1908: 1.

—.12 Dec 1908: 1.

—. 16 Jan 1909: 1.

MacDonald, J. Gitanmaax History: Portion of Hazelton Community Plan. Dec. 15, 1980. N. pub, Photocopy author's possession.

Mackie, R.S. *Trading Beyond the Mountains: The British Fur Trade on the Pacific 1793-1843.* Vancouver: UBC Press, 1997.

"Maik George Winds up his Biggest Season." *The Omineca Herald* 11 April 1928: 1.

Mandell, Louise. "Speaking Notes Prepared for Gitxsan Government Commission Community Meeting", Hazelton, British Columbia, Jan. 19, 2015, 15 pages.

Marsden, S. "Defending the Mouth of the Skeena: Perspectives on Tsimshian Tlingit Relations." Presented at the 29th Ann. Meeting of the Can. Arch. Assn., Halifax, N.S., May 1996.

—. "An Historical and Cultural Overview of the Gitxsan." Vols. I-II, unpublished, Jan 1987.
McGillivray, S. "Journal of Voyage to Simpson's River by Land, Summer 1833." HBCA (B188/a/18).
McLeod, I. with H. McNeil. *Prospectors Promoters and Hard Rock Miners: Tales of the Stewart, BC and Hyder, Alaska Camps.* Kelowna: S.H. Co. Ltd, 2004.
Meilleur, H. *A Pour of Rain.* Victoria: Sono Nis Press, 1980.
Miller, B. *Wires in the Wilderness: the Story of the Yukon Telegraph.* Surrey: Heritage House, 2004.
Moeran, J.W.W. *McCullagh of Aiyansh.* London: Marshall Brothers Ltd., 1923.
Moore, D. P., P. Eng, P. Geo. "Babine River Slide Hazard Assessment." Nov. 25, 1993.
Monet, Don and Ardythe Wilson. *Colonialism on Trial.* Gabriola Island, BC: New Society Publishers, 1992.
Morin, M. H. *Niwhts'ide'ni Hibi'it'en: The Ways of Our Ancestors.* Smithers: School District 54, 2011.
Morison, C.F. "A Brief Narrative History of Early British Columbia from 1872 to 1876." J. W. Morison, ed. 1926 BCPA (MSS 424).
—. Letter to Rev. A.C. Pound of Nakusp, BC 1926 BCPA (MSS 424).
—. BC Pioneers Biography, Provincial Library, nd, BCPA (MSS 424).
Morrow, T. A. *Cataline: Packer Extraordinaire.* Prince George: Talisman Publications, 2013.
Murray, P. *The Devil and Mr. Duncan: A History of the Two Metlakatlas.* Victoria: Sono Nis Press, 1985.
"Native Badly Mutilated by Grizzly Bear." *The Omineca Herald* 29 Sept. 1922: 1.
Newman, P. C. *Caesars of the Wilderness.* Markham, Ontario: Penguin, 1988.
Orchard, Imbert. *Martin: The Story of a Young Fur Trader.* Victoria: Province of BC, 1981.
Provincial Archives of British Columbia (PABC):
- Registration of Voters, Legislative Electorates and Elections Act, May 10, 1894, BC Gazette, Victoria.
- Crown Land Registry Services, 1896-1915 (GR-3097, Vol. 0083, 2403 to 2488).
- Inquisitions 1906, 1909.
- Starrett, Robert transfer of land to Charles Starrett.
- Loring, R.E. letter to R. E. Gosnell, Librarian to Legislative Assembly, Sept. 5, 1896.
- Methodist Church, Port Essington, Baptisms, MF 94A, 1883-1946 Register.
- Sargent, R.S.: "Notes of a conversation with Richard Strong Sargent, Hazelton, September 22 and 24, 1929." PABC (E/E/Sa 7, Env. S. 345).
- Surveyor Generals Office, Victoria.
- Hankin, Thomas:
  - Preemption application May 5, 1863, GR 1182, File No. 1, p. 22.
  - Preemption application Dec. 17, 1870, granted Dec. 19, 1870, GR 1182, B1332.
  - To/from colonial governor re: postal services, Feb. 1871, B1332, file 708.
  - Hankin and colonial Governor.
  - Hankin Survey, Cert. of Improvement, Lot 695, Cassiar, B1332, file 708 no. 1502, 1890.
  - Hankin *et al* to Lt. Governor of BC, 1878 GR-0444, Vol. 47, File 6.
- O'Reilly, P. IRC, January 23, 1892 to the Chief Commissioner of Lands & Works, Victoria (GR-2982, Box 5, File 4, Minutes of Decision 23 Jan. 1892).

"Packing Contract Let: Supplies for Yukon Telegraph Line to be carried by 'Cataline.'" *The Omineca Herald* April 2, 1910: 1.
Pang, K. "An Island Dies, an Empire Falls" *Discover Magazine* April 1994: 14.
Parkin, R. *H.M. Bark Endeavour: Her Place in Australian History.* Melbourne: Mieghunyah Press, 2006.
Patenaude, B.C. *Golden Nuggets: Roadhouse Portraits along the Cariboo's Gold-Rush Trail.* Surrey, BC: Heritage House, 1998.
—. *The Gold Miners Journal.* Victoria: Trafford Publishing, 2004.
Perry, K.E. *Frontier Forts & Posts: During the Fur Trade and Gold Rush Period.* Surrey: Hancock, 2006.
Pierce, W.H. *From Potlatch to Pulpit, Being the Autobiography of William Henry Pierce.* J. P. Hiles, ed. Vancouver: Vancouver Bindery, 1933.
Pringle, H. "The First Americans." *Scientific American* (March 2013): 36-45.

Raibmon, P. *Authentic Indians: Episodes of Encounter from the Late-Nineteenth-Century Northwest Coast.* Durham and London: Duke University Press, 2005.

Ream, P. T. *The Fort on the Saskatchewan: A Resource Book on Fort Saskatchewan and District.* Edmonton: Metropolitan, 1974.

Robinson, W. and W. Wright. *Men of M'deek and Wars of M'deek.* Red Deer: Skytone Printing, 2003.

Rogers, L.L. 1981. "A Bear in its Lair. *Natural History Magazine* 70 (10): 64-70. (www.bearstudy.org/website/images/stories/Publications/A_bear_in_its_Lair.pdf June 18, 2015.)

Rush, S. "Aboriginal Title: The Path to Coexistence." Native Title in Perspective: Selected Papers from the Native Title Research Unit, 1998-2000. Ed. Lisa Strelein and Kado Muir. Canberra: AIATSIS, 2000.

Sargent, P. Essay n.d. Polly Sargent fonds, Hazelton Public Library.

Shervill, R. L. "Olof "Tie" Hanson." *Whistle Punk* (Spring 1986).

Sherwood, J. *Surveying Northern British Columbia: A Photojournal of Frank Swannell.* Prince George: Caitlin Press 2004.

Smith, R. L. "The Hankin Appointment, 1868." *BC Studies* 22 (Summer 1974).

"Starrett (Fri. Jan. 1, 1904)." Deaths. *Edmonton Daily*. 4 Jan. 1904.

Starrett, V. *Born in a Bookshop: Chapters from the Chicago Renaissance.* Norman: University of Oklahoma Press, 1965.

"Steamboats of the Skeena River: The Hudson's Bay Company and Robert Cunningham." (en.wikipedia.org/wiki May 30, 2014.)

Sterritt, N.J., S. Marsden *et al. Tribal Boundaries in the Nass Watershed.* Vancouver: UBC Press 1998.

Sterritt, N.B. "Peavies, Pike Poles & Percherons: Hand Logging on the Upper Skeena in the Early Days," Dec. 1993, (unpublished manuscript, author's possession).

Stewart, H. *Indian Fishing: Early Methods on the Northwest Coast.* Vancouver: Douglas & McIntyre, 1977.

St. Peter's Anglican Church, Hazelton:
- Hazelton Mission, Hazelton, BC, nd, no author, 23 pages.
- Baptisms (1886-1955); Marriages (1886-1944).

Stumpf, A. J., B. E. Boster and V. M. Lawson. "Glacial Stratigraphy of the Bulkley River Region: A Depositional Framework for the Late Pleistocene in Central British Columbia." *Geographique Physique et Quaternaire* 58 2-3 (2004).

"Tenders Called for 140 Miles." *The Omineca Herald* 17 July, 1909: 1.

Tomlinson, G. with J. Young. *Challenge the Wilderness.* Anchorage: Great Northwest Publishing, 1991.

Tomlinson, R. "Ankitlas: The First Mission of the Kispiox." 1968 (unpublished, author's possession).

Trueman, A. S. "Placer Gold Mining in Northern British Columbia: 1860 to 1880." MA Thesis. UBC, 1935.

Turner, N. *Plants in British Columbia Indian Technology.* Victoria: British Columbia Museum, 1979.

Turner-Turner, J. *Three Years Hunting and Trapping in America and the Great Northwest.* London: MacLure & Co., 1888.

Usher, J. *William Duncan of Metlakatla: A Victorian Missionary in British Columbia.* Ottawa: National Museum of Canada, 1974.

Vancouver, G. & J. Vancouver. *A Voyage of Discovery to the North Pacific Ocean, and Round the World.* Vol. IV. London: J. Stockdale, 1801.

Vibert, P. Ed., *Heads of Households in British Columbia in 1874.* Vancouver: BCGS, 1984.

Walbran, J. T. *British Columbia Coast Names: 1592-1906, Their Origin and History.* Vancouver: Douglas, 1971.

Watson, T. "American Indian Sailed to Europe With Vikings?" *National Geographic News* 26 Nov. 2010. (news.nationalgeographic.com May 25, 2015.)

Wicken, W. C. "Treaty of Peace and Friendship 1760: Early History." Aboriginal Affairs and Northern Development Canada. (www.aadnc-aandc.gc.ca/search May 24, 2015).

Williams, D. R. *Trapline Outlaw: Simon Peter Gunanoot.* Victoria: Sono Nis Press, 1982.

Wright, E. and W. Beynon. "Txamsem Brings Fresh Water to the People." *Tsimshian Narratives I: Tricksters, Shamans and Heroes.* J. J. Cove and G. F. MacDonald, eds. Ottawa: Canadian Museum of Civilization, Mercury Series, 1987: 16.

Index

Notes: CMS denotes Anglican Church Missionary Society; SCC, Supreme Court of Canada; "(f)" after a page reference denotes footnote; "(g)," a glossary entry; "(i)," a photograph or illustration; "(m)," a map

A

Abraham, Peter (Miinhl Gan), 54, 61(i)
Adams, Alfred, 296–297
Allied Tribes of British Columbia, 296
Alling, Lillian, 248
Alphonse, Dennis, 297
Aluugigat (first peoples), ix, 12–13, 144
Amax Exploration, 7, 183–185
Ames, Kenneth, 70
Anglican Church Missionary Society (CMS): Cunningham as missionary, 129; Duncan's term with, 132, 146(i), 148–150, 163, 166; Tomlinson's term with, 146(i), 148–150
Angus, James, 242
Angus, Peter, 249
animals, consequences of disrespect, 28–30, 71–74, 79
Ankitlas, 145, 146(i), 149
ansgiyast (Gitxsan cemetery). *See* Gitxsan funeral and burial customs
Ansi'suuxs. *See* Gitanmaax
An'spa'yaxw. *See* Kispiox
ant'gelaa (Gitanmaax cremation site), 269. *See also* Gitxsan funeral and burial customs
Antgulilbixs/Mary Johnson, 249, 303(i)
Atlantic Telegraph Company, 117
Austin, Kenneth, 50–52
Australia, 144, 286–288

B

Babine Lake, 13, 102–103, 103(i)
Babine River *(Xsugwin Lik'insxw)*, 13, 84, 85(i), 260–261
Babine Slide Road, 261, 263
Banner, Stuart, 287
Barbeau, Marius, 18, 52, 127, 150
Barker, William "Billy," 129
Barney, Peter (Woosimlaxha), 209(i), 215, 217, 256, 261, 263
Barrett, Charles, 207, 212
Bear Lake, meeting re boundaries, 54–55
Beirnes, George, 207, 226, 247–249
bentwood boxes, 77, 81
Berens, Henry Hulse, 128
berries in Gitxsan diet, 75, 81–83
Beynon, William, 18, 296–297
Bird, Billy, 242
Blackstock, Bob, 263

Blackwater, Bill, 88–90
Blackwater, Bill Sr., 270, 304
Blackwater, David, 87, 88(i)
Blackwater, Walter, 87, 88(i)
Bloody Sunday (Ireland), 184–185
Bob, Alec (Haatix Lax Nok), 54, 61(i)
Book Builders of 'Ksan, 18, 19(f), 78–79
Bratzine, Henry, 200
bridges: at Kuldo, 84–86; over Bulkley River, 228(i); over Suskwa River, 120(i); suspension bridge over Babine River, 84, 85(i); suspension bridge over Bulkley River, 84, 86, 119, 134
British Columbia government: belief in *terra nullius* doctrine, 288, 299; claim against (see *Delgamuukw v. BC*); on extinguishment of aboriginal title, 307, 316, 317; recognition of aboriginal rights (1991), 317(f)
Brown, Edith (Wiilixsha'os), 236, 237, 240–242
Brown, John (Gwiiyeehl), 63, 59–62, 120–121
Brown, Jonathan, 256, 261
Brown, Joseph (Gwiiyeehl), 237, 238–239
Brown, Martha (Kliiyeemlaxha), 259
Brown, William: about, 102, 107; building of Fort Kilmaurs, 102–103; competition for furs from coastal traders, 103–105; on fur trade potential of Gitxsan, 105–107; land tenure system of Nedut'en and Gitxsan, 101; on population of Gitanmaax nation, 106; "voyage of discovery" down Babine River, 105
Bulkley, Charles, 162
Bulkley River: fish traps at rockfall, 80(i); major tributary of Skeena River, 13; rockfall and salmon migration, 65–66, 68–69; terraces along the river, 15
Bulkley Slough, 32, 33(i)

C

Cabot, John, 95–96
Calder, Arthur, 296
Calder, Frank, 298
Calder v. BC (1973), 298
Canadian National Railway, 180
Carleton University (Ottawa), 306
Carrier peoples (Dakelh), 53–55. *See also* Wet'suwet'en
Carrier-Sekani Tribal Council, 63(i)
Cataline (Jean Caux), 207, 209(i), 274
Caux, Jean (Cataline), 207, 209(i), 274

cedar (Am Hat'al). *See* logging and cedar pole business
cemeteries. *See* Gitxsan funeral and burial customs
Charleson, Edward Ebbs ('Ned'): Diamond D Ranch owner, 207, 212; on government pack train, 214(i); re fight between telegraphers, 172; road-building confrontation near Hazelton, 177; work on Yukon Telegraph, 169
Charleson, J.B., 169, 229
Charlie, William (Wosi'midiik), 54, 55(i)
Chrétien, Jean, 297, 298
Clah, Arthur Wellington, 132
Clifford, Charles W.D., 152–153, 158
Clifford, Charlie (Gidumgaldo): one of "two Charlies" (with Charlie Sterritt), 208–209, 215–216; at opening of Hazelton Amalgamated School, 3(i); work on telegraph, 229
Clifton, Heber L., 297
Clifton, Johnny, 297
Clifton, Robert, 297
Clifton, Patricia, 297
Collins, Perry, 117
Collins Overland Telegraph (COT): aboriginal suspicion about "talking wire," 120–121; blockhouse built at Kispiox (1866), 130, 162; cancellation, 122, 162; contract for BC telegraph, 117; line lease taken over by federal government (1871), 168; to link North America and Europe, 116; transporting materials to The Forks, 117–119
Colnett, James, 98
Columbus, Christopher, 94–95
Cook, James, 286–287
Cordilleran Glacier, 14–15
Cox, Constance: photos, 38(i), 126(i); stories of life in Hazelton, 127–128; story of boy almost cremated alive, 369–370; on taboo re multiple births, 37–38; translator for Marius Barbeau, 127; work on behalf of aboriginal peoples, 125, 127
Cox, Mazel, 126, 204
Cox, Ruxton, 126–127
Crosby, Thomas, 159, 172
Cunningham, Robert: HBC trader at The Forks, 111; meeting with Charles Morison, 122; pre-emption of land at The Forks, 131; private business after HBC, 123, 128, 131–132; purchase of lots in Hazelton, 158; work before HBC, 129
Cussons, George, 162–163

D

Dakelh (Carrier peoples), 53–55. *See also* Carrier-Sekani Tribal Council

Dawson, George M., 87, 135–136
Dawson City Board of Trade, 168
Delgamuukw/Albert Tait. *See* Tait, Albert (Delgamuukw)
Delgamuukw/Earl Muldon, 43, 45
Delgamuukw v. BC: BC Court of Appeal's overturning BCSC's decision (1993), 317; BC Supreme Court's dismissal of case (1991), 308, 309(i), 314–316; BC Treaty Commission process (1994–96), 317; BC's denial of aboriginal title, 307, 316; decision to go to court, reasons, 306–307; documenting Gitxsan and Wet'suwet'en place names/boundaries, 303–304, 306; elders and chiefs as main witnesses, 312–314, 316; genealogy research, 282; Gitxsan House boundaries, internal (1987), 308, 309(i), 310–312; Gitxsan research team, 304, 306; Gitxsan/Wet'suwet'en boundaries, external (1977), 304, 305(i), 320; legacy of case, 319–322; political cartoon (Don Monet), 315(i); SCC's ruling on aboriginal title (1997), 318–319; statement of claim (1984), 53, 300(i), 308
Dewdney, Edgar, 125, 131, 132–133
Diamond D Ranch, 207, 212
Dias, Bartolomeu, 94
Dinii/Alvin Weget, 45
Douglas, James (governor of Vancouver Island), 54, 111–112, 288
Douglas, James (president of Royal Society), 287
Downie, William Downie, 112–115
Dudoward, Rufus, 296–297
Duff, Wilson, 127, 304, 310(f)
Duncan, William: conflict with Bishop Ridley, 148–150, 163, 166; educational program at Metlakatla, 162; George Cussons as mentor, 162–163; mentor to Clah, 132; religious avocation/training, 162–163; tenure with CMS, 132, 150, 162

E

Eastern Canada, map, xxiii
education, 1–3
Elliott, Albert, 253
Elliott, David W., 298
European exploration in New Caledonia: Charles Morison (telegraph) (1866), 115–123; Simon McGillivray (trade expansion, 1833), 107–111; William Brown (exploration/trading, 1822–26), 102–107; William Downie (re mineral prospects, 1859), 112–115
European migration to America: arrival on Atlantic coast, 94–96; exploration of Skeena area, 99–101; mapping of BC coast, 97–99; search for route to Asia, 93–94; Spanish and Russians, 97

Evans, Ezra, 156

F

family trees: Haaxxw, xxviii; Hankin, xxv; Russell and Weir, xxvii; Starrett and Cummins, xxvi; Wiik'aax, xxix
Faulkner, Hugh, 304
festivities (feasts, gambling, games of strength and skill), 77, 83–84
Field, Cyrus W., 117
Finlayson, Roderick, 111, 129
First Ministers' Conference on Aboriginal Rights (1983), 299–300, 306–307
Fisher, Robin, 289
Fort Kilmaurs (Old Fort), 102–103
Fort Simpson, 107, 111, 122, 123(i)
Fort St. James, 99–100
Fowler, Luke, 260
Frizzell, George John, 173–174
fur trade: "Boston men" (American free traders), 205; fur trade potential of Gitxsan, 105–107; by Gitxsan/Wet'suwet'en at Mission Flats, 100–101, 103–105; HBC and coastal traders, 103–105, 130; inter-tribal conflict at Bear Lake, 55; Legaic's power over trade on Skeena River, 205; in Skeena watershed with Europeans, 99–101; in Western Canada (map), xviii

G

Gai'nim, 52
Gamayam/Charles Mark, 136–137, 139, 152, 276–279
Gamble, Edward, 297
Gans'Niigyamks pole (House of Haaxxw), 51(i), 52, 218, 219
gawaganii (peace ceremony), 50–52, 327(g)
Geel/Big Louis, 208, 210(i), 239
Gelakgen, Jacob and Elizabeth, 244
George, Bear Lake, 281–282
George, Herb, 306
George, Marvin, 308, 309(i), 310–312, 313
Gidumgaldo, House of: clemency sought for killer of Billy Owen, 278–279; large house in Gitanmaax (1881), 207; lawyers needed for land rights claims, 285, 300; pole (*Ts'akim Eek* or Nose like Coho) at Gitanmaax, 150–152; Wet'suwet'en permitted to fish below the rock fall, 65–66
Gidumgaldo/Charlie Clifford. *See* Clifford, Charlie (Gidumgaldo)
Gidumgaldo's pole (*Ts'akim Eek* or Nose like Coho), 4(i), 8(i), 9, 150–152
Gisday Wa/Alfred Joseph. *See* Joseph, Alfred (Gisday Wa)

Gitangasx, 12, 54, 55, 56–59
Gitanmaax: census by Tomlinson (1881), 145–148; common destination by 1859 for Europeans, 113; description before European arrival, 76–77; description by Horetzky, 133; employment, 4; funeral customs (*see* Gitxsan funeral and burial customs); hub for supplies and packing (1901), 207–208(i); locations, 76–77, 135; maps of town and region, xiv, xv–xix; name's origin ("Torchlight People"), 33–37; population (1893), 157; reserve at, 9, 157–158; role of chief Nola, 29–30, 33, 76; routes to Fort Fraser, 113–115. *See also* Omineca gold fields; telegraph; The Forks
Gitanyow: concern re incursion of settlers, 178–179; *Histories, Territories, and Laws of the Kitwancool*, 127; reserve, 158; settlement by Ts'iiyee, 29, 39; totem pole agreement with BC Provincial Museum, 127
Gitksan-Carrier Tribal Council: author's land and land rights work with, 187, 304, 320; political action re land rights, 297, 303 *See also* Gitxsan-Wet'suwet'en Tribal Council
Gitluudaahlxw, Alexander, 42(i), 268
Gitluudaahlxw, House of: author and family as members, 45; chiefs, 45; headstone of Alexander Gitluudaahlxw, 42(i), 268; *Madiigam Gyamk* (supernatural grizzly of the sun) pole, 42, 44(i); Moses Morrison as heir, 43; new name of House of Yee'l, 42(i), 43; revival through *ts'imil guut* (adoption), 43
Gitluudaahlxw/Alvin Weget, 45
Gitluudaahlxw/Moses Morrison, 43
Gitluudaahlxw/Peter Muldon, 45
Gitsegukla, 29–30, 113, 158
Gitxsan: adoption law (*ts'imil guut*), 41–43; alienation of Gitxsan land and reserves, 156–159; Aluugigat or first peoples, 12; ancestral village (*see* Temlaham); belief in reincarnation, 270–271; census (1881), 145–148; confluence of K'amksi'wa and Aluugigat, 144; death (*see* Gitxsan funeral and burial customs); diet (*see also* salmon), 75, 77–79, 81–83; eastern boundary confirmed with Sekani, 62–63; before final settlement in upper Skeena, 16–17; House membership, 45; House names, 76; inter-tribal conflict at Bear Lake due to fur trade, 55; killing of Gitxsan at Wisanskit by Tsetsaut, 59–62; land tenure system, 101; migration from Gitangasx to Kisgegas, 54; multiple births, taboo around, 37–38; new vision and revival of values needed, 321; Nisga'a (Nass River) raiders, 205–206; packing contests, 217; salmon, access to, 69; seasonal cycle (*see* Gitxsan seasonal

cycle); sports, love of, 217–218; technology (see Gitxsan technology); territories (see *Delgamuukw v. BC*); Young People's Educational Association, 217.

Gitxsan clans: Eagle Clan, 17; Fireweed Clan (Gisk'aast), 17, 26–27, 55, 61; Frog Clan (House of Haaxxw), 17; Frog-Raven Clan (Lax See'l or Lax Ganada), 29–30, 33, 55, 76; Raven Clan, 26; Wolf Clan, 17, 42, 55, 61, 76, 264.

Gitxsan diet, 75, 77–79, 81–83. See also salmon

Gitxsan funeral and burial customs: *ansgiyast* (cemetery), 268; *ant'gelaa* (Gitanmaax cremation site), 269; belief in reincarnation, 270–271; cremation, 268–270, 272; customary law re accidental death, 277–279; grave houses, 271–273; gravestones, 273–275; map of marked and unmarked gravesites, 282–283; new cemetery for whites at Two Mile, 271–272; orientation of Gitxsan vs white graves, 274; stonemasons in headstone business, 273–275

Gitxsan seasonal cycle: fall, 77, 81, 83–84; spring, 77–81; summer, 77, 79–80; winter, 77, 83

Gitxsan technology: canal to bring water to the village, 87–89; fish weirs and traps, 66–67, 68(i), 69, 79–81; snowshoes, 76, 89, 223. *See also* bridges

Gitxsan-Wet'suwet'en Tribal Council, 300(i), 308

glaciers, 14–15

Glen, John, 216–217

Glen Vowell: agricultural potential, 138; baseball and hockey teams, 217; birthplace of author's father, 1; Christmas at, 244; confrontation over land (1909), 178–180; founding, 237–238, 239(i); Indian Day School (Salvation Army), 173; population (1901, 1915), 158, 241; reserve, 158, 180

Goff, Fannie Parker, 194

gold discoveries: Klondike, 168, 209–211; Omineca gold fields, xxi(m), 131–133, 162, 227–228

Gold Miner's Journal (Patenaude), 155

Gottesfeld, Allen, 15–16, 30–31

Gouin, Leon, 185

Grand Trunk Pacific railway: Hagwilget area's potential, 114, 115; impact on sternwheelers on Skeena, 174(i); importance in obtaining agricultural land, 175; need for poles and lumber, 250; takeover by Canadian National Railway, 180; way station opposite Legate Creek, 237

Grant, Peter, 314

Gray, John Hamilton, 214

Great Britain: 1793 Royal Proclamation on treaties with aboriginal nations, 286–287; colonial land policy applied inconsistently, 287; colonization of Australia, 287–288

Green, Bella, 75
Green, David, 312(i)
Guedon, Marie Françoise, 304
Gunanoot, Sammy, 75
Gunanoot, Simon: fight and feud with Alex McIntosh, 212–213, 246; guide for hunters, 226, 229; murder of Max LeClair, 213; at Xsuwii Aks, 241
Gutgwinuxs/Billy Williams, 176
Guu Saxtoosw/Freddy Jackson, 18–19, 220
Guuhadak/Thomas Wright, 17, 55, 235
Guuxwo'ot/Peter John, 65–66
Gwa'gayee/Mark Holland, 150–152
Gwiiyeehl/John Brown, 63, 59–62, 120–121
Gwiiyeehl/Joseph Brown, 237, 238–239
Gwilagantxw, 57–59
Gwiniiho'osxw/Alfred Shanoss, 238
Gwininitxw/Solomon Jack, 261, 270
Gwits'enxsim Sim'oogit/Philip Turner, 27–28

H

Haatix Lax Nok/Alec Bob, 54, 61(i)
Ha'atu (murder of Charlie Yeomans), 277–279
Haaxxw, House of: Frog Clan, 16; *Gans'Niigyamks* pole, 51(i), 52, 218, 219; story of Liluxws and fight with Nisga'a, 46–50
Haaxxw/Mark Sampson. 50
Hagen, George, 263
Hagwilget (also called Tsë Cakh, and Rocher Deboule): common destination by 1859 for Europeans, 113; cooperation among Gitxsan and Wet'suwet'en fishermen, 66–69; descriptions, 108, 134–135; different names for village, 66; home of many Wet'suwet'en, 65; map, xv; new village after rockfall, 66, 105; reserve (under name Rocher Deboule), 158; rockfall in Bulkley River, impact on salmon, 65–66, 68–69, 105
Hagwilget Canyon, 69–70
Hagwilget Peak, 13–14
halayt (Gitxsan shaman), 71–74
Hankin, Arthur, 62, 209, 256
Hankin, Charles, 125, 128–129
Hankin, Graham, 125, 129
Hankin, Philip, 125, 128
Hankin, Thomas: arrival in BC, 125; death and estate, 141; establishment of HBC at The Forks (1866), 130; exploration up the Skeena, 130; at Hazelton, 128, 132, 133; HBC trader on Nass and at The Forks, 111; horses and livestock at Hazelton, 136, 137–138; marriage with Margaret MacAulay, 125, 131; petition to BC governor, 139–140; pre-emption of land at Gisgamaawin (1874), 128(i), 138, 156, 159; pre-emption of land at The Forks, 131; pre-emption of land in

Cariboo district (1863), 125, 129; private business at The Forks, 123, 128, 131–132; ranch near Glen Vowell, 140(i); title to land at Woodcock's Landing, 139; work with Robert Cunningham, 129. *See also* Hankin store
Hankin Store, 131–133, 137(i)
Hanson, Olof, 250–251, 253
Hanson Lumber and Timber Company, 250, 253, 259
Harmon, Daniel, 99–101, 286
Harris, Chris (Luus), 304
Harris, Cole, 157–158
Harris, Frank, 6
Harris, Heather, 232–234, 270–271, 282
Harris, Irene (author's great-aunt), 236–237
Harris, John, 207, 209–211
Harris, Walter, 297
Hazelton: aerial photo, 114(i); census (1891), 153; descriptions of town, 1–3, 5(i), 8, 133, 135–136; differences with Gitanmaax, 8–9; flood (1936), 202–203; founding, 128, 132; funeral customs (*see* Gitxsan funeral and burial customs); hub of north for supplies and packing (1901), 207–208(i); hub of pole/railway tie industry, 251–252, 263; impact of glaciers on geography, 14–15; maps of area, xv–xix; No. 1 Reserve chief's refusal to answer McKenna–McBride Commission, 293–295; Old Hazelton, xiv(m); population (1890s), 153; Skeena Treasure House Museum, 185
Hazelton Amalgamated School, 2, 3(i)
Hazelton Peak (Andamixw/Moonlight Mountain), 72–74
Hazelton Superior School, 2, 2(i)
HBC. *See* Hudson's Bay Company (HBC)
Heath, Bill, 7
hemlock bark, uses, 77–79
hemlock bark in Gitxsan diet, 77–79
The Histories, Territories, and Laws of the Kitwancool, 127
Holland, Mark (Gwa'gayee), 150–152
Holland, William, 293–295
Horetzky, Charles, 133–135
Houston, Richard, 190
Hudson's Bay Company (HBC): ascent of Skeena by *Caledonia* (1891), 158–159; coastal traders and, 103–105, 130; exploration of Skeena (1866), 130; fur trade potential of Gitxsan, 105–107; headquarters for New Caledonia District, 99–100; outpost at The Forks, 130–131; packers of freight from Hazelton, 207, 208(i); purchase of lots in Hazelton, 158; recommendation to expand trade to Nass and Skeena rivers, 111; return to upper Skeena (1880), 152–153; use of Legaic's trade canoes, 122, 130

I
Indian Act: abolishing of cultural practices, 4(f); aboriginal land claims prohibited in court (pre-1950s), 285(f); McKenna–McBride Royal Commission on, 295
Inlander (sternwheeler), 173–174

J
Jack, Solomon (Gwininitxw), 261, 270
Jackson, Freddy (Guu Saxtoosw), 18–19, 220
Jim, Victor (Misilos), 297, 300(i)
John, Edward: Bear Lake discussion of tribal boundaries, 55(i); on discovery of Spaagh and his family, 281–282; leader of Carrier-Sekani Tribal Council, 54(f), 55(i); meeting with Alan Williams re land rights, 299; at Wisanskit where Gitxsan hunters were killed by Tsetsaut, 54, 61(i)
John, Peter (Guuxwo'ot), 65–66
Johnson, Jonathan (Wii Muugilsxw), 39–40, 225–227, 237
Johnson, Joshua, 79
Johnson, Mark, 177
Johnson, Mary (Antgulilbixs), 249, 303(i)
Johnson, Samuel, 79, 80–81
Johnson, Solomon, 79, 221–222
Johnson, Sophia, 221–222
Johnson, William, 177
Joint Committee of Canadian Parliament (1926), 296
Jones, Ray (Niis Noohl), 297
Joseph, Alfred (Gisday Wa): claim against BC government (1984), 53, 300, 308; lead plaintiff for Wet'suwet'en in *Delgamuukw*, 308, 310(i); map of internal House boundaries (1987), 308, 309(i), 310–312, 313

K
K'aatim Hayatsxw/Andrew Mowatt, 215
K'amksi'waa (white people), xi, 91–92, 144. *See also* European migration to America; European exploration in New Caledonia
Kelly, Peter R., 296, 297
Kennco Explorations, 7
Keynton, Bessie, 208
Keynton, William, 159
Kisgegas, 17, 105–106, 158, 236
Kispiox (An'spa'yaxw): description, 39; feast at, 43(i); Liluxws–Naxwan story, 46–50; *Madiigam Gyamk* (supernatural grizzly of the sun) pole, 42, 44(i); religious rivalry

between Methodists and Salvation Army, 237–238, 239(i); reserve, 158; settlement story, 30, 39–40; totem poles of Kispiox chiefs, 41(i). *See also* Haa<u>x</u>xw, House of

Kispiox Jim. *See* Liluxws/Kispiox Jim

Kispiox Louis (Big Louis), 208, 210(i), 239

Kispiox Margaret, 208, 210(i)

Kliiyeemlaxha, House of, 43(i), 45(n)

Kliiyeemlaxha/Martha Brown, 259

Klondike, 168, 209–211

'Ksan Indian Village and Museum: author's employer, 32, 186–187; Book Builders of 'Ksan, 18, 19(f), 78–79; showcase of Gitxsan culture, 186(i)

L

laax wan (double bladed knife), 46(i), 47, 330(g)

Ladaix (Kitanmaax Jimmy), 207

Laforce, Vital, 131

land and land rights, pre-1950s: 1793 Royal Proclamation, application west of Rockies, 289; 1793 Royal Proclamation on treaties with aboriginal nations, 286–287, 289; Abel Oakes' understanding of whites' laws re land (1920), 284–286; aboriginal claims in court prohibited pre-1950s, 285(f); aboriginal provincial organization lacking, 295–296; alienation of Gitxsan land (1890s), 156–159; Allied Tribes of British Columbia's actions (1915), 296; "BC Special," annuity, 296; Captain James Cook, 286–287; Charles Martin as aboriginal land rights advocate, 175–181, 213; chiefs' position re ownership of land (1909), 175; Committee of Skeena River petition (1910), 178, 179(i), 291–292(i); constitutional protection for aboriginal rights, 299–300; consultation with aboriginal peoples lacking, 175–176; Douglas treaties and lack of extinguishment language, 288; Duncan–Ridley dispute over CMS land in Metlakatla, 289–290; fight at Kispiox (1910), 176–178; Gitxsan organizing against reserves and Indian Act (1909), 178–180; Hazelton-to-Kispiox-Valley road (1909), 175–176, 178; importance of agricultural land in BC, 175; Joint Committee of Parliament on land claims (1926), 296; McKenna–McBride Royal Commission (1915), 290–296; Native Brotherhood of BC (1931), 296–297; Nisga'a/Gitxsan statements to Mackenzie King (1924), 179–180; North West Co. employee's recognition of territories' ownership (1812), 286; "Numbered Treaties" with Canadian government, 288; *terra nullius* doctrine, 288, 299; Trutch's hostility to aboriginal people, 286, 289

land and land rights, after 1950s: aboriginal involvement in constitutional talks, 299–300, 306–307; author's land rights work with Gitksan-Carrier Tribal Council, 187, 304, 320; *Calder v. BC* (1973), impact, 298; Delgamuukw case (see *Delgamuukw v. BC*)

Larahritz, John *(halayt),* 72(i)

Laurentian Glacier, 14–15

LeClair, Max, 213

Lee, Norman, 209–211

Legaic of Metlakatla, 106, 122, 130, 164, 205

Liluxws/Kispiox Jim, 46–50, 162, 164–165, 178, 181

logging and cedar pole business: cedar, uses for, 250; Charlie Sterritt's work in, 252; clear-cutting vs selective logging, 259; Gitxsan families in business, 251–252; Hanson Lumber and Timber Co., 250, 253, 259; harvesting cedar and hemlock, 77–78; hauling poles, sleigh vs truck, 262(i); "herding" logs downriver and log jams, 256–257; log chutes, 254–256; Neil B. Sterritt's involvement, 6–7, 252, 253–256, 259–263; for railways, 251; skidways and peavies, 261, 263

Loring, Richard, 213–214, 279–280, 281

Lulaxs, Johnny, 269–270

Lumm, Ah, 153–155

Lumm, Jessie (wife of Charlie Sterritt), 7, 153, 154–155, 156(i)

Luu Uuxs/Kathleen Morrison. *See* Morrison, Kathleen (Luu Uuxs) (author's grandmother)

Luus/Chris Harris, 304

Lyon, Joseph, 207

Lyons, Joseph H., 152–153

M

MacAulay, Donald, 131

MacAulay, Margaret, 125, 126(i), 131

MacDonald, George, 70

Mackenzie, Alexander, 99

Madiigam Gyamk (supernatural grizzly of the sun) pole, 42, 44(i)

Madiigam Ts'uwii Aks (Madiik) and landslide at Sealy Lake, 28–29

Madiik and landslide at Sealy Lake, 28–29

Maik George, 251

Maitland, Bill, 263

Maitland, Heber, 297

Manson, Donald, 111

Manson, William, 111, 129

Mark, Charles (Gamayam), 136–137, 139, 152, 276–279

Marsden, Susan, 235

Marshall, Gary, 6(i)

Marshall, Jane, 32

Marshall, Tom, 275
Marshall, Ward: genealogical information from cemetery, 282; logging for cedar poles, 251, 259; moving HBC warehouse, 200; on religious rivalry in Kispiox, 237; on totem poles in Hagwilget Canyon, 69–70; undertaker, 275
Marshall Brothers Trucking, 4, 5, 70
Martin, Charles (Wiilaxhaa): at Aiyansh and New Aiyansh, 166–167; baptism (1885), 165; business in Hazelton, 173–175; care for Kate Sterritt and children, 240; church involvement, 167, 172–173; death, 181; education at Metlakatla, 162, 164–165, 181; fight with McCullagh and prison sentence, 167–168; land rights advocate, 175–181, 213, 291(i); servant for John Field, 166; Simon Gunanoot business, 213–214; story of his father (Liluxws) and Nisga'a, 46–50, 178; telegraph key, 171(i); work as miner, 166; work on CNR, 180; work with Yukon Telegraph, 169–172
May, James J., 155–156
McBride, Richard, 290. *See also* McKenna–McBride Royal Commission
McCullagh, James B., 166–168
McDougall, Edith and Al, 32
McDougall, James, 100
McEachern, Allan, 314, 316–317
McGillivray, Simon, 107–111
McIntosh, Alexander, 212–214
McIntosh, Angus, 159
McIntosh, Donald, 30, 159
McKenna, J. A. J., 90
McKenna–McBride Royal Commission (1915), 290–295
McKenzie, Mary, 156
McLaren, Dick, 228
McLean, Joshua, 263, 312(i)
McLean, Maggie, 251
McLeod, James and Isabella, 274–275
McNeill, Lucy Margaret, 152, 162(f)
McNeill, William, 162
Metlakatla: Anglican mission, 146(i), 148–149, 163; Charles Morison's death at, 116, 123; Duncan–Ridley dispute over CMS land, 289–290; education of Charles Martin (Wiilaxhaa), 164–165; educational program, 162; winter quarters for aboriginal peoples, 122
migration routes: across Beringia, 15; ancient and European, xiii, 15
Miinhl Gan/Peter Abraham, 54, 61(i)
Miller, Bill, 248
Misilos/Victor Jim, 297, 300(i)
Mission Flats, 100–101, 103–105, 114(i)

missionaries. *See* Anglican Church Missionary Society (CMS)
Monet, Don, 315(i)
Moogasxw/Jack Wright, 264
Moore, George, 242
Moore, Johnny (Xsemgitgiigeenix), 84–86
Morison, Charles: with Collins Overland Telegraph, 117, 119, 121; description of Fort Simpson, 122; efforts to ascend Bulkley in loaded canoes, 119; with HBC, 122–123; jobs in BC prior to telegraph work, 115–116
Morrison, Herbert, 243–244
Morrison, James, 247, 261, 312(i)
Morrison, Kathleen (Luu Uuxs) (author's grandmother): early life with parents, 236; at Glen Vowell, 239–240; intentions re totem pole, 218–219(f); logging ability, 4; marriage to Charlie Sterritt, 240–241, 243(i); marriage to Joseph Brown, 237, 238–239; parents, 236; photo, 240(i); work at cannery, 245
Morrison, Moses (Gitluudaahlxw), 43
Mowatt, Alexander, 266
Mowatt, Andrew (K'aatim Hayatsxw), 215, 216(i), 217, 242
Mowatt, Arthur (Skawats'eekx), 66–67, 152
Mowatt, Charles (Yal), 266
Muirhead, Cecil, 199
Muldoe, Johnny (Anda Ap), 66
Muldoe, Ken (Delgamuukw), 314
Muldoe, Beal (Guuhadak), 275
Muldon, Earl (Delgamuukw), 43, 45
Muldon, Peter (Gitluudaahlxw), 45
Mumford (sternwheeler), 117–118
Murie, Adolf, 127
Myros, Charley, 32

N

Naalaxha/Abel Oakes, 12, 284–286, 300
Nahanee, Ed, 297
Nass River, 98–99, 107
National Transcontinental Railway, 197
Native Brotherhood of British Columbia, 296–297
Naxwan, story of Liluxws and Nigitxw, 46–50
Nedut'en peoples, 100–101
Nelson, Arthur, 271
New England map, xxiii
New Metlakatla, 166
Newfoundland map, xxiii
Nigitxw, 46–47
Niis Noohl/Ray Jones, 297
Nisga'a: beginnings (according to Ska'woo), 26–27; *Calder v. BC* (1973), 298; land rights statements to Mackenzie King (1924), 179–180; Nass River raiders in Gitxsan territory, 205–206; Nishga Land Committee, 296; "Nishga Petition" (1912), 296; story of

Liluxws and fight with Nisga'a, 46–50, 178; Temlaham as ancestral village, 12, 25; trade with Gitxsan and Tsimshian, 77
Nola, Chief, 29–30, 33, 76
Nole, John, 89–90
North West Mounted Policemen, 176

O

Oakes, Abel (Naalaxha), 12, 284–286, 300
Ogden, Peter Skene, 110
Old Hazelton, xiv(m)
Old Kuldo (Gowal Mihl), 87–89, 158
Omagh, Ireland (Ulster), 184–185
O'Meara, Arthur, 296
Omineca gold fields: discovery of gold (1869), 131; employment for Gitxsan people, 162; freighting to mining camp, 227–228; report from civil engineer, 132–133; routes to, xxi(m)
O'Neill, Margaret, 140(i)
O'Reilly, Peter, 157–158
Overstall, Richard, 313
Owen, Billy, 276–279

P

Patenaude, Bronwen, 155
Patsey, Gary, 303, 306
Patsey, Johnny (Spooksw), 70
Paull, Andrew, 296
peavies, 261, 263
Perkins Bull, William, 188
Perkins Bull Historical Series, 188
Pierce, William H., 172, 237
Port Essington, 98, 131
potlaches and the Indian Act (1880), 4(f)
The Private Life of Sherlock Holmes (Vincent Starrett), 191

R

railways, 114, 115, 180, 197. *See also* Grand Trunk Pacific railway
Reid, Ambrose, 296–297
reserves: on Gitxsan land (1890s), 9, 157–159; Glen Vowell, 158, 180; Hazelton No. 1 Reserve at McKenna–McBride Commission, 293–295; McKenna–McBride Commission (1915), 290–296; Trutch's refusal to recognize reserves' legitimacy, 289
residential schools, 2–3
Ridley, William: bishop of New Caledonia (1879), 148–149, 163, 165(i); Charles Martin as live-in boarder, 164–165; conflict with Tomlinson and Duncan, 148, 149–150, 163, 166; dispute with Duncan over CMS land in Metlakatla, 289–290; purchase of Hankin's store for CMS, 139, 149, 163; visit to Ankitlas, 149
Rigsby, Bruce, 304
Robinson, Victor, 282
Rocher Deboule Mountain (Stekyawden), 13–14
Rolls, Charlie, 166
Ross, Charles, 62
Royal Proclamation (1793), 286–287, 289, 297
Royal Society, sponsor of Cook's voyage, 286–287
Rudge, George, 274
Russell, Bertie, 197–199, 198(i)
Russell, Jean. *See* Sterritt, Jean (née Russell, author's mother)
Russell, Louise (later Matthews) (author's aunt), 198(i), 200
Russell, Shirley Ann (author's aunt), 196, 200–201
Russell, William (Russell William Smith) (author's grandfather): author's visits in Vancouver, 126–127; death of son, "Bertie," 198–199; divorce and re-marriage, 204; family, 195–196, 198(i); in Fort George in Quebec, 195–197; with HBC, 195–196, 199–200
Ryan, Don, 306

S

Sabasuuxw ('Bas) (later Selena Simpson), 206
salmon: consequences of disrespect, 28–30, 71–74, 79; drawing of first spring salmon, 30(i); drying fish at Hagwilget, 82(i); fish weirs and traps, 66–67, 68(i), 69, 79–81; fishing at Temlaham, 27–28; fishing methods of Hagwilget, 66–67, 68(i), 69; fishing technology re *wo'o* (fish traps), 79–81; rockfall on Buckley River, 65–69
Salvation Army, 172–173, 237–238
Sampare, Alfred, 152
Sampson, Arthur P. (Smax), 56–59, 271
Sampson, Charles ('Niist): built house for Charlie Sterritt, 246; logging, 39, 256, 261; on salmon near Kispiox, 39; woodsmanship, 222
Sampson, Edward, 257
Sampson, Mark (Haaxxw), 50
Sampson, Perry, 84, 256–257, 261
Sampson, Tom, 271
Sargent, Dick, 18, 152–153, 154(i), 159, 173
Sargent, Polly, 159, 185
Sealy Lake, 28–29, 29n
Sekani peoples: Bear Lake discussion of tribal boundaries, 54, 55(i); claim against BC government, 53; eastern boundary with Gitxsan, 62–63; Gitxsan crest and clan system, 62; inter-tribal conflict at Bear Lake due to fur trade, 55. *See also* Carrier-Sekani Tribal Council

Seymour, Charles. T., 129
Shanoss, Alfred (Gwiniiho'osxw), 209(i), 238
Shanoss, Moses, 268, 271
Sibley, Hirram, 117
Simpson, Lucy, 187, 188, 206–207
Simpson, Selena (Sabasuuxw or 'Bas), 206, 246
Sinclair, William, 152
Skawats'eekx. See Gidumgaldo
Skawill, Daniel, 273, 274(i)
Ska'woo and settlement at Temlaham, 26–28
Skeena River: ascent by HBC's *Caledonia* (1891), 158–159; bottomland between it and Bulkley River, 14, 16(i); confusion with Nass River, 107; danger of, 243–244; European settlement (*see* European exploration in New Caledonia); glacier action, 14–15; maps of, xvi–xix; name ("river of mist"), origin, 28; river and tributaries, 13–15; terraces along river, 15
Skulsh, Isaac, 79
Smax/Arthur P. Sampson. See Sampson, Arthur P. (Smax)
Smiak, Artha, 58(i)
Smith, Diane, 288
Smith, Gordon, 84
Smith, Herbert Elmer, 194
Smith, John, 256
Smith, Mickey, 6(i)
Snaaxw, Margaret, 131
snowshoes, 76, 89, 223
Spaagh, James (Spookxw), 280–282
Spookxw/Johnny Patsey, 70
Spookxw/Edward Spouk, 290, 293, 295
Spookxw/James Spaagh, 280–282
Spooner, Leo, 251
Spouk, Edward (Spookxw), 290, 293, 295
St. Mary Magdalen Catholic Church, 18
St. Peter's Anglican Church, 5(i), 8(i), 9, 135(i)
St. Pierre, Joseph, 169–172
St. Theresa of the Child Jesus Church, 6
Starrett, Andrew (author's great-great-great-grandfather), 190
Starrett, Charles (author's great-grandfather), 188–189, 206–207
Starrett, Martin, 215
Starrett, Robert Jr., 190
Starrett, Robert Sr., 188, 189(i), 190, 191
Starrett, Vincent, 183, 191
Stekyawden (Rocher Deboule Mountain), 13–14, 110
Sterritt, Arthur (author's brother), 297(f), 304
Sterritt, Arthur (author's uncle), 241, 243(i), 258
Sterritt, Charlie (Haaxxw) (author's grandfather): acceptance of name Haaxxw, 218(f); attraction to Salvation Army, 237; birthplace in Gitanmaax, 9; catching wild horses, 208–209; cedar pole logging, 252; journey to Telegraph Creek, 7–8; Klondike cattle drive, 209–211; love of good stories, 18, 220; marriage to Kate Morrison, 240–241, 243(i); marriage to Margaret Johnson, 221–222, 241–244; move to Hazelton, 246–247; one of "two Charlies" (with Charlie Clifford), 208, 215–216; packer, work as, 208–209, 212, 214–215; packing ability, 216–217; parents, 188, 206–207; photo on outing to Vancouver, 156(i); pre-empting land on Kispiox River, 242; pre-empting land on Skeena, 221; totem poles, 218–219; trapping at Xsuwii Aks, 247; work at Diamond D Ranch, 212
Sterritt, Gordon (author's son), 184, 185, 186, 224(i), 231(i)
Sterritt, Jack, 243(i)
Sterritt, Jamey, 6(i), 203
Sterritt, Jamie (author's son), 187(i), 231(i)
Sterritt, Jean (née Russell; author's mother): courtship and marriage, 201, 203; death of brother, "Bertie," 198–199; early life in Newfoundland, 193–194, 198(i); in Fort George and Sennetere, Quebec, 195–198; in Hazelton, 203–204
Sterritt, Jessie (wife of Charlie Sterritt, née Lumm), 7, 153, 154–155, 156(i)
Sterritt, Kathleen. See Morrison, Kathleen (Luu Uuxs) (author's grandmother)
Sterritt, Margaret (later Heath) (author's aunt), 7, 51(i), 156(i)
Sterritt, Neil B. (Wiik'aax) (author's father): acceptance of name Wiik'aax, 263–265; Bear Lake discussion of tribal boundaries, 55; birth in Glen Vowell (1913), 241; children's self-reliance, 244–245; Christmas at Glen Vowell, 244; early years, 241–247; family photos, 232(i), 243(i); female grizzly attack, 265–266; Gans'Niigyamks pole, 51(i), 52, 218, 219; Geological Survey of Canada work, 257; hauling poles, sleigh vs truck, 262(i); logging and cedar pole business, 6–7, 252, 253–256, 259–263; move to Hazelton, 246; spelling of surname, 189; trapping, 258–259; on Wet'suwet'en good qualities, 67–68; in WWII, 257–258
Sterritt, Neil J. (author): on cover of industry magazine, 184(i); drawing of first spring salmon, 30(i); early life and education, 1, 2(i), 5–7; fight for constitutional protection for aboriginal rights, 299–300; genealogical sleuthing, 187–192, 282; Gitxsan names, 45, 45(n); on goat hunting trip, 6(i); with grandfather on trip to Vancouver, 208–209; at Hazelton school, 2(i); Irish connections of family, 190; at 'Ksan Indian Village and Museum, 186–187; life at Temlaham, 25, 30–31; life in Gitanmaax, 32; member of House

of Gitluudaahlxw, 45; storytelling ability, x; with Uncle Percy, sons, and snowshoes, 231(i); wife and sons adopted into Percy Sterritt's House, 232; work with Amax, 7, 183–185

Sterritt, Neil J. (author) and *Delgamuukw v. BC*: assistance for land claim research, 302–303, 304; drawing of author on stand, 315(i); filing claim against BC government (1984), 300(i), 308; on Gitxsan research team, 306; land rights work with Gitksan-Carrier Tribal Council, 187, 304; map of Gitxsan internal House boundaries (1987), 308, 309(i), 310–312; mapping Gitxsan territory to obtain financing (1977), 303–304, 305(i); re Gitxsan eastern borders (1985), 53–55

Sterritt, Percy (Wii Bowax) (author's uncle): adoption of author's wife and sons into House, 232; on Charles Sampson, 222; early life, 221–222; family life and games, 230–232; freight to mining camp, 227–228; hunting guide, 226–227; inheriting name Wii Bowax, 221; on pack train, 225–226, 227; photo with brother, 232(i); poem about his stories, 232–234; snowshoe expertise, 76, 223, 231(i); story of bear hibernation and hunting, 223–224; trapping at Xsuwii Aks, 247; trapping in bitterly cold weather, 229–230; use of Gitxsan place names, 76

Sterritt, Walter (author's uncle): early years with Neil B., 241–243; journey with Neil J., 8; logging and mining, 260, 261(i); trapping at Xsuwii Aks, 247–249; during WWII years, 258

Sterritt family tree (from 1882), xxx

Stevens, Charles, 242

Stewart-Vowell Commission (1909), 175

Storrings, Phyllis, 260

Sullivan, Charlotte, 153–155

Supreme Court of Canada (SCC): alignment with UN Declaration on the Rights of Indigenous Peoples, 319; *Calder v. BC* ruling (1973), 298; *Delgamuukw* ruling (1997), 318–319; landmark legal principles on aboriginal title, 321; ruling that "Crown must act honourably" re aboriginal peoples, 319; Tsilhqot'in and aboriginal title (2014), 319

Sustut River, 13

T

Tait, Albert (Delgamuukw): claim against BC government (1984), 53, 300, 300(i), 308; death just before *Delgamuukw* trial (1987), 313–314; hauling of fish trap, 81; lead plaintiff for Gitxsan in *Delgamuukw*, 308; mapping external boundaries of Gitxsan territory, 303; mapping Gitxsan territory at Old Kuldo, 87, 88(i)

Teegee, Daniel, 281–282

telegraph between North America and Europe: overland link, 116; suspicion/superstition about "talking wire," 120–121; trans-Atlantic cable, success, 116, 121–122, 162; transporting materials to The Forks, 117–119; Yukon Telegraph, 168–172

Temlaham: ancestral village of Gitxsan, Nisga'a and Tsimshian, 12, 25; catching salmon, 27–28; dispersal story, 29–30; evidence of village's existence, 30–31; pre-emption of land by settlers, 30, 159; story of landslide at Sealy Lake (Madiik), 28–29, 29n; story of settlement: Ska'woo, 26–28

Temlaham Ranch, 25

Tens, Isaac (Ts'igwii), 277–278

terra nullius doctrine, 288, 299

The Forks (Gitanmaax): aerial photo of area, 114(i); gathering place for feasts and trade, 130; HBC outpost failed (1866), 130–131; interest by European traders, 104, 106, 111; routes to Fort Fraser, 113–115

Thorkildson, J.P., 172–173

Tolmie, W.F., 130

Tomlinson, Alice, 168

Tomlinson, Robert Jr., 149, 150, 159, 237–238

Tomlinson, Robert Sr.: census of Gitanmaax (1881), 145–148; conversion of Christians in Kispiox, 237; help with fishing materials for Gitxsan, 81; personal/religious history, 148–149; tenure at CMS, 146(i), 148–150

"Torchlight People" (Gitanmaax), 33–37

totem poles: *Gans'Niigyamks* pole (House of Haaxxw), 51(i), 52, 218, 219; Gidumgaldo's (*Ts'akim Eek* or Nose like Coho), 4(i), 8(i), 9, 150–152; Gitanyow's agreement with BC Provincial Museum, 127; of Kispiox chiefs, 41(i); *Madiigam Gyamk* (supernatural grizzly of the sun) pole, 42, 44(i); poles removed from Hagwilget Canyon, 69–70; Totem Park in Gitanmaax, 218, 219

trade (non-fur): hides and other with Nisga'a and Tsimshian, 77; oolichan oil brought in, 77

Trudeau, Pierre Elliott, 297, 298

Trutch, Joseph, 286, 289

Tsetsaut (Luu Tsabim Tsim Yip): allies of fur traders, 55–56; considered intruders by early Gitxsan, 56; story of defeat by Gwilagantxw, 56–59; story of killing of Gitxsan at Wisanskit, 59–62

Ts'igwii/Isaac Tens, 277–278

Ts'iibaasaa, Joshua, 26–27

Ts'iiyee, 39–40

Tsilhqot'in and aboriginal title, 319

ts'imil guut (adoption law of Gitxsan), 41–43

Tsimshian, 12, 26–27
Ts'ugyet/James Green, 52
Turner, Elijah (Wiiyagadeets), 27–28, 237
Turner, Philip (Gwits'enxsim Sim'oogit), 27–28

U

Ullman, Anna Mae, 248–249
UN Declaration on the Rights of Indigenous Peoples, 319
Union of BC Indian Chiefs, 297

V

Vancouver, George, 97–99
Veith & Borland, 207
Vowell, Arthur Wellesley, 157–158, 238(f), 281

W

Wale, Howard, 297
Weget, Alvin (Dinii; also Gitluudaahlxw), 45
Weir, Ann (author's grandmother), 194–197, 199, 202, 204
Weir, Frank (author's great-grandfather), 194, 196
Weir, Hannah (author's great-grandmother, née Oxford), 194, 196
Wet'suwet'en people: Bear Lake discussion of tribal boundaries, 53, 55(i); claim against BC government, 53; map with external Gitxsan and Wet'suwet'en boundaries (1977), 304, 305(i); move to Hagwilget, 65; qualities according to author, 67–68; rockfall in Bulkley River, impact on salmon, 65–66, 68–69, 105; trade in furs with Europeans, 100, 103–105
Whidby, Joseph, 98
White, James (Skawats'eekx), 152
White Paper on aboriginal rights (1969), 297, 298
white people, migration. See European migration to America
Wii Bowax/Percy Sterritt. See Sterritt, Percy (Wii Bowax) (author's uncle)
Wii Muugilsxw/Jonathan Johnson, 39–40, 225–227, 237
Wiigaak, Daniel. See Wiik'aax, Daniel
Wiigyet: as "essence of human frailty," 18–19; place among Tsimshian speaking peoples, 18–19; story: bringing light to the world, 19–20; story: bringing water to the world, 21; story: giving tufted ears to the lynx, 21–22; story: Wiigyet and the abalone, 23–24
Wiik'aax, Daniel, 241–242, 249, 264, 306, 307(i)
Wiik'aax, House of: family tree, xxix; Neil B. Sterritt as Wiik'aax, 264–265; settlement on upper Skeena, 17; story of Tsetsaut's defeat and Gitxsan move to Kisgegas, 56–59

Wiik'aax/Neil B. Sterritt. See Sterritt, Neil B. (Wiik'aax) (author's father)
Wiilaxhaa/Charles Martin. See Martin, Charles (Wiilaxhaa)
Wiilixsha'os/Edith Brown, 236, 237, 240–242
Wiiyagadeets/Elijah Turner, 27–28, 237
Williams, Alan, 298–300
Williams, Billy (Gutgwinuxs), 176
Williams, David Ricardo, 212, 213
Williams, Guy, 297
Williams, Jimmy (Woosimlaxha), 41–43, 138
Williams, Johnson, 237
Williston, Ray, 3(i)
Wilson, Ardythe, 306, 312–313
Wilson, Long Frank, 275
Wilson, Philip (Wo'os Sa'lo'op), 222–227
Wilson, Robert, 223–224
Wires in the Wilderness (Miller), 248
Witset, 66, 103–104
The Wolves of Mount McKinley (Murie), 127
Woods, Helen, 151(i)
Wo'os Sa'lo'op/Philip Wilson, 222–227
Woosimlaxha/Jimmy Williams, 41–43, 138
Woosimlaxha/Peter Barney, 209(i), 215, 217, **256**, 261, 263
Wosi'midiik/William Charlie, 54, 55(i)
Wright, Emma, 27
Wright, Henry, 312(i)
Wright, Jack (Moogasxw), 264, 303(i)
Wright, Simon, 264(f)
Wright, Thomas (Guuhadak), 17, 55, 235

X

Xsemgitgiigeenix/Johnny Moore, 84–86
Xsimxsan, 46–50
Xsuwii Aks: author's father's early years at, 241–247; Simon Gunanoot at, 241; trapping at, 247–249

Y

Yee'l, House of, 42–45. See also Gitluudaahlxw, House of
Yee'l (the warrior), 30, 39–40
Yeomans, Charlie, 276–279
Young People's Educational Association (YPEA), 217
Yukon Telegraph, 168–172
Yukon Telegraph Trail, map, xxii